LEGAL AID AND THE FUTURE OF ACCESS TO JUSTICE

This open access book provides a snapshot of the state of contemporary access to justice in England and Wales.

Legal aid lawyers provide a critical function in supporting individuals to address a range of problems. These are problems that commonly intersect with issues of social justice, including crime, homelessness, domestic violence, family breakdown and educational exclusion. However, the past few decades have seen a clear retreat from the tenets of the welfare state, including, as part of this, the reduced availability of legal aid. This book examines the impact of austerity and related policies on those at the coalface of the legal profession. It documents the current state of the sector as well as the social and economic factors that make working in the legal aid profession more challenging than ever before.

Through data collected via the Legal Aid Census 2021, the book is underpinned by the accounts of over 1000 current and former legal aid lawyers. These accounts offer a detailed demography and insight into the financial, cultural and other pressures forcing lawyers to give up publicly funded work. This book combines a mixture of quantitative and qualitative analysis, allowing readers a broad appreciation of trends in the legal aid profession.

This book will equip readers with a thorough knowledge of legal aid lawyers in England and Wales, and aims to stimulate debate as to the fate of access to justice and legal aid in the future.

Legal Aid and the Future of Access to Justice

Catrina Denvir
Jacqueline Kinghan
Jessica Mant
and
Daniel Newman

• HART •
OXFORD • LONDON • NEW YORK • NEW DELHI • SYDNEY

HART PUBLISHING

Bloomsbury Publishing Plc

Kemp House, Chawley Park, Cumnor Hill, Oxford, OX2 9PH, UK

1385 Broadway, New York, NY 10018, USA

29 Earlsfort Terrace, Dublin 2, Ireland

First published in Great Britain 2023

A catalogue record for this book is available from the British Library.

A catalogue record for this book is available from the Library of Congress.

ISBN: HB: 978-1-50995-780-4
ePDF: 978-1-50995-782-8
ePub: 978-1-50995-781-1

Typeset by Compuscript Ltd, Shannon

FOREWORD

'Law has gone away …'
WH Auden

I am writing on International Human Rights Day having just read *Legal Aid and the Future of Access to Justice*. Congratulations to Catrina Denvir, Jacqui Kinghan, Jess Mant and Daniel Newman on a work of scholarship and humanity that paints a bleak picture whilst never giving up hope.

So much has been written and argued about the distinctions between civil and political and social and economic rights. Still, it has always been clear to me that the most essential bridge between the two categories of fundamental protections is access to justice on the basis of need and not just wealth.

I am increasingly impatient with the orthodoxies that suggest that economics has anything other than politics at its heart; that it is somehow a science with the 'trickle-down' theory being as irrefutable as the law of gravity. I have watched wealth not merely trickling, but being positively sucked upwards in one of the wealthiest countries on Earth. Austerity is always a political choice; yet never was it so ideological and even spiteful as with the destruction of legal aid.

In its early pages, this book explains how in the post-war era, access to justice was installed as a key component of the welfare state, only subsequently to be undermined at the turn of the century and especially after 2010. Why so spiteful? Because, in addition to the general attack on the poor, the elderly, the disabled, women and ethnic minorities that austerity always brings, cutting legal aid protects those who govern from those for whom the state is often the provider of income, housing, health and even refuge. It is a deliberate and certain way to facilitate abuses of government power against the most vulnerable in society. Vital areas of administrative law that are constantly amended by statute and a complex web of regulations are converted into an unenforceable dead letter, unintelligible to those in need of support.

As these cuts have been accompanied by a denigration of legal aid lawyers, judges and even human rights by those in government, we have seen not so much a vicious circle as a downward spiral of derision and despair. Denvir, Kinghan, Mant and Newman are all the more compelling for basing their analysis upon the Legal Aid Census, the results of which are so extensive as to be impossible to refute. They present their case with painstaking detail and considerable subtlety.

Far from being the so-called 'fat cats' of many an anti-lawyer political rant, legal aid practitioners are well motivated in the public interest, but find it increasingly impossible to make a reasonable living in its pursuit.

Law students are having the idealism squeezed out of them by the domination of city law firms over the solicitors' profession in particular, and their corresponding and disproportionate influence upon the content of a legal education. This influence places wealth generation and protection over the ethical quest for equal justice as the hallmarks of professional prestige. It deters many, and shuts out even more, from public service and ill-prepares those who attempt this path. This is exacerbated by wider societal inequality, prohibitive tuition fees and student debt. The practical elements of pre-qualification experience are still too difficult to access for too many, particularly those from poorer, non-white and immigrant backgrounds.

As legal aid has been undermined, so inevitably has the profession of those who serve it. It is ever harder to recruit and retain these lawyers who must endure increasingly stressful terms and conditions in some of the most un-level playing fields in the English and Welsh legal system.

The ultimate victims are not even these hard-pressed and dedicated professionals, but the public they seek to serve. When criminal barristers went on an indefinite strike in the autumn of 2022, they rightly cited the underfunding and undermining of the whole system as well as their real earnings fall of 28 per cent since 2006. Sadly, it took the possibility of custody time limits expiring and remand prisoners being released for the Government to relent and offer a 15 per cent increase in legal aid fees for most cases in the Crown Court. Of course, civil and welfare lawyers lack the same trump card, and the less reasonable Dominic Raab has replaced Brandon Lewis at the Justice Department where he also hopes to fulfill his lifelong ambition of scrapping the Human Rights Act.

So in a winter of food and fuel inflation and industrial discontent, those in greatest need of legal advice and assistance will once more feel a cold wind. With the shortage in social housing allowing private landlords to inflate rents to extortionate levels, how many tenants really understand their rights to challenge unfair increases before a tribunal? With low pay, high living costs and unaddressed health conditions forcing so many people to be reliant upon universal credit, who is really equipped to challenge negative decisions without expert help? And as ministers ratchet up the hostile environment for foreign nationals including genuine refugees still further, there will be no shortage of work and fees for those who act in furtherance of the Government's cause. By contrast those fleeing persecution will increasingly find advice deserts in a supposed country of safety.

In the end, we must choose what kind of society we want to be. A civilised one built upon the rule of law and access to justice, or a lawless one where only the venal and most abusive thrive? For a while at least, the pandemic reminded many of the dangers of inequality and value of community. However, it should also have shown us the extent to which unchecked power corrupts. During this health emergency, the United Kingdom lost at least twice as many civilians as during World War II. If that war prompted a societal reset, this important book should help our communities and especially its public interest lawyers argue that another is long overdue.

Shami Chakrabarti
January 2023

ACKNOWLEDGEMENTS

We would like to express our appreciation to Shami Chakrabarti, CBE and Spike Mullings for contributing the foreword and afterword to this book.

Our sincerest thanks to Chris Minnoch and Rohini Teather at the Legal Aid Practitioner's Group for commissioning the Legal Aid Census, providing funding to ensure this book could be made widely available on an open access basis, and for their support throughout the various stages of this research.

Thanks also to Sasha Aristotle, for her research assistance and editorial support, Seb Krumins for his work on the empirical components of the project, Chao Cheng for his assistance with manuscript preparation, and Professor Simon Burtonshaw-Gunn for his support in refining the final text. We are grateful to the Baring Foundation for providing funding for this research assistance.

Finally, we owe a debt of gratitude to those who helped refine the project during the pilot stage, as well as to all those participants who took the time to respond to the Legal Aid Census. Thank you for making this research possible. It is our hope that by giving voice to your concerns, this research will support the creation of policy that safeguards a sustainable future for legal aid.

Catrina Denvir, Jacqueline Kinghan, Jessica Mant and Daniel Newman
March 2023

CONTENTS

LIST OF TABLES

LIST OF FIGURES

LIST OF ABBREVIATIONS

BAME	Black, Asian and Minority Ethnic
BME	Black and Minority Ethnic
BVC	Bar Vocational Course
CBA	Criminal Bar Association
CCMS	Client and Cost Management System
CILEX	Chartered Institute of Legal Executives
CPS	Crown Prosecution Service
ECHR	European Convention on Human Rights
FRCs	Fixed recoverable costs
GDL	Graduate Diploma in Law
LAA	Legal Aid Agency
LAPG	Legal Aid Practitioners Group
LASPO	The Legal Aid, Sentencing and Punishment of Offenders Act 2012
LLB	Bachelor of Laws
LLM	Masters of Laws
LPC	Legal Practice Course
PPE	Pages of Prosecution Evidence
SQE	Solicitors Qualifying Exam
QLD	Qualifying Law Degree
YLAL	Young Legal Aid Lawyers

1

Introduction

Legal aid is a crucial component in the fabric of the justice system in England and Wales. It plays a key role in facilitating access to justice by helping to ensure legal needs are met and that individuals can establish or enforce their rights across various areas of law. Legal aid practitioners work at the frontline of the justice system. They assist clients with a wide range of issues, including but not limited to those relating to criminal defence, family matters, education, housing, immigration, discrimination, debt, community care and employment. Legal aid services are typically provided for communities and clients through private law firms, not-for-profit advice agencies, local law centres and national charities. However, the legal aid system is experiencing unprecedented pressures and challenges.[1] The COVID-19 pandemic,[2] changes brought about by the Legal Aid, Sentencing and Punishment of Offenders Act 2012 (LASPO),[3] fee arrangements,[4] court closures[5] and wider attempts to reduce legal aid spending[6] are just a few of the conditions and events that have contributed to concerns that the sector is increasingly unviable.

A review of the legal aid landscape which elevates the perspectives of those working day-to-day in the sector is vital and long overdue. Pre-existing data on the specifics of legal aid practice has been piecemeal, lacking context and insufficiently able to elucidate conditions on the ground. This book presents and analyses the results of the most comprehensive census of legal aid practitioners ever conducted in England and Wales. It provides a greater and more accurate understanding of a sector adversely impacted by repeated crises and challenges. In the decade since the enactment of LASPO and the aftermath of COVID-19 lockdowns, legal aid practitioners reveal the true extent of the current state of legal aid in response to the five surveys that comprise the Legal Aid Census.

[1] The Westminster Commission on Legal Aid, 'Inquiry into the Sustainability and Recovery of the Legal Aid Sector' (All-Party Parliamentary Group on Legal Aid, 2021).

[2] The Law Society of England and Wales, 'Law Under Lockdown: The Impact of Covid-19 Measures on Access to Justice and Vulnerable People' (The Law Society, September 2020).

[3] James Organ and Jennifer Sigafoos, 'The Impact of LASPO on Routes to Justice' (Equality and Human Rights Commission, 2018).

[4] House of Commons Justice Committee, 'The Future of Legal Aid: Third Report of Session 2021–22' (Her Majesty's Stationery Office, 2021).

[5] Jack S Caird, 'Court and Tribunal Closures' (House of Commons Library, 21 March 2016).

[6] James Thornton, 'Is Publicly Funded Criminal Defence Sustainable? Legal Aid Cuts, Morale, Recruitment and Retention in the English Criminal Law Professions' (2020) 40 *Legal Studies* 230.

I. The Role of Legal Aid

Legal aid facilitates access to justice in England and Wales through the provision of legal advice, mediation and legal representation for individuals who are otherwise unable to pay for a lawyer. The provision of legal aid can help individuals assert their rights and entitlements, understand and be empowered to use the law, and be represented in courts and tribunals. By allowing substantive access to justice, legal aid plays a critical role in enhancing citizenship and reducing social exclusion in society.[7]

Legal aid is therefore an important device through which the legal profession responds to legal need. The concept of legal need refers to the scale and nature of need for legal support among the public. In England and Wales, clear trends in respect of this need have been identified through decades of empirical legal research in the field of civil justice. For example, 'legal need surveys' are a key resource for understanding the extent to which the general public experience 'justiciable' problems – that is, problems that have a legal dimension – and the support that they may require if they do. These surveys indicate that approximately a third of adults in England and Wales will experience a civil, family or administrative justice problem at any one time.[8] Despite the prevalence of justiciable problems, not all require action to be taken and very few will escalate to the point of needing formal legal intervention.[9]

Justiciable problems are, however, disproportionately experienced by particular populations in society. For instance, people are more likely to experience legal problems if they are relying on welfare benefits or social housing.[10] High legal problem prevalence is also generally associated with poverty, disability and the experience of physical or mental ill-health conditions.[11] These factors also create a higher likelihood of more frequent, complex and interrelated problems. To that extent, legal problems tend to 'cluster';[12] if people are contending with one legal

[7] Hilary Sommerlad, 'Some Reflections on the Relationship between Citizenship, Access to Justice and the Reform of Legal Aid' (2004) 31 *Journal of Law and Society* 345.

[8] Hazel Genn, *Paths to Justice: What People Do and Think About Going to Law* (Hart, 1999); Pascoe Pleasence et al, *Causes of Action: Civil Law and Social Justice*, 1st edn (Legal Services Commission, 2006); Pascoe Pleasence et al, *Causes of Action: Civil Law and Social Justice*, 2nd edn (Legal Services Commission, 2010); Pascoe Pleasence and Nigel Balmer, 'How People Resolve "Legal" Problems' (Legal Services Board, 2014); Isabella Pereira et al, 'The Varying Paths to Justice: Mapping Problem Resolution Routes for Users and Non-users of the Civil, Administrative and Family Justice Systems' (Ministry of Justice Analytical Series, 2015).

[9] See: Pleasence and Balmer (n 8); World Justice Project, 'Global Insights on Access to Justice' (World Justice Project, 2019); Pascoe Pleasence et al, 'How People Understand and Interact with the Law' (Legal Education Foundation, 2015); Rebecca L Sandefur, 'The Importance of Doing Nothing: Everyday Problems and Responses of Inaction' in Pascoe Pleasence et al (ed), *Transforming Lives* (Legal Services Commission, 2007).

[10] Pleasance and Balmer (n 8) 20; Ramona Franklyn et al, 'Key Findings from the Legal Problem and Resolution Survey 2014–15' (Ministry of Justice Analytical Series, 2017) 14–17.

[11] Pascoe Pleasence et al, 'Paths to Justice: A Past, Present and Future Roadmap' (UCL Centre for Empirical Legal Studies, 2013) iv.

[12] Pascoe Pleasence et al, 'Multiple Justiciable Problems: Common Clusters and Their Social and Demographic Indicators' (2004) 1 *Journal of Empirical Legal Studies* 301.

problem, they are more likely to experience further legal problems. This may be due to the impact of that legal problem on their health, well-being or financial security. It may also be due to the nature of that problem as one which necessarily 'triggers' other problems. For example, relationship breakdown is rarely a standalone family law problem because of the way that it implicates changes that instigate other issues related to immigration law, housing law or social security.

There are a broad range of strategies that people may take when they experience a legal problem. However, problem-solving varies significantly according to the *type* of problem. For instance, there are different consequences and costs for pursuing or not pursuing resolutions for different problems. Indeed, there may be no need to take any action at all in relation to some problems – many are trivial or will quickly resolve themselves. Additionally, some problems are more associated with 'law' than others. While relationship breakdown is heavily associated with privately funded lawyers and courts, few people think of issues with welfare in the same way.[13] In many ways, this is related to the structure of the legal services market itself; traditional legal practices are not inclined to offer services relating to basic and unprofitable welfare issues.[14] People experiencing social welfare problems are therefore far more likely to rely on the advice sector for help. These individuals often need to be referred by other service providers such as doctors or local authorities, because they may conceive these problems as the result of 'bad luck' rather than legal disputes in and of themselves.[15]

The actions that people take also vary significantly across population groups. In other words, the actions people take depend heavily on who people are and what opportunities and resources they are able to draw upon when they experience these problems. Additionally, not everyone who experiences a serious problem will take steps to resolve it. It is therefore imperative not to conflate levels of demand for legal services with levels of legal need. Rather, need for legal assistance and advice is often characterised by structural and institutional barriers which relate to the ways that people are positioned within society. For example, on this point, scholars have discussed the importance of 'legal empowerment' and 'legal capability'. These concepts refer not only to the difficulties that people may face when they try to seek help, but also to the confidence that is required for people to believe that they can take action, and that doing so will improve their situation or resolve their problem.[16] Certain population groups are not only more likely to experience legal problems, but are also more likely to face barriers that may prevent them from accessing assistance to resolve those problems. The extent to which people are empowered to articulate their legal needs and to make use of available support is much more constrained for particular groups who face broader barriers within society. For these groups, the availability of free assistance through legal aid is an

[13] Pleasence and Balmer (n 8).

[14] ibid 102.

[15] ibid 9; Franklyn et al (n 10) 64–65, 71, 81–84.

[16] Martin Gramatikov and Robert Benjamin Porter 'Yes, I Can: Subjective Legal Empowerment' (2011) 18 *Georgetown Journal on Poverty Law and Policy* 169; Pleasence and Balmer (n 8) 2.

essential resource through which to address and prevent legal problems. Through services funded by legal aid, some may be able to negotiate a solution informally with the other party and thereby avoid the need for action or discussion of legal rights. If necessary, others may be supported to use more formal processes such as dispute resolution or court procedures to obtain a resolution. Often, advice funded by legal aid is needed simply so that people can seek guidance about what their options are and which route would be most appropriate for them given the nature of their problem and their individual circumstances. This advice may be from a law firm or from the broader advice sector, both of which play a crucial role in the fabric of legal assistance, advice and support in England and Wales.

In the criminal justice context, legal aid plays a critical role in ensuring that the right to a fair trial is upheld, especially in complex cases and where individuals are at risk of imprisonment. Under Article 6(3) of the European Convention on Human Rights (ECHR), which, at the time of writing, is still incorporated by the Human Rights Act 1998, everyone charged with a criminal offence has a range of minimum rights entitlements. These include the right 'to defend himself in person or through legal assistance of his own choosing or, if he has not sufficient means to pay for legal assistance, to be given it free when the interests of justice so require'.[17] Importantly, legal aid also ensures the availability of early advice and representation when suspects are charged at the police station; this is critical in view of the experience of vulnerability at this stage of the criminal process.[18] Legal aid therefore plays a crucial role in meeting legal need. Importantly, legal aid not only provides support to those seeking assistance, but also is supposed to provide a safety net to those clients who cannot seek out this support. Many legal needs, for instance, are 'unmet' in the sense that there is either no suitable help available or because people are not able to make use of help that is available. Those experiencing unmet legal need might never seek help to resolve their problem. Alternatively, they might begin to seek assistance, but end up letting the matter drop because they experience 'referral fatigue' or otherwise feel they have exhausted all of their options.[19] In either circumstance, people with unmet legal needs often end up contacting advice services at a later point when their circumstances have escalated into multiple or far more serious problems, which are much more difficult and complicated to resolve.[20]

II. The Foundations of Legal Aid

Legal aid in England and Wales was formally and widely introduced by the Legal Aid and Advice Act 1949 as part of the post-war expansion of the British welfare

[17] Art 6(3)(c) European Convention on Human Rights.

[18] Roxanna Dehaghani, *Vulnerability and Police Custody: Police Decision Making and the Appropriate Adult Safeguard*, 1st edn (Routledge, 2019).

[19] Pleasence and Balmer (n 8) 4; Pleasence et al (2006) (n 8) 77.

[20] Pereira et al (n 8) 27–30.

state. Before 1949, the UK relied upon a piecemeal system to provide assistance to people who could not afford to access the courts or pay for advice from a lawyer. There were thus great limits to the Magna Carta's principle, established in the thirteenth century, that 'to none will we sell, to none will we deny, or delay, the right of justice'. As Henry Brooke explains in his leading account of the history of legal aid:

> Although access to the courts was recognised as a constitutional right, there was no constitutional right to the provision of legal assistance at public expense if one could not afford a lawyer, although from time to time statutory or quasi-statutory arrangements provided some form of help .... There was always a tradition by which lawyers on occasion provided pro bono services on an ad hoc basis, but this was an unpredictable source of assistance and attracted a strong social stigma because of its explicit link with the concept of pauperism.[21]

The limited provisions which existed prior to 1949 included the Poor Prisoners Defence Act 1903, which determined that legal aid would be paid once it was decided that a prisoner had a defence. They also included the Poor Man's Lawyers movement, which included charitable approaches of *pro bono* help which stopped short of representation in court. In the lead-up to the enactment of the modern legal aid system, it was increasingly accepted that the limited nature of legal aid undermined access to justice:

> Why legal aid should have developed so slowly in the land that gave birth to the ideal of freedom and equality of justice for all men is hard to understand. Conditions were so bad that Gurney Champion in his Justice and the Poor in England ironically proposed that Parliament should, in so far as the poor were concerned, repeal the fortieth paragraph of Magna Carta – 'to no man will we deny, sell or delay right or justice'.[22]

The Legal Aid and Advice Act 1949 therefore moved beyond ad hoc measures and philanthropy; it introduced a concerted, state-centred approach in England and Wales which, crucially, was premised on need.

The concept of the legal aid system was articulated substantively in the Beveridge report,[23] first published in 1942 at the height of the Second World War. William Beveridge, an economist and subsequent Liberal Member of Parliament, sought to reform the system of social welfare to address what he termed the 'five giants on the road of reconstruction': want, disease, ignorance, squalor and idleness.[24] Beveridge's report served this end by setting out the foundational ideas of what would subsequently become the welfare state, promoting the notion that there would be rewards for citizens' wartime sacrifices and offering a state commitment to the provision of services 'from the cradle to the grave'.[25] In practice, this

[21] Henry Brooke, *The History of Legal Aid 1945–2010* (Henry Brooke, 2016), available at sirhenrybrooke.me/2016/07/16/the-history-of-legal-aid-1945-to-2010/#_ftnref4.

[22] Reginald Heber Smith, 'Legal Aid and Advice: The Rushcliffe Report as a Landmark' (1947) 33 *American Bar Association Journal* 445.

[23] William Beveridge, 'Social Insurance and Allied Services' (His Majesty's Stationery Office, 1942).

[24] ibid.

[25] ibid.

comprised four pillars of the welfare state: the National Health Service, social security, universal education and universal housing. While legal aid was certainly not one of the pillars of the welfare state, it nevertheless underpinned its architecture. Beveridge's recommendations asserted that legal aid should be available in those types of cases in which lawyers normally represented private individual clients; furthermore, it should not be limited to those people 'normally classed as poor' but should instead include those of 'small or moderate means'. As such, there was to be an increasing scale of contributions payable by those with income or capital above minimum levels, below which legal aid would be free.[26] In addition to the means test, cases were to be subjected to a merit test which involved assessment by legal practitioners independent of government on a similar basis to that which was applied to private clients.

In turn, the Rushcliffe Committee was charged with investigating the feasibility of such a legal aid scheme, and their work in doing so has subsequently been referred to as 'legal aid's founding text'.[27] The Committee was established in 1944 and produced its report in 1945, the month after the war in Europe ended. The Committee's Chair was Lord Rushcliffe, a barrister and former Conservative MP, who had served in Ramsay MacDonald's national government. The remit of his Committee was:

> To enquire what facilities at present exist in England and Wales for giving legal advice and assistance to poor persons, and to make such recommendations as appear to be desirable for the purpose of securing that poor persons in need of legal advice may have such facilities at their disposal, and for modifying and improving, so far as seems expedient, the existing system whereby legal aid is available to poor persons in the conduct of litigation in which they are concerned, whether in civil or criminal courts.[28]

This would be the most thorough examination of legal aid that had been conducted. In its report, the Committee found that: 'The great increase in legislation and the growing complexity of modern life have created a situation in which increasing numbers of people must have recourse to professional legal assistance'.[29]

The Committee therefore found that there was a growing need for legal aid. The Committee recognised that it was essential for individuals to have assistance when they sought to navigate the law and for this assistance to be available to all those who were unable to afford it. However, change was needed if such arrangements were to be possible:

> A service which was at best somewhat patchy has become totally inadequate and that this condition will become worse. If all members of the community are to secure the

[26] ibid.

[27] Michael Cross, 'Legal Aid's Founding Text Turns 70' (The Law Society Gazette, 2015), available at www.lawgazette.co.uk/commentary-and-opinion/legal-aids-founding-text-turns-70/5048898.article.

[28] The Rushcliffe Committee, 'Rushcliffe Committee Report on Legal Aid and Legal Advice in England and Wales' (CM6641, 1945) 1.

[29] ibid, 23.

> legal assistance they require, barristers and solicitors cannot be expected in future to provide that assistance to a considerable section as a voluntary service.[30]

As such, the report recommended that there was a need to establish a comprehensive scheme under which legal aid would be available in all courts. This was to be administered by the legal profession but funded by the state. At the time, the Committee recommended that 'barristers and solicitors should receive adequate remuneration for their services',[31] and that 'it would be impossible for a Solicitor adequately to prepare a case without being seriously out of pocket at the present rate of remuneration'.[32] The Committee assured that legal aid should be available to a wider income group than 'those who are normally classed as poor' and, indeed, suggested that 'the term "poor person" should be discarded and the term "assisted person" adopted'.[33] An assisted person would be a man or woman whose net income (after deduction of income tax and certain other items) did not exceed £420 a year, and they would be expected to contribute 'what (if anything) he could afford'.[34]

The recommendations of the Rushcliffe Committee were accepted by the post-war Labour Government. The legal aid scheme was intended 'To provide legal advice for those of slender means and resources' such that 'no one would be financially unable to prosecute a just and reasonable claim or defend a legal right; and to allow counsel and solicitors to be remunerated for their services'.[35]

This was a broad and expansive vision for legal aid, with the scheme conceptualised as an important means of realising the principle of access to justice. It in this spirit that the then-Attorney General, Sir Hartley Shawcross, introduced the Legal Aid and Advice Act to the House of Commons:

> I should be inclined to call this Bill a charter. It is the charter of the little man to the British courts of justice. It is a Bill which will open the doors of the courts freely to all persons who may wish to avail themselves of British justice without regard to the question of their wealth or ability to pay … going back further to the time when Magna Charta decreed that: To no one will we sell, deny, or delay right or justice. – it is an interesting historical reflection that our legal system, admirable though it is, has always been in many respects open to, and it has received, grave criticisms on account of the fact that its benefits were only fully available to those who had purses sufficiently long to pay for them.[36]

This charter was one designed to empower the ordinary citizen. While the welfare state is often thought of as a safety net, this approach meant that legal aid was considered a safety net *for the safety net* because it would provide people with the

[30] ibid.
[31] ibid.
[32] ibid, 26.
[33] ibid.
[34] ibid, n 28.
[35] Lord Chancellor's Department, 'Striking the Balance: The Future of Legal Aid in England and Wales' (His Majesty's Stationery Office, 1996).
[36] Legal Aid and Advice Bill HC Deb 15 December 1948.

ability to enforce their rights in relation to other components of the state. Under the Act, legal aid was to be available in all courts and tribunals where lawyers normally appeared for private clients. The fundamental principle of the system was that if a citizen with a legal problem could satisfy both the means test and the merits test, then they would be entitled to legal aid. This marked an important shift whereby legal aid was designed to be led by the demands of those experiencing legal need:

> Since its inception, legal aid has technically been 'demand led'. Tests of eligibility were set, in crime, based on the longstanding Widgery criteria and in civil cases, on a test of reasonableness, and applicants within financial eligibility obtained legal aid.[37]

The legal aid scheme was implemented in stages, beginning with funding to cover representation in matrimonial cases in the High Court in 1950. It was introduced gradually into other areas of civil work and other courts, and was most significantly expanded to include funding for legal advice. Criminal legal aid also expanded in the 1960s – and again in the 1970s and 1980s – which involved establishing duty solicitors in magistrates' courts and police stations.

III. The History of Legal Aid

The legal aid system has undergone a multitude of changes since its enactment in 1949. Although the scheme has persisted to the present day, the optimistic and ambitious aspirations of the Rushcliffe Committee have never quite been realised. In reality, political changes and reforms have characterised the lifetime of the legal aid scheme by decline and wavering support.[38] To understand the historical context that has shaped the journey from the lofty ambitions of the Rushcliffe report to the present day, it is useful to consider Brooke's 'six eras' of legal aid.[39] Until the 1980s, there was a period of political consensus around legal aid in which the scheme was generally accepted as an important part of state welfare provision. If the foundation of legal aid is considered the first era of legal aid, this second era was one of growth as legal aid expanded to the extent that legal aid lawyers started to form a larger part of the legal profession. This was facilitated, for example, by the introduction of the green form for advice and assistance on any matter of English law, which relied only upon a simplified test of income and expenditure. At this time, legal professionals were able to use legal aid to assist a range of different population groups with various legal problems by providing them with the knowledge and understanding of their rights, as well as assisting them to take action, if required.

[37] Roger Smith, 'Legal Aid on an Ebbing Tide' (1996) 23 *Journal of Law and Society* 570, 571.
[38] ibid.
[39] Brooke (n 21).

However, the mid-1980s heralded the beginning of the first challenges to legal aid's rapid growth. Between 1986 and 1997, the Conservative Party began to prioritise cost-saving measures within public services. As a taxpayer-funded scheme that was rapidly expanding in terms of its scope and demand, the legal aid budget was an unsurprising target for such policies in the face of rising costs. In fact, during this time period legal aid expenditure rose from £306 million in 1986 to £1.4 billion by 1997. To facilitate increased accountability among the profession who were making use of the scheme, the Thatcher-led administration reallocated responsibility for the administration of legal aid to the Legal Aid Board 1986, under the logic that removing control from the profession would help to prevent mismanagement or overinflated costs. However, concerns about the cost of legal aid endured, and these culminated in policy which set out to reduce costs by imposing limitations on the scope of civil legal aid eligibility.[40]

The fourth era of legal aid occurred under Tony Blair's Labour administration from 1997 to 2005. During this period, the Government's legal aid policies were characterised by continued adherence to the Conservative Party's ambitions of reducing expenditure within the scheme. Most notably, this era saw the enactment of the Access to Justice Act 1999, which represented the biggest overhaul of legal aid since 1949. This statute replaced the Legal Aid Board with the Legal Services Commission, with a remit to be more selective in the administration of legal aid contracts. It also removed legal aid eligibility for personal injury cases and introduced an overall cap on legal aid expenditure. The impact of these changes was intended to be mitigated by the Act's creation of a new Community Legal Service and Criminal Defence Service. However, by 2005 it was clear that these initiatives had ultimately failed because legal aid costs were increasing at an exponential rate. This was partly caused by the absorption of criminal legal aid in the Crown Court and the higher courts into the mainstream legal aid budget.

The fifth and penultimate era of legal aid is the shortest, running between 2005 and 2010. At this stage, the legal aid budget had been significantly curtailed, with governments on both sides of the political spectrum having achieved their goals of bringing spiralling costs under control, at a figure of £2.1 billion.[41] Nevertheless, there remained a dispute between the Labour Government and the legal profession over the Government's desire to introduce arrangements for price-competitive tendering for legal aid contracts. The Carter Review in 2006[42] led to the ultimate implementation of this change, prioritising a system of best-value tendering. This has been criticised by members of the profession for leading to fragmentation of legal services as well as increased bureaucratisation and rigidity in relation to fee arrangements for those services relying on legal aid as a source of funding.[43]

[40] Lord Chancellor's Department (n 35).

[41] Brooke (n 21).

[42] Lord Carter of Coles, *Legal Aid: A Market-Based Approach to Reform* (Ministry of Justice, 2006).

[43] Una Padel, 'The Criminal Justice System Gets Carter' (Centre for Crime and Justice Studies, 2007), available at www.crimeandjustice.org.uk/sites/crimeandjustice.org.uk/files/09627250308553556.pdf.

It is the sixth of Brooke's eras – the age of austerity – that occupies most attention in current scholarship and practitioner literature concerning legal aid. This era began in 2010 with the election of the Conservative–Liberal Democrat coalition government. This administration introduced a wide range of policies geared towards curtailing public expenditure in response to the global financial crisis of 2008. As many scholars have argued, this crisis has frequently been relied upon as a justification for neoliberal transformation in which states have generally reduced their commitments to social provision and focused their efforts instead on promoting free trade and property rights.[44] In terms of legal aid, this was most notably evident in the enactment of LASPO, which came into effect in April 2013 and established the parameters of the current legal aid scheme. In proposing this legislation, the Ministry of Justice asserted that LASPO would achieve four key aims. First, it would discourage unnecessary and adversarial litigation at public expense; second, it would target legal aid to those who need it most; third, it would make significant savings to the cost of the legal aid scheme; and finally, it would deliver better overall value for money for the taxpayer. In pursuit of these aims, the LASPO reform introduced the most substantive range of cuts to legal aid eligibility since the scheme was introduced in 1949 by ambitiously seeking to cut £350 million per year from the legal aid budget. In doing so, it fundamentally overhauled the post-war premise that underpinned the Rushcliffe Committee's original proposals, by creating a default of 'non-eligibility'; as such, legal aid was no longer dependent on the satisfaction of means and merits tests, but instead was available only in specific, exceptional circumstances. In many ways, this sixth era of legal aid therefore marked the dismantling of post-war political commitments to the pursuit of equal access to justice. The legal aid sector is currently dealing with the ongoing legacy of the coalition period, and it is the ongoing impact of LASPO – and the culmination of the reforms that preceded it – that frame the present reality of legal aid services and the support that citizens can expect when they experience legal need.

The vast majority of the cost-savings achieved by LASPO came from the way that it altered the scope of civil and family legal aid. This included the almost wholesale removal of private family, employment, welfare benefits, housing, debt, clinical negligence and non-asylum immigration law matters from scope. A limited number of exceptions exist in relation to cases that involve, for example, domestic violence as associated with immigration and asylum or private family law problems, or a risk of homelessness as may be associated with debt or housing law problems.[45] To mitigate the stark impact this reform was likely to have on those with learning disabilities or mental health problems that would prevent them from managing their own legal problems, an Exceptional Case Funding scheme was established to provide legal aid in cases where a failure to do so would be a breach of an individual's rights under the ECHR. However, a stringent and

[44] David Harvey, *A Brief History of Neoliberalism* (Oxford University Press, 2005).
[45] Legal Aid, Sentencing and Punishment of Offenders Act 2012, Sch 1.

time-consuming application process as well as strict criteria meant that this option was rarely used in practice, with few advice providers capable of investing the time necessary to make use of the scheme.[46] Unsurprisingly, the newly limited scope of legal aid resulted in reduced volumes of publicly funded cases, with expenditure falling by approximately £90 million in civil cases and £160 million in family law cases in the first six years after LASPO's enactment.[47] Applicants for legal aid must now satisfy three tests: they must establish that their legal matter be one of the exceptional issues that remains in scope of legal aid, as well as fulfil a merits test and a means test. Broadly speaking, the merits test considers the likelihood of success of the case and whether it justifies the use of publicly funded legal advice or representation. The means test considers the applicant's financial situation and whether they qualify for legal aid. Under LASPO, economic savings were also made by altering the details of the financial means test for areas of law that remained in scope of legal aid. This included ending automatic eligibility for those in receipt of means-tested benefits and reducing the limit on the maximum income and capital an individual can have if they are to qualify for legal aid. Specifically, these can be categorised into four key changes: applying capital eligibility test to all legal aid applicants; increasing Income Contributions for Contributory Clients; capping the subject matter of dispute disregard at £100,000; and removing legal aid in cases with borderline prospects of success. The application of these changes to the means test has saved an estimated additional £9 million per year from the legal aid budget.[48]

At the same time as imposing these restrictions on eligibility, LASPO also reduced the fees paid to lawyers undertaking legal aid work in civil and family matters, by introducing a blanket 10 per cent reduction to fees in most civil legal aid cases. In addition, the uplifts for some hourly rates were capped or removed, and remuneration for pre-permission work on judicial review cases was limited.[49] This aspect of the reform led to annual spending reductions of £60 million in family law and £6 million in civil cases.[50] In respect of criminal law, LASPO also made a number of changes to the fees that lawyers could claim as well as the provision of legal aid to prisoners. Criminal reductions cut litigators fees by 8.75 per cent for cases in the Crown Court (other than Very High Cost Cases), in the Court of Appeal, and in other cases covered by the Standard Crime Contract such as magistrates' court cases, police station attendance and Parole Board cases. The fee

[46] Emma Marshall, 'Almost Four out 10 Legal Aid Firms Do Not Use "Safety Net2 Scheme' (The Justice Gap, 2020), available at www.thejusticegap.com/almost-four-out-10-legal-aid-firms-do-not-use-safety-net-scheme.

[47] Lord Chancellor and Secretary of State for Justice, 'Post-Implementation Review of Part 1 of the Legal Aid, Sentencing and Punishment of Offenders Act 2012 (LASPO)' (His Majesty's Stationery Office, 2019).

[48] ibid.

[49] Ministry of Justice, 'Proposals for the Reform of Legal Aid in England and Wales' (Ministry of Justice, 2010).

[50] Lord Chancellor and Secretary of State for Justice (n 47).

changes have saved £140 million per annum.[51] Regulations under LASPO also reformed the fees paid to experts in civil, family and criminal proceedings. These policies reduced the budget by approximately £30 million per annum.[52]

In alignment with earlier legislative reform, the enactment of LASPO also came with another overhaul of legal aid governance. Just as the Legal Aid Board had been replaced with the Legal Services Commission, the responsibility of administering legal aid under LASPO was relocated to the Legal Aid Agency (LAA). The LAA takes the form of a new executive agency of the Ministry of Justice, meaning the Government now has more direct control over the legal aid budget. While the Legal Services Commission was already unpopular among the legal profession, there was a great deal of further anxiety created by the relocation of legal aid administration to an agency within the hierarchical structure of the Ministry of Justice. In practice, this signalled a blurring between government and legal aid administration and the increased politicisation of legal aid.

The long-awaited post-legislative review of LASPO was produced in response to extensive evidence from legal professionals and academics about the damage that the Act had caused to the justice system, legal services, and the capacity of the sector to meet legal need. In recognition of the challenges that had emerged as a result of LASPO, the Government committed to providing £8 million of additional funding.[53] This funding was to be spent across all areas of law, and largely targeted towards improving technology and digital services. The report also acknowledged the need for further research examining the longer-term sustainability of the sector and the need to trial new solutions that could improve access to justice for those citizens who were no longer eligible for legal aid. The review was accompanied by a supplementary Legal Support Action Plan,[54] which stressed the importance of such innovations focusing on early legal advice, and committed to investigating the effectiveness of new forms of advice provision, such as health justice partnerships. Importantly, the review was unequivocal in ruling out any possibility of reinstating legal aid funding, and clearly articulated that future priorities would be focused upon non-legal help so as to empower people to solve their own legal problems rather than relying on taxpayer-funded assistance. Unfortunately, the commitments to further research were impaired due to delays associated with the outbreak of the COVID-19 pandemic, and the findings of such explorations have not yet emerged. Furthermore, the additional financial commitments made in this review represented little more than two per cent of the £350 million of annual cuts to the legal aid budget that had been made and have had little effect on the scale of damage to the sector.

[51] ibid.
[52] ibid.
[53] ibid.
[54] Ministry of Justice, 'Legal Support: The Way Ahead' (Ministry of Justice, 2019).

IV. The Current State of Legal Aid

The legal aid system in England and Wales has thus endured significant challenges in recent decades. As a result, the ability of legal aid practitioners to respond to the often complex and multifaceted needs of their clients has been hindered by the lack of early legal advice and representation across many areas of law. Those most adversely impacted by the changes include children and young people, migrants and refugees, disabled people and those with mental and physical ill-health.[55] In 2018, Philip Alston, the United Nations' special rapporteur on extreme poverty and human rights, embarked on a fact-finding mission to the UK and – early on in his observations – implicated legal aid in the exacerbation of and entrenchment of poverty in the country. For Alston:

> There have been dramatic reductions in the availability of legal aid in England and Wales since 2012 and these have overwhelmingly affected the poor and people with disabilities, many of whom cannot otherwise afford to challenge benefit denials or reductions and are thus effectively deprived of their human right to a remedy.[56]

Legal aid was duly included in his final report the following year.[57] According to this report, one in five people in the UK lived in poverty in 2019, and close to four in 10 children would do so within the following two years. Alston drew on the seventeenth-century English philosopher Thomas Hobbes to articulate how these lives were likely to be 'solitary, poor, nasty, brutish, and short'. His analysis demonstrated that austerity politics, including the roll-out of Universal Credit, had contributed to the 'systematic immiseration of millions'. He cited legal aid cuts as part of this process:

> Legal aid has been dramatically reduced in England and Wales since 2012. The LASPO Act (Legal Aid, Sentencing and Punishment of Offenders Act) made most housing, family and benefits cases ineligible for aid; ratcheted up eligibility criteria; and replaced many face-to-face advice services with telephone lines. Consequently, the number of civil legal aid cases declined by a staggering 82 per cent between 2010–2011 and 2017–2018. As a result, many poor people are unable to effectively claim and enforce their rights, have lost access to critical support, and some have even reportedly lost custody of their children. Lack of access to legal aid also exacerbates extreme poverty, since justiciable problems that could have been resolved with legal representation go unaddressed.[58]

[55] Amnesty International, 'Cuts That Hurt: The Impact of Legal Aid Cuts on Access to Justice in England and Wales' (Amnesty International, 2016).

[56] Phillip Alston, 'Statement on Visit to the United Kingdom, by Professor Philip Alston, United Nations Special Rapporteur on extreme poverty and human rights' (United Nations Human Rights Office of the High Commissioner, 2018) 13.

[57] Phillip Alston, 'Visit to the United Kingdom of Great Britain and Northern Ireland: report of the Special Rapporteur on Extreme Poverty and Human Rights' (United Nations Human Rights Office of the High Commissioner, 2019).

[58] ibid, 9–10.

It is important to understand LASPO within the wider context of austerity. In the year before the reforms, 91,000 people received legal advice for welfare benefits cases. In the year after LASPO, legal advice fell by 99.5 per cent to just 478 people. This intersected with simultaneous changes including the introduction of complicated, problematic new benefits such as Universal Credit and the 'cruel and humiliating' fit-to-work tests, which meant people were likely to need advice more than ever.[59]

The wider austerity cuts that brought about changes such as welfare reform and reductions in local government funding have combined to make the legal aid landscape all the more challenging for practitioners in recent years. Research shows that the housing crisis and deepening levels of inequality in society, even before the COVID-19 pandemic, presented lawyers with almost insurmountable difficulties day-to-day in their casework especially given the inability to resolve issues in their early stages.[60] A 2018 survey of Members of Parliament similarly indicated that more than half had seen an increase in the number of constituents seeking advice, and that advice was especially needed in the areas of welfare benefits and housing.[61] These challenges are not restricted to civil legal aid provision, having also been prevalent in criminal legal aid where resource constraints in the system have had considerable impacts on clients.[62]

Legal aid practitioners have been struggling to sustain legal aid service provision amidst these pressures. In 2013, there were 1,592 firms with criminal legal aid contracts[63] and 1,881 firms with civil legal aid contracts, but these numbers had dropped to 1,104[64] and 1,445 respectively by March 2021. The Law Society's Otterburn Report, published in 2014, noted that most criminal solicitors' firms' finances were 'precarious', with profit margins near five per cent.[65] Recent research also shows expansive legal advice deserts across England and Wales; in some areas, there is simply no provision available for community care and housing law as well as significantly reduced provision in immigration and asylum, social welfare and education.[66] Researchers repeatedly note the disconnect between the stated impact of policy changes that would work to improve

[59] Camilla Hodgson, *Cruel and Humiliating: Why Fit-for-work Tests are Failing People with Disabilities* (*The Guardian*, 22 May 2017), available at www.theguardian.com/careers/2017/may/22/cruel-and-humiliating-why-fit-for-work-tests-are-failing-people-with-disabilities.

[60] Jon Robins and Daniel Newman, *Justice in a Time of Austerity: Stories from a System in Crisis* (Bristol University Press, 2021).

[61] APPG on Legal Aid, 'MP Casework Survey Findings' (APPG on Legal Aid, 2018), available at www.apg-legalaid.org/sites/default/files/APPG%20on%20Legal%20Aid%20-%20MP%20casework%20survey%20findings%207%20Sept%202018.pdf.

[62] Roxanna Dehaghani and Daniel Newman, 'The Crisis in Legally Aided Defence in Wales: Bringing Wales into Discussions of England and Wales' (2021) 41 *Legal Studies* 234.

[63] Legal Services Commission, 'Legal Services Commission Annual Report and Accounts 2012–13' (His Majesty's Stationery Office, 2013), 15.

[64] Alex Chalk MP, 'Written Questions: Legal Aid Scheme: Contracts' (UIN 166396, 16 March 2021).

[65] Otterburn Legal Consulting, 'Transforming Legal Aid: Next Steps – A Report for the Law Society of England and Wales and the Ministry of Justice' (Otterburn Legal Consulting LLP, 2014).

[66] The Law Society of England and Wales, 'Civil Legal Aid: A Review of its Sustainability and the Challenges to its Viability' (The Law Society, 2021).

access to justice through streamlining and efficiency, and the reality on the ground of a deeply compromised system.[67] For example, marketisation in immigration and has shown that the supply of legal aid services is unable to meet the demand.[68] Likewise, while the intention was that limiting legal aid in private family law to mediation and exceptional circumstances would incentivise people to avoid adversarial court processes, research demonstrates an increase in the number of cases issued in court.[69] In social welfare law, legal aid is said to be 'withering on the vine' as people who might be eligible for what remains of the scheme are unlikely to access assistance because they do not understand that they could be helped, incorrectly assume it will not be available, or else cannot find someone who can help them.[70] For those pursuing family court proceedings, LASPO has led to a significant reduction in the availability of advice and representation and an increase in litigants in person presenting with a diversity of support needs.[71] Criminal justice has seen the drive to speed up and rationalise defence services working to marginalised and exclude defendants as their lawyers have not got enough time to work on their cases fully.[72]

Against this background, the disillusionment experienced by legal aid lawyers as a result of negative perceptions of their work – both from government actors[73] and in the public sphere – has been profound, and high levels of resilience and persistence are required to overcome ongoing challenges and constraints.[74] It has been further noted that the negative public perception of legal aid practitioners as being 'fat cats' or 'activists' has caused undue harm to the sector generally.[75] This combination of resource constraints, challenging working conditions and wider negative perceptions of legal aid work has led to a sustainability crisis in the profession, with poor rates of retention and an 'ageing demographic' of legal aid practitioners.[76]

The pandemic has exacerbated existing problems by creating new and urgent legal issues for clients while simultaneously inhibiting opportunities for individuals to access justice.[77] It has consequently strained minimal resources for

[67] Luke Clements, 'Clustered Injustice and the Level Green' (Legal Action Group, 2020).

[68] Jo Wilding, *The Legal Aid Market: Challenges for publicly funded immigration and asylum legal representation* (Policy Press, 2021).

[69] Anne Barlow et al, *Mapping Paths to Family Justice: Resolving Family Disputes in Neoliberal Times* (Palgrave MacMillan, 2017).

[70] Robins and Newman (n 60).

[71] Jess Mant, 'Placing litigants in person at the centre of the post-LASPO court process' (2020) 32 *Child and Family Law Quarterly* 421.

[72] Lucy Welsh, *Access to Justice in Magistrates' Courts: A Study of Defendant Marginalisation* (Hart, 2022).

[73] Lizzie Deardon, 'Government Attacks on Lawyers 'Undermine Rule of Law' says Lord Chief Justice' (*The Independent*, 10 November 2020), available at www.independent.co.uk/news/uk/politics/government-priti-patel-lawyers-activists-attacks-rule-law-b1720428.html.

[74] Jacqueline Kinghan, *Lawyers, Networks and Progressive Social Change: Lawyers Changing Lives* (Hart, 2021) 147–67.

[75] Westminster Commission (n 1) 19.

[76] ibid, 94.

[77] Law Society of England and Wales (n 2).

practitioners and arguably worsened an existing well-being crisis in the legal aid profession.[78] For instance, Young Legal Aid Lawyers reported in its first COVID-19 Report in April 2020 that 25 per cent of its members were required to put themselves at risk of infection because of their job; 67.5 per cent stated that their work volume had 'decreased', 'significantly decreased' or been 'decimated' since the start of the pandemic; and 80 per cent of junior legal barristers stated that their work had 'significantly decreased' or been 'decimated'.[79] Research from Newman et al shows the huge levels of demand being faced in social welfare law as the pandemic brought vast numbers of new client on board at a time in which the sector was struggling to reach out to its existing client base.[80] Relatedly, Mant et al document the way that both clients and practitioners across debt, housing and welfare benefits advice are having to adapt to new ways of working, which raises considerable well-being issues for both sides.[81]

The pandemic has also led to an overwhelming case backlog in the criminal justice system. Statistics show that there were almost 61,000 cases received but not completed in the Crown Court and 364,000 cases in the magistrates' courts by June 2021.[82] A move to digital court hearings has raised wider access to justice concerns for groups at risk of digital exclusion.[83] Even before the pandemic, the digital court reform agenda proposed by the Ministry of Justice had been criticised for being based upon cost savings rather than improving access to justice. Given the lack of funding within the system, and the wider supply and demand issues brought about by the pandemic, these concerns persist. There are also significant concerns about the consequences for those groups who have traditionally relied upon face-to-face services who have 'disappeared' from services during the pandemic and who are at risk of further exclusion due to services being overwhelmed by the influx of pandemic-induced legal need among those with higher levels of legal capability.[84] In 2020, the Government pledged £500 million to support the justice system in light of the pandemic, with a key emphasis on reducing court backlogs. The legal professions, however, did not view this as sufficient to deal with the deeper effects of years of neglect for access to justice.[85] This is the present situation

[78] See: LawCare, 'Life in the Law 2020/21' (LawCare, 2021), available at www.lawcare.org.uk/media/14vhquzz/lawcare-lifeinthelaw-v6-final.pdf.

[79] Young Legal Aid Lawyers, 'Covid-19 Report' (Young Legal Aid Lawyers, 2020), available at www.younglegalaidlawyers.org/covid19report.

[80] Daniel Newman et al, 'Vulnerability, Legal Need and Technology' (2021) 23 *International Journal of Discrimination and the Law* 230.

[81] Jessica Mant et al, 'Blended Advice and Access to Justice' (Ministry of Justice and the Access to Justice Foundation 2022).

[82] National Audit Office, 'Reducing the Backlog in Criminal Courts' (National Audit Office, 2021) 5.

[83] Catrina Denvir and Amanda D Selvarajah, 'Safeguarding Access to Justice in the Age of the Online Court' (2021) 85 *MLR* 25.

[84] Newman et al (n 80).

[85] The Law Society of England and Wales, '£500m justice funding boost welcomed, but much more still needs to be done' (The Law Society, 25 November 2020), available at www.lawsociety.org.uk/Contact-or-visit-us/Press-office/Press-releases/500m-justice-funding-boost-welcomed-but-much-more-still-needs-to-be-done.

of a legal aid sector that seeks to uphold access to justice despite decades' worth of political neglect, hostility and ill-fortune. This context has inspired the research that underpins this book and underscores the importance of building a knowledge base that can assist with understanding what the future holds for legal aid.

V. Investigating Legal Aid

There have been numerous attempts to review the sustainability of legal aid and make recommendations for reform in recent years. Here, we will set out the most significant of these reviews and the evidence base they offer, so as to provide an important grounding in the existing evidence that preceded the Legal Aid Census as well as the significant evidence gaps that the Census sought to address. In particular, these reports demonstrate the destructive impact of LASPO, the need to examine the implications of this reform and the compounding impact of the pandemic in order to more fully understand the role of the legal aid sector in protecting and promoting access to justice.

In 2014, the Legal Action Group established the Low Commission to develop a strategy for the future provision of advice and legal support on social welfare law in England and Wales in the wake of LASPO being introduced.[86] The Commission's main report called for urgent reforms to ensure that ordinary people can access the help they need to deal with employment, debt, housing and other social welfare law problems. Some of the key principles underpinning the Low Commission's suggested approach were: early intervention and action rather than allowing problems to escalate; investment for prevention to avoid the wasted costs generated by the failure of public services; simplifying the legal system; developing different service offerings to meet different types of need; investing in a basic level of provision of information and advice; and embedding advice in settings where people regularly go, such as GP surgeries and community centres. The Commission called for greater use to be made of new technology and helplines for those who can manage to access these forms of communication and are not digitally excluded and for more emphasis to be placed on public legal education throughout the national curriculum.

In a report entitled 'Cuts that Hurt', Amnesty International set out a series of recommendations in relation to legal aid reforms.[87] The most fundamental of these was that the UK Government needed to ensure that children and vulnerable young people are entitled to legal aid, regardless of the legal issue at stake. The report asserted that children and families without sufficient means should be able to obtain legal advice, assistance, and where litigation is contemplated, legal representation free of charge in any case where a child's best interests are

[86] The Low Commission, 'Tackling the Advice Deficit: A Strategy for Access to Advice and Legal Support on Social Welfare Law in England and Wales' (Legal Action Group, 2014).
[87] Amnesty International (n 55).

engaged. The report called for a restoration of legal advice to those areas of civil and family justice taken out of scope by LASPO. It also called for an overhaul to the Exceptional Case Funding system so as to make it fully accessible to members of the public and ensure that all those who are potentially eligible for Exceptional Case Funding have the opportunity to receive advice on their entitlement and funded assistance in making an application.

In the same year, the Trades Union Congress published a report on access to justice and legal aid, entitled 'Justice Denied'.[88] This report called for the government to ensure that access to legal aid is based on need and sufficiently enables people to enforce their human rights. The report recommended that the Ministry of Justice carry out immediate and in-depth assessments of the access to justice impacts of budget cuts, LASPO and reforms to court services. The report asserted that such assessments should be undertaken in collaboration with trade unions, other organisations with expertise in the field, those who use the justice system and other government departments. The assessments should include the impacts on equalities; whether LASPO enables the UK to meet its obligations under ratified international conventions; the wider impacts on access to justice; the wider costs to the public sector and knock-on costs of the reforms; and the impacts on court services and on the ability of the justice system to deliver justice fairly, effectively and efficiently. The report called for justice services to be viewed as interconnected and interdependent, and based within the context of wider public services. Overall, the report argued that the justice system should be recognised as a public service and a public good, and future government reforms should commit to using evidence-based approaches in relation to similar reforms in the future.

Following these influential reports, the Fabian Society published its report, 'The Right to Justice' in 2017, after its author Lord Bach was invited by then-leader of the Labour opposition, Jeremy Corbyn, to develop policy proposals on legal aid.[89] A raft of proposals were suggested but were underpinned by the radical call for a new statutory right to justice. The report recommended that the Government should consider how to simplify and clarify the means-testing process in criminal courts, as well as the evidence requirements for civil and criminal legal aid applications, in order to prevent people from being forced to abandon their legal problems. The key principle underpinning Lord Bach's proposal was that 'everyone charged with a criminal offence should have equality of arms in the presentation of their defence.'

In 2019, the Law Society launched a campaign entitled End Legal Aid Deserts.[90] Legal aid deserts occur when even those who remain eligible for legal aid and are facing important legal issues struggle to get the local face-to-face advice they need due to a shortage of advice organisations and law firms able to offer legal

[88] Speak Up for Justice, 'Justice Denied: Impacts of the Government's Reforms to Legal Aid and Court Services on Access to Justice' (Trades Union Congress, 2016).

[89] Fabian Society, 'The Right to Justice: Final Report of the Bach Commission' (Fabians, 2017).

[90] The Law Society of England and Wales, 'Legal Aid Deserts' (The Law Society, 22nd August 2022), available at www.lawsociety.org.uk/campaigns/legal-aid-deserts.

aid-funded advice. The Law Society produced extensive data to demonstrate the geographical areas where there were only one or no legal aid providers. This indicates, for example, that over a third of the population live in a local authority area with no housing legal aid providers. On the basis of this data, the Law Society has called on the Government to independently review the sustainability of the legal aid system, so as to ensure that every area in England and Wales has an acceptable number of legal aid providers.

In 2020, the House of Commons Justice Committee conducted an inquiry post-LASPO that formed the 'Future of Legal Aid Report' in order to 'set out the core problems within the current legal aid framework and to identify the solutions that could improve the long-term future of legal aid.'[91] They found that there was an 'urgent need to overhaul the system so that providers are paid for all the work they do to support their clients, especially at the early stages of the process'. To this extent, the inquiry concluded that the structure of the fee scheme did not support high-quality service to clients, and the legal aid scheme generally lacked flexibility. It is notable that the report references the frustration of those who responded to the inquiry at the repeated similar findings of inquiries and reviews into civil legal aid with no sign of change. The Government responded to the inquiry in 2021 and emphasised its commitments to undertaking a review of the means test for legal aid as well as to the forthcoming publication of the Independent Review of Criminal Legal Aid. The Government indicated that it was planning to increase criminal legal aid by £51 million per annum, and that many of the other recommendations in the criminal legal aid context would be addressed later that year. The Government also re-emphasised its commitment to undertaking a pilot study to test the impact of early advice in social welfare law and an allocation of £3 million to support litigants in person, both of which were set out in the 2019 post-legislative review but were ultimately curtailed by the pandemic.

As promised, the Ministry of Justice published the Independent Review of Criminal Legal Aid in 2021.[92] This review was led by Sir Christopher Bellamy QC and explored what more could be done to improve criminal legal aid for providers and the public. It had wide-ranging terms of reference including reform of legal aid schemes in criminal legal aid, recruitment and retention of legal aid practitioners and the wider market for criminal legal aid services. The report made the case for funding for criminal legal aid to be increased for solicitors and barristers as soon as possible to an annual level of 'at least 15%' above present levels to ensure that a 'level playing field' between defendants and prosecutors was maintained. For Bellamy, '£135m is, in my view, the minimum necessary as the first step in nursing the system of criminal legal aid back to health after years of neglect'. The Government responded to this review with a commitment to increase fees by up to 15 per cent, but these figures were contested by professional groups such as the Law Society, who argued that the real-terms effects of this would be lower in

[91] House of Commons Justice Committee (n 4).

[92] Christopher Bellamy, 'Independent Review of Criminal Legal Aid' (Ministry of Justice, 2021).

practice.[93] The lacklustre response from the Government resulted in a four-week criminal barrister strike led by the Criminal Bar Association, which later ended with acceptance of a 15 per cent pay increase and additional funding, including £5 million per year for the youth courts.[94]

In March 2021, The House of Lords Constitution Select Committee reported on COVID-19 and the courts.[95] This report highlighted several challenges faced by lawyers, judges and clients in remote hearings and raised access to justice concerns in relation to delays and wide-ranging challenges faced by litigants. The report concluded that the justice system is 'under strain' and that 'actions that might have been capable of alleviating the effects of the pandemic' had not been taken. It highlighted 'data deficiencies' in the justice system and also found that the backlog of cases in the criminal courts, which was unacceptably high before the pandemic, had now reached 'crisis levels'. In the same year, the Westminster Commission on Legal Aid conducted an inquiry into the sustainability of legal aid and heard comprehensive evidence from legal aid practitioners and clients from October 2020 to March 2021, and reported later in 2021. The Commission demonstrated that there were 'significant issues' in terms of the accessibility of the justice system that had only been exacerbated by the pandemic. Problems with recruitment and retention of practitioners were widely reported, with firms struggling to support trainees. A number of recommendations were proposed including raising fees in line with inflation, reversing the 8.75 per cent cut to criminal legal aid, bringing social welfare advice back into scope and simplifying the exceptional case funding regime.[96] As detailed here, there has been no shortage of prior work that seeks to ascertain the scale and depth of the impact of legal aid reforms on different areas of legal need and access to justice. Each of these reviews has produced important evidence concerning the way that LASPO has impacted upon the legal aid sector and its clients. Each has also had variable success in instigating political action in response to the problems identified, with some inspiring incremental financial and research commitments from the UK Government, but none has yet been able to capture the widespread and deep-rooted nature of these problems in a way that has reinvigorated commitments to recognising the important role of legal aid. Moreover, none has yet been capable of capturing a detailed and large-scale view of the intersecting implications of austerity measures, legal aid reform, and the COVID-19 pandemic. In order to address this important gap, the Legal Aid Census builds upon the individual strengths of these investigations by providing

[93] Ministry of Justice, 'Response to Independent Review of Criminal Legal Aid' (Ministry of Justice, 2022), available at www.gov.uk/government/consultations/response-to-independent-review-of-criminal-legal-aid/response-to-independent-review-of-criminal-legal-aid.

[94] Judith Burns, 'Barristers Start Indefinite Strike Action Over Pay in England and Wales' (*BBC News*, 1 September 2022), available at www.bbc.com/news/uk-62757099; Haroon Sadique, 'Criminal barristers in England and Wales vote to end strike action' (*The Guardian*, 10 October 2022), available at www.theguardian.com/law/2022/oct/10/barristers-in-england-and-wales-vote-to-end-strike-action.

[95] Westminster Commission (n 1).

[96] House of Lords Select Committee, 'Covid-19 and the Courts' (House of Lords, 2021), available at publications.parliament.uk/pa/ld5801/ldselect/ldconst/257/25704.htm.

the first comprehensive view of the legal aid sector in England and Wales from the perspectives of those working at its frontline.

VI. The Legal Aid Census

The Legal Aid Census was born out of the need for a specific evidence base on the experiences, perspectives, and motivations of practitioners working across the legal aid sector, as well as the need for insight into the common challenges they face and aspirations they have for the future of legal aid. The need for such a comprehensive view of the sector as a whole has long been acknowledged within the sector, which often finds itself resigned to siloed working in different areas of law, or to engaging in sporadic campaigns as opportunities arise to do so. As such, the research team was commissioned by the Legal Aid Practitioners' Group (LAPG),[97] a membership body representing legal aid practitioners across England and Wales, to design and implement a workforce census that could provide vitally important insight into the demographics and characteristics of the sector, and identify issues that are commonly experienced across the legal aid workforce. The consequent Legal Aid Census, which ultimately comprised five surveys, therefore emerged in response to calls for robust and wide-ranging data from practitioner groups comprising the LAPG's membership. These included organisations responsible for representing key groups within the sector, such as the Black Solicitors Network,[98] the Housing Law Practitioners Association,[99] Legal Action Group,[100] and Shelter,[101] to acquire a more representative and thorough understanding of the legal aid landscape. As explored throughout this chapter, pre-existing data concerning the reality of legal aid practice has so far been piecemeal and incapable of elucidating comprehensive conditions on the ground. To address this important evidence gap, our research team was supported by the LAPG to produce the most comprehensive study of past, present and aspiring legal aid practitioners ever conducted in England and Wales.

The underpinning objectives of the Census were to develop a baseline demographic profile of legal aid practitioners, as well as a comprehensive understanding of practitioners' education and training backgrounds, salaries, fee arrangements and job satisfaction levels. In order to achieve this, the Census sought to identify routes into the profession, lawyers' perceptions on barriers faced and correlations between these perceptions and socio-economic background. The Census

[97] The Legal Aid Practitioners Group is a membership organisation that represents and provides support for legal aid practitioners; see lapg.co.uk.

[98] The primary voice of black solicitors in England and Wales; see www.blacksolicitorsnetwork.co.uk.

[99] A forum for practitioners working in the housing field; see www.hlpa.org.uk/cms.

[100] An independent charity promoting access to justice; see www.lag.org.uk.

[101] An independent charity that supports people who have lost their homes or are facing eviction; see www.shelter.org.uk.

also aimed to identify and describe the key challenges facing legal aid lawyers across different areas of law, and to provide an indication of how legal aid advice providers may have been affected by legal aid cuts, wider austerity reforms and the COVID-19 pandemic. Finally, the Census sought to capture how legal aid practitioners have adapted to the changing legal aid landscape and what they believe is needed to sustain the legal aid sector in future.

A. Census Respondents

The Legal Aid Census comprised five surveys, voluntarily self-administered online[102] by respondents from each of the following stakeholder groups:

1. Former legal aid practitioners who have left the legal aid sector
2. Current legal aid practitioners currently working in the legal aid sector
3. Chambers engaged in the provision of legal aid services
4. Organisations engaged in the provision of legal aid services
5. Current law students undertaking a law degree.

Respondents in the first four stakeholder groups were asked questions in order to ascertain their perspectives on a range of topics including but not limited to: the delivery of legal aid; their personal experiences in the industry; the impact of factors such as LASPO and the pandemic on the sector; the LAA; salaries and remuneration; recruitment, retention, training and professional development; and working conditions. The final stakeholder group were asked questions regarding their interest in pursuing a career in legal aid and any factors that deterred them from such a career. Those who indicated an interest in pursuing a career in legal aid ('Prospective Legal Aid Practitioners') were asked a series of more detailed questions regarding their experiences of legal education and training as well as their motivations for pursuing a career in legal aid. The first four surveys – excluding the fifth, which targeted current students – were tested as pilots in March 2021. For each, a representative group of stakeholders participated in trial versions of the surveys and provided feedback on the survey instruments in order to ensure that questions aligned with the research aims and that the surveys were sufficiently clear to interpret. In response to suggestions made by these stakeholders, a number of changes were made to the surveys in order to revise question structure and clarify question framing prior to wider dissemination in April 2021. Stakeholder groups were able to submit responses between 12 April 2021 and 11 June 2021; additionally, the LAPG disseminated invitations to participate in the Census to practitioners based within its 334 membership organisations at regular intervals

[102] All data and responses were stored securely, managed in accordance with relevant data legislative requirements, and pseudo-anonymised as appropriate. The recruitment strategy, methods of data analysis, and data management plan received ethical approval from Cardiff University (Ethics Reference number: SREC/030221/02).

during this data-collection period. Calls to participate in the Census were also shared through practitioner networks and social media.

Student respondents were able to submit responses to the fifth survey between 14 June 2021 and 12 July 2021. Invitations to participate and background information about the Census were disseminated to law students in England and Wales via social media platforms and relevant academic networks, including heads of law departments across universities in England and Wales, the Clinical Legal Education Organisation and Young Legal Aid Lawyers.

The Census ultimately gathered a wide range of data from managers and directors of legal aid organisations, barristers, solicitors, legal executives, clerks, paralegals, caseworkers, students, aspiring legal aid practitioners, and former legal aid practitioners. In total, 255 former legal aid practitioners, 1,208 current practitioners, 369 organisations, 32 chambers, and 376 students responded to the Legal Aid Census.[103] The scale of the Census means that it can provide unprecedented insights from across the legal aid sector, including from those who have recently left as well as those who hope to enter it in the near future.

B. Census Design

The five surveys that comprised the Census included questions that were both closed and open-ended in nature. In order to gain insights across the totality of responses provided with respect to any one open-ended question, the research team coded open-ended questions for key themes. In total, six researchers were involved in coding the open-ended questions posed across the five surveys. To commence, open-ended questions across all of the surveys were thematically grouped, with each thematic group of questions assigned to a single coder. This facilitated a consistent approach to the coding of similar questions across the different surveys. Where multiple themes were raised in a single response, only the main three issues were coded.[104] Codes were devised following a review of all the open-ended responses with respect to a particular question. As per the method outlined in Montgomery and Crittenden, each response to a particular open-ended question was evaluated in turn, with new codes created where an open-ended response raised a theme that did not fit into any of the existing codes.[105] The coding of all open-ended questions passed through an initial phase in which preliminary codes were evaluated for thematic completeness by the same

[103] This excludes 56 respondents who were removed from the practitioner survey as they either did not complete the Census in its entirety, or were identified as current students who responded to the practitioners' survey in error.

[104] In instances where more than three issues were raised, researchers assessed which of those issues were the 'main' issues with reference to the order in which the issues were raised and the level of detail provided.

[105] Andrew Montgomery and Kateleen Crittenden, 'Improving Coding Reliability for Open-Ended Questions (1977) 41 *The Public Opinion Quarterly* 235.

single member of the research team, prior to finalisation. Once coding of the full set of responses for each question was completed, a random subset of the total number of open-ended responses given in respect of each question was reviewed by a second coder. The purpose of the second coding was to confirm that the codes attributed to each response by the first coder were relevant and appropriate. For questions where more than 100 responses were received, a minimum of 20 per cent were subject to second coding. For questions with less than 100 responses, the percentage subject to second coding increased on a sliding scale.[106] Agreement between the first and second coder across the full set of open-ended questions analysed was high. On average, the second coder agreed with 99.6 per cent of the codes assigned by the first coder. Statistics presented are those derived from the codes assigned by the first coder. The text indicates where descriptive statistics relate to coded open-ended questions. Descriptive statistics used throughout are coupled with quotes extracted from the open-ended responses in order to provide greater context for findings and to illuminate the perspectives of respondents in their own words. Percentages reported exclude those who did not answer the question and as respondents were not forced to answer questions, the total number of respondents differs slightly from question to question. In addition, percentages exclude responses to qualitative questions where a respondent indicated in their open-ended response that the question was 'not relevant'. This book analyses findings from all five surveys that comprised the Census and relies upon descriptive statistics to set out key findings.

C. Impact of the Legal Aid Census

The headline findings of the Legal Aid Census were published as a report of approximately 100 pages in March 2022.[107] The report, entitled 'We Are Legal Aid: Findings from the Legal Aid Census 2021', was designed to present a clear and accessible summary of key Census findings in order to encourage broad engagement with the data among those working within the legal aid sector. It was intended to serve as an educational and pragmatic resource for practitioners that could be used to raise broader awareness of legal aid work both within and beyond the sector, as well as a foundational evidence base for campaign work where appropriate.

The launch of the 'We Are Legal Aid' report was eagerly received by the legal aid sector. The findings prompted an open letter to the Lord Chancellor, signed

[106] Where fewer than 50 responses were provided to a question 100% of responses were subject to second coding. Where 50–100 responses were received, between 30–50% of responses underwent second coding.

[107] Catrina Denvir et al, 'We Are Legal Aid: Findings From the 2021 Legal Aid Census' (Legal Aid Practitioners Group, 2021).

by leading figures across the legal aid sector of England and Wales.[108] Signatories included AdviceUK,[109] Association of Costs Lawyers,[110] International Federation of Women Lawyers,[111] Housing Law Practitioners Association,[112] Law Centres Network,[113] The Law Society of England and Wales' Junior Lawyers Division,[114] Legal Action Group,[115] Public Law Project,[116] Resolution,[117] Society of Labour Lawyers,[118] and Young Legal Aid Lawyers,[119] as well as the LAPG, which first commissioned the Census. These groups strongly supported the Census and its ability to demonstrate a realistic view of the present-day legal aid sector to the UK Government:

> The Legal Aid Census provides the robust evidence that we need to demonstrate what life is really like for practitioners and organisations on the legal aid front line. You have accepted the perilous state of the criminal legal aid sector and the need for urgent investment in the system and its people if we are to ensure that legal representation is there for those who need it. The same is no less true for those in civil legal aid where years of cuts and underfunding have taken their toll. The Census demonstrates that practitioners are highly motivated and committed to their clients and to social justice. However, a lack of investment has caused significant issues across the legal aid sector.[120]

For the sector, the Census demonstrated the urgent need for government action to ensure that legal aid organisations are sustainable and that practitioners are able to continue their work in responding to legal need. Representatives of the sector used the Census as a basis for arguing that: 'The government must recognise legal aid organisations as part of the backbone of the high street and a vital part of levelling up our communities' and furthermore 'must address burgeoning legal aid deserts to make access to justice a reality for all.'[121]

[108] Legal Aid Practitioners Group, 'Joint Open Letter to the Lord Chancellor' (Legal Aid Practitioners Group, 31 March 2022), available at lapg.co.uk/wp-content/uploads/Joint-open-letter-to-the-Lord-Chancellor.pdf.

[109] A support network for independent advice organisations; see www.adviceuk.org.uk.

[110] The representative body for costs lawyers; see www.associationofcostslawyers.co.uk.

[111] A non-governmental organisation geared towards promoting and preserving the rights of women and children; see fidafederation.org/en.

[112] See n 98.

[113] A network of specialist, community-based legal advice providers; see www.lawcentres.org.uk.

[114] A representative branch of the Law Society representing lawyers early in their career; see www.lawsociety.org.uk/topics/junior-lawyers.

[115] See n 99.

[116] A national charity geared towards promoting the accessibility of public law remedies; see publiclawproject.org.uk.

[117] A membership group of family lawyers geared towards promoting constructive dispute resolution; see resolution.org.uk.

[118] The legal think tank of the Labour party; see societyoflabourlawyers.org.uk.

[119] A network of junior lawyers working in areas of law that have traditionally been publicly funded; see www.younglegalaidlawyers.org/about.

[120] Legal Aid Practitioners Group (n 108).

[121] ibid.

As such, the 'We Are Legal Aid' report acted as a springboard for the launch of a new campaign within the sector to make legal aid sustainable. For the signatories of the letter, the Census findings offered a clear indication that 'now is the time for the government to stand up and be counted on all aspects of the legal aid system'.[122]

While it is encouraging to see that the 'We Are Legal Aid' report was capable of having this impact within the sector, this publication marked only the beginning of the journey towards meaningful change. The Census is the most comprehensive evidence base ever compiled on the legal aid sector, and consequently holds significant potential value in terms of firmly demonstrating the relevance of legal aid to broader issues of access to justice. As such, this book builds on the 'We Are Legal Aid' report to deepen and widen the analysis in three key ways. First, this book provides a more detailed view of the sector by drawing on an extensive range of qualitative data in order to bring together the varied voices of practitioners across the sector. Second, the report was designed to operate as a succinct document which focused tightly on a small number of key, policy-relevant issues. In contrast, this book explores many of the other issues that were of concern to respondents across the sector, such as perspectives on the lack of legal aid content in undergraduate legal education and the prevalence of bullying and harassment. Third, this book contextualises the issues, experiences, problems and concerns identified in the Census by drawing thematic connections with wider academic literature on access to justice and the legal professions. In doing so, it provides a rigorous and original contribution to the literature in these fields, challenging assumptions that underpin accepted knowledge through empirical data informed by frontline perspectives of legal aid.

VII. Structure of the Book

Chapter two sets out a foundational view of the modern legal aid profession. It draws together data collected about demographic, employment and educational characteristics of current legal aid practitioners with organisational characteristics about the chambers and legal aid organisations within which they work. The chapter also explores the demographic and educational characteristics of law students who responded to the census, focusing on those who indicated an interest in pursuing a legal aid career. Drawing on this data, chapter two paints what we have termed a 'portrait of the profession', offering a detailed view of the people and organisations who currently make up the legal aid sector, as well as those who are likely to form its next generation, as informed by Census responses.

Chapter three builds upon this foundational portrait by exploring in detail the educational backgrounds of current practitioners. Here, we examine and compare the specific opportunities and experiences that shaped the journeys that current

[122] ibid.

practitioners have taken into a legal aid career. In doing so, this chapter reflects upon the educational factors that motivated current practitioners to pursue a career in legal aid, and draws upon their first-hand experiences to identify the challenges and barriers that may make such a decision more difficult.

Chapter four examines the working conditions and practices that characterise the legal aid sector, drawing out the realities of daily practice for those working across the sector. In doing so, this chapter reflects on the high-stakes nature of legal aid work and the way that such work is frequently underpinned by strong social justice values. It considers the challenges faced by the legal aid workforce, using understandings of vulnerability in order to understand the impact of working conditions on those charged with upholding the operation of the sector. It reflects on the ways that legal aid work is underpinned by several challenges relating to well-being, stressors, workplace bullying and harassment, as well as significant tensions surrounding working hours and remuneration that frame the working environments of legal aid practitioners. All of these challenges are viewed in light of the levels of job satisfaction reported by current legal aid practitioners and the efficacy of the coping strategies that are taken across the sector to manage these challenges.

Chapter five delves further into important questions about the sustainability of the legal aid sector, by reporting on the level and nature of fees on which legal aid practitioners and organisations rely. This chapter asserts that the current rates of remuneration, coupled with the rigidity and complexity of legal aid fee arrangements, pose considerable challenges for legal aid practitioners. Building on chapter four, this analysis provides further reinforcement for the daily reality of practitioners needing to work beyond set hours to meet demand, and struggling to fit work around their family life and personal commitments. By clearly outlining the extent to which legal aid practitioners engage in unpaid work, this chapter provides a crucial challenge to prevailing media narratives concerning the motivations and working realities of legal aid lawyers.

Chapter six reflects on how the sector has been impacted by the COVID-19 pandemic. In doing so, it establishes an insight into the initial impact of government-imposed lockdowns, as well as the challenges that are likely to endure for the sector in the longer term. It explores how practitioners have adapted to the new world of remote working, providing advice and representing clients virtually and via telephone. For practitioners, this has meant an enormous increase in both demand and workload, as they balance the tasks of supporting vulnerable groups as well as a new 'COVID cohort' of clients, maintaining a supportive and cohesive workplace community and a healthy work–life balance, and proper supervision and training provision for junior staff. The chapter reveals that the pandemic has also brought significant concerns about economic sustainability for organisations, chambers and individual practitioners. Additionally, several practitioners reported concerns about pandemic-related economic insecurity, stemming from large outstanding caseloads subject to delays in the wider justice system, as well as pre-existing concerns about the financial viability of legal aid work and economic precarity within the sector. Taken together, this chapter demonstrates that the legal aid sector is facing significant challenges as it moves beyond the immediate repercussions of the pandemic, and begins to look towards the post-COVID future of the legal aid workforce.

Chapter seven turns to consider the implications of these findings for the future of the legal aid sector. Here, the book considers the observations of those who responded to the Census on behalf of their organisations or chambers, with specific reference to their experiences of recruiting and retaining practitioners. It sets out the key challenges for organisations and chambers in terms of attracting and keeping legal aid lawyers, given the low levels of remuneration compared to other areas. It also reflects upon the extent to which legal aid is perceived as viable from an organisational perspective, drawing together information about the number of organisations and chambers who reported abandoning legal aid work with reasons that individual practitioners have chosen to exit the sector. In order to provide a view of how these problems may shape the future sustainability of legal aid, this chapter also examines the reasons that deter students from pursuing careers in legal aid, including poor pay, lack of legal aid contracts, difficulty in affording to work in legal aid, as well as a lack of information provided regarding legal aid as a career.

Chapter eight draws together the key findings presented in this book and sets out an agenda for thinking through the future of legal aid in light of the Census findings. This concluding chapter asserts that the Legal Aid Census should mark the beginning of a new era of research that seeks to monitor, evaluate and understand legal aid, as well as serve as a call for immediate action in terms of policy and reform. While each of the previous chapters highlight challenges facing the sector, this chapter draws together practitioners' views and perspectives on what is needed in the future to address these challenges. Here, we purposely centre practitioners' voices by reflecting on the responses that were received from practitioners when they were asked if there were any final parting words that they would like to contribute to their Census submissions. This chapter consequently reveals the core concerns and hopes that practitioners hold for the sector and the future of legal aid. Building on this, the chapter sets out an agenda for both future policy reform and future research activities that are necessary for furthering and sustaining legal aid.

2

A Portrait of the Profession

I. Introduction

Legal aid lawyers are frequently regarded as forming part of a broader profession which is seen as greedy, manipulative and corrupt and driven by financial rewards.[1] These views often derive from a presumption that all lawyers earn high salaries or come from elite and privileged backgrounds that effectively divorce their concerns, motivations and perspectives from those of ordinary people. These presumptions are particularly deleterious for legal aid lawyers due to the fact that their salaries are derived from public funding. As such, legal aid lawyers are associated not only with these presumptions, but also with concerns about whether their salaries are a legitimate use of taxpayers' contributions, or whether they truly provide a service that offers value for money. These attitudes toxify the public debate around legal aid funding, such that when legal aid lawyers express resistance to efforts to restrict funding or when they urge higher rates of pay, they are derided in the media as part of a clowder of 'fat cats'.[2] In this first substantive chapter, we assess the validity of these presumptions by setting out the demographics and backgrounds of the members of the legal aid sector who responded to the Legal Aid Census. By exploring who legal aid lawyers are, what kinds of background they come from and who chooses a career in legal aid, we provide a basis for the findings presented throughout this book and paint a portrait of the legal aid profession that contrasts with many of the misconceptions currently framing their public denigration.

[1] Leo J Shapiro, 'Public Perception of Lawyers: Consumer Research Findings' (American Bar Association, 2002), available at www.americanbar.org/content/dam/aba/administrative/market_research/public_perception_of_lawyers_2002.pdf.

[2] Helen O'Nions, '"Fat Cat" Lawyers and "Illegal" Migrants: The Impact of Intersecting Hostilities and Toxic Narrative on Access to Justice' (2020) 42 *Journal of Social Welfare and Family Law* 319.

II. The Legal Profession of England and Wales

Across the legal profession as a whole, there are 17,263 practising barristers,[3] 156,965 practising solicitors,[4] and approximately 20,000 Chartered Institute of Legal Executives (CILEX) professionals[5] registered within England and Wales. These individuals form part of a cohort which differs from the broader population of England and Wales in a number of ways. Notably, the legal profession comprises a higher proportion of individuals educated at fee-paying schools and elite universities[6] and a lower proportion of individuals from lower socio-economic and working-class backgrounds.[7] Estimates in respect of the number of barristers that attend fee-paying schools have varied from 18.1 per cent[8] to 37 per cent.[9] Whilst the Solicitor's Regulation Authority reported in 2022 that 23 per cent of solicitors in England and Wales attended fee-paying schools.[10] This compares to a population average of seven per cent.[11] These differences are exacerbated amongst certain sections of the profession, with the Sutton Trust and the Social Mobility Commission reporting in 2019 that 'Senior judges are the most socially exclusive groups of all the professions … with the highest numbers of both independent school and Oxbridge alumni.'[12]

[3] As of December 2021. Bar Standards Board, 'Statistics on Practising Barristers' (Bar Standards Board, 2022), available at www.barstandardsboard.org.uk/news-publications/research-and-statistics/statistics-about-the-bar/practising-barristers.html.

[4] As of July 2022. Solicitors Regulation Authority, 'Population of Solicitors in England and Wales' (Solicitors Regulation Authority, 2022), available at www.sra.org.uk/sra/research-publications/regulated-community-statistics/data/population_solicitors.

[5] As of August 2022. Chartered Institute of Legal Executives, 'Facts, Figures, Statistics' (Chartered Institute of Legal Executives, 2022), available at www.cilex.org.uk/media/interesting_facts/facts__figures.

[6] Legal Services Board, 'The State of Legal Services 2020 – Evidence Compendium' (2020), available at legalservicesboard.org.uk/wp-content/uploads/2020/11/The-State-of-Legal-Services-Evidence-Compendium-FINAL.pdf; The Sutton Trust and the Social Mobility Commission, 'Elitist Britain 2019: The Educational Backgrounds of Britain's Leading People' (The Sutton Trust and the Social Mobility Commission, 2019), available at www.suttontrust.com/wp-content/uploads/2019/12/Elitist-Britain-2019.pdf, 55; The Bridge Group, 'Socio-Economic Background and Progression to Partner in the Law' (The Bridge Group, 2020), available at https://static1.squarespace.com/static/5c18e090b40b9d6b43b093d8/t/5f6c69ea4d0d1b29037581f3/1600940523386/BG_SEB_Partner_Law_Sep2020_SUMMARY_FINAL.pdf.

[7] Solicitors Regulation Authority, 'How Diverse is the Solicitors' Profession' (Solicitors Regulation Authority, 2022), available at www.sra.org.uk/sra/equality-diversity/diversity-profession/diverse-legal-profession; Bar Standards Board, 'Diversity At the Bar 2021: A Summary of the Latest Available Diversity for the Bar' (Bar Standards Board, 2022), available at www.barstandardsboard.org.uk/uploads/assets/be522642-160b-433b-af03a910a5636233/BSB-Report-on-Diversity-at-the-Bar-2021.pdf, 24.

[8] Legal Services Board (n 6); Young Legal Aid Lawyers, 'Young Legal Aid Lawyers: Social Mobility in a Time of Austerity' (Young Legal Aid Lawyers, 2018), available at www.younglegalaidlawyers.org/sites/default/files/Soc Mob Report – edited.pdf.

[9] Bar Standards Board (n 7).

[10] Solicitors Regulation Authority (n 7).

[11] Legal Services Board (n 6).

[12] The Sutton Trust and the Social Mobility Commission (n 6).

Whilst certain aspects of the profession's diversity have changed over time – for example, there is greater representation in respect of gender and ethnicity[13] – these changes have been slow to reflect within the hierarchy of the profession. So whilst the Law Society reports that since 1990 over 60 per cent of new entrants into the legal profession in England and Wales have been women,[14] women are less well-represented in senior roles and in the judiciary.[15] They are also less likely to be barristers, according to the Bar Standards Board.[16] Women are also reported to be overrepresented in some areas of legal aid work such as family law.[17]

With regards to socio-economic status, educational background and ethnicity, the picture is slightly different for those working in legal aid. For example, whilst white graduates from higher socio-economic backgrounds are overrepresented in city firms, Black and minority ethnic women from lower socio-economic groups are overrepresented in high-street firms.[18] The Bar Council has also found that Black and Asian minority ethnic and state-educated barristers are more likely to be represented in publicly funded work, which is itself the most diverse part of the Bar. A greater proportion of ethnic minority barristers – relative to white barristers – also earn over half of their income from legal aid work.[19]

Efforts to understand these patterns both across and within the profession have looked to individual choice as a key determinant. Such explanations seek to ascribe responsibility to the individual and to assume that differences either reflect a failure on the part of these groups to meet the demands of entry to the profession or the requirements of certain roles, specialisms or firms. Alternative explanations may instead frame a career in legal aid as reflecting a positive choice to pursue (or not to pursue) specific careers or roles.[20]

[13] Hilary Sommerlad et al, 'Diversity in the Legal Profession in England and Wales: A Qualitative Study of Barriers and Individual Choices' (University of Westminster Law Press, 2013).

[14] The Law Society of England and Wales, 'Women in Law' (The Law Society, 2018), available at www.lawsociety.org.uk/en/campaigns/women-in-leadership-in-law/features/women-in-law.

[15] Ministry of Justice, 'Diversity of the Judiciary: Legal Professions, New Appointments and Current Post Holders – 2020 Statistics' (Ministry of Justice, 2020), available at https://assets.publishing.service.gov.uk/government/uploads/system/uploads/attachment_data/file/918529/diversity-of-the-judiciary-2020-statistics-web.pdf.

[16] Solicitors Regulation Authority (n 7); Bar Standards Board (n 7); Legal Services Board, The State of Legal Services 2020: A Reflection on Ten Years of Regulation (Legal Services Board, 2020), available at https://legalservicesboard.org.uk/wp-content/uploads/2020/11/The-State-of-Legal-Services-Narrative-Volume_Final.pdf.

[17] Nick Hilborne, 'Family Lawyers "Disproportionately Female and White"' (Legal Futures, 2020), available at www.legalfutures.co.uk/latest-news/family-lawyers-disproportionately-female-and-white.

[18] Sommerlad (n 13).

[19] The Bar Council, Bar Survey Summary Findings April 2020 (The Bar Council, 2020), available at www.barcouncil.org.uk/resource/bar-survey-summary-findings-april-2020.html The Bar Council, 'Bar Survey Summary Findings July 2020' (The Bar Council, 2020), available at at www.barcouncil.org.uk/resource/bar-survey-summary-findings-july-2020-pdf.html; Women Barristers' Alliance, 'Written Evidence from Themis: The Intersectional Women Barristers' Alliance' (Women Barristers' Alliance, 2020), available at committees.parliament.uk/writtenevidence/13811/html.

[20] Sommerlad (n 13).

As it relates to the latter, there is certainly evidence that many practitioners seek a career in legal aid. This choice may derive from a desire to contribute to their community and the belief that lawyering can exist as a force for social good. A commitment to this ideal necessarily influences career trajectory given that, whilst opportunities for such work may be offered within *pro bono* schemes at City Firms, the scope and scale of this work is substantially more limited than is the case in legal aid. A career in legal aid may also follow from an interest in certain subject areas such as criminal law, where much of the work is publicly funded.[21] However, the possibility that those entering into legal aid are driven by altruistic motives co-exists with the less flattering view of legal aid lawyers depicted at the opening of this chapter. On this view, legal aid lawyers are as financially motivated as the rest of the legal profession, but somewhat more problematically, their financial enrichment – unlike that of corporate lawyers – comes at taxpayers' expense.

While individual agency may play a role in dictating career outcomes, it is also recognised that both structural and cultural barriers operate to curtail individual agency and can ultimately push certain groups towards certain forms of work. These barriers are reflected in employment practices which fail to offer flexible working conditions, or which organise work and promotion on the assumption that employees are 'unencumbered' by caring responsibilities.[22] Structural barriers are also reflected in the geography of the job market and barriers to entry.

To date, 'a partnership position in a large corporate law firm has almost universally been held out as the singular mark of success for those with a law degree',[23] while lawyers dealing with 'small-timers' in criminal law, personal injury or family law have been deemed to be lower in the prestige rankings of the profession.[24] On this view, corporate law is positioned as the aspiration, with legal aid work the 'fallback' career. However, given that many students express a desire to pursue a career in public-interest work at the outset of their degrees,[25] the inverse may be true. The fact that this inclination has been shown in some studies to decline over the course of an individual's legal education points to the impact of a range of structural factors that divert students away from legal aid. These factors might conceivably include the implicit and explicit messaging relating to a career in legal aid received during legal education,[26] the burden of debt accumulated during

[21] For example, Sherr and Webb found a strong preference among students at all years in their law degree to specialise in criminal law, welfare, family and housing in spite of the relatively limited employment market in these areas. Avrom Sherr and Julian Webb, 'Law Students, the External Market, and Socialization: Do We Make Them Turn to the City?' (1989) 16 *Journal of Law and Society* 225.

[22] Sommerlad (n 13).

[23] Ronit Dinovitzer and Bryant Garth, 'The New Place of Corporate Law Firms in the Structuring of Elite Legal Careers' (2020) 45 *Law and Social Inquiry* 339.

[24] John J Bonsignore, 'Elite Law Practice and Anti-Social Corporate Behavior' (1997) 21 *Legal Studies Forum* 333.

[25] Howard S Erlanger et al, 'Law Student Idealism and Job Choice: Some New Data on an Old Question' (1996) 30 *Law and Society Review* 851.

[26] See eg Andrew Boon, 'From Public Service to Service Industry: The Impact of Socialisation and Work on the Motivation and Values of Lawyers' (2005) 12 *International Journal of the Legal Profession* 229.

education,[27] and/or a lack of training or employment opportunities. These and other barriers are discussed in more detail in chapter three.

Structural barriers co-exist with cultural barriers which reflect a more implicit and pernicious constraint upon the free exercise of agency. To draw on the work of Bourdieu,[28] culture describes how the ways of thinking, perceiving and feeling that are common to a group operate to embed assumptions about gender, race or class.[29] This culture is reflected variously in professional attire, behavioural norms, dialect and patterns of socialising which come naturally to those with 'prior positioning' on account of their background, education and family. This has the effect of 'othering' those who do not share these practices or demonstrate these qualities[30] and who are then forced to assimilate, compromise or disengage.[31] Where an individual perceives a mismatch between a prospective employer or employment sphere, some will invariably 'opt-out' in favour of more fitting environs,[32] as reflected in the fact that 'BME professionals tend to seek employers who share a similar ethnic background'.[33] Whilst culture exists within different workplaces, sectors and professions, it also exists in legal education. This is reflected in the tendency of legal education to reinforce the existing legal hierarchy in which public interest work is considered 'morally exalted', but incapable of providing a 'standard of living appropriate to a lawyer'.[34] As 'students believe what they are told, explicitly and implicitly, about the world they are entering, they behave in ways that fulfil the prophecies the system makes about them and about that world.'[35] Culture has therefore been said to present a 'major obstacle to diversity'.[36]

Opting out is not confined to the point in time when individuals are making initial decisions about which careers to pursue. Ensuring that a diverse group of individuals are encouraged to and can gain a foothold in the profession is important, but so too is ensuring that conditions within the profession enable the retention of diversity. To date, the retention debate in legal aid has often focused on a generation of practitioners 'ageing out' of the profession who are not being replaced with new entrants. However, as the literature makes clear, these barriers do not disappear simply because an individual has managed to gain entry to a profession. Indeed, where some individuals are forced to jump more hurdles than others to enter into

[27] Jesse Rothstein and Cecilia Rouse, 'Constrained after College: Student Loans and Early-Career Occupational Choices' (2011) 95 *Journal of Public Economics* 149, 150.

[28] Pierre Bourdieu, *The Logic of Practice* (Stanford University Press, 1990).

[29] Sommerlad (n 13) 9.

[30] See Andrew Francis, 'Legal Education, Social Mobility, and Employability: Possible Selves, Curriculum Intervention, and the Role of Legal Work Experience' (2015) 42 *Journal of Law and Society* 173.

[31] Sommerlad (n 13) 60.

[32] Elea nor Rowan and Steven Vaughan, 'Fitting in and "Opting out": Exploring How Law Students Self-Select Law Firm Employers' (2018) 52 *Law Teacher* 216.

[33] Sommerlad (n 13) 59.

[34] Duncan Kennedy, 'Legal Education as Training for Hierarchy' in David Kairys (ed), *The Politics of Law: A Progressive Critique* (Pantheon Books, 1990) 64.

[35] ibid, 54.

[36] Sommerlad (n 13) 8.

a profession, it only serves to reaffirm the existence and persistence of these barriers. Problematically, these groups are not heterogeneous, with Sommerlad et al's study revealing that individuals from an ethnic minority or lower socio-economic background or who attended a new university more often reported having to resort to paralegal work 'in the hope of gaining a training contract through hard work and exemplary performance'.[37] It has also been noted that those from ethnic minority backgrounds find it more difficult to secure training contracts[38] and to achieve career progression across the profession as a whole.[39] Similarly, the persistence of certain barriers in the profession means that women more often leave criminal law where last-minute work and long hours make for a difficult balance with caring responsibilities.[40] These considerations are discussed in greater detail in chapter seven.

Against this backdrop, the Conservative Government's recent agenda of social mobility and 'levelling up' is particularly Janus-faced, with the LASPO Act widely viewed as having increased the barriers to the recruitment and retention of diverse groups in legal aid.[41] However, the effect of LASPO spans beyond the level of individual employment. Pleasence, Balmer and Moorhead observed in 2012 that firms where a majority of partners were from ethnic minority backgrounds were more likely to provide most of their services to legally aided individuals.[42] Such firms were also more often practising in the areas of law that were funded through legal aid prior to the introduction of LASPO, such as immigration.[43] On this basis, ethnic minority firms are more likely to have been affected by the changes introduced in the Act than other groups.

LASPO has also been associated with an adverse impact on the geographic distribution of advice and the availability of advice across different areas of law, as discussed in chapter one. Byrom's 2013 study for example, identified that the South West faced a disproportionate risk of agencies ceasing to provide specialist casework in response to LASPO, with the Midlands exhibiting a higher number of services at risk of closure.[44] According to the Independent Review of Criminal

[37] ibid, 59.

[38] Pascoe Pleasence et al, 'A Time of Change: Solicitors' Firms in England and Wales' (The Law Society, Legal Services Board, Ministry of Justice, 2012) 9.

[39] Byfield Consultancy, 'Opening Up of Shutting Out' (Byfield Consultancy, 2015), available at byfieldconsultancy.com/wp-content/uploads/2021/03/Opening-up-or-shutting-out_Social-mobility-in-the-legal-profession.pdf, 20.

[40] Sommerlad (n 13) 63.

[41] Initiatives proposed by the Department of Levelling Up, Housing and Communities, for instance, have frequently been abandoned due to consultations revealing that such initiatives would not work within the current limitations on legal aid. See, for instance, Department of Levelling Up, Housing and Communities, 'Call for Evidence to Consider the Case for a Housing Court: The Government Response' (Gov.uk, 16 June 2022), available at www.gov.uk/government/consultations/considering-the-case-for-a-housing-court-call-for-evidence/outcome/call-for-evidence-to-consider-the-case-for-a-housing-court-government-response.

[42] Pleasence et al (n 38).

[43] ibid.

[44] Natalie Byrom, 'The State of the Sector: The Impact of Cuts to Civil Legal Aid on Practitioners and their Clients' (The University of Warwick, 2022), available at warwick.ac.uk/fac/soc/law/research/centres/chrp/spendingcuts/153064_statesector_report-final.pdf, 5.

Legal Aid, for instance, the number of criminal legal aid firms in England and Wales dropped from 1,510 in 2014/15 to 1,220 in 2019/2020.[45] Firms dealing with criminal legal aid cases have decreased by 35 per cent since 2012[46] and by around 50 per cent since 2007.[47] Similarly, the Law Society has shown that the number of housing law providers decreased from 286 to 260 between the September 2018 and September 2020 legal aid contract commencement,[48] while the number of civil legal aid providers decreased from 2,401 in 2010/11 to 1,254 in 2019/20.[49] The funding of criminal legal aid work has also been implicated in the fact that 10 per cent of criminal barristers who took on legal aid work between April 2021 and April 2022 later withdrew from these cases.[50]

As such, there is significant merit in considering the composition of legal aid suppliers and of current, former and prospective practitioners, as well as better understanding what factors motivate individuals to pursue a career in the sector. This analysis is not intended to be representative of the legal aid population at large given the sampling method used to gather Census data. Where differences between groups are observed or inferences are drawn, they are subject to this over-riding limitation. Nonetheless, the findings discussed here frame the analysis of data that follows in subsequent chapters. This includes the extent to which structural barriers inhibit entry to the profession (as discussed further in chapter three), and/or encourage exit from the profession (as discussed in chapter seven). The evidence presented here also challenges the assumptions of privilege that tends to attach to lawyers, and clearly refutes the proposition that legal aid is a 'fall back' career or one that individuals pursue with the intention of achieving financial enrichment.

III. Current, Former and Prospective Practitioners

In total, 1,208 current legal aid practitioners, 255 former legal aid practitioners and 376 students responded to the Census. Of the 376 students who responded to the Census, 52.9 per cent (n=199) were considering a career in legal aid whilst 47.1 per cent (n=177) were not.

[45] Independent Review of Criminal Legal Aid, 'Independent Review of Criminal Legal Aid: Summary Information on Publicly Funded Criminal Legal Services' (Ministry of Justice, 2021), available at assets.publishing.service.gov.uk/government/uploads/system/uploads/attachment_data/file/960290/data-compendium.pdf, 8.

[46] BBC News, 'Thousands of Barristers Take Action Over Legal Aid' (BBC, 11 April 2022), available at www.bbc.com/news/uk-61062627.

[47] The Law Society of England and Wales, 'Defending the Future of Criminal Legal Aid: What We are Doing for Members' (The Law Society, 2022), available at lawsociety.org.uk/topics/legal-aid/defending-the-future-of-criminal-legal-aid.

[48] The Law Society of England and Wales, 'Written Evidence Submitted by the Law Society of England and Wales to the Justice Select Committee on the Future of Legal Aid' (The Law Society of England and Wales, 2020).

[49] Stephanie Boyce, 'Civil Legal Aid is Under Threat: It's Time to Act' (The Law Society, 2022), available at www.lawsociety.org.uk/topics/blogs/civil-legal-aid-is-under-threat-its-time-to-act.

[50] BBC News (n 46).

A. Demographic Characteristics

Table 2.1 below details the key demographic characteristics of current and former practitioners and those students who responded. While all student responses are useful for understanding the issues facing those at the point of deciding whether to pursue a career in legal aid, these responses have been divided into two cohorts for clarity: all students, and the sub-set of those students who indicated that they were actively considering a career in legal aid ('prospective practitioners').

The majority of current practitioners were aged 40 years and over (53.9 per cent, n=648), with the highest proportion of respondents aged 41–50 years old (22.7 per cent, n=273). The fact that more than half of these respondents were over 40 years old seems to align with reports on the increasing age profile of those engaged in legal aid work.[51] This figure contrasts with the average ages of 30 (males) and 29.3 (females) of all qualified solicitors admitted to the roll reported by the Law Society and the Solicitors Regulation Authority.[52] The age distribution of former practitioners hints at the possibility that withdrawal from the profession is not simply a matter of older practitioners retiring. The majority of former practitioners were aged between 36 and 59 years and were therefore likely to be in the middle of their careers. Nevertheless, retirement is still likely to be an issue that is not well reflected in our data given that those who are no longer active in the profession may not have received an invitation to participate in the Census. Unsurprisingly, given that higher education tends to coincide with early adulthood, most of the students who responded to the Census were aged between 18–21 years (46.5 per cent, n=175); however, fewer of those who expressed an interest in a career in legal aid (prospective practitioners) fell into this age category (37.7 per cent, n=75).

In total, 60.9 per cent (n=732) of current practitioners identified as female and 38.3 per cent (n=460) identified as male. Whilst a similar proportion of female-identifying respondents were among the cohort of former practitioners (57.6 per cent, n=147), a greater proportion of student respondents identified as female (73.6 per cent, n=276). This may reflect the higher number of women entering into the profession.[53]

Over three-quarters of current practitioners (77.4 per cent, n=927) identified as white British, a figure that is slightly lower than the wider England and Wales population (80.5 per cent).[54] Taken together, the number of current practitioners from Asian, Asian British, Black, African, Caribbean, Black, Mixed or

[51] The Westminster Commission on Legal Aid, 'Inquiry into the Sustainability and Recovery of the Legal Aid Sector' (All-Party Parliamentary Group on Legal Aid, 2021) 94.

[52] The Law Society of England and Wales, 'Entry Trends: Undergraduates and Graduates in Law' (The Law Society, 2020), available at www.lawsociety.org.uk/career-advice/becoming-a-solicitor/entry-trends.

[53] The Law Society of England and Wales (n 14).

[54] Office for National Statistics, 'Population of England and Wales' (UK Government, 2018), available at www.ethnicity-facts-figures.service.gov.uk/uk-population-by-ethnicity/national-and-regional-populations/population-of-england-and-wales/latest.

multiple ethnic groups was 14.6 per cent. This broadly corresponds to existing data which establishes the proportion of barristers from ethnic minority backgrounds at 15 per cent[55] and proportion of solicitors from minority ethnic groups at 14.0 per cent.[56] It contrasts, however, with the ethnic diversity of clients as legal aid client diversity data reveals that 74 per cent of clients were ethnic minority compared to 28 per cent white in 2019/20.[57]

Fewer current practitioners reported a disability (9.0 per cent, n=108) as compared to 15.4 per cent (n=39) of former practitioners and 15.5 per cent (n=30) of prospective practitioners. These numbers place Census respondents closer to the overall UK workforce with a disability rate of 13–15 per cent, than the rate of 4–6 per cent reported by the Legal Services Board and the Solicitors Regulation Authority in respect of barristers and legal executives.[58] That fewer current practitioners report a disability as compared to prospective practitioners may reflect the difficulty faced by those with a disability in establishing a career in the sector, as observed in Foster and Hirst's study.[59]

The experience of a long-term/chronic illness, disease or condition was the most common reported form of disability for current and former practitioners, whilst a mental health condition was the most common condition for all students and those students identified as prospective practitioners. Almost two in three prospective practitioners with a disability reported a mental health condition. The rate at which current practitioners reported a mental health condition (24.3 per cent, n=26) was slightly higher than that reported by McManus et al's 2007 Household Survey of Adult psychiatric morbidity (23.0 per cent), whilst the rate for prospective practitioners (63.3 per cent, n=19) was considerably higher. Nevertheless, differences between survey methods and specifically the reliance on self-reporting in the Legal Aid Census means direct comparison is problematic.[60]

Nearly half of the current practitioners who responded were based in London (46.4 per cent, n=558) as was the case with former practitioners (48.6 per cent, n=122), with much smaller numbers based in Wales. Statistics from Young Legal Aid Lawyers on the distribution of their membership, reveals a similarly 'London-centric' pattern, with 49.0 per cent of their respondents working in London, 13.5 per cent working in North West England, and 10.6 per cent working

[55] Legal Services Board (n 16).

[56] The Law Society (n 520.

[57] Bolt Burdon Kemp, Inequality within Britain's Legal Aid Funding System (Bolt Burdon Kemp), available at www.boltburdonkemp.co.uk/our-insights/campaigns/inequality-in-britains-legal-aid-funding-system.

[58] Legal Services Board (n 16); Solicitors Regulation Authority (n 7).

[59] See eg Debbie Foster and Natasha Hirst, 'Legally Disabled? The Career Experiences of Disabled People Working in the Legal Profession' (Cardiff University, 2020), available at legallydisabled.com/wp-content/uploads/2020/01/Legally-Disabled-full-report-FINAL.pdf, 106.

[60] Sally McManus et al, 'Adult Psychiatric Morbidity in England, 2007: Results of a Household Survey' (National Health Service, 2009).

in Yorkshire and the Humber, and in the Midlands respectively.[61] The distribution of current practitioners in this study therefore reaffirms the broad pattern of 'advice deserts' in which advice services are concentrated in London.[62] All students, as well as the sub-set of those who identified as prospective practitioners, exhibited a less London-centric distribution with approximately a quarter in each group living in London and greater numbers living in Wales. This difference may reflect the tendency of graduates to move to larger metropolitan areas in order to secure employment.

Table 2.1 Key demographic characteristics of current, former and prospective legal aid practitioners

	PRACTITIONERS						STUDENTS	
	Current		Former		Prospective		All	
	N	%	N	%	N	%	N	%
Age	(n=1203)		(n=254)		(n=199)		(n=376)	
18–21	4	0.3	0	0.0	75	37.7	175	46.5
22–25	77	6.4	6	2.4	59	29.6	101	26.9
26–30	165	13.7	16	6.3	24	12.1	39	10.4
31–35	170	14.1	23	9.1	15	7.5	23	6.1
36–40	139	11.6	40	15.7	10	5.0	14	3.7
41–50	273	22.7	67	26.4	11	5.5	19	5.1
51–59	234	19.5	60	23.6	5	2.5	5	1.3
60+	141	11.7	42	16.5	0	0.0	0	0.0
Gender	(n=1202)		(n=255)		(n=199)		(n=375)	
Male	460	38.3	101	39.6	44	22.1	90	24.0
Female	732	60.9	147	57.6	150	75.4	276	73.6
Non-binary/prefer to self-identify	2	0.2	2	0.8	3	1.5	5	1.3
Prefer not to disclose	8	0.7	5	2.0	2	1.0	4	1.1
Ethnicity	(n=1197)		(n=252)		(n=199)		(n=376)	
Asian or Asian British	85	7.1	14	5.6	26	13.1	55	14.6
Black, African, Caribbean or Black British	33	2.8	5	2.0	10	5.0	18	4.8

(continued)

[61] Young Legal Aid Lawyers, 'Second Covid-19 Report' (Young Legal Aid Lawyers, 2020), available at www.younglegalaidlawyers.org/sites/default/files/Second%20COVID-19%20Report%2025%20May%202020.pdf, 5–7.

[62] The Law Society of England and Wales, 'Legal Aid Deserts' (The Law Society, 22 August 2022), available at www.lawsociety.org.uk/campaigns/legal-aid-deserts.

Table 2.1 ***(Continued)***

	PRACTITIONERS						STUDENTS	
	Current		Former		Prospective		All	
	N	%	N	%	N	%	N	%
Mixed or multiple ethnic groups	56	4.7	11	4.4	13	6.5	20	5.3
White British	927	77.4	203	80.6	113	56.8	216	57.4
White Other	0	0.0	0	0.0	29	14.6	47	12.5
Other ethnic group	96	8.0	19	7.5	4	2.0	10	2.7
Prefer not to disclose	0	0.0	0	0.0	5	2.5	11	2.9
Disability	(n=1198)		(n=253)		(n=199)		(n=375)	
No	1090	91.0	214	84.6	159	79.7	304	81.1
Yes	108	9.0	39	15.4	30	15.5	54	14.4
Prefer not to disclose	–	–	–	–	10	5.0	17	4.5
Disability Type	(n=107)		(n=39)		(n=30)		(n=54)	
Deafness or partial hearing loss	6	5.6	4	10.3	3	10.0	3	5.6
Blindness or partial sight loss	6	5.6	0	0.0	1	3.3	1	1.9
Learning disability	10	9.3	2	5.1	5	16.7	13	24.1
Learning difficulty or developmental disorder	9	8.4	1	2.6	4	13.3	8	14.8
Physical disability	17	15.9	8	20.5	5	16.7	7	13.0
Mental health condition	26	24.3	12	30.8	19	63.3	32	59.3
Long-term/chronic illness, disease or condition	46	43.0	20	51.3	13	43.3	25	46.3
Neurodevelopmental disorder	2	1.8	0	0.0	0	0.0	0	0.0
Other	2	1.8	3	7.7	0	0.0	0	0.0
Location	(n=1202)		(n=251)		(n=199)		(n=365)	
London	558	46.4	122	48.6	47	23.6	93	25.5
South East England	142	11.8	51	20.3	39	19.6	59	16.2
South West England	114	9.5	19	7.6	14	7.0	27	7.4
English Midlands	138	11.5	23	9.2	27	13.6	52	14.2
North East England	134	11.1	24	9.6	24	12.1	46	12.6
North West England	125	10.4	38	15.1	28	14.1	57	15.6

(continued)

Table 2.1 ***(Continued)***

	PRACTITIONERS						STUDENTS	
	Current		Former		Prospective		All	
	N	%	N	%	N	%	N	%
North Wales	11	0.9	1	0.4	3	1.5	7	1.9
West Wales	2	0.2	1	0.4	1	0.5	2	0.5
Mid Wales	0	0.0	0	0.0	1	0.5	1	0.3
South Wales	29	2.4	10	4.0	11	5.5	21	5.8

B. Employment Characteristics

The employment characteristics of practitioners are set out in Table 2.2. Current practitioners reported working in legal aid for a considerable period of time. A third of respondents (33.2 per cent, n=400) had been in the sector for 21 years or more, and just under a quarter (24.3 per cent, n=293) had been in the sector for 11–20 years. This may reflect a commitment to work that is viewed as socially important, or a lack of alternative career options (as discussed in chapter seven), rather than necessarily reflecting a high degree of satisfaction with working conditions (as is discussed in chapter four). Fewer former practitioners reported having worked in the sector for 21 or more years (18 per cent, n=46), which may reflect smaller numbers of retired practitioners in this cohort. Just under half of all former practitioners left legal aid having worked in the sector for between one and 10 years.

Most current practitioners worked in organisations that provided services other than legal aid. 88.4 per cent (n=1,055) reported that their organisation also undertook work that was not funded by legal aid, with only 11.6 per cent (n=139) providing solely legal aid-funded work. Nearly half of all practitioners (48.3 per cent, n=580) worked in for-profit firms with legal aid contracts, while over a third (35.3 per cent, n=424) worked in chambers. Smaller numbers worked in not-for-profit specialist advice (5.3 per cent, n=64) and law centres (5.1 per cent, n=61).

A similar number of current practitioners reported their principal role as 'solicitor' (35.1 per cent, n=424) or as 'barrister' (33.7 per cent, n=407). In contrast, solicitors comprised almost half (49.8 per cent, n=127) of the respondents who reported that they had left legal aid, followed by barristers (27.5 per cent, n=70) and paralegals (10.6 per cent, n=27). In addition to their roles, 7.2 per cent of current practitioners (n=87) indicated that they held an additional role with 6.4 per cent (n=77) holding one or more managerial or administrative roles (practice manager, director, head of chambers, head of department, billing clerk). 0.8 per cent (n=9) reported holding an 'other role' and 0.1 per cent (n=1) described holding additional managerial and other roles.

Most practitioners worked full time in their roles (66.3 per cent, n=795), with 21.9 per cent (n=262) working variable hours, 10.1 per cent (n=121) working part time, 1.7 per cent (n=20) working condensed hours and 0.1 per cent (n=1) reporting an 'other' form of working schedule. More women in the sample reported working part time than men (13.1 per cent, n=95 versus 5.5 per cent, n=25).

The majority of current practitioners in this study (57.2 per cent, n=689) worked across more than one area of law. Of the 516 practitioners who indicated that they worked in only one area of law, the majority (48.8 per cent n=252) were crime practitioners. Across all current practitioners, the greatest number reported working in public family law (31.9 per cent, n=384), followed by crime (29.6 per cent, n=357) and private family law (29.0 per cent, n=349). These figures differ from those reported by Young Legal Aid Lawyers in 2020, where 36.5 per cent of their respondents reported working crime, and 18.3 per cent worked in family law (with no distinction made between public and private family law).[63] Higher numbers of former practitioners who responded to the Census reported having worked in crime (34.5 per cent, n=88) and family law, with 31.4 per cent (n=80) in public family law and 25.9 per cent (n=66) in private family law. Additionally, 22.7 per cent (n=58) of former practitioners had left housing law.

Significant attention has recently been given to the sustainability of criminal legal aid via the Independent Review of Criminal Legal Aid, the Westminster Commission on Legal Aid and the House of Commons Justice Committee's Inquiry into the Future of Legal Aid.[64] That the highest number of former practitioners in our sample were working in criminal law reinforces concerns regarding sustainability and a year-on-year decrease in the number of solicitors working for criminal legal aid firms. This issue, as detailed in Miller's statement to the House of Commons Justice Committee, is one of 'an ageing criminal defence profession and areas where there were no lawyers under 35 doing the work at all.'[65] Further analysis of Census data reaffirms this pattern, with 39.0 per cent (n=138) of crime practitioners aged 40 or under, and 61.0 per cent (n=216) aged over 40. This compares to 43.5 per cent of family (public), 48.1 of family (private) and 51.4 per cent of housing law practitioners aged 40 or under.

Table 2.2 Employment characteristics of current and former legal aid practitioners

	Current		Former	
	N	%	N	%
Length of time in legal aid	(n=1205)		(n=255)	
Less than 1 year	66	5.5	14	5.5
1–5 years	289	24.0	68	26.7

(continued)

[63] Young Legal Aid Lawyers (n 61).

[64] Christopher Bellamy, 'Independent Review of Criminal Legal Aid' (Ministry of Justice, 2021); Westminster Commission on Legal Aid (n 51); House of Commons Justice Committee, 'The Future of Legal Aid: Third Report of Session 2021–22' (Her Majesty's Stationery Office, 2021) 15.

[65] House of Commons Justice Committee (n 64).

Table 2.2 (Continued)

	Current		Former	
	N	%	N	%
6–10 years	157	13.0	59	23.1
11–20 years	293	24.3	68	26.7
21+ years	400	33.2	46	18.0
Employment status	(n=1203)			
Permanent	598	49.7	–	–
Fixed term	64	5.3	–	–
Ad hoc (in days or hours)	4	0.3	–	–
I am self-employed	533	44.3	–	–
I don't have an employment contract	13	1.1	–	–
Unknown	10	0.8	–	–
Employer type	(n =1200)			
Chambers	424	35.3	–	–
For-profit firm with legal aid contracts	580	48.3	–	–
Not-for-profit specialist advice provider	64	5.3	–	–
Law centre	61	5.1	–	–
University law clinic	2	0.2	–	–
Sole practitioner	16	1.3	–	–
Other	53	4.4	–	–
Provision of non-legal aid services	(n=1194)			
Yes	1055	88.4	–	–
No	139	11.6	–	–
Principal role	(n=1206)		(n=255)	
Head of department	53	4.4	–	–
Solicitor	424	35.1	127	49.8
Barrister	407	33.7	70	27.5
Legal executive	24	2.0	8	3.1
Trainee/pupil/legal apprentice	125	10.3	1	0.4
Caseworker	43	3.6	12	4.7
Clerk	2	0.2	–	–
Practice manager	12	1.0	–	–
Director	43	3.6	–	–
Head of chambers	10	0.8	–	–

(continued)

Table 2.2 ***(Continued)***

	Current		Former	
	N	%	N	%
Billing clerk	24	2.0	–	–
Other	16	1.3	1	0.4
Paralegal	23	1.9	27	10.6
Costs lawyer	–	–	5	2.0
Advisor	–	–	4	1.6
Work schedule	(n = 1199)			
Full-time	795	66.3	–	–
Part-time	121	10.1	–	–
Condensed hours	20	1.7	–	–
Variable hours	262	21.9	–	–
Other	1	0.1	–	–
Current practice areas	(n=1205)		(n=255)	
Crime	357	29.6	88	34.5
Prison law	59	4.9	14	5.5
Claims against public authorities	147	12.2	16	6.3
Community care	139	11.5	21	8.2
Debt	14	1.2	20	7.8
Discrimination	74	6.1	11	4.3
Education	33	2.7	9	3.5
Mediation	13	1.1	2	0.8
Housing	222	18.4	58	22.7
Immigration and asylum	123	10.2	44	17.3
Family (public)	384	31.9	80	31.4
Family (private)	349	29.0	66	25.9
Clinical negligence	15	1.2	13	5.1
Mental health	85	7.1	10	3.9
Public law	299	24.8	–	–
Welfare benefits	49	4.1	32	12.5
Court of Protection	141	11.7	10	3.9
Other	8	0.7	17	6.7
Inquest and public inquiries	18	1.5	7	2.7
AATP	2	0.2	9	3.5
Employment	3	0.2	–	–

C. Educational Background

As set out in Table 2.3, the vast majority of current practitioners (93.0 per cent, n=1,108) attended school in the UK, with 7.0 per cent (n=84) reporting that they attended school overseas. A higher number of current students who identified as prospective practitioners attended school outside of the UK (20.6 per cent, n=41). Of those current practitioners who attended school in the UK, approximately two-thirds (64.1 per cent, n=705) attended a state comprehensive school, with just under a quarter (23.4 per cent, n=257) attending a fee-paying school and just under one-fifth (19 per cent, n=209) attending a grammar school. Prospective practitioners exhibited a rate of fee-paying school attendance that was much lower at 10.9 per cent (n=17) and closer to the UK average of seven per cent.[66]

Most current practitioners had attended or were attending university (93.8 per cent, n=1,133). Of those who indicated they had or were attending university, 24.5 per cent (n=274) had or were currently studying for a postgraduate Master of Laws (LLM), with a further 5.4 per cent (n=60) studying for a non-LLM Masters-level course in a law-related subject. The majority of prospective practitioners were working towards the completion of an undergraduate Bachelor of Laws (LLB) (54.3 per cent, n=108). A further 17.1 per cent (n=34) were completing their Legal Practice Course (LPC), 8.5 per cent (n=17) were completing their accredited vocational training course (Bar Course), 7.0 per cent (n=14) were completing their Graduate Diploma in Law (GDL), a postgraduate law conversion course, and 1.0 per cent (n=2) were completing studies for their Solicitors Qualifying Exam (SQE), which is due to replace the LPC exams by 2023. A small number (12.0 per cent, n=24) reported that they were completing a non-practice LLM, an 'other' degree, an 'other' undergraduate degree, or did not specify their degree. The number of prospective practitioners undertaking an LLB reaffirms the role of the LLB as a main route into the profession, as discussed further in chapter three. Current practitioners tended to enter into the profession via a pupillage or training contract.

Just under a fifth of practitioners (18.5 per cent, n=221) were in receipt of state benefits or were eligible for free school meals during their primary or secondary education. This rate was higher among prospective practitioners at 29.4 per cent (n=58). The majority of current practitioners did not have parents or other caregivers who went to university (54.9 per cent, n=655 of 1,193), as was the case for prospective practitioners (52.8 per cent, n=105). These figures are slightly higher than the rate for barristers reported by the Bar Standards Board in 2020 of 47.2 per cent, and the rate of 49.0 per cent reported in respect of solicitors by the SRA.[67] More than three quarters of current practitioners were first generation lawyers, with 80.5 per cent (n=965 of 1,199) having no other legal professionals in their immediate family.

[66] Legal Services Board (n 6).

[67] Unlike the BSB, the SRA does not ask whether an individual was the first in their family to attend university, but rather whether their parents attended university. 51 per cent reported to the SRA that they had a parent who attended university. By implication, 49 per cent did not.

Table 2.3 Educational background of current and prospective legal aid practitioners

	Current		**Prospective**	
	N	**%**	**N**	**%**
School location	(n=1192)		(n=199)	
Outside of the UK	84	7.0	41	20.6
UK	1108	93.0	158	79.4
School type	(n=1100)		(n=157)	
State comprehensive	705	64.1	126	80.3
Fee-paying independent school	257	23.4	17	10.9
Grammar school	209	19.0	12	7.6
Other	29	2.6	2	1.3
Attended/attending university	(n=1208)			
No	75	6.2		
Yes	1133	93.8		
Undertaking a graduate degree	(n=1119)		(n=199)	
No	785	70.2	–	–
Yes – LLM	274	24.5	–	–
Yes – a non-LLM Masters-level course in a law-related subject	60	5.4	–	–
LLB	–	–	108	54.3
GDL	–	–	14	7.0
LLM (non-practice)	–	–	15	7.5
Bar course (including combined LLM courses)	–	–	17	8.5
LPC (including combined LLM courses)	–	–	34	17.1
Other undergraduate degree	–	–	3	1.5
Other	–	–	3	1.5
SQE	–	–	2	1.0
Not specified	–	–	3	1.5
State benefits/free school meals during education	(n=1197)		(n=197)	
No	976	81.5	139	70.6
Yes	221	18.5	58	29.4
Parents/step-parents/carers or guardians attended University	(n=1193)		(n=199)	
No	655	54.9	105	52.8
Yes	538	45.1	94	47.2

(continued)

Table 2.3 *(Continued)*

	Current		Prospective	
	N	%	N	%
Legal professionals in immediate family	(n=1199)			
No	965	80.5	–	–
Yes	234	19.5	–	–
Route to current role	(n=1189)			
Training contract	381	32.0	–	–
Pupillage	369	31.0	–	–
Paralegal route	107	9.0	–	–
Solicitor apprenticeship	15	1.3	–	–
CILEX qualifications	33	2.8	–	–
Other route	284	23.9	–	–

D. Choosing a Career in Legal Aid

As has been discussed, the literature makes clear that a number of motivations exist for pursuing work in legal aid, and current, prospective and former practitioners acknowledged this when asked to indicate what motivated them to seek a career in the field.

Overall, responses among current and prospective practitioners revealed a strong desire to enhance access to justice and support those experiencing disadvantage. As shown Table 2.4, for both current and prospective practitioners the same four reasons were most commonly selected: the 'opportunity to help those facing economic, cultural or social disadvantage', the 'opportunity to make access to justice more equitable', the 'opportunity to have a positive impact on society' and the 'opportunity to improve access to justice'. Other factors such as the opportunity to 'make a fairer society' or 'a difference in the community' featured more highly amongst prospective rather than current practitioners, but were still prevalent.

Some practitioners noted motivations that might be viewed as offering personal gratification (for example, those directed at gaining experience or at flexible working); however, the number indicating that these factors attract/ed an individual to a career in legal aid was relatively low. It is striking that comparatively few respondents gravitated towards the profession in search of an income, as only six practitioners (0.5 per cent, n=6) indicated that financial reasons motivated them to join the sector. Of these, four practitioners indicated that they found employment in legal aid because they required an income, whilst two indicated that they were initially attracted to the area because it was possible to make a decent living. Both of these practitioners added the caveat that this was no longer possible, with one practitioner specifically attributing this to post-1995 legal aid policy changes.

The motivations detailed below also make clear that the decision to enter legal aid was, for the vast majority, an intentional choice as opposed to being a function of a lack of other options. Very few current practitioners fell into the sector, or pursued it to obtain experience or a training contract; however, the opportunity to gain experience or get a training contract was higher amongst current students. The data also showed some evidence to support the proposition that individuals seek careers where they will be surrounded by individuals with whom they share what Bourdieu refers to as 'culture'.[68] Over a third of current and prospective practitioners identified 'like-minded people' as an attraction, with approximately a third drawn to the 'shared values' of the profession and approximately one-fifth drawn by a 'sense of community or belonging'.

Table 2.4 What attracted/s current and prospective legal aid practitioners to a career in legal aid?

	Current (n=1180)		**Prospective** (n=196)	
	N	**%**	**N**	**%**
Opportunity to help those facing economic, cultural or social disadvantage	893	75.7	170	86.7
Opportunity to make access to justice more equitable	840	71.2	162	82.7
Opportunity to have a positive impact on society	833	70.6	157	80.1
Opportunity to improve access to justice	756	64.1	146	74.5
Opportunity to apply my skills to help others	723	61.3	124	63.3
Sense of fulfilment or personal reward	653	55.3	101	51.5
Opportunity to make a fairer society	594	50.3	132	67.3
Opportunity to enable social change	532	45.1	131	66.8
Opportunity to make a difference to my community	497	42.1	104	53.1
Like-minded people	437	37.0	71	36.2
Opportunity to hold the government accountable	435	36.9	118	60.2
Sense of professional obligation	416	35.3	56	28.6
Shared values	362	30.7	68	34.7
Opportunity to change or make better laws	345	29.2	112	57.1
Sense of community or belonging	227	19.2	42	21.4
Opportunity to gain experience/get a training contract	221	18.7	63	32.1
Inclusivity of the sector	167	14.2	39	19.9
Flexible working conditions	118	10	27	13.8
The sector's collective voice	108	9.2	24	12.2

(continued)

[68] Bourdieu (n 28).

Table 2.4 ***(Continued)***

	Current (n=1180)		**Prospective** (n=196)	
	N	**%**	**N**	**%**
Only work available in my area of practice interest	22	1.9	–	–
Fell into it	10	0.8	–	–
I needed an income/pay used to be good	6	0.5	–	–
Other	4	0.3	2	1.0

Prospective practitioners were also asked whether their previous life experience had played a role in influencing their decision to pursue a career in legal aid. Of those who gave an answer (n=80), 90.0 per cent (n=72) confirmed that their background or life experience was an influence on their choice of career. An analysis of open-ended responses revealed that students who personally experienced injustice or poverty (46.3 per cent, n=37) and witnessed or heard about injustice (50.0 per cent, n=40) were influenced by their experiences to become legal aid practitioners. As one narrative elucidated:

> Being mixed-race, particularly in an overwhelmingly white area of the country [and] [s]eeing injustice that is done time and again to marginalised groups makes me want to pursue my vision of a fairer society and a more accountable government. This particularly applies as my grandparents are part of the Windrush Generation affected by the Windrush Scandal.[69]

Other prospective practitioners indicated their previous work or employment experience (17.5 per cent, n=14), previous experience volunteering with a charity or NGO (7.5 per cent, n=6) and own beliefs and values or privilege (20.0 per cent, n=16) were influential. One respondent explained that 'Many friends and those who I worked with as a youth worker have benefitted from legal aid representation and I want to help ensure it remains a viable option and is of a high standard.'[70] Another spoke to how the combination of personal experience and work experience proved transformative, explaining:

> I was briefly homeless due to poor mental health. I also worked at a local council's homeless department and was appalled by how they treated clients, often making unlawful decisions as they didn't think a client would get legal advice. This motivated me to learn housing law and become a caseworker. I eventually wanted to do even more for my clients so [I] [w]ent back to uni to get my law qualifications.[71]

These responses reinforce that individuals are drawn to legal aid because of the social importance of the work and the potential to contribute to social justice as a legal aid practitioner. Importantly these responses clearly refute the presumption

[69] Student Respondent Number 250.
[70] Student Respondent Number 317.
[71] Student Respondent Number 349.

implicit in accusations of 'fat cat lawyers', highlighted in the introduction to this chapter, that individuals pursue a career in legal aid with the intention of advancing their own interests.[72]

When former practitioners were given the opportunity to indicate what they liked most about working in legal aid in their own words, coding of these responses (n=197) revealed 65.5 per cent (n=129) liked 'making a difference in people's lives or helping those facing disadvantage' and a further 15.7 per cent (n=31) liked helping to provide access to justice. 9.1 per cent (n=18) indicated they liked 'holding the government/public sector/organisations to account'. Responses that indicated a degree of personal satisfaction also featured. For example, 15.2 per cent (n=30) indicated that they found the job satisfying or enjoyable, 15.2 per cent indicated they enjoyed the intellectual challenge of the work, 13.2 per cent (n=26) enjoyed face-to-face client work and 10.2 per cent (n=20) enjoyed the camaraderie with like-minded colleagues. Financial remuneration was notable for its absence – not a single former practitioner mentioned this factor in respect to what they liked about the sector, but a considerable number observed the inability to survive on current salaries as a reason for leaving the sector (as discussed further in chapter seven).

IV. Chambers and Organisations

The chambers responding to the Census were larger in size, with 64.5 per cent (n=20) reporting more than 41 barristers in residence including pupils but not including door tenants or associated tenants (see Table 2.5). There were no chambers with fewer than 10 barristers in residence in the sample. In spite of respondent chambers tending towards the larger side, the number of King's Counsel (Queen's Counsel, at the time of the Census) in residence reported by chambers (n=25) were small, with 68.0 per cent (n=17) of chambers having one to five QCs. While eight per cent (n=4) had 6–10 and 16–20 respectively, 12 per cent (n=3) had more than 26 QCs and 4.0 per cent (n=1) had 21–25 QCs.

The majority of organisations were on the small side, with 41.4 per cent (n=152) reporting a headcount of less than 10 employees, as shown in Table 2.5. As would be expected in light of this, organisations (n=364) also reported smaller numbers of fee-earners. For 4.4 per cent (n=16), no full-time equivalent fee-earners were reported. 45.1 per cent (n=164) reported one to four full-time-equivalent fee-earners, 31.6 per cent (n=115) reported more than four to 10 or fewer fee-earners, 14.6 per cent (n=53) reported more than 10 to 30 or fewer fee-earners, and 4.3 per cent (n= 16) reported more than 30.

The majority of the 369 organisations captured by the Census were for-profit firms providing both private and legal aid services (67.8 per cent, n=250).

[72] O'Nions (n 2).

Only 10.6 per cent (n=39) indicated that they were for-profit firms providing only legal aid services and 8.1 per cent (n=30) reported they were a not-for-profit specialist advice provider. Law centres comprised 7.6 per cent (n=28) of the sample and 6.0 per cent (n=22) of organisations specified an 'other' organisational type but did not elaborate further. Organisations tended towards being long-standing service providers, with 58.1 per cent (n=208) of 358 organisations having provided legal aid services for longer than 21 years. A further 17.0 per cent (n=61) had provided legal aid services for 1–10 years and 24.8 per cent (n=89) had provided services for 11–20 years.

In line with the tendency for practitioners to aggregate in London, 46.9 per cent (n=15) of the chambers who responded to the Census were located in London, followed by the English Midlands (15.6 per cent, n=5). There was no representation from chambers in the South East of England. Similarly, organisations were mostly based in London (31.6 per cent, n=116); however, the spread of organisations encompassed all parts of England and Wales.

As was the case for current and former practitioners, the most common area of work for respondent chambers was crime (65.6 per cent, n=21), followed by public and private family law (56.3 per cent, n=18). There were also a number of chambers undertaking Court of Protection work (50.0 per cent, n=16). Fewer chambers reported members predominantly working in employment (3.1 per cent, n=1), welfare benefits (6.3 per cent, n=2), debt (6.3 per cent, n=2) and prison law (9.4 per cent, n=3), or across all areas of law (3.1 per cent, n=1).

Most organisations (93.1 per cent, n=337 of 362) held a legal aid contract. Contracts were predominantly held in crime (44.5 per cent, n=150), public (39.8 per cent, n=134) and private (35.3 per cent, n=119) family, and housing law (26.4 per cent, n=89). As per the LAA's Directory of Providers from July 2021, this compares to 47.9 per cent (n=1,572) of providers working in crime, 47.4 per cent (n=1,555) working in family and 12.2 per cent (n=399) working in housing.[73] Seventy-three organisations indicated that they also held other contracts. Of these, 50.7 per cent (n=37) held Housing Possession Court Duty Scheme contracts, 41.1 per cent (n=30) held Very High Costs Crime contracts, 9.6 per cent (n=7) held Civil Legal Aid Discrimination contracts, 2.7 per cent (n=2) held Civil Legal Aid Education contracts and 6.8 per cent (n=5) held other contracts (including other telephone advice).[74]

[73] Numbers calculated from Legal Aid Agency, 'Legal Aid Provider Spreadsheet' (Legal Aid Agency, 20 July 2021), available at https://assets.publishing.service.gov.uk/government/uploads/system/uploads/attachment_data/file/1008746/210720_Data_to_share_on_GOV.UK.xlsx.

[74] Of those organisations who answered 'other' one indicated they held a CLA Telephone contract for family law, two held CDD contracts, one held a housing contract, and one held housing, debt and welfare benefit contracts.

Table 2.5 Characteristics of chambers and organisations

	Chambers		Organisations	
	N	%	N	%
Location	(n=32)		(n=367)	
London	15	46.9	116	31.6
South East England	0	0.0	57	15.5
South West England	4	12.5	37	10.1
English Midlands	5	15.6	48	13.1
North East England	2	6.3	36	9.8
North West England	4	12.5	46	12.5
Wales	2	6.2	27	6.4
Practice/contract areas	(n=32)		(n=337)	
Crime	21	65.6	150	44.5
Prison law	3	9.4	24	7.1
Claims against public authorities	9	28.1	22	6.5
Community care	6	18.8	28	8.3
Debt	2	6.3	23	6.8
Discrimination	7	21.9	14	4.2
Education	6	18.8	4	1.2
Mediation	6	18.8	12	3.6
Housing	10	31.3	89	26.4
Immigration and asylum	7	21.9	47	13.9
Family (public)	18	56.3	134	39.8
Family (private)	18	56.3	119	35.3
Clinical negligence	7	21.9	11	3.3
Mental health	6	18.8	41	12.2
Public law	11	34.4	44	13.1
Welfare benefits	2	6.3	16	4.7
Court of Protection	16	50.0	15	4.5
Inquest and public inquiries	13	40.6	–	–
Employment	1	3.1	0	0.0
All of these areas	1	3.1	–	–
Other	–	–	6	1.8

(continued)

Table 2.5 ***(Continued)***

	Chambers		Organisations	
	N	%	N	%
Headcount	Barristers (n=31)		Total (n=367)	
1–10	0	0.0	152	41.4
11–20	3	9.7	79	21.5
21–40	8	25.8	65	17.7
41+	20	64.5	71	19.3

V. Implications of Findings

Whilst the findings detailed above do not speak to the population of legal aid practitioners and providers as a whole, the current practitioners, chambers and organisations who responded to the Census exhibit a number of features that echo trends in the sector and in the profession that have been documented elsewhere.

Respondents to the current practitioners' survey presented as largely white, female, aged 40 and over, and working in London. Practitioners were often longstanding members of the legal aid community; approximately a third of practitioners had worked in legal aid for 21 years or more, while around a quarter had worked in the sector for 11–20 years. The vast majority of practitioners reported being employed at organisations providing both private and legal aid services. All areas of legal aid were represented by the practitioner group, but the majority of practitioners working solely in one area of practice were working in crime and the most common areas of practice overall were family law (both public and private) and crime. The overwhelming majority of practitioners attended school in the UK, and around two-thirds of respondents attended a state comprehensive school. Similarly, over 90 per cent of respondents had attended or were attending university. Just under a fifth of practitioners received state benefits or were eligible for free school meals during their primary or secondary education. Most practitioners did not have parents or caregivers who attended university, and just over 80 per cent of practitioners were the first legal professionals in their immediate family.

Prospective practitioners also self-identified as mostly female and white British. Whilst most were aged 18–21, more of those considering a career in legal aid were older as compared to the student cohort as a whole. The largest proportion of prospective practitioners were living in London and/or studying for their LLB. A higher proportion of prospective practitioners stated that their families were on benefits or were eligible for free school meals relative to current practitioners, while a slightly higher proportion of prospective practitioners indicated that their parents or guardians attended university as compared to current practitioners. Prospective practitioners were more often from ethnic minority backgrounds than current practitioners. They were also more likely to report a disability, and specifically reported much higher rates of mental ill-health.

Former practitioners largely self-identified as white British, female, former legal aid solicitors, between the ages of 41 and 59, who had worked in London, and practised in the areas of crime and family law. The majority had worked for at least a year in legal aid, and almost half had worked in the sector for over a decade.

Chambers were largely based in London, were of a larger size, and had members undertaking work predominantly in the areas of crime and family law. Organisations mostly presented as for-profit firms – providing both private and legal aid services – out of London. Organisations tended to have smaller head-counts, were nearly all legal aid contract-holders, and had mostly been providing legal aid services for decades.

These figures reveal that the legal aid sector may attract greater diversity than is the case for the legal profession as a whole, particularly as it relates to ethnic minority and socio-economic status. Findings also tend to reinforce the retreat of practitioners from certain areas of practice such as crime, and concerns regarding an ageing workforce. Similarly, findings in respect of the distribution of practitioners, chambers and organisations and the representation of different genders within the legal aid profession reaffirm known patterns.

Media narratives around legal aid have typically exacerbated perceptions that legal practitioners are an elite group motivated primarily by money. The responses provided by current, former and prospective practitioners documented in this chapter suggest otherwise. The motivations expressed by these individuals are firmly grounded in widening access to justice and serving those who have experienced disadvantage. Prospective practitioners are also often motivated by experiences in their personal lives and past employment, which inspire them to pursue careers fighting for social justice. The situations presented in this chapter challenge perceptions of purported privilege that underpin many wider assumptions about the legal profession. What emerges instead is a largely state-schooled cohort of legal aid practitioners, many of whom were first generation students at university and the first person to qualify as a lawyer in their immediate family. Prospective practitioners report an even greater incidence of state-schooling than current practitioners and the legal profession more broadly.

Notwithstanding the limitations of our sample, the higher proportion of prospective practitioners who report coming from a ethnic minority and/or state-school background or having a disability, as compared to the proportion of these groups represented within the cohort of current practitioners, may point to the barriers faced by these groups in obtaining entry into the profession. This discrepancy suggests the existence of structural and/or cultural barriers that prevent the more diverse population of prospective practitioners from successfully establishing a career in legal aid. Building on this, in the next chapter we consider the experiences and challenges faced by current, former and prospective practitioners in preparing for a career in legal aid, and we examine their associated implications.

3

Preparing for a Career in Legal Aid

I. Introduction

For much of the twentieth century, legal education in England and Wales was organised into separate academic and vocational stages of training. Requirements for the academic stage and the mandatory topics to be covered were set out in a joint statement by the Law Society and the General Council of the Bar.[1] These were organised by Law Schools into a set of seven units (Contract Law, Criminal Law, Tort Law, Public Law, Equity and Trusts, Land Law, and European Union Law). When taken together in the context of an LLB or a one-year GDL 'conversion course', these units formed the basis of a qualifying law degree (QLD). Upon completion of the academic stage, prospective barristers proceed to a Bar Course, followed by a year-long pupillage with a chamber. Alternately, prospective solicitors undertake a Legal Practice Course and a two-year period of workplace training with a recognised training provider.[2]

This model of legal education and training has attracted a number of criticisms over the decades, during which it has persisted largely unchanged. Of particular relevance for present purposes is the way in which the structural dimensions of the employment and education market, the cost of education and training relative to graduate earnings, and the nature of legal education itself dissuade students from pursuing a career in legal aid and leaves them underprepared for the reality of working within the sector. In this chapter, we begin by exploring several of the tensions that underpin legal education and training in England and Wales, before drawing together key findings from current and prospective legal aid practitioners who responded to the Legal Aid Census. In doing so, this chapter provides important insights into the extent to which the education and training framework can support or inhibit entry into the legal aid sector.

[1] Solicitors Regulation Authority and Bar Standards Board, 'Academic Stage Handbook' (Solicitors Regulation Authority and Bar Standards Board, 2014), available at www.sra.org.uk/globalassets/documents/students/academic-stage/academic-stage-handbook.pdf?version=4a1ac3, 15–20.

[2] Whilst training as a solicitor or barrister are not the only routes into the legal aid profession, as reported in ch 2, 63% of current practitioners entered into the legal aid profession via a training contract or pupillage.

II. Tensions in Legal Education

Despite the training paths demarcating vocational and academic stages, the academic study of law has regularly come under pressure to incorporate a broader range of vocationally relevant competencies.[3] As Webb explains,

> the intellectual battle lines are … drawn increasingly sharply (at the extremes) between those academics who tend to see engagement with practice and employability skills as anti-academic and inconsistent with the liberal ideal, and those … critical of the more theoretical and abstract drift of legal scholarship and law teaching.[4]

At the same time, efforts to bring the study of law closer to practice have given rise to concerns regarding the extent to which this enables 'corporate creep' through which 'the market gains an opportunity to determine curricula content'.[5] In the context of legal education, this market has been dominated by large corporate firms who, as the primary supplier of training contracts to LLB and conversion course graduates,[6] have enjoyed primacy in the employment market. This primacy has been a function of their ability to underwrite the costs of a trainee's LPC and to offer the organisational infrastructure and breadth of practice areas necessary to receive authorisation as a registered training provider. When coupled with a generous salary during training and, in some instances, the provision of signing bonuses, there has been little basis upon which smaller high-street and not-for-profit legal aid providers have been able to compete to attract graduates.

These opportunities for corporate influence have proliferated in a climate of decreased public funding in which law firms and business enterprises 'are increasingly invited to financially support university-based legal education under a privatised model'.[7] As Thornton argues, this has been accelerated by the neoliberal transformation of higher education and market fundamentalism, which has operated to rebrand legal education as a private rather than a public good. As a result, 'those aspects associated with social justice, theory and critique are perceived as

[3] See eg James Gray and Mick Woodley, 'The Relationship between Academic Legal Education and the Legal Profession: The Review of Legal Education in England and Wales and the Teaching Hospital Model' (2005) 2 *European Journal of Legal Education* 1; Julian Webb, 'The LETRs (Still) in the Post: The Legal Education and Training Review and the Reform of Legal Services Education and Training – A Personal (Re)View.' in Hilary Sommerlad et al (eds), *The Futures of Legal Education and the Legal Profession* (Hart, 2018). For a similar discussion in the context of US legal education see eg Harry Edwards, 'The Growing Disjunction between Legal Education and the Legal Profession' (1992) 91 *Michigan Law Review* 34; Ray W Campbell, 'The End of Law Schools: Legal Education in the Era of Legal Service Businesses' (2016) 85 *Mississippi Law Journal* 1.

[4] Webb (n 3) 110.

[5] Susan B Boyd, 'Corporatism and Legal Education in Canada' (2005) 14 *Social and Legal Studies* 287, 288.

[6] Training contracts are offers given to students in which a law firm will pay for the costs of their LPC and will provide them with two years' paid work experience to fulfil the requirements that until 2021 were set down by the Solicitors Regulation Authority (SRA).

[7] Boyd (n 5) 288.

having little "use value" within the market paradigm, thereby rendering them dispensable'.[8]

The neoliberalisation of legal education has also resulted in significant competition between education providers, with universities drawing on a range of metrics and specifically their graduate employment outcomes as markers of distinction. These market forces mean that recruiters' demands for graduates capable of delivering on 'day one' results in an incremental shift in pedagogical priorities in favour of the needs of large corporate law firms.[9] Whereas once this might once have been viewed more critically as a threat to the independence of legal education, such concerns have been increasingly silenced as the 'employability agenda' in higher education has gained momentum. The result, according to Nicolson, is that 'a university education has been transformed from a public good into a commodity marketed to student "consumers" who … seem more interested in gaining credentials to compete on the labour market than intellectual and personal growth'.[10]

Invariably, the 'employability' needs of those segments of the employment market associated with lower salaries and fewer training contracts – such as legal aid – are routinely overlooked. This outcome is especially problematic in terms of attracting new entrants to the legal aid profession and preparing them for their role within it. In this environment, even clinical legal education opportunities which offer 'the most promising means of encouraging students to take [access to justice] seriously … through exposure to those most in need of legal services',[11] become 'padding' for the CVs of those seeking a corporate law career. This is not because the skills, knowledge and experience students gain within these settings is considered particularly relevant to such a career. As Francis's empirical research with legal recruiters and current employees at large law firms makes clear, firms value only that which is taught on their own formal vacation scheme. Instead, clinical placement completion presents as a form of virtue signalling – offering evidence of a graduate's commitment to the pursuit of a career in law.[12]

The influence of large corporate law firms in graduate employment and graduate training necessarily leads to their greater representation at university career fairs and events which they commonly sponsor. As such, awareness of alternative careers in law and especially careers in legal aid may be low among students, and the pursuit of such careers may be actively minimised by law schools who are keen to maximise graduate employment and wary of the future of legal aid.

The economic realities many students face during study and upon graduation compound these effects. Over the last decade, the cost of university education has

[8] Margaret Thornton, 'The Law School, the Market and the New Knowledge Economy' (2007) 17 *Legal Education Review* 1.

[9] Andrew Francis, 'Legal Education, Social Mobility, and Employability: Possible Selves, Curriculum Intervention, and the Role of Legal Work Experience' (2015) 42 *Journal of Law and Society* 173, 196–17.

[10] Donald Nicolson, 'Legal Education, Ethics and Access to Justice: Forging Warriors for Justice in a Neo-Liberal World' (2015) 22 *International Journal of the Legal Profession* 51, 53.

[11] ibid, 57.

[12] Francis (n 9) 196–97.

risen more than threefold as a result of the coalition Government's decision in 2010 to lift the cap on university fees to £9,000 from 2012/13 onwards. Greater educational debt brought about as a result of higher student fees and increased living costs invariably results in some students – who would otherwise be attracted to legal aid – prioritising the paid work experience, training opportunities and higher graduate starting salaries provided within corporate law. Consequently, in England and Wales as in the USA, it is 'difficult for a student to turn down an early, lucrative offer from a large firm for the insecurity of hoping to find a low paying public interest job'.[13]

These external forces act in concert with the implicit influences that students are exposed to during legal education on account of the way law is approached as a subject of study. In the process of learning to think like a lawyer, students are taught that they must 'set aside their common sense, their view of social policy, their sense of justice, and any other form of "woozy thinking",[14] including their humanity,[15] that would run the risk of interfering with a valueless and scientific approach to the facts'.[16] As such, legal education's dogmatic adherence to the rules-based paradigm and a commitment to moral neutrality[17] which emphasises 'the ability to think precisely, to analyse coldly, to work within a body of materials that are given',[18] has been accused of extinguishing the idealism that may have brought students to law school in the first place.

This focus on teaching students the objective application of the law to a particular fact scenario as opposed to 'attempt(ing) to teach how the power of law is used to maintain a particular social order and what the alternatives to the prevailing order might exist' means that legal education offers little in the way of a justice agenda, at least as is stands in relation to the core units required for professional practice in England and Wales.[19] It is perhaps not surprising that this environment and the form of thinking it seeks to instil within students may have the unintentional effect of extinguishing a student's desire to work for social justice.[20]

As such, it remains that 'We are always teaching more than law when we teach students to think like lawyers.'[21] The method of instruction that dominates legal education does more than teach students the craft of law. It explicitly and implicitly

[13] Daniel Greenberg, 'Reflections on the New Mexico Conference: What Would You Have Said Before You Came to Law School' (1989) 19 *New Mexico Law Review* 171, 174.

[14] ibid.

[15] Karl N Llewellyn, *The Bramble Bush: On Our Law and Its Study*, 2nd edn (Oceana, 1960) 116.

[16] James R Elkins, 'Thinking Like a Lawyer: Second Thoughts' (1996) 47 *Mercer Law Review* 511, 523.

[17] Roger Burridge and Julian Webb, 'The Values of Common Law Legal Education Reprised' (2010) 42 *The Law Teacher* 263, 267–69.

[18] Llewellyn (n 15) 116.

[19] Elkins (n 16) 514–15. Whilst this argument was initially advanced in respect of legal education in the US, the argument is as relevant in England and Wales, as it is in the US.

[20] Stephen Wizner, 'Is Learning to "Think Like a Lawyer" Enough?' (1998) 17 *Yale Law and Policy Review* 589.

[21] Elkins (n 16).

conveys an understanding of what the profession values.[22] What is valued is also signalled implicitly and explicitly in the prioritisation of certain substantive areas of legal knowledge as part of a 'qualifying degree'; the availability (or lack thereof) of elective units relevant to social justice such as social welfare law, family law and immigration law; the availability of paid work experience of different forms; and the extent to which careers in legal aid are given coverage over the duration of the law degree.

These features specific to the legal education and training pathway help explain why over the course of legal education, students exhibit a shift away from idealism towards instrumentalism and move away from their previously expressed intention to pursue legal aid, public service or government work.[23] Of course, the academic components of legal education may suppress the social justice dimensions of the law and the benefits of pursuing a career to that end; however, we cannot discount the effect of other factors such as the stranglehold that large corporate firms have managed to maintain over the graduate workforce (and *ipso facto* the curriculum). This outcome is made possible because the cost of qualification and the work experience requirements set down by the SRA to date have made it increasingly difficult for legal aid providers – particularly those providers who perform only legal aid work – to attract graduates.

For this reason, recent changes to the qualification process enacted by the Solicitors' Regulatory Authority (SRA) in 2021 which make possible a significant departure in form for legal education, may be viewed in a positive light. Whilst retaining both an academic and vocational component to the qualification process, the SRA has done away with the requirement for prospective solicitors to complete an LLB or conversion course. In its place, any undergraduate degree coupled with a requisite amount of work experience and a pass on both stages of a newly introduced SQE will render an individual eligible for registration as a solicitor in England and Wales.

In introducing these changes, the SRA sought – among other objectives – to address the systemic lack of competition engendered by the existing qualifying process. First, by removing the QLD, the SRA argued that universities would no longer be 'protected from competition by a requirement, which only they can meet'.[24] Second, by mandating two years of work experience but removing the requirement for this experience to be completed with a registered training provider, the changes addressed large corporate firms' stranglehold over vocational training and, *ipso facto*, the admittance of solicitors to practice.

In relinquishing the grip that corporate law has on the market for professional qualification, these changes hint at the possibility of the emergence of a

[22] Wizner (n 20).

[23] Andrew Boon, 'From Public Service to Service Industry: The Impact of Socialisation and Work on the Motivation and Values of Lawyers' (2005) 12 *International Journal of the Legal Profession* 229, 232 citing findings from a number of different studies.

[24] Brannan J and Marrs R, 'Paths to Practice: Regulating for Innovation in Legal Education and Training' in Catrina Denvir (ed), *Modernising Legal Education* (Cambridge University Press, 2020), 234. We might question the validity of this argument given that prospective solicitors are still required to possess an undergraduate degree.

new generation of legal aid lawyers whose entry into the profession is aided by new models of legal education which better integrate academic study, professional learning and work experience. Innovations such as solicitor-apprenticeships, sandwich degrees and embedded clinical work which enable graduates to be admitted to practice upon completion of their degree may go some way to addressing the financial challenges associated with the length of the current training pathway for solicitors.

With the route to qualifying via the LPC retained only for those who commenced their legal training prior to 1 September 2021, the impact of these changes will not be seen until at least 2023. Yet in spite of the fact that the SQE does not require previous legal knowledge or qualifications, there is good reason to believe that the law degree will continue to represent the main route of entry into the profession. BPP, a private academic and professional legal training provider, for example, advises students in respect of the SQE that 'the assessments are rigorous and demanding in testing skills and knowledge' and as such it 'strongly recommend[s] that non-law graduates take a course that gets them to the same level of knowledge that an LLB, GDL or PGDL graduate would have.'[25]

Moreover, whilst providers such as the University of Law and BPP have sought to include coverage of the foundations of law alongside preparation for SQE1 and 2 in their Masters degree programmes, it remains that completion of a law degree still holds symbolic value for students beyond the instrument value it has held to date in relation to solicitor qualification. For students, this symbolic value is enshrined in societal perception of law as a difficult subject which is capable of study by only the most able, as well as the perceived experiential value of the degree derived from studying a subject that is of interest.[26] For those students who are undecided as to whether to qualify as a barrister or solicitor, the requirement of a legal qualification for those intending on going to the bar means that a law degree will offer students the greatest number of career options.

Irrespective of which pathway will dominate following the SRA changes, there are a number of features of the education and training pathway which undermine the desirability and feasibility of pursuing a career in legal aid. As such, this chapter explores legal education and training as preparation for legal aid practice by examining how practitioners went about qualifying for their role in legal aid and draws on the roles of legal education, work experience and training in this process. A key focus of the chapter is the extent to which choosing a career in legal aid can be challenging in light of a lack of specific modules or wider opportunities tailored towards legal aid. A relative lack of information or focus upon careers in legal aid at both the undergraduate and vocational stage – as compared to careers in corporate law – can also exacerbate this challenge. This chapter also considers the

[25] BPP, 'Should I do the LPC or SQE?' (BPP, 9 December 2021), available at www.bpp.com/insights/lpc-or-sqe-key-differences.

[26] Alex Nicholson and Paul Johnson, 'The Value of a Law Degree – Part 3: A Student Perspective' (2021) 55 *The Law Teacher* 431.

financial and personal barriers which arise in the process of preparing for a career in legal aid, including the high levels of debt incurred by current and prospective practitioners and the relative scarcity of training positions in legal aid practice. Findings set out how the current legal education and training pathway operates to divert students away from a career in legal aid whilst leaving those who remain committed to such a career largely unprepared for its reality.

Given that much of the forthcoming analysis examines specific aspects of legal education, the analysis of student data excludes those students who were not considering a career in legal aid, as well as those not currently studying the degrees necessary for qualification as a barrister or solicitor (ie the LLB, GDL, LPC, Bar Course or SQE studies).[27] As such, this chapter refers to 'law students' rather than 'prospective practitioners'.

III. Educational Experiences

A. Courses Relevant to Legal Aid

Up until the 1970s, the legal profession trained new entrants via an apprenticeship model. This changed following the publication of the Ormrod Report on Legal Education in 1971, which recommended that the legal profession of England and Wales become a graduate profession. At the time, training for the profession for non-graduates consisted of four years of articles plus the completion of a one-year recognised course of education and the passage of two parts of a qualifying exam. With only 40 per cent of solicitor graduates at the time (as compared to 80 per cent of barristers), the proposal set down in Ormrod represented a considerable step-change particularly for the solicitors' profession.[28] The result was an expansion of the academic component of training at the expense of its vocational component. In effect, a three-year law degree would see the previous four years of vocational training demanded of non-graduates reduced to two.[29]

In the 50 years since the reforms heralded by Ormrod, there has been wide-scale growth in the number of universities, law schools and law degrees available. Correspondingly, there has also been continued growth in the number of law students. Individuals graduating with legal qualifications have doubled from

[27] Notwithstanding that it is recognised that changes to the qualifying routes for prospective solicitors are due to be enacted with the commencement of the SQE. See Ben Waters, 'The Solicitors Qualification Examination: Something for All? Some Challenges Facing Law Schools in England and Wales' (2018) 52 *The Law Teacher* 519. 199 students indicated they were interested in a career in legal aid. Of these, 175 were studying for the LLB, GDL, LPC, Bar Course or SQE.

[28] Patricia Leighton, 'Legal Education in England and Wales: What Next?' (2021) 55 *The Law Teacher* 405.

[29] Phillip A Thomas and Geoff M Mungham, 'English Legal Education: A Commentary on the Ormrod Report' (1972) 7 *Valparaiso University Law Review* 87.

around 15,000 in 1994 to over 30,000 in 2016.[30] Whilst law has very much become part of the mainstream offering of universities, it has continued to attract criticism. For those within academia it has been viewed as insufficiently academic,[31] whilst for those outside of academia it has been deemed insufficiently vocational. This debate is in part a product of disagreement as to the purpose of a law degree: should it be a form of legal education or lawyer education? If it is the latter, how might this be reconciled with the fact that many of those who study law do not go on to qualify?[32] If a law degree is intended to produce both Pericles and the Plumber, to what extent can it effectively produce either?[33]

On the training of students for a career in legal aid, findings from the Census suggest that opportunities to study topics relevant to legal aid were more prevalent in the conversion or vocational stages (as they exist at the time of writing) than during the undergraduate stage of legal education. Of those current practitioners who had an LLB (n=836), just under half (49.6 per cent, n=415) were given the opportunity to study modules or topics relevant to civil or criminal legal aid during their LLB. However, of the practitioners who undertook a conversion course or vocational training (n=1,092), more than half (61.1 per cent, n=667) were given the opportunity to study modules or topics relevant to civil or criminal legal aid during their conversion or vocational stage (GDL, LPC or Bar Course), substantially outweighing those who were not given such opportunities (38.9 per cent, n=425).

Table 3.1 Modules relevant to civil or criminal legal aid that current legal aid practitioners were given the opportunity to study during their legal education

	Undergraduate (LLB) stage (n=412)		**Conversion/vocational stage** (n=665)	
	N	%	N	%
Family law	322	78.2	515	77.4
Immigration	48	11.7	175	26.3
Welfare benefits	37	9.0	77	11.6
Housing	64	15.5	130	19.5

(continued)

[30] Matthew Williams et al, 'Research to Inform Workforce Planning and Career Development in Legal Services Employment: Trends, Workforce Projections and Solicitor Firm Perspectives' (Institute of Employment Studies, 2019) 33.

[31] Leighton (n 28).

[32] James Thornton, 'Is Publicly Funded Criminal Defence Sustainable? Legal Aid Cuts, Morale, Recruitment and Retention in the English Criminal Law Professions' (2020) 40 *Legal Studies* 230.

[33] William Twining, 'Pericles and the Plumber' in William Twining (ed), *Law in Context: Enlarging a Discipline* (Oxford University Press, 1997), 64. Twining referred to Pericles as 'the lawgiver, the enlightened policy-maker, the wise judge' and the Plumber as 'someone who is master of certain specialized knowledge, 'the law', and certain technical skills'.

Table 3.1 ***(Continued)***

	Undergraduate (LLB) stage (n=412)		**Conversion/vocational stage** (n=665)	
	N	**%**	**N**	**%**
Equality and discrimination	45	10.9	35	5.3
Education	13	3.2	9	1.4
Criminal litigation	334	81.1	591	88.9
Other	32	7.8	41	6.2

As shown in Table 3.1 above, the most common relevant modules offered to current practitioners at both the undergraduate and vocational stages were family law and criminal litigation. It is noteworthy that only a small number of respondents had the opportunity to study modules relevant to wider areas of social welfare law, especially at the undergraduate stage where modules in immigration, welfare benefits and education were infrequently offered. In terms of 'other' subjects offered during undergraduate legal education deemed relevant to criminal or civil legal aid, respondents noted a wide range of areas including administrative law, employment, community care, criminal, European law, public law, human rights, mental health, public interest law, trusts, landlord and tenant, evidence and banking law. Some respondents also referenced judicial review and other subjects that examined issues pertaining to access to justice, legal service delivery and legal need. The 'other' subjects mentioned as being offered during the conversion, vocational, and/or Bar Course stage included civil and personal injury litigation, conveyancing, labour, contract, wills and probate, employment, landlord and tenant, and public and mental health law. Furthermore, two respondents indicated a specific 'legal aid add-on' module was offered.

Data drawn from law students largely aligns with the findings in respect of current practitioners and indicates an increase in the availability of legal aid related modules at the undergraduate stage. Of those who had previously studied or were currently studying for their LLB or GDL (n=171), 62.6 per cent (n=107) indicated they were given the opportunity to study modules or topics relevant to legal aid, whilst 26.3 per cent (n=45) were not.

As shown in Table 3.2 below, the most commonly offered LLB/GDL module relevant to legal aid was family law (78.1 per cent, n=82), followed by employment law (53.3 per cent, n=56) and modules related to the legal profession, such as professional ethics (42.9 per cent, n=45). Again, modules on social welfare law (5.7 per cent, n=6) and housing law (13.3 per cent, n=14) were far less commonly offered. A small number of respondents (6.7 per cent, n=7) indicated that they were offered other modules relevant to legal aid. These 'other' modules included programmes related to gender and the law, clinical education programmes, civil dispute resolution, and criminal process and inquest law.

Of those students studying for a vocational degree (LPC or Bar Course) or for their SQE (n=44), 79.5 per cent (n=35)[34] were given the opportunity to study modules relevant to legal aid. As with undergraduate studies, the modules most commonly offered that were relevant to legal aid included family law (85.7 per cent, n=30) and employment (62.9 per cent, n=22). In contrast to the offerings at the LLB/GDL stage, students at the vocational stage were more often offered immigration law modules (40.0 per cent, n=14), and were offered fewer modules related to social justice (5.7 per cent, n=2), social welfare (2.9 per cent, n=1) or the legal profession (2.9 per cent, n=1).

Table 3.2 Proportion of law students offered modules relevant to legal aid during their LLB/GDL studies or LPC/Bar Course/SQE training

	Modules relevant to legal aid that were offered during LLB/GDL (n=105)		**Modules relevant to legal aid that were offered during the LPC/ Bar Course/SQE Training** (n=35)	
	N	%	**N**	%
Family law	82	78.1	30	85.7
Immigration	26	24.8	14	40.0
Housing	14	13.3	4	11.4
Social welfare	6	5.7	1	2.9
Employment	56	53.3	22	62.9
Modules related to the legal profession	45	42.9	1	2.9
Social justice (or similar)	40	38.1	2	5.7
Other	7	6.7	4	11.4

Whilst the findings make clear that there is at least some provision of courses of study that are necessary for those considering a career in legal aid, there remains a gap in provision. When asked what courses during the LLB/GDL stage would be most useful to their future careers in legal aid, it is noteworthy that the 32 law students who answered referenced modules that were not commonly offered such as immigration law (43.8 per cent, n=14), social welfare (28.1 per cent, n=9) and housing law (25.0 per cent, n=8). A sizable proportion of responses also nominated other modules (37.5 per cent, n=12). 'Other' suggested modules included human rights, public law and topics covering the law in relation to children, social care, debt and mental health. 'Other' modules also included those with a specific

[34] This percentage includes an additional one student who did not answer this question but went on to provide information regarding the modules they were offered and so has been presumed to have answered 'yes' to this question.

focus on the history, operation and policy of legal aid, as well as modules providing clinical legal education.

Of the law students who answered in respect of the vocational/SQE stage (n=10), housing was more often viewed by vocational/SQE students (60.0 per cent, n=6) as enhancing the legal aid relevance of their studies. Vocational stage students also expressed greater demand for modules that were infrequently offered such as social welfare law (50 per cent, n=5). As was the case for the LLB/GDL stage, some students (20.0 per cent n=2) suggested 'other' modules to enhance the legal aid relevance of their vocational studies. These included debt, mental health law and prison law. Modules in relation to the legal profession and social justice were more commonly reported being offered at the LLB/GDL stage, perhaps reflecting the broader liberal arts orientation of this stage of legal education.

It is notable that no students reported being offered modules or indicated that it would be helpful to have modules that dealt with broader employment skills at any point during their studies. This is interesting because legal recruiters have previously observed the need for graduates to be equipped to enter the world of work and to have a better understanding of how to navigate an office environment, tailor their communication style for different audiences, practice effective email etiquette, and deal with work overload and underload.[35]

Despite the well-being concerns expressed by the profession (see chapter four) and observed by students during work placements as described below, no responses referenced the need for training on the aspects of legal practice that negatively impact mental well-being. Legal recruiters in previous studies have observed that 'We know in our sector, mental health concerns are prevalent, and yet we do nothing to prepare people for the rigours … if [legal education could incorporate] mental health support, we'd have it sorted, I think.'[36] That these types of subjects were not mentioned by student respondents may reflect what Nicholson refers to as the '"employability paradox": the idea that often the very skills that employers value are those that students do not enjoy developing.'[37]

It is also interesting to note that despite the complexity of the funding rules that govern legal aid, the need for units focusing on these areas were not mentioned by graduates undertaking vocational training. This may be a case of students not knowing what they do not know. While many new trainees find out the hard way that this knowledge is required, often from day one, unless they have had exposure to legal aid practice, the importance of this knowledge prior to then may not be appreciated.

Although findings make clear that opportunities to study modules relevant to legal aid do exist, the data also suggests that such opportunities tend to be

[35] Alex Nicholson, 'The Value of a Law Degree – Part 4: A Perspective from Employers' (2022) 56 *The Law Teacher* 171.

[36] ibid.

[37] ibid, 182.

unevenly distributed. As one student noted, their LPC was 'frustratingly commercial focussed – even civil litigation which is obviously relevant to public social welfare law and e.g. civil claims against public authorities is taught through a commercial [lens].'[38] Another put the point rather more succinctly: 'The course was not aimed at people who want to go into Legal Aid.'[39]

Given that the LPC offered by three of the main providers – BPP Law School, Nottingham Law School, and the Oxford Institute of Legal Practice – was actually a product of consultation between the providers and a number of 'heavyweight' law firms with the purpose of producing a course that was better suited to the 'realities of city practice', this lack of legal aid focus is of no surprise.[40] Certainly it is no surprise to those involved in the development of LPC education.[41] Whether students – and particularly those who embark upon a self-funded LPC – have knowledge of this history, or the implications it poses for unit options, is a different matter. It is correct to say that many LPCs are not aimed at those who wish to go into legal aid, and this is deliberately so.[42] As Kennedy notes in the context of US legal education, institutions 'act in more concrete ways to guarantee that their students will fit themselves into their appropriate niches in the existing system of practice' and 'the actual content of what is taught in a given school will incapacitate students from any other form of practice than that allotted to graduates of that institution'.[43] Similarly, efforts by providers to tailor LPC content to regional corporate firms operating outside of London[44] have also introduced greater fracture. That the legal aid sector has not attempted to collaborate to shape an LPC in its own image may be the product of a range of different factors. This includes reduced market power; as Kalsi and Sharpley noted in 2010 amidst widescale changes to legal aid, it is 'unlikely that LPC providers will, for example, deliver a course that devotes a significant number of litigation hours to criminal practice in the current market when criminal legal aid is under threat.'[45] Added to this is the breadth of work the sector undertakes which may inhibit a common focus and the lower levels of recruitment that occur within the sector and the absence of readily available LPC funding opportunities. Perhaps most problematic though, is the inability of the legal aid sector to shift focus away from their current workload to focus on more strategic objectives. As Kalsi and Sharpley observe, this means that

[38] Student Respondent Number 327.

[39] Student Respondent Number 346.

[40] Allen & Overy, Clifford Chance, Freshfields Bruckhaus Deringer, Herbert Smith, Linklaters, Lovells, Norton Rose, and Slaughter & May. James Faulconbridge, 'Alliance "Capitalism" and Legal Education: An English Perspective' (2012) 80 *Fordham Law Review* 2651, 2653.

[41] As Kalsi and Sharpley note: 'The LPC … as it stands it does not serve as best it could students who want to do legal aid work': Sonia Kalsi and Deborah Sharpley, 'Pathways in Legal Education: Taking the Right Route?' Learning in Law Annual Conference (College of Law, 2010) 5.

[42] Faulconbridge (n 40); Julian Webb, 'Regulating Lawyers in a Liberalized Legal Services Market: The Role of Education and Training' (2013) 24 *Stanford Law and Policy Review* 533.

[43] Duncan Kennedy, 'Legal Education as Training for Hierarchy' in David Kairys (ed), *The Politics of Law: A Progressive Critique* (Pantheon Books, 1990) 64.

[44] Faulconbridge (n 40) 2651.

[45] Kalsi and Sharpley (n 41) 5.

in the context of joint curriculum development, 'the already financially squeezed legal aid firms would find it difficult if not impossible to become involved in the same way.'[46]

For that reason, in 2006 the College of Law introduced a Legal Aid Route to completion of the LPC, the purpose of which was to address some of the ethical and funding dimensions of legal aid work necessary for practice, require a clinical component, as well as requiring students choose elective units where legal aid funding was (at the time) available. The components of the route existed in addition to the ordinary requirements of the LPC, resulting not in an additional qualification but rather a statement of recognition by the College that the student had successfully completed the legal aid route and its associated requirements. It is not clear when this offering ceased, but the fact that it did – in spite of its seeming popularity – tells us something important about the market for legal aid education.[47]

B. *Pro Bono*, Clinics and Work Experience

In the absence of units related to legal aid or designed to equip students with the skills needed for legal aid practice, clinical work experience has been the default method of facilitating 'on the job' learning. Such opportunities provide students with exposure to careers beyond the corporate law or high-street paradigm and are therefore necessary from both an awareness-raising and skills-development perspective.

It is therefore unsurprising that *pro bono* projects featured quite strongly in current practitioners' experience of legal education. Just over half (53.0 per cent, n=589) of those respondents who went to university (n=1,112) undertook *pro bono* work during their time at university (either at undergraduate level or during the vocational stage) compared to 47.0 per cent (n=523) who did not. Additionally, 26.4 per cent (n=288) of 1,089 practitioner respondents indicated that they were offered the opportunity to work in a student legal advice clinic service during their undergraduate degree whereas 73.6 per cent (n=801) were not.

In spite of what is generally seen as a growth in the number and availability of clinical legal education opportunities, including *pro bono* activities, on account of its perceived contribution to the employability agenda in higher education,[48] the responses provided by law students suggest a drop in the number of opportunities either made available or taken up by those currently engaged in education and training. From the 174 law students undertaking their LLB/GDL/LPC/Bar Course/SQE who answered, a total of 42.5 per cent (n=74) of students had undertaken *pro bono* projects and/or activities arranged by their institution during

[46] ibid, 8.
[47] ibid.
[48] Francis (n 9) 196–97; Nicolson (n 10) 53.

their legal studies, with 90 respondents (51.7 per cent) not having done so and 10 respondents (5.7 per cent) indicating that they didn't know.

Within the context of legal employability more generally, participation in external 'informal' opportunities have previously been viewed as very important, not just in establishing an employability narrative, but also in securing other forms of work experience including vacation schemes.[49] In addition to opportunities made available by their university, a total of 90.6 per cent (n=1,026 of 1,133) of current practitioners undertook work experience arranged independently prior to their qualification and/or training. The most common forms of work experience were paralegal work (51.3 per cent, n=526) followed by different forms of *pro bono* or voluntary work outside of law school (46.6 per cent, n=478). Only 23.7 per cent (n=243) of those practitioners who had attended or were attending university indicated that they had undertaken vacation schemes as a form of work experience. This figure is relatively low compared with the prevalence of vacation schemes for those pursuing careers in corporate law.[50] The rate of undertaking independently arginali work experience was lower for those current practitioners who had not attended or were not attending university (74.7 per cent, n=56 of 75), with paralegal work (62.5 per cent, n=35) and *pro bono* or voluntary work (14.3 per cent, n=8) the most common types of work undertaken.

This rate was lower still for current law students, where only 98 respondents (56.3 per cent) had undertaken independently arranged work experience. Of those current students who had undertaken independently arginali work experience, 37.8 per cent of students (n=37) indicated that this experience was in legal aid, 56.1 per cent (n=55) indicated it was not, whilst 6.1 per cent (n=6) did not know. For current students, the most common form of experience was charity volunteering (40.8 per cent, n=40), followed by internships (37.8 per cent n=37), mini pupillages (33.7 per cent, n=33), *pro bono* work (30.6 per cent, n=30), marshalling/judicial shadowing (17.3 per cent, n=17), paralegal work (15.3 per cent, n=15), case work (14.3 per cent, n=14), legal administration (13.3 per cent, n=13) and 'other' activities (13.3 per cent, n=13). An even smaller number of students reported undertaking vacation schemes (14.3 per cent, n=14) compared to the rate reported by current practitioners.

Analysis of open-ended responses provided by law students in relation to work experience and *pro bono* experiences helps provide a potential explanation for this apparent drop in access to university facilitated and independently arranged work experience. Students revealed the challenges of the COVID-19 pandemic in terms of being able to access work experience; problems included office closures, work experience opportunities repeatedly being cancelled, having fewer opportunities being offered and subsequently more competition for places, and home-schooling commitments resulting in less time available to pursue work experience opportunities.

[49] Francis (n 9) 187–88.

[50] Students were not asked this question in the student survey.

The relatively low number of current practitioners and law students who report participating in a vacation scheme – what is viewed as a mainstay of training – may reflect the fact that those who pursue a career in legal aid know early on that this is the path in law they wish to pursue and so do not engage in unrelated forms of work experience. Conversely, it may reflect the occurrence of self-selection in which non-traditional students (those we would argue are more commonly represented in the legal aid sector on the basis of the findings outlined in chapter two) gravitate towards the legal aid sector because of a belief that they do not exhibit the characteristics demanded of recruiters in the corporate sector. Given that these characteristics include extra-curricular activities, exemplary A-level grades and what recruiters describe as an 'X factor', it is not difficult to see how those from arginalized backgrounds who have experienced disruption to their education or a lack of opportunity to participate in sporting, cultural, political or other endeavours may find it difficult to compete.[51] Early access to work experience often operates as a prerequisite to securing external formal work experience opportunities such as vacation schemes; those who are unable to access such opportunities can therefore face heightened barriers.

Invariably, those with connections to informal work experience have an advantage, with one study showing that students with connections to the profession through either family or friends were twice as likely to secure work experience during high school compared to those who did not.[52] This poses clear problems for law students from non-traditional backgrounds, as it has typically been assumed that students will have access to this type of work experience via their networks.[53] Whilst this was true in Francis' study of law students at two universities in the UK, it was not the case amongst respondents to the Census. The majority of current practitioners who had attended or were attending university who responded (n=1,121) said they did not have access to work experience through family or friends (68.9 per cent, n=772) with the same true of those who had not attended university (87.8 per cent, n=65 of 74). This disparity runs the risk of excluding students from non-traditional backgrounds, or those who are the first in their family to seek a career in law. Of those who did have access to work experience through personal networks (31.1 per cent, n=349 for those who attended university and 12.2 per cent, n=9 for those who did not), the majority said they had a friend of the family in the legal profession (64.5 per cent, n=225 and 66.7 per cent, n=6 respectively). Law student responses largely echoed these findings, with 77.5 per cent (n=76 of 98) indicating they did not have access to work experience via family and friends. Of the 22 students (22.5 per cent) who did have access via family and friends, 59.1 per cent (n=13) had a friend of the family in the legal profession.

[51] Francis (n 9) 187–88.
[52] ibid, 186.
[53] Francis (n 9).

Legal work experience, whether acquired during clinical legal education, *pro bono* work or other opportunities, has previously been associated with producing a number of gains relevant to students' career preparation. Specifically, it has been said that experience in clinical settings involving interaction with real clients and cases aids in the development of social responsibility, fosters empathy and interpersonal skills, enables networking and integration with legal professionals and promotes ethical behaviour.[54] It has also been shown in other studies that experiential opportunities in higher education has a formative impact on the 'habits of mind, work ethic, behaviours and professional identity' of students learners that are critical to strengthening student employability,[55] as well as being associated with improvements in an individual's own perception of their knowledge, writing, speaking and problem-solving skills.[56]

This notion of integration and professional identity is particularly important, given that there are questions as to whether employability exists as a set of skills and attributes that can be taught (via, for example, work/clinical experience opportunities). Some have instead proposed that work experience exists as a narrative that demonstrates to recruiters that an individual has the necessary 'habitus' – 'the durable ways of `speaking, walking and thereby of feeling and thinking' – needed to signal that they are `objectively compatible' with a profession (or section thereof).[57] That work experience may enable individuals to understand more effectively what is required in terms of outward behaviour, enable them to fit in and demonstrate their compatibility, is beneficial in employability terms. However, evidence from the Census suggests that work experience was less effective in exposing law student respondents to the reality of their career choice and what this would mean in terms of their quality of life, financial security and psychological well-being. Nor did it appear that these were insights that individuals were necessarily capable of gleaning from short stints of work experience.

Taking those who attended university and those who did not as a whole (n=1,123), around half of practitioners either strongly agreed (19.3 per cent, n=217) or agreed (33.2 per cent, n=373) that their work experience prepared them well for their careers in legal aid. From those who provided an explanation for their answer in the form of an open-ended response (n=458), a number of themes emerged in the coding. Overall, 14.8 per cent (n=68) of respondents observed that their work experience provided no preparation for the emotional and/or financial hardships of legal aid work. This comment was particularly prominent amongst those who disagreed or strongly disagreed with the view

[54] Francina Cantatore et al, 'A Comparative Study into Legal Education and Graduate Employability Skills in Law Students through pro Bono Law Clinics' (2021) 55 *Law Teacher* 314, 315–16.

[55] Francina Cantatore, 'The Impact of Pro Bono Law Clinics on Employability and Work Readiness in Law Students' (2018) 28 *International Journal of Clinical Legal Education* 147, 168.

[56] See eg ibid, 168.

[57] Francis (n 9) 179, 187.

that their work experience prepared them for their career in legal aid. As one respondent noted,

> I don't think a short period of work experience can prepare you for the demoralising effect of doing substantial hours of work unpaid in legal aid and having difficult work paid less and less well year after year after year.[58]

Another respondent emphasised that their lack of work experience specifically in the field of legal aid meant that 'the trauma of practising in this area is much harder than I ever could have anticipated.'[59]

While some respondents indicated that the emotional and/or financial aspects of legal aid practice could not be adequately conveyed during work experience, others observed the value of being exposed to the practicalities of legal aid work and understanding the needs of legal aid clients. For these respondents, their work experience was valuable insofar as it enhanced their professional capabilities, as the following quote exemplifies:

> I spent 6 years working in various charity and international organisation posts before commencing my recognised period of training and I think that really helped to be able to take a holistic approach to clients (not have tunnel vision just to look at one legal issue without taking the context of the client's personal circumstances into account) which also helps to anticipate potential future barriers likely to be faced by clients (e.g. we resolve homelessness issue[s] but then the client is likely to face a benefits issue due to the way the [Universal Credit] system works and the client's challenges in engaging with the system)[60]

Importantly, however, the length of the work experience to which the respondent refers is vastly longer than that most students acquire, and thus indicative of a career change, rather than career preparation. Others observed that legal aid work required a specific skillset best understood through broader forms of experience: 'Working with marginalised and vulnerable groups has provided me with skills that are important to legal aid work.'[61] For other respondents, work experience was important in helping them clarify their interest in a legal career and refining the type of career they wished to pursue, rather than as a skills acquisition opportunity. As one respondent explained, 'I understood from the experience that I did want a career in law and that I would be better suited for a high street firm rather than a larger firm.'[62]

These insights suggest that longer periods of work with related client groups may facilitate the type of skills acquisition that is valuable to legal aid work. In the context of the legal education and training pathway, however, we might expect that the acquisition of such work experience is likely to be limited to those who

[58] Practitioner Respondent Number 1084.
[59] Practitioner Respondent Number 438.
[60] Practitioner Respondent Number 670.
[61] Practitioner Respondent Number 537.
[62] Practitioner Respondent Number 1031.

are changing careers and re-training to enter law. For the majority of students who undertake shorter placements, the experience they gather may be most beneficial insofar as it enables them to confirm their overall career direction and consolidate an impression in the eyes of prospective recruiters that they are sufficiently committed to that direction. Importantly, the existence of formal vacation schemes facilitated by corporate firms are distinct from the opportunities (or lack thereof) made available to students in legal aid. Formal vacation schemes are highly structured, rigorously planned and constitute a significant investment by firms as part of their overall recruitment strategy which sees a certain number of trainees recruited into a firm each year.[63] No such equivalent exists for the legal aid sector, a field in which recruitment is generally more sporadic. Whilst alternative opportunities may be provided by large high-street firms, they are unlikely to challenge the scale of opportunities provided by corporate law firms. As such, most exposure to legal aid work comes by way of volunteering in a community advice setting or undertaking paid paralegal work.

C. Careers Information

Invariably, viewing legal work experience as a means by which to confirm one's interest in practising in legal aid will be viewed by some as an overly modest objective. Nevertheless, it is an objective that takes on a heightened importance in light of the seeming absence of other opportunities to learn about careers in legal aid during undergraduate and graduate training. Data reveal that only 34.4 per cent (n=379) of current practitioners (n=1,101) who attended university had access to careers events and/or information about careers in legal aid whilst at university. As shown in Figure 3.1, this information was mostly provided at the LLB stage (54.4 per cent, n=205) and only a minority of current practitioners had access to such information when studying for another undergraduate degree (12.2 per cent, n=46). A considerable proportion of current practitioners (40.1 per cent, n=151) also said they received information during the LPC. Where 'other' stages were mentioned, practitioners reported having received information during school, CILEX training, non-law postgraduate study or their solicitor-apprenticeship.

According to 372 current practitioners, where information was provided it was disseminated via the university careers service (68.8 per cent, n=256), *pro bono* projects/clinical casework (32.3 per cent, n=120), individual academic members of staff (29.8 per cent, n=111), student societies (27.4 per cent, n=102) or legal aid firms giving presentations (21.8 per cent, n=81).

When asked why they thought they had no access to careers events and/or information about careers in legal aid at university, 345 current practitioners provided an open-ended response. Consistent with the focus on corporate law that

[63] Francis (n 9) 190.

Figure 3.1 Stage of university when current legal aid practitioners were given access to careers events and/or information about careers in legal aid (n=377)

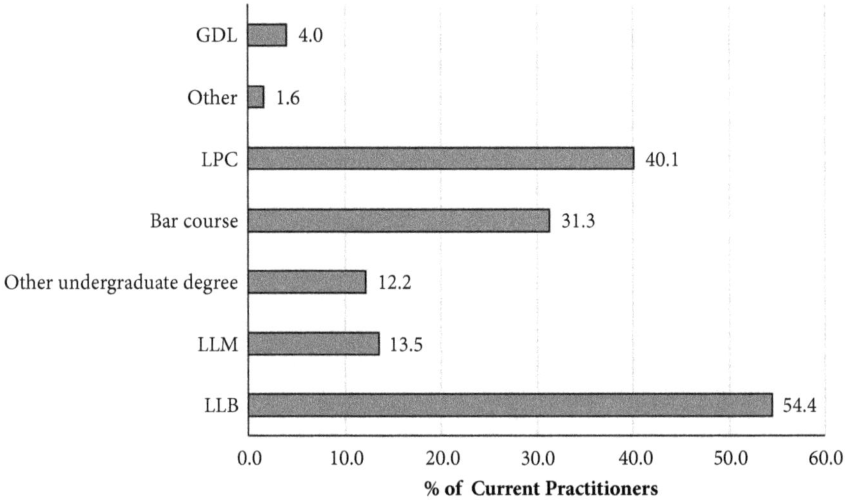

emerged in discussions regarding the elective units available to students during their study, a large proportion of respondents (44.1 per cent, n=152) indicated that there was a strong focus on corporate law, and legal aid was either discouraged or disregarded at their institutions, while 58.0 per cent (n=200) reported that they did not have careers advice at all. There was a strong feeling amongst these practitioners that there had been a bias towards corporate law: 'Careers events were geared towards commercial firms and commercial routes.'[64] There was also a sentiment that the universities were not interested in highlighting legal aid as a career option: 'lecturers saw legal aid as a career dead end and did not promote it.'[65] Harris, Dehaghani and Newman have explored the issue that lecturers are wary of encouraging students to pursue what they recognise is a challenging, low-paid and potentially unsustainable career path.[66] This problem also accords with the aforementioned pressures that universities face in a competitive higher education environment where student employment statistics and graduate destination outcomes are used to distinguish providers in the higher education market. As Kennedy observes, faculties 'propagat[e] myths about the character of the different kinds of practice' so as to channel their students into jobs in the hierarchy of the profession according to their own standing in the hierarchy of schools. Thus, any job outside the established hierarchy is denigrated, including delivering legal services for the poor, which 'although morally exalted' are characterised as

[64] Practitioner Respondent Number 603.
[65] Practitioner Respondent Number 835.
[66] Nicola Harris et al, 'Vulnerability, the Future of the Criminal Defence Profession, and the Implications for Teaching and Learning' (2021) 55 *The Law Teacher* 57.

'hopelessly dull and unchallenging' and come with the significant drawback that 'the possibilities of reaching a standard of living appropriate to a lawyer are slim or non-existent'.[67]

As employers observed in Nicholson's study, however, it is critical to have an understanding of the range of careers open to students and what different types of client work entails. This is particularly true of certain areas of law where, in spite of being excellent on paper and high-achieving academically, many of those who sought work in private law did not have it in them to 'sit across from a homeless alcoholic telling them that they're not going to see their kids again' and were not aware that this was the job.[68] In this regard, career information can bridge the gap between graduates' expectations and the reality of legal aid practice, as well as give students insights into the profession that would encourage them to reflect on their suitability for different sectors. Such information ought to precede the completion of work experience, since limited work experience opportunities in the legal aid ought to go to those most likely to pursue a career in the sector.

The absence of careers information was not always a deliberate choice, however; some simply considered it a function of the time. Practitioners who qualified more than 20 years ago explained that 'It was so long ago, I don't think it was really thought about back then!'[69] and 'It was another world! Careers advice was rudimentary.'[70] Many respondents presumed that with the passage of time, legal aid careers advice would now be more available and accessible: 'I studied 30 years ago – there just wasn't the information that there is now.'[71]

The presumption that such information must be more readily available now is largely incorrect, as law student data indicated only a small increase in the availability of legal aid careers advice for current students. For those students who were or who had undertaken an LLB or GDL, or who were undertaking a vocational degree, who answered the question (n=175), 45.1 per cent (n=79) reported having had access to careers events and/or information about careers in legal aid, whilst 40.0 per cent (n=70) did not, and 14.9 per cent (n=26) were unsure. When asked why they did not have access to events and/or information about careers in legal aid, those who provided an open-ended response (n=60) gave a number of reasons. The largest proportion of law students advanced the view that the focus at their institution was on corporate law (40.0 per cent, n=24). By extension, 25.0 per cent (n=15) of students indicated that their institution perceived no demand for career information in legal aid or did not see legal aid as a priority. As one student explained, 'I doubt it would've been a popular choice among my cohort. Legal aid has a reputation for being difficult work without much pay.'[72]

[67] Kennedy (n 43) 64.
[68] Nicholson (n 35) 11.
[69] Practitioner Respondent Number 892.
[70] Practitioner Respondent Number 75.
[71] Practitioner Respondent Number 478.
[72] Student Respondent Number 265.

A further 11 students (18.3 per cent) indicated that the messaging provided by staff within their institution was that there was no future in legal aid and that students were dissuaded from pursuing a career in the field. As one student put it, 'when I mentioned that I was interested in a career in legal aid, specifically as a criminal barrister, I was told that there was little point pursuing this career path as there is no money in it.'[73] Consistent with themes emerging in the literature, another student observed the pressures that graduate employment statistics may play in discouraging students from a career in legal aid: 'as legal aid has limited jobs, encouraging students to pursue this career is not beneficial to universities who want to keep their "alumni employment levels" as high as possible.'[74] As with practitioners, there was a concern amongst current students that the university was focused on corporate law: 'The university seems to push everyone down the commercial law route, with the events they give and the law firms that come on campus.'[75] In line with empirical findings in other studies,[76] some students also identified the trend for legal aid to appear more as a means to fill a CV through *pro bono* work or volunteering rather than being offered as a career in its own right: 'legal aid is never represented as a career or training option, only as a way to gain experience!'[77]

Additionally, nine students (15 per cent) attributed the lack of events and/or information in legal aid to the emergence of COVID-19 and the subsequent restrictions on public gatherings, whilst a smaller number (8.3 per cent, n=5) suggested that communication from their university was poor overall. A small number of students (6.7 per cent, n=4) attributed the lack of events and/or career information to the fact that legal aid providers did not have money to sponsor these types of events.

Evidently, the representation of careers in legal aid during education and training is relatively low. When coupled with an LLB and LPC that seemingly offers few opportunities for students to gain knowledge and skills relevant to a career in legal aid, there are questions regarding the extent to which the current legal education and training regime adequately prepares students for this field of practice. The answer to this question takes on more importance in light of the shift to outcomes-based regulation enshrined in the SQE. Whilst the SQE may introduce greater flexibility into the education pathway and open opportunities for students to acquire knowledge outside of the foundation areas, we might expect that the pressures that have shaped education and training to date will continue to shape how it organises itself in response to the introduction of the SQE.

[73] Student Respondent Number 234.
[74] Student Respondent Number 278.
[75] Student Respondent Number 235.
[76] Francis (n 9) 196–97.
[77] Student Respondent Number 349.

D. Legal Education as Preparation for Legal Aid Practice

Of the law students who provided a response (n=174), more tended to disagree (29.9 per cent, n=52) or strongly disagree (8.0 per cent, n=14) with the view that their legal education to date had prepared them well for a career in legal aid relative to those who agreed (25.9 per cent, n=45) or strongly agreed (6.9 per cent, n=12). Almost a third of student respondents neither agreed nor disagreed (29.3 per cent, n=51) with the proposition that their legal education to date had prepared them well for a career in legal aid. These responses are depicted in Figure 3.2 below.

Figure 3.2 Whether law students thought their legal education had prepared them for a career in legal aid (n=174)

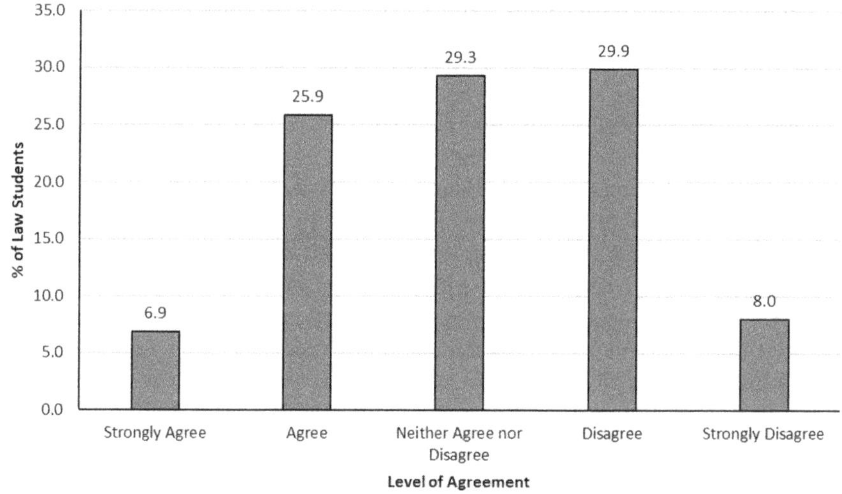

A number of justifications emerged from respondents who further explained their views in an open-ended follow-up question (n=74). For those whose views were favourably inclined, students often said that their institution did as well as it could have done or provide some exposure to content deemed relevant to legal aid (28.4 per cent, n=21). Often, this line of reasoning was contextualised via reference to the relatively short length of their degree and the required content that needed to be covered. Others, however, made the distinction that feeling well-prepared for a career in legal aid was insufficient in practice. As one respondent explained,

> I think my education prepared me as best it could, as I had ample real world experience helping clients and did a lot of comprehensive reading, writing and discussions on legal aid topics across multiple jurisdictions over the year. However, I don't think any amount of education can make a career in legal aid seem worth it enough to pay off the student

> loans. My heart is fully in legal aid, and if it meant I could support myself and buy a home and hopefully raise a family on the wages offered to legal aid lawyers, I would obviously be the first to sign up. The issue is the lack of funding and attention afforded by governments to civil issues of broad public interest.[78]

Overall, however, it is interesting to note that half of student respondents (50 per cent, n=37) indicated that the lack of modules relevant to legal aid and the lack of career events and/or information provided about careers in legal aid left them feeling unprepared for a career in the field. One student noted that

> even if there are some events and pro bono opportunities, the [law] course is entirely angled towards commercial/private law … I believe social justice/legal aid is completely neglected by universities at an undergraduate level, and if you do not have the personal passion for it [to find] events, journals, [and] opportunities yourself, universities will not push you towards the legal aid world.[79]

By extension, 23.0 per cent (n=17) of students explained that they only became acquainted with legal aid via *pro bono*, volunteer and/or clinical work, with 12.2 per cent (n=9) indicating that they lacked practical understanding of legal aid work despite having taken relevant modules.

When asked to explain what had been the most valuable aspect of their legal education to date for preparing them for a career in legal aid, two clear themes emerged from the open-ended responses provided by 109 law students. These answers aligned with responses to wider Census questions on legal education, with law students noting the provision of 'specific modules' relevant to legal aid (43.1 per cent, n=47) and 'pro-bono/clinical/volunteer' work undertaken as part of their studies (42.2 per cent, n=46). A further 6.4 per cent of respondents (n=7) nominated external work experience they had secured and 5.5 per cent (n=6) identified professional events/guest speakers/networks as being most valuable. A total of 9.2 per cent of respondents (n=10) offered 'other' explanations, which included the requirement to balance study and work under pressure, the conversations they engaged in with peers, holding student office, learning how to undertake legal research, and participating in mooting, advocacy training or practical activities. Finally, 5.5 per cent (n=6) of law students indicated that 'nothing' had been most valuable whilst 1.8 per cent (n=2) indicated that they did not know or that it was too early to tell. Law student findings therefore reiterate the perceived importance of modules relevant to legal aid as well as the availability of experiential learning opportunities (either by way of pro bono projects or clinical legal education) as a factor in supporting students towards a future career in legal aid.

[78] Student Respondent Number 252.
[79] Student Respondent Number 279.

IV. Barriers to Entry into the Sector

A. The Cost of Legal Education and Training

Whether calculated in terms of course fees, student time, or unpaid work, the training pathway to registration as a solicitor or barrister comes at significant cost. Average fees for a three-year LLB degree are generally set at the maximum rate of £9,250 per year (with living costs an additional expense), whilst those undertaking a GDL will pay approximately £8,400 for the year, on top of the cost of their undergraduate education. Added to this is the cost of an LPC, which ranges from £9,000 to £17,000, and the Bar Vocational Course or qualifying course for future barristers (BVC) costs £13,000 at a minimum.[80] As a result, the cost of entry into the legal aid profession as a barrister or solicitor is significant and growing year-on-year.

Whilst the introduction of the SQE will do away with some of these expenses for those intended to qualify as a solicitor, the cost of an undergraduate degree will remain. The costs of SQE preparation courses compound this burden and can vary from £3,000 to £16,000.[81] Furthermore, the cost of sitting the SQE itself is £1,622 for SQE 1, and £2,493 for the year 2022/23, up 3.4 per cent from the previous year.[82] Preparation costs are optional since a student could theoretically study for the SQE without completing such a course; however, it is important to note that re-sitting the SQE requires a repayment of the full fee for the SQE component failed.[83] With the SQE payment required up-front, one would have to be exceptionally confident to attempt the SQE without the aid of a formal preparatory course, which also typically require upfront payment. Individuals who cannot afford upfront fees may opt to complete their SQE preparation as part of a more expensive yet loan-eligible LLM degree which, at one institution, ranges from £11,500 for law graduates to £13,500 for non-law graduates.[84] Although such degrees are more expensive, they enable students to secure a postgraduate loan of up to £11,836 which facilitates a deferral of costs.[85] Ultimately, the £4,115 for the exam and approximately £11,500 for a preparatory Masters degree will not be all that dissimilar to the cost of an LPC, which can range from £13,930 to £17,706 at BPP depending on location.

[80] The Lawyer Portal, 'Course Comparison Table' (The Lawyer Portal), available at www.thelawyerportal.com/study-law/gdl/gdl-course-comparison-table.

[81] Niamh Murphy, 'Sponsorship, Scholarship or Save: How to Fund the SQE' (Legal Cheek, 10 June 2021), available at www.legalcheek.com/lc-careers-posts/sponsorship-scholarship-or-save-how-to-fund-the-sqe.

[82] Solicitors Regulation Authority, 'Cost and Fees' (Solicitors Regulation Authority), available at sqe.sra.org.uk/about-sqe/costs-and-fees.

[83] SQE1 provides an exception to this where a student fails either FLK1 or FLK2 in SQE1, they will only pay 50% of the full fee to retake the failed component. If they fail both FLK1 and FLK2 they are liable to pay the full fee to re-sit.

[84] BPP, 'Complete SQE 1 and 2 Training' (BPP), available at www.bpp.com/courses/law/postgraduate/sqe/complete-sqe-training.

[85] See eg BPP (n 84).

What is different, however, is that the SQE enables students to accumulate work experience in a variety of environments, rather than restricting eligible work experience to that accumulated via a training contract. This permits unpaid work experience to qualify towards the SQE's two-year full-time training requirement. At present, paralegal work, a placement during a law degree, work at Citizen's Advice or at a student law clinic all qualify.[86] It remains that corporate law firms will continue to provide training contracts which will cover the cost of SQE preparation, maintenance grants and paid work experience. However, for other legal service areas the SQE runs the risk of facilitating a wholesale shift in the burden of training costs from employers to students. Under the existing system, whilst legal service providers do not always fund the LPC, they are required to pay a wage during the two-year training contract period. This wage requirement will no longer apply to work experience accumulated for the SQE which may induce students into undertaking unpaid work for the promise of paid work once they have qualified. This is a concerning phenomenon that predates the SQE and yet is not remedied by it.[87]

As a result, in addition to covering the costs of preparing for and sitting the SQE, students will potentially face two years of unpaid work experience. Indeed, for those seeking to acquire training via a student law clinic, this may actually amount to paying for the privilege of acquiring work experience since the cost of running a student law clinic is not neutral for educational institutions and is passed on to students via course fees. Similarly, whilst sandwich degrees involving a period of industry placement are lauded by employers,[88] students are unpaid for the duration, whilst simultaneously being required to pay course fees for the duration of their placement.

Although these changes are likely to see an increase in the number of qualified solicitors and a subsequent decrease in the number of students who undertake a law degree yet do not proceed to qualification, it will come at the expense of greater student debt and an exacerbation of the already widespread phenomenon of unpaid work experience. Further, it is not clear that it will necessarily result in an increased number of newly qualified solicitors seeking a career in legal aid. As documented in The Future of Legal Aid enquiry, 'the level of student debt, combined with the impact of LASPO has provided little incentive to choose a career in publicly funded work.'[89] According one Law Centre Director quoted in that report, 'ten years ago we got 80 applications [per vacancy], now we would be lucky to get 10, if that.'[90]

[86] Solicitors Regulation Authority, 'Qualifying Work Experience for Candidates' (Solicitors Regulation Authority, 5 April 2022), available at www.sra.org.uk/become-solicitor/sqe/qualifying-work-experience-candidates.

[87] See eg Kevin Poulter, 'When, If Ever, Is Exploitation Acceptable' (*The Guardian*, 28 May 2010), available at www.theguardian.com/law/2010/may/28/when-exploitation-acceptable.

[88] Nicholson (n 35) 14.

[89] House of Commons Justice Committee, 'The Future of Legal Aid: Third Report of Session 2021–22' (Her Majesty's Stationery Office, 2021) 53.

[90] ibid.

Findings from the Census make clear the scale of debt accumulated during the education and training pathway of current practitioners. There were different experiences of debt between current practitioners and law students, but both cohorts experienced it to some degree. Over the course of their legal education, a third of current practitioners (38.4 per cent, n=431 of 1,123) indicated that they had accrued debt, while 61.6 per cent (n=692) indicated that they had no debt. In comparison, the majority of law students studying for their LLB/GDL/LPC/Bar Course/SQE (85.1 per cent, n=148 of 174) indicated that they did or would have debt at the end of their legal education. As shown in Figure 3.3 below, the most commonly cited amount of debt for current practitioners was within the range of £10,000–£19,999 which was reported by 23.1 per cent (n=99) of respondents. Even with the impact of inflation, current students reported higher levels of debt; the most commonly cited amount for students was £50,000+ as identified by 32.7 per cent (n=48). The data suggests a marked escalation of debt issues among current law students interested in a career in legal aid.

Figure 3.3 Size of debt incurred from legal education by current legal aid practitioners (n=429) and law students (n=147)

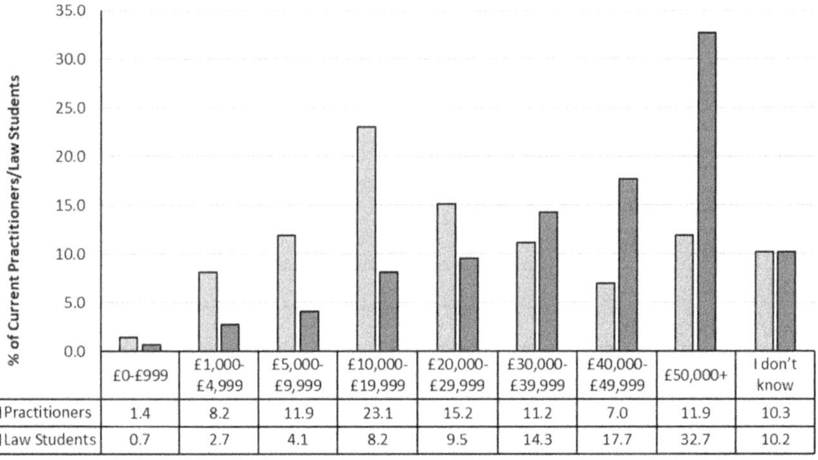

	£0-£999	£1,000-£4,999	£5,000-£9,999	£10,000-£19,999	£20,000-£29,999	£30,000-£39,999	£40,000-£49,999	£50,000+	I don't know
Practitioners	1.4	8.2	11.9	23.1	15.2	11.2	7.0	11.9	10.3
Law Students	0.7	2.7	4.1	8.2	9.5	14.3	17.7	32.7	10.2

Debt Incurred from Legal Education

For law students, the majority of student debt was in the form of student loans (87.8 per cent, n=130 of 148). Other sources of debt included bank loans (15.5 per cent, n=23), credit cards (13.5 per cent, n=20) and family members (16.9 per cent, n=25), with fewer respondents indicating debt would be owed to a local authority (1.4 per cent, n=2). Those who said 'other' (1.4 per cent, n=2) indicated that their debt was owed to a friend.

The increase in debt coincides with a decrease in the availability of local authority grants and an increase in the proportion of law students taking out loans to fund education. As shown in Table 3.3, a greater proportion of law students reported that they had received or were receiving financial support for their undergraduate studies (71.8 per cent, n=122) compared to current practitioners (63.0 per cent, n=703).[91] This was also true of vocational training, with 54.7 per cent (n=35) receiving financial support compared to 34.6 per cent (n=384) of current practitioners.[92]

With far fewer students reporting reliance on local authority grants (1.6 per cent, n=2 at the undergraduate stage, and none at the graduate stage), there was a higher reliance on student grants among law students (37.7 per cent, n=46 at the undergraduate stage and 17.1 per cent, n=6 at the graduate stage). A far greater proportion of law students also reported receiving financial support via student loan, with 91.0 per cent (n=111) of students relying on a student loan during their undergraduate degree (compared to 55.8 per cent of current practitioners) and 68.6 per cent (n=24) relying on a student loan during their GDL/vocational training (compared to 15.7 per cent of current practitioners).

Table 3.3 Sources of support received by current legal aid practitioners and law students during their studies

	Current practitioners		**Law students**	
	N	**%**	**N**	**%**
Funded support received for undergraduate studies	(n=1120)		(n=170)	
No	414	37.0	48	28.2
Yes	706	63.0	122	71.8
Source of support for undergraduate studies	(n=706)		(n=122)	
Student loan	394	55.8	111	91.0
Student grant	–	–	46	37.7
Local authority grant	369	52.3	2	1.6
Access scheme	17	2.4	7	5.7
Scholarship	50	7.1	23	18.9
Family support	212	30.0	37	30.3
Other	45	6.4	4	3.3

(continued)

[91] Other sources of support reported by current practitioners in respect of undergraduate studies included university grants or discounts, government assistance in the form of means tested bursaries and grants, working full or part time to fund studies, receiving charitable funding, studying prior to the introduction of tuition fees or having an employer pay their fees. A further four responses did not indicate the nature of the 'other' support received. Responses from current students included working part time and relying upon hardship support and carer financial support.

[92] Other sources of support reported by current practitioners in respect of GDL or vocational legal studies included bank loans, university grant, bursary or scholarship, employer-funded studies, working full or part time, obtaining charitable loans, or securing other scholarships/bursaries funded by the profession (eg Inns of Courts, Law Society). Other responses from current students included friends, SQE apprenticeship, private loans, and institutional or university scholarships.

Table 3.3 ***(Continued)***

	Current practitioners		Law students	
	N	%	N	%
Funded support received for GDL or vocational legal studies	(n=1100)		(n=64)	
No	726	65.4	29	45.3
Yes	384	34.6	35	54.7
Source of support for GDL or vocational legal studies	(n=383)		(n=35)	
Student loan	60	15.7	24	68.6
Student grant	–	–	6	17.1
Local authority grant	127	33.2	0	0.0
Access scheme	5	1.3	0	0.0
Inns of Court scholarship	92	24.0	9	25.7
Advance pupillage award	4	1.0	1	2.9
Training contract funding	20	5.2	1	2.9
Family support	126	32.9	11	31.4
Other	75	19.6	14	40.0

Whilst the increase in the number of law students relying on financial support compared to current practitioners may suggest a widening of access to education, it may also reveal an increased need for support in light of the increased costs of education and training. Worryingly, the explosion in the numbers of students relying on loans at the undergraduate and graduate level compared to current practitioners presents real concerns as to the viability of these students pursuing a career in legal aid. This reinforces the Justice Committee's concerns that:

> Even if there are enough [practitioners] in the next few years, with rising levels of student debt, the longer-term pipeline looks much more problematic, especially in terms of the next generation of mid-career practitioners, who are needed for the most complex publicly funded cases.[93]

As has been observed in other studies across all occupations and not just law, 'debt leads graduates to choose higher-salary jobs' and 'appears to reduce the probability that students choose low-paid "public interest" jobs'.[94] Indeed, the Young Legal Aid Lawyers group has observed in three consecutive reports that unpaid work

[93] House of Commons Justice Committee (n 89) 33.

[94] Jesse Rothstein and Cecilia Rouse, 'Constrained after College: Student Loans and Early-Career Occupational Choices' (2011) 95 *Journal of Public Economics* 149, 150.

experience is a barrier to social mobility, but that such work experience is necessary to establish a career in legal aid.[95]

Even where debt does not deter students from entering into legal aid, it can have the effect of inhibiting the retention of practitioners, particularly in certain areas of practice. As was reported by James Mulholland QC, Chair of the Criminal Bar Association (CBA) and documented in 'The Future of Legal Aid' report, many criminal barristers are leaving because of substantial student debt.[96] When considered in light of the rising costs of living, including higher house prices, it is not surprising that a student's desire to contribute to the social good may ultimately be eclipsed by their need for financial security. Particularly since, notwithstanding the fact that the scale of student debt in England and Wales is lower than that in the US, one of the key initiatives intended to encourage students into public interest work in the US – the Public Service Loan Forgiveness Program – has no equivalent in England and Wales.[97]

Within the neoliberal paradigm, the availability of student loans has generally been framed as a public good insofar as it makes education accessible for those without means, and leads to a well-funded higher education sector. Thus, the increased rate of students relying on student loans during their studies implies equality of access, with the increased availability of loans theoretically equalising the playing field for entry. In spite of this, Census findings reveal increased numbers of younger practitioners experiencing financial barriers during the process of qualifying. Of those current practitioners who did and did not attend university, 38.5 per cent (n=452 of 1,174) indicated that they experienced or were experiencing financial barriers towards qualifying as a legal aid practitioner. 41.9 per cent (n=188) of those aged 18–35 reporting financial barriers compared to 35.9 per cent (n=161) of those aged 36–50, and 22.3 per cent (n=100) of those aged 51 and above.

Open-ended responses provided by those current practitioners who did and did not report financial barriers identified the cost of study, training and qualification as the most widely experienced problem (38.4 per cent, n=199 of 518). Where other issues were mentioned, they appeared to stem from the cost of study training and qualification; reliance on family support (26.3 per cent, n=136), reliance on additional work and extra jobs (24.9 per cent, n=129), the low levels of remuneration in legal aid work (23.6 per cent, n=122) and reliance on loans and borrowing (13.5 per cent, n=70) were mentioned.[98]

[95] Young Legal Aid Lawyers, 'Young Legal Aid Lawyers: Social Mobility in a Time of Austerity' (Young Legal Aid Lawyers, 2018), available at www.younglegalaidlawyers.org/sites/default/files/Soc Mob Report – edited.pdf.

[96] House of Commons Justice Committee (n 89) 16.

[97] Though as CJ Ryan, 'Paying for Law School: Law Student Loan Indebtedness and Career Choices' (2021) 1 *University of Illinois Law Review* 97, 114 notes, the likelihood of securing forgiveness through this programme is low and as such, the scheme is not without difficulty.

[98] Additional responses included: concerns around debt (n=57, 11.0%); costs incurred through work experience and pupillages (n=51, 9.8%); reliant on grant, scholarship, apprenticeship or funding (n=50,

The rates at which law students reported that they were experiencing or had experienced financial barriers was even higher, at 64.7 per cent (n=112 of 173). As with current practitioners, open-ended responses provided by law students identified the cost of study, training and qualification as the most widely experienced problem (75.3 per cent, n=64 of 85). Where other issues were mentioned by students, they likewise appeared to stem from the cost of study training and qualification. This included reliance on loans and borrowing (27.1 per cent, n=23), reliance on family support (20.0 per cent, n=17), the low levels of remuneration in legal aid work (18.8 per cent, n=16) which would make repaying debts challenging, the lack of training contracts/sponsorship (17.6 per cent, n=15), reliance on additional work and extra jobs (15.3 per cent, n=13) and the requirement to self-fund the qualification process (15.3 per cent, n=13).[99]

The requirement to self-fund often extends to funding the work experience opportunities that are increasingly considered vital to student employability. These roles may be remunerated by way of course credits which incur course fees but are typically not financially remunerated (save for some instances where travel costs may be covered). The incidence of unpaid work experience was relatively high amongst current practitioners, with 78.0 per cent (n=884 of 1,133) of practitioners having undertaken forms of work experience that were unpaid or expenses-only. 880 respondents provided further detail as to how this work experience was funded, citing family support (53.0 per cent, n=466), part-time work (48.2 per cent, n=424), savings (25.6 per cent, n=225), working full time (13.9 per cent, n=122), welfare benefits (2.5 per cent, n=22), student loans/overdraft (1.9 per cent, n=17), other means (1.4 per cent, n=12), or scholarships/grants/bursaries (1.0 per cent, n=9). Those who indicated 'other' reported that they engaged in squatting, they stayed with family friends, their partner was working, or that the experience did not cost them anything.

The rate of unpaid work experience was higher amongst law students, with 87.8 per cent (n=86 of 98) reporting that some of their work experience had been unpaid or expenses-only. Of the 86 students who had undertaken work experience opportunities that were unpaid or expenses-only, these opportunities were largely

9.7%); other eg not having appropriate work clothes, the lack of job certainty, and the requirement to self-fund the qualification process (n=46, 8.9%); accommodation costs/cost of living (n=40, 7.7%); reliant on savings (n=28, 5.4%); not relevant/can't answer/no answer (n=24, 4.6%); lack of grants and affordable loans (n=23, 4.4%); lack of family support (n=23, 4.4%); different areas of law (n=21, 4.1%); lack of training contracts/sponsorship (n=20, 3.9%); things used to be easier for legal aid work (n=18, 3.5%); transport and travel costs (n=15, 2.9%); welfare benefits (n=10, 1.9%); Impact on family (n=8, 1.5%); Restricted choice of university (n=6, 1.2%); lack of legal aid work (n=5, 1.0%).

[99] Other responses included: concerns around debt (n=12, 14.1%); costs incurred through work experience and pupillages (n=10, 11.8%); reliant on grant, scholarship, apprenticeship or funding (n=10,11.8%); lack of job certainty (n=5, 5.9%); other including visa restrictions for international students and lack of connections in industry (n=4, 4.7%); accommodation costs/cost of living (n=7, 8.2%); reliant on savings (n=10, 11.8%); not relevant/can't answer/no answer (n=2, 2.4%); lack of grants and affordable loans (n=3, 3.5%); lack of family support (n=3, 3.5%); transport and travel costs (n=2,2.4%); impact on family (n=6, 7.1%); lack of legal aid work (n=3, 3.5%).

funded by working part time (47.7 per cent, n=41), personal savings (41.9 per cent, n=36) or via family support (39.5 per cent, n=34). Fewer respondents indicated that funding was not required (9.3 per cent, n=8) or that they were working full time (4.7 per cent, n=4).

As indicated previously, Census findings reveal the increased number of law students who report having accumulated in excess of £50,000 relative to current practitioners. For those students who expressed concern in their open-ended responses as to the amount of debt they had accumulated, responses indicated that some had spent between £60,000 and £70,000 on financing their undergraduate education alone. The Westminster Commission has observed that 'junior practitioners starting now can expect to incur debts of between £50,000 and £70,000 depending on their undergraduate degree and postgraduate qualifications',[100] as fees for an entire LLB are now approximately £30,000; consequently, an estimate of £50,000 to £70,000 sounds increasingly conservative once vocational training, living expenses and stints of unpaid work experience are considered.

With such high levels of debt accumulated just from undergraduate education, it is not surprising that students are questioning the financial viability of qualifying further. As one respondent indicated, 'I cannot afford to qualify beyond my LLB and therefore am unable to pursue a legal career'.[101] This reliance on debt to fund education and training is particularly problematic at the vocational stage, where the establishment of combined LPC/LLM degrees which are eligible for student loans encourages students to self-fund further education despite there being no guarantee that they will secure a training contract. The absence of training contracts for those seeking a career in legal aid has been exacerbated since 2010 following the cessation of the Government's training contract grants for legal aid firms which had provided for approximately 85 training contracts annually.[102] In its place is the Legal Education Foundation's Justice First Fellowship scheme, which has funded 121 fellows for training contracts and seven fellows for pupillage since 2014. Over the course of seven years this equates to a substantially more modest 17 training contracts and one pupillage a year as compared to the government scheme.[103]

In their responses, students also reflected on the extent to which their backgrounds could create and worsen these financial barriers. For instance, some respondents noted that law can be perceived as an elitist pursuit in which it was harder to get by for those from less privileged backgrounds. Given that legal aid work does not pay as well as other areas of law, many students felt unable to pursue

[100] The Westminster Commission on Legal Aid, 'Inquiry into the Sustainability and Recovery of the Legal Aid Sector' (All-Party Parliamentary Group on Legal Aid, 2021) 95.

[101] Student Respondent Number 181.

[102] The Westminster Commission on Legal Aid (n 100) 96.

[103] Justice First Fellowship, 'Supporting the Next Generation of Social Justice Lawyers' (Justice First Fellowship), available at jff.thelegaleducationfoundation.org.

it because they simply could not afford to after incurring the costs of qualifying. According to one respondent:

> Legal aid work simply isn't as lucrative as non-legal aid routes. People in higher classes can sacrifice a dip in a paycheck because their family can help, people in higher classes can sacrifice their summer to an unpaid internship at a legal aid firm because their family can sustain them financially over the summer. I simply can't do that. I must earn money in the summer and I have my enormous debts to pay off in the future.[104]

Another respondent observed that they were facing financial barriers because of 'A lack of funding support and access opportunities for marginalised communities.'[105] Concerns over the viability of legal aid as a practice area were pronounced amongst those who already had financial concerns, with one student stating that 'There is little support, the work is demanding, the hours are long and the pay is poor.'[106] These combined issues call into question whether the gains seen over the last five decades in the socio-demographic diversity of the profession are likely to be sustained going forward. More worryingly, in light of an ageing legal aid profession, the role that financial concerns play in dictating the viability of a career in legal aid when combined with evidence of rising debt levels, offer little in the way of reassurance that legal aid can remain sustainable in the longer term. This is particularly true given that the cost of education and training is rarely the only barrier individuals are likely to face during the qualifying process. As indicated in open-ended responses by both law students and practitioners with dependants, the decision to pursue a career in legal aid must be considered in light of the impact on a respondent's dependants and conversely, in light of the impact of dependants on a career in legal aid.

B. Personal Circumstances and Characteristics

In total, 14.0 per cent (n=158 of 1,125) of current practitioners indicated that they had or have had dependants/caring responsibilities during their legal studies/training. In a follow-up question, 242 practitioners provided an open-ended response detailing the impact of debt and dependants upon their career progression and 93 practitioners described the issue of dependent/caring responsibilities specifically. Of these 93 practitioners, nearly half (49.5 per cent, n=46) of the responses noted that having dependants slowed down and/or stopped the practitioners career progression, and 29.0 per cent (n=27) of practitioners suggested that having dependants negatively affected their studies and/or ability to qualify as a lawyer. A further 12.9 per cent (n=12) reported that having dependants meant they had to work longer hours to support the family. For 11.8 per cent (n=11)

[104] Student Respondent Number 209.
[105] Student Respondent Number 281.
[106] Student Respondent Number 340.

maternity leave or returning to work from maternity leave affected their career progression and 10.8 per cent (n=10) indicated that dependants made studying difficult. For 6.5 per cent (n=6), having dependants made finding work harder whilst for 5.4 per cent (n=5) dependants made pupillage and work experience more difficult. Only a minority of respondents (16.1 per cent, n=15) reported that having dependants did not affect their career negatively.

Whilst law students were not asked about the impact of caring responsibilities specifically, they were asked to indicate whether they had experienced a range of other barriers in their attempt to work as a legal aid lawyer. A total of 94 law students indicated that they had faced other barriers. Of these, 67.0 per cent (n=63) believed that their social class presented a barrier to work as a legal aid lawyer, with 37.2 per cent (n=35) citing their age as a barrier and 25.5 per cent (n=24) citing their gender as a barrier. Nationality as well as caring responsibilities were believed to be a barrier by 19.1 per cent (n=18) of respondents, followed by ethnicity (17.0 per cent, n=16), race (13.8 per cent, n=13), sex (11.7 per cent, n=11), religion (5.3 per cent, n=5) and sexuality (3.2 per cent, n=3).

When asked to elaborate on the nature of the barriers faced, one student described that he saw his age and caring responsibilities as having impeded his work opportunities. As he explained,

> I'm 37 and have a 2-year-old son. I struggle to get to interview unless I take my date of birth off applications. I'm often asked if I can handle looking after a child with work at interview, and sometimes asked why my partner doesn't just do it all so I can work full time.[107]

Another student noted the challenges of studying whilst facing substantial caring responsibilities and socio-economic barriers, both of which had impacted upon their grades and consequently their employability:

> I'm from a state school and I had caring responsibilities at home as my parents suffered with alcohol and mental illnesses. At school we were not encouraged to attend [u]niversity, I didn't have revision or study skills so I've winged my way through the LLB without having the study skills I needed so my grades are pretty bad. I've had to juggle studying with working and caring for my family too, they have both been a huge barrier.[108]

As discussed previously, the difficulties faced by those having to self-fund their legal studies were a consistent theme in the verbatim responses provided by law students, yet sometimes this presented as only one of many barriers faced. This was explained by one student as follows:

> I am originally from Hungary, from a very poor family. In my own country I could not afford to work and study parallel. Here in the UK as a mature student (30) I felt that this and my nationality were affecting my chances. Additionally, I was working sometimes

[107] Student Respondent Number 354.
[108] Student Respondent Number 209.

> 50+ hours to [make ends meet] and I achieved far worse grades than I would have been capable of.[109]

Discrimination on the basis of immigration status was also a factor for one law student post-Brexit, who noted that:

> Because of Brexit my immigration status in the UK had become much more precarious (I am on a pre-settled status) with difficult decisions to make and the risk of losing my status and therefore my ability to work in the UK if I go abroad to gain international legal experience.[110]

In addition, a small number of law students noted that their disability was a barrier for them, particularly where their disability impeded their performance on standardised recruitment tests or where it meant they required part-time work. This accords with previous research which has observed that the disabled are the most under-represented group in the legal profession. This research documents that poor experiences of accessibility were more common in respect of work experience, pupillage, paralegal work and the BPTC, with the reverse true in relation to university undergraduate courses and the CPE/GDL.[111] As such, whilst access to a career in law is challenging for those with disabilities irrespective of their intended role, access to careers at the bar for those with a disability may prove especially challenging.

Whilst the diversity of the legal profession has grown over time,[112] it is not surprising that given the challenges detailed above, 'the better off are still 80 per cent more likely to make it into professional positions than those from working-class backgrounds'.[113] That those from working class backgrounds are struggling to enter into the profession they have received specific training to enter, undermines much of the social mobility agenda behind efforts to widen access to higher education. Moreover, it undermines much of the progress that has been made in equalising access to the legal profession so as to shift it away from 'a hobby profession for wealthy white men'.[114] As our findings make clear, in line with observations made elsewhere, if the intended graduate destination is legal aid, successfully qualifying is exceptionally challenging; necessitating reliance on parental support or graduate loans to underwrite education costs.[115] Even where

[109] Student Respondent Number 267.

[110] Student Respondent Number 294.

[111] See eg Debbie Foster and Natasha Hirst, 'Legally Disabled? The Career Experiences of Disabled People Working in the Legal Profession' (Cardiff University, 2020), available at legallydisabled.com/wp-content/uploads/2020/01/Legally-Disabled-full-report-FINAL.pdf, 106.

[112] Legal Services Board, 'The State of Legal Services 2020 – Evidence Compendium' (Legal Services Board, 2020), available at legalservicesboard.org.uk/wp-content/uploads/2020/11/The-State-of-Legal-Services-Evidence-Compendium-FINAL.pdf.

[113] Tina McKee et al, 'The Fairness Project: The Role of Legal Educators as Catalysts for Change. Engaging in Difficult Dialogues on the Impact of Diversity Barriers to Entry and Progression in the Legal Profession' (2021) 55 *The Law Teacher* 283, 284.

[114] House of Commons Justice Committee (n 89) 20.

[115] ibid.

individuals have recourse to such support, the lack of positions for trainees and the newly qualified calls into question the economic rationality of pursuing a career in legal aid. News media reports show that the lack of attractiveness of legal aid for both students and practitioners has been an issue for almost two decades.[116] In spite of this, little has been done to address the sustainability of the profession, a problem which is only likely to get worse in the near future given the increasing costs of education, training and living.

C. Availability of Training and Employment Opportunities

As expressed in the census and reported above, one of the key concerns for law students in amassing significant amounts of education debt was the scarcity of opportunities in legal aid. Evidence from the sector suggests that this is because providers have neither the time nor the money to train new entrants to the profession.[117] This has led, in the words of the Westminster Commission, to a situation in which there is 'an ageing demographic, difficulty with succession planning, fewer juniors coming through, declining numbers of positions and an inability of firms to justify the costs associated with training the next generation given the current fee structure.'[118]

Findings from the Census indicate that the availability of training and employment opportunities tends to differ by practitioner type. Whilst 93.3 per cent (n=28 of 30) of chambers indicated that they currently trained pupil barristers, for legal services organisations the rate was much lower. Here 57.5 per cent (n=210 of 365) of organisations reported training practitioners compared to 41.1 per cent (n=150) who did not and 1.4 per cent (n=5) who reported not to know.

Of those organisations who did train practitioners, a clear majority focused on training solicitors (93.8 per cent, n=197 of 210). 31.0 per cent (n=65) also trained CILEX professionals, with far fewer organisations training caseworkers (2.9 per cent, n=6), paralegals (4.8 per cent, n=10), or apprentices (2.4 per cent, n=5). 5.7 per cent of organisations (n=12) reported training 'other' professionals.

When asked to provide an open-ended response to why they did not train practitioners, organisations most often suggested that limited funding, capacity, resources, infrastructure and time impeded their capacity. 43.8 per cent (n=56 of 128) of organisations referenced that training practitioners was not cost effective or that they could not afford it, while 24.2 per cent (n=31) referenced minimal

[116] See eg Clare Dyer, 'Legal Aid "Crisis" as Poor Pay Deters Trainees' (*The Guardian*, 22 March 2004), available at www.theguardian.com/uk/2004/mar/22/ukcrime.prisonsandprobation; Aishah Hussain, 'Aspiring Lawyers Divided over Career in Legal Aid' (Legal Cheek, 30 June 2021), available at www.legalcheek.com/2021/06/aspiring-lawyers-divided-over-career-in-legal-aid; Clare Dyer, 'Solicitors Shunning Legal Aid Work as Pay Rates Fall, Survey Reveals' (*The Guardian*, 7 January 2008), available at www.theguardian.com/uk/2008/jan/07/law.children.

[117] House of Commons Justice Committee (n 89) 17.

[118] The Westminster Commission on Legal Aid (n 100) 94.

capacity, the small or niche nature of the area in which they practised or their inability to offer relevant training. A further 16.4 per cent (n=21) referenced insufficient resources and infrastructure, with 12.5 per cent (n=16) indicating that they had no time to do so, 5.5 per cent (n=7) reporting that they had no lawyers on staff or only offered mediation services, 4.7 per cent citing a lack of funding, and 3.9 per cent (n=5) indicating the impact of COVID-19 and difficulties recruiting respectively. In contrast, 6.3 per cent of organisations (n=8) indicated that they were currently trying to recruit trainees or that they had had some trainees in the past.

In addition to this, almost three-quarters of organisations (73.2 per cent, n=265 of 362) indicated that they were not recruiting or expanding, contrasting with 26.8 per cent (n=97) who were. The lack of growth in the sector may have adverse implications for the availability of student training in legal aid going forward. The lack of training contracts or opportunities for paid qualifying experience will continue to form an additional barrier for students looking to move into legal aid work and operate to deter students from pursuing a career in the field.

V. Implications of Findings

Education has traditionally been framed as a mechanism for enabling social mobility; by extension, law as a largely stable profession capable of securing for the individual a decent standard of living has been an aspirational career for many. As discussed in chapter two, the legal profession has witnessed good gains in diversity and now represents a more heterogeneous group – particularly in socio-economic terms – than was the case 50 years ago. As this chapter reveals, however, the fact that a more diverse range of individuals are drawn to legal aid work seems to have relatively little to do with the promotion of legal aid within legal education. As our findings suggest, law students who identified as prospective practitioners report having been actively discouraged from pursuing such a career. Instead – and taken together with the findings in chapter two – the lure of a career in legal aid may have more to do with the fact that it is one of few careers where an individual can make a tangible contribution to enhancing social justice. This is a contribution that appears especially important for those who have experienced disadvantage, exclusion or injustice.

These aspirations are laudable and ought to be encouraged, but there is a point at which pragmatism trumps altruism. Problematically, this point is likely to occur earlier for those from less affluent backgrounds. As this chapter makes clear, there are a number of features of the current education and training pathway that not only prevent students from converting an interest in legal aid into a career, but also tend to hasten a commitment to one path over another at an early point. Chief among these concerns is the growing cost of education vis-a-vis legal aid salaries. Current and prospective practitioners reported being reliant on grants or loans to fund their education and dependent on family support, part-time jobs or other funding to make their work experience viable. Practitioners also reported experiencing financial barriers such as debt as a result of grants and loans being less readily available and a majority of prospective practitioners expressed concerns about debt. These issues are not without consequence and are likely to push students towards careers that offer the safest return on their investment in their education. Good intentions alone cannot sustain an individual through a long and expensive education and training pathway, nor should they be expected to when legal aid is a public good.

The limited space within the curriculum given over to teaching the knowledge and skills that may be demanded of legal aid lawyers compounds these issues. Less than half of practitioners who undertook undergraduate legal education reported having had the opportunity to take courses relevant to legal aid. Social welfare law and related social justice areas, in particular, have emerged as areas of practice that students may have been denied access to. Census results indicate that only a small number of educational opportunities were made available to current practitioners in areas such as immigration, housing, welfare benefits, education and community care at the undergraduate level. Efforts to embed opportunities for clinical experience throughout the law degree which have been initiated by the vast majority of providers,[119] have increased the opportunities for students to come into contact with the types of clients that they may serve if they were to pursue a career in legal aid. However, in light of the foregoing, it is hard to view these clinical opportunities as a genuine effort to support the skills development of those intending to pursue a career in legal aid. We ought to be concerned about using vulnerable populations in the service of higher education's employability agenda and justifying doing so on the basis that these populations are equal beneficiaries.

The introduction of the SQE for solicitors and the retention of the qualifying law degree for barristers will no doubt catalyse a period of existential reflection for many education and training institutions, although it is unlikely that this will do much for legal aid. Opportunities to study legal-aid-relevant courses improved at the conversion or vocational stage for many practitioners; however, this important source of experience is one that may not continue with the introduction of the SQE. Regulators have been keen to advance the view that the new system provides greater flexibility for institutions to serve the market. Nevertheless, opening up possibilities for new forms of education that better cater to the needs of specific legal sectors, as has been noted above, assumes those legal sectors have the time and capacity to shape that education. At present, the legal aid sector – preoccupied as it is with surviving in the present – has limited scope to plan for a future which appears increasingly bleak. For example, the reason the College of Law Legal Aid Route LPC was discontinued is publicly unknown, but Kalsi

[119] See eg Nicholson and Johnson (n 26); Nicholson (n 35).

and Sharpley's perspectives on its development may hold clues. They observe that in the absence of more specific requirements from regulators, providers would be driven by market concerns and unlikely to devote a significant number of hours to areas of legal practice which were considered 'under threat'.[120] As Francis makes clear, 'Although the regulators have shown limited interest in dictating the detail of employability, the broader drivers of "what recruiters want" more informally shapes concerns within legal education. Even as formal regulatory ties are loosened.'[121] This tends to suggest that liberalising the regulation of legal education will have the effect of cementing the myopic focus of many legal education providers on servicing the corporate market, to the detriment of those wishing to pursue a career in legal aid.

Having explored several of the structural and cultural factors that may affect lawyers' decisions and capabilities to pursue a career in legal aid, this book will now turn to consider some of the factors that may affect lawyers' experiences of working in this sector. In doing so, it will draw common threads between the deterrence and challenges that prospective legal aid lawyers encounter during their legal education, and those that they continually face throughout their working lives as legal aid practitioners.

[120] Kalsi and Sharpley (n 41) 5.
[121] Francis (n 9) 178.

4

Working Conditions in Legal Aid

I. Introduction

This chapter explores working conditions and practices in the legal aid sector. Building upon the insights this book has already provided into the identities and backgrounds of practitioners that comprise the legal aid sector – as well as the various factors that influence how and why they pursue careers in this sector – it highlights a significant number of issues encountered by practitioners currently working in legal aid. In doing so, it focuses upon the humanity of the practitioners at the heart of this book and seeks to understand some of the problems and concerns that they encounter on a daily basis. Recent work on legal aid lawyers in England and Wales has pointed to the value of using vulnerability as a theoretical framing through which to understand the issue such practitioners face working in the midst of, first, austerity and, thereafter, the COVID-19 pandemic.[1] This chapter employs this theory as a device through which to move beyond traditional conceptions of the elite legal profession explored in chapter two. By examining reported issues such as workplace stressors, bullying and salary concerns through this lens, this chapter provides a basis from which to develop more accurate and cohesive notions of the structural conditions that frame their work.

The chapter begins by considering issues around well-being, thereon identifying some of the key stressors experienced by practitioners. It moves on to consider the prevalence of workplace bullying and harassment as further evidence of the difficulties that practitioners can face in the sector. The chapter then discusses concerns around salary and working hours, with practitioners offering their reflections around the inadequacy of current sectoral arrangements. The chapter then reflects on overall perceptions of job satisfaction in light of the aforementioned problems before considering the extent to which legal aid professionals utilise professional networks, and the availability and accessibility of opportunities for training and development as means through which to address these challenges.

[1] Daniel Newman et al, 'Vulnerability, Legal Need and Technology' (2021) 23 *International Journal of Discrimination and the Law* 230; Daniel Newman and Roxanna Dehaghani, *Experiences of Criminal Justice: Perspectives from Wales on a System in Crisis* (Bristol University Press, 2022); Daniel Newman and Jon Robins, 'The Demise of Legal Aid'? Access to Justice and Social Welfare Law after Austerity (2022) 3 *Amicus Curiae* 448.

II. The Vulnerability of the Legal Aid Sector

To these ends, the topic of lawyer working conditions in this chapter is loosely grounded by the work Fineman has conducted on vulnerability theory.[2] Vulnerability theory is founded on the need to move away from the notion of 'the liberal legal subject', which is rooted in the idea that rational individuals operate in a meritocracy characterised by equal opportunities. Instead, vulnerability theory challenges this assumption by substituting in the notion of 'the vulnerable subject', which is more capable of recognising the common experience of facing struggles in a structurally unfair society. This reveals that the liberal legal subject is a snapshot of a person taken on their best day, shorn of context or perspective, and exposes how the reality is often inherently more complicated by messier circumstances and fluctuating situations.

Fineman's thesis purports that everyone is vulnerable, although some people are more resilient than others. Fineman asserts that vulnerability should not be reduced to a category that captures those who are supposedly victimised, dependent or weak.[3] In contrast, it is more likely that justice occurs if the state is 'built around the recognition of the vulnerable subject' – a device which recognises that all citizens are vulnerable and that vulnerability is not a cause for shame but a simple statement of reality.[4] The state should 'act to fulfil a well-defined responsibility to implement a comprehensive and just equality regime that ensures access and opportunity for all'.[5] For Fineman, vulnerability is 'universal and constant when considering the general human condition, [but] must be simultaneously understood as particular, varied, and unique on the individual level'.[6] She has identified two particular forms of difference – the first includes 'physical, mental, intellectual, and other variations in human embodiment'; the second involves 'social and constructed, resulting from the fact that individuals are situated within overlapping and complex webs of economic and institutional relationships'.[7] Vulnerability arises from our embodiment, an embodiment that exposes us to harm. As Fineman notes, 'individuals can attempt to lessen the risk or mitigate the impact of such events, but they cannot eliminate their possibility'.[8]

One of the most distinct features of vulnerability theory is that not only are individuals vulnerable but also institutions. As Fineman explains:

> Institutions as well as individuals are vulnerable to both internal and external forces. They can be captured and corrupted. They can be damaged and outgrown. They can

[2] Martha A Fineman, 'Equality, autonomy, and the vulnerable subject in law and politics' in MA Fineman and A Grear (eds), *Vulnerability: Reflections on a New Ethical Foundation for Law and Politics* (Routledge, 2013) 12–28.

[3] Martha A Fineman, 'The Vulnerable Subject: Anchoring Equality in the Human Condition' (2008) 20 *Yale Journal of Law and Feminism* 8.

[4] ibid, 10.

[5] Martha A Fineman, 'The Vulnerable Subject and the Responsive State' (2010) 60 *Emory Law Review* 251, 273–74.

[6] Fineman (n 2) 21.

[7] ibid.

[8] Fineman (n 3) 9.

> be compromised by legacies of practices, patterns of behavior and entrenched interests that were formed during periods of exclusion and discrimination, but are not invisible in a haze of lost history.[9]

This institutional vulnerability can alter the response of the institution towards individuals and may serve to further perpetuate disadvantage, whether intentionally or otherwise. It is important here to raise the issue of resilience because it is as a vehicle for enhancing resilience that institutions are most relevant in the social justice context that underpins this book. For Fineman, 'the counterpoint to vulnerability is not invulnerability, for that is impossible to achieve, but rather the resilience that comes from having some means with which to address and confront misfortune'.[10] Resilience is a set of advantages; different groups with varying levels of privilege will find they have more or less resilience. Resilience on the individual level can be bolstered by institutions, helping people deal with the issues they face and the legal aid sector can be understood as a crucial component of this. Such institutions play a key role 'in lessening, ameliorating, and compensating for vulnerability' so that the state needs to respond to human vulnerability when considering the 'the effectiveness and the justice of the operation of those institutions'.[11]

While vulnerability theory has been applied across the breadth of legal studies, recent scholarship has called for its specific application to legal aid lawyers to help encourage a wider understanding of the challenging working conditions practitioners in this sector can face. Such work pushes us to think about groups – such as lawyers, traditionally regarded as high-status professionals – as potentially vulnerable. Indeed, Dehaghani and Newman have made the argument that criminal legal aid lawyers need to be understood through a vulnerability lens.[12] They note that understanding these lawyers as vulnerable requires new ways of looking at vulnerability:

> Readers … should be comfortable with the assumption that the defendant is in a vulnerable position, because others such as the police (or lawyers) have power, thus meaning that principles should protect defendants … The idea that the police who control their liberty while constructing cases against them, or the lawyers who push them towards guilty pleas and manipulate clientele to serve their own ends might be seen as vulnerable somehow on a par with the inherently weak individual who has the might of the state pitched against them might appear perverse … it feels somewhat odd to challenge this traditional view and give such credence to the powerful parties in this relationship.[13]

[9] ibid, 18.

[10] Fineman (n 5) 269.

[11] ibid.

[12] Roxanna Dehaghani and Daniel Newman, "We're Vulnerable Too': An (Alternative) Analysis of Vulnerability within English Criminal Legal Aid and Police Custody' (2017) 7 *Onati Socio-Legal Series* 1199.

[13] ibid, 1203.

However, they go on to note that:

> Austerity justice under-funding key institutions such as the police and legal aid systems means that practitioners are vulnerable as they are unable to operate at their optimum level and this predisposes them to malfunctioning as an increasingly threadbare service … It is, then, important to recognise that even those powerful instructions and professionals are vulnerable – even if doing so might feel uncomfortable.[14]

Newman and Robins have followed this work by advocating for legal aid lawyers working in social welfare law to be understood similarly, highlighting their lacking more resilience relative to criminal lawyers.[15] Newman et al have made a call for the vulnerability of legal aid lawyers across the sector to be especially recognised following the pandemic, which has further weakened institutional resilience and made the shared vulnerability of everyone all the more obvious.[16]

A far cry from grand theory, vulnerability theory is best conceived of as a middle range theory and a conceptual device which comprises limited numbers of variables and scope.[17] Such theories can be valuable for helping us to grasp specific social segments and situations, eschewing grand theory in favour of an approach that prioritises findings that emerge within empirical data. Such theories can play an important role in helping us understand a phenomenon on its own concrete terms, rather than abstracting to a level that makes it difficult to propose solutions to problems. In other words, vulnerability theory can be applied on a pragmatic basis, as and when it is considered relevant rather than requiring wholesale commitment to the thesis. It is in such a spirit that this chapter grounds its consideration of legal aid lawyers' challenging working conditions in vulnerability theory; it offers value for us as an heuristic device that centres the experiences and perceptions of the practitioners who responded to the Legal Aid Census and, as such, the issues they face while working in the legal aid sector.[18]

These issues were already a concern before the Census but not necessarily understood in the level of depth that we present in this book, especially via vulnerability theory. To a degree, these issues have already been partly identified

[14] ibid, 1203–04.

[15] Newman and Robins (n 1).

[16] ibid.

[17] Robert K Merton, 'On Sociological Theories of the Middle Range', in Robert K Merton, *On Theoretical Sociology: Five Essays, Old and New* (Free Press, 1967) as cited by Martha A Fineman, 'Vulnerability and Social Justice' (2019) 53 *Valparaiso University Law Review* 341.

[18] Of course, it is entirely possible to consider the working conditions of legal aid lawyers through the kind of grand theory that is the apotheosis of a middle range theory. For example, Newman (2016) has elsewhere considered criminal legal aid lawyers applying perhaps the most famous grand theory of all, Marx and Engels' historical materialism, particularly drawing out the notion of alienation. Powerful as a grand theory approach such as Marxism might be in providing impactful accounts of the issues faced by these lawyers in their practice, this chapter is informed by an approach that foregrounds the experiences of the lawyers to help give a flavour of the reality of their working conditions. In doing so, it is hoped that an understanding of this lived reality will be valuable in informing broader debates, both later in this book and more widely amongst those who read it. See further Daniel Newman, 'Are Lawyers Alienated Workers?' (2016) 22 *European Journal of Current Legal Issues* 1.

by various inquiries and reports of the type discussed in chapter one. However, the issues are not yet fully acknowledged or understood from the perspectives of legal aid practitioners themselves.

For example, in the Westminster Commission, practitioners gave evidence about how unsustainable their practices were. The Report notes that:

> The overwhelming consensus from the evidence that was heard throughout the Inquiry was that legal aid work and the rates payable are not financially viable for practitioners. What came across was that for so many the work is a vocation not just a career. However, practitioners are forced to leave legal aid in order to make a more comfortable living and improve their work/life balance and wellbeing. Some practitioners remain in legal aid but choose to undertake more privately paid work in order to pay their bills and turn a profit.[19]

The Commission further draws on powerful quotes such as the following from Jenny Beck QC:

> Firms are not managing. In family law firms are turning to more private work in order to balance. 80% of my team do publicly funded work. However, the spread of our income is 50/50. So, 20% that do private provide 50% of fee income. This is the only way we can survive.[20]

Considering the importance of these issues for the sector, it is appropriate that we seek to better understand them from the perspective of practitioners. And, with our grounding in vulnerability theory now set out, that is what we do in the following sections of this chapter through consideration of the Census data.

III. Well-being and Stressors

A. Well-being

A major problem for the legal profession relates to their professional well-being. There is a wealth of research that has been conducted on lawyers' experiences which highlights negative well-being in legal work. This is a global issue, with a third of respondents to the International Bar Association's recent research claiming that working in the legal profession had an overall negative impact on lawyers' well-being.[21] For example, in Australia, the 'Courting the Blues' study found that 31 per cent of solicitors had high levels of distress on the Kessler Psychological

[19] The Westminster Commission on Legal Aid, Inquiry into the Sustainability and Recovery of the Legal Aid Sector (All-Party Parliamentary Group on Legal Aid, 2021) 103.

[20] ibid.

[21] International Bar Association, 'Mental Wellbeing in the Legal Profession: A Global Study' (International Bar Association, 2021).

Distress Scale compared to 13 per cent of adults in the general population.[22] Within England and Wales, legal professionals are considered to have higher levels of mental health issues and lower levels of well-being than the general population according to leading academic contemporary scholarship.[23] Law Care, the legal mental health charity, found that 69 per cent of lawyers had experienced mental ill-health.[24] Meanwhile, the Law Society well-being report for its Junior Lawyers Division has most recently shown that 48 per cent of respondents had experienced a mental health problem in the month prior to its survey.[25] The Bar Council well-being report shows 31.5 per cent indicating a current low level of well-being at the time of the study.[26] Adding to this research, our Census looks at the well-being experiences of lawyers working in the legal aid sector specifically.

The practitioner survey revealed the impact of legal aid work on the mental well-being of current legal aid professionals. Of the 1,179 practitioners who responded, almost half of responses claimed their work in legal aid had an overall negative effect, with 39.3 per cent (n=463) identifying work having a 'negative' impact on their mental well-being, and 9.7 per cent (n=114) reporting that work had an 'extremely negative effect'. These responses compare to 27.8 per cent (n=328) who cited work as having a neutral impact, 1.4 per cent (n=17) who indicated that they did not know, and less than a quarter citing work as having a positive impact (20.0 per cent, n=236), or an 'extremely positive' impact (1.8 per cent, n=21). The relatively low numbers of current practitioner respondents citing work as having a positive or extremely positive impact on their mental well-being (21.8 per cent) as opposed to a negative or extremely negative impact on their well-being (49.0 per cent) reflects the mental toll that working in legal aid has on practitioners.

When asked to explain the impact of their work on their mental well-being, 533 respondents provided context via responses to an open-ended question. Coding of these answers revealed a number of common themes. Whilst many of the responses simply reasserted the role their work played in enhancing or diminishing their mental well-being, a number of more substantive responses provide insight into the factors contributing towards diminished well-being. There is a degree of overlap across these themes and what emerges is a complex web of interrelated well-being problems faced by practitioners. Digging into these themes thus

[22] Ian Hickie et al, 'Courting the Blues: Attitudes towards Depression in Australian Law Students and Lawyers' (Brain and Mind Research Institute, University of Sydney, 2019).

[23] Emma Jones et al, *Mental Health and Wellbeing in the Legal Profession* (Bristol University Press, 2020).

[24] LawCare, 'New Research Into Lawyer Wellbeing Makes the Case For Profession-Wide Change' (LawCare, 2021), available at www.lawcare.org.uk/latest-news/life-in-the-law-new-research-into-lawyer-wellbeing.

[25] The Law Society of England and Wales, 'JLD Campaign: Wellbeing' (The Law Society), available at www.lawsociety.org.uk/campaigns/junior-lawyers-division-campaigns/wellbeing.

[26] The Bar Council, 'Barrister's Working Lives Survey: Barrister Wellbeing (BWB) Analysis' (The Bar Council, 2021), available at www.barcouncil.org.uk/uploads/assets/55b160bc-35c7-48a6-b105e68526019ca5/8a57305c-4c3e-46c9-af444c221354e2b7/Working-Lives-2021-wellbeing-analysis.pdf.

provides for a greater understanding of individual difficulties for practitioners around well-being as well as the overall well-being predicament facing this sector as a whole.

The most common response saw 52.3 per cent (n=279) of respondents indicate that their work had caused them anxiety or stress or had otherwise negatively affected their mental well-being. Amongst the majority detailing anxiety or stress, a common sentiment was how hard-wired these feelings were into the role: 'Once or twice per week I feel anxious about my work, to the extent that I lose sleep'.[27] What emerges is the normalisation of these feelings. It is an accepted part of the job to the extent that, as one practitioner suggested, 'Colleagues who are unable to cope leave the sector … it is sink or swim'.[28] For some, the anxiety and stress came from the plight of their clients: 'I experience huge anxiety as a result of the importance of my clients' cases and the injustice of the system'.[29] There were also concerns about the high-stakes nature of work for practitioners themselves: 'I am haunted by cases and by decisions, every day you risk everything … one wrong move and you are struck off or disgraced or lose your contract'.[30]

The next most reported theme (23.1 per cent, n=123)was that the workload is too large, leading to burn-out. The near quarter of responses cautioning about such burn-out discussed how difficult they found it to switch off from work. Typical experiences were that 'my workload and work-related issues are always on my mind including during weekends and time off',[31] and that 'I'm just completely burnt out and wherever I am and whatever I'm doing I'm always thinking about work'.[32] Many practitioners told how much they liked working in legal aid but that doing what they wanted was causing them harm, and that their passion was not enough to mitigate the negative impact on their well-being:

> I love my job and wouldn't want to do anything else but it is not sustainable to carry on in the way that I am. I have to work in almost all my free time and offer work all weekend and every evening until 10/11pm. This is necessary simply to get all the work done and keep on top of upcoming cases. It is draining and unsustainable.[33]

Indeed, several practitioners reported that the problems were reaching a crisis point for them as in the following: 'I think I am approaching burn out' and have 'an appointment booked with my GP on Monday'.[34]

17.8 per cent (n=95) of current practitioners reported that balancing work and their personal life caused stress, as exemplified in the following: 'I do not have a

[27] Practitioner Respondent Number 327.
[28] Practitioner Respondent Number 123.
[29] Practitioner Respondent Number 477.
[30] Practitioner Respondent Number 760.
[31] Practitioner Respondent Number 768.
[32] Practitioner Respondent Number 659.
[33] Practitioner Respondent Number 591.
[34] Practitioner Respondent Number 1090.

proper work–life balance at all'.[35] Lawyers of all genders reported that they 'miss out on family life',[36] though there was a particularly gendered impact due to there being 'lots of mum-guilt'.[37] Respondents often reported finding it 'difficult to find respite from work', as in this example:

> Work, or thinking about work, occupies all waking hours during the week. Some respite can be had at the weekend, but almost every Sunday is substantially taken up with preparation. Pre-booked annual leave is the best remedy, but maintaining this often involves refusing work which is offered after the leave is booked and it is common to have to respond to emails even when on holiday for example to approve orders circulated the week prior.[38]

The weekend working trend described in this quote has become known as 'Sunday homework club' on legal Twitter as lawyers express their solidarity for one another working to prepare cases for the following week.

A smaller but concerning issue arose with the 7.1 per cent (n=38) of respondents who indicated that they found the subject matter of their work traumatising. Lawyering has been considered emotionally charged labour for the way practitioners have to deal with the stressful events of their clients.[39] It was frequently reported that 'vicarious trauma is huge',[40] while others noted that there was 'insufficient support to manage the effect of vicarious trauma'.[41] The notion of vicarious trauma has recently become a prominent talking point amongst legal aid lawyers particularly since Fleck and Francis published their work on the prevalence of this condition for those working in the sector.[42] Their work was borne out of concern that lawyers working in legal aid regularly work with traumatic cases without adequate training or support. Indeed, in one study, lawyers working on asylum cases reported 'feeling like a sponge' in their interactions with clients.[43] Allied to the already reported issues such as anxiety, burn-out and lack of work–life balance, the concern is that lawyers dealing with traumatised clients lack the resilience to avoid becoming themselves traumatised in turn.

Despite the distressing accounts above and the fact that 38.6 per cent (n=206) of respondents indicated that work was sometimes stressful or hard, it may be reassuring to note that many found their work enjoyable, satisfying or otherwise having an overall positive effect on their mental well-being. However, it is crucial

[35] Practitioner Respondent Number 1053.
[36] Practitioner Respondent Number 512.
[37] Practitioner Respondent Number 936.
[38] Practitioner Respondent Number 1106.
[39] Joy Kadowaki, 'Maintaining Professionalism: Emotional Labor Among Lawyers as Client Advisors' (2015) 22 *International Journal of the Legal Profession* 323.
[40] Practitioner Respondent Number 308.
[41] Practitioner Respondent Number 537.
[42] Rachel Francis and Joanna Fleck, 'Vicarious Trauma in the Legal Profession: A Practical Guide to Trauma, Burnout and Collective Care' (Legal Action Group, 2021).
[43] Chalen Westaby, '"Feeling Like a Sponge": The Emotional Labour Produced by Solicitors in Their Interactions with Clients Seeking Asylum' (2010) 17 *International Journal of the Legal Profession* 153.

to also note that these positive takes were often very qualified with a long list of downsides despite an overall positive spin. Sentiments commonly expressed were that 'the role is very rewarding but there are times when it can be very overwhelming making you extremely anxious, unable to sleep and burnt out'.[44] Practitioners were thus able to, 'feel like I'm doing something good and meaningful, even if it is sometimes stressful'.[45]

Considering the way positives are drawn out from negatives, it is important to provide full quotes to express the balance that practitioners make – lest the positive aspect be uncritically removed from its wider, less reassuring context. This respondent provides a powerful example of this trend:

> The rewarding nature of the job has given me meaning in my life. It is so important to my mental health to do a job that I love. I love my clients and helping them. However, this has a negative impact too as I want to do my best for them but I am underpaid and overworked as a result. I have had to really battle against the huge demands on me professionally in an effort to put myself first. At many points I considered just giving up on my work as the pressure from all angles seemed to[o] much. However I feel that would be to give in a system that is unfair and I don't want to let that system win – I don't want my clients to be without lawyers who really care about them so I have kept going. I do the best I can whilst also investing time and my own money in therapy to ensure myself care has improved to enable me to continue doing the job I love.[46]

Over a third of responses identified positives amongst the negatives, which speaks to both the scale of the well-being problem faced in the sector as well as some of the reasons practitioners remain and how they rationalise working in a sector they find so damaging.

B. Stressors

To deepen the understanding of how practitioner well-being is adversely impacted by working in the sector, the Census explored specific stressors that practitioners may face. Stress has been identified as the second most common issue faced by legal aid lawyers in research by the Young Legal Aid Lawyers group.[47] These were broadly grouped into two areas: client-related stressors; and more general stressors.

Table 4.1 sets out the five most common client-related and general stressors identified. As shown, the most frequent stressor/challenge selected by 67.7 per cent (n=795) of practitioner respondents was the challenge of supporting clients with complex legal and other needs. This was followed by 50 per cent (n=588) who identified 'providing a quality service within the available time and resources',

[44] Practitioner Respondent Number 31.
[45] Practitioner Respondent Number 872.
[46] Practitioner Respondent Number 882.
[47] Young Legal Aid Lawyers, 'Social Mobility in a Time of Austerity' (Young Legal Aid Lawyers, 2018), available at www.younglegalaidlawyers.org/sites/default/files/Soc Mob Report – edited.pdf.

49.7 per cent (n=584) who identified 'abusive, threatening or difficult clients', and 48.1 per cent (n= 565) who identified 'worry about client outcomes' in their responses. Only a small minority (3.1 per cent, n=36) of practitioners specified that they did not face any of these challenges or stressors in their work.[48] As it relates to more general stressors in their work, four key stressors were selected by more than half of the respondents: the under-resourced justice system (71.8 per cent, n=837); managing work–life balance (65.7 per cent, n=766); dealing with the LAA (59.7 per cent, n=696); and meeting tight deadlines (50.5 per cent, n=589).[49]

When given the opportunity to offer an open-ended response to 'other' client or general stresses faced, 53 practitioners provided further commentary.[50] Coding of these responses revealed a number of additional issues, the most frequently mentioned being financial sustainability for the practitioner or their practice and the requirement to perform non-remunerated work (41.5 per cent, n=22).[51]

Table 4.1 Five most common client-related, general and other challenges and stressors identified by current legal aid practitioners in relation to their work

		N	%
Client-related (n=1175)	Clients with complex legal/other needs	795	67.7
	Providing quality with the available time and resources	588	50.0
	Abusive, threatening or difficult clients	584	49.7
	Worry about client outcomes	565	48.1
	Complexity and severity of clients' legal matters	546	46.5
General (n=1166)	Under-resourced justice system	837	71.8
	Managing work–life balance	766	65.7
	Dealing with the Legal Aid Agency	696	59.7
	Meeting tight deadlines	589	50.5
	Fluctuating workload	356	30.5

(continued)

[48] Other responses not detailed in Table 4.1 include: traumatic nature of the work (including experiences of clients and colleagues etc) (n=546, 46.5%); unrealistic client expectations (n=523, 44.5%); insufficient resources to provide the help clients need (n=511, 43.5%); number of incoming referrals (n=350, 29.8%); not enough staff to meet client demand (n=323, 27.5%); limited referral and other service options (n=255, 21.7%); none of these issues (n=36, 3.1%); other (n=29, 2.5%).

[49] Other responses not detailed in Table 4.1 include: performance targets (n=299, 25.6%); limited career pathways or progression (n=240, 20.6%); tenuous job security (n=202, 17.3%); lack of opportunity for, or access to, training and support (n=178, 15.3%); dealing with colleagues (n=165, 14.2%); working environment (n=149, 12.8%); safety concerns (n=104, 8.9%); other 'general' (n=32, 2.7%).

[50] Due to the similarity between 'Other Responses' in relation to the 'Other (Client) Issues' and 'Other (General) Issues' reported by practitioner respondents, 'Other Responses' were coded jointly. Although 29 respondents indicated that there were 'other (Client) stressors' and 32 indicated there were other (General) stressors, the percentages in this table are calculated with a denominator 53 rather than 61 which refers to the number of unique respondents.

[51] Other responses not detailed in Table 4.1 include: language barriers (n=3, 5.7%); retaining staff (n=2, 3.8%); public opinion/government rhetoric (n=2, 3.8%); lack of variety of work (n=1, 1.9%);

Table 4.1 ***(Continued)***

		N	%
Other (n=53)	Financial sustainability/requirement to perform non-remunerated work	22	41.5
	Failures in other elements of the system that adversely impact client outcomes	11	20.8
	Unrealistic expectations of judiciary/bullying judges/inconsistent judicial decision-making	11	20.8
	Administrative battles with LAA/financial management of legal aid files/inability to get paid in a timely fashion/inability to secure legal aid funding for clients	6	11.3
	Client mental health problems	5	9.4

Taken together, the responses provided suggest that current legal aid practitioners face a broad range of stressors which relate to both their relationships with clients as well as the wider working conditions within the sector. Importantly, it is possible to draw parallels between the financial sustainability issues cited as reasons for leaving legal aid by former legal aid practitioners and the difficulties that continue to be faced by current legal aid practitioners. These issues will be discussed further in chapter five.

C. Workplace Bullying, Harassment and Discrimination

Another prominent issue that impacted lawyers was bullying, harassment and discrimination at work. Bullying is a problem in the legal profession of England and Wales according to reports from Law Care.[52] In addition to identifying issues concerning mental well-being within the sector, practitioners were thus also asked to indicate whether they had experienced bullying, harassment and/or discrimination in the workplace in the last five years. Of the 1,188 practitioners who answered, most had not experienced bullying, harassment and/or discrimination (70.8 per cent, n=841), while 26.9 per cent (n=320) confirmed that they had, and 2.3 per cent (n=7) preferred not to say.

Of those who had experienced bullying, harassment and/or discrimination (n=320), 73.8 per cent (n=236) reported experiencing bullying, 36.3 per cent (n=116) reported discrimination and 22.2 per cent (n=71) reported experiencing

seeing how unjust society is (n=1, 1.9%); lack of supervision (n=1, 1.9%); gender discrimination (n=1, 1.9%).

[52] LawCare, 'LawCare 2020 Figures: Sharp Increase in Legal Professionals Seeking Help for Anxiety' (LawCare, 2020), available at www.lawcare.org.uk/latest-news/lawcare-figures-show-increase-in-legal-professionals-seeking-anxiety-help.

harassment.[53] Open-ended responses provided illustrations of the kinds of incidents and experiences of professionals. For example, exploring the frequency of each incident type on the basis of role – as shown in Figure 4.1 – revealed that bullying was the most common of the three across all role-types. Bullying accounted for almost two thirds of the behaviour reported by both trainees/pupils/paralegals (62.5 per cent, n=20) and caseworkers (65 per cent, n=10). Discrimination was most commonly reported form of poor treatment by billing clerks (40 per cent, n=2) and those with 'other' role types (50 per cent, n=3), while harassment was most often reported by legal executives (25 per cent, n=2), caseworkers (25 per cent, n=4) and directors (25 per cent, n=3).[54]

When it came to identifying the perpetrators of the bullying, harassment and/or discrimination, judges (32.5 per cent, n=102) were the most frequently identified source. Respondents told that, 'judges [are] frequently misogynist bullies taking out their stress on female advocates',[55] while 'judges have belittled me at times and mocked my (regional) accent'.[56] The bad behaviour could take place in court ('a judge in a trial was consistently rude and sarcastic towards me and at one point stood up and screamed at me')[57] or outside of court ('a judge sent very rude emails repeatedly').[58] In their recent research on criminal legal aid lawyers, for example, Newman and Dehaghani reported concerns from lawyers about judicial bullying as one of the most prominent challenges facing those working in this area.[59]

After judges, the most common responses related to peers in the workplace (23.9 per cent, n=75 of 314). Senior partners/senior colleagues (16.9 per cent, n=53) and line managers/supervisors (14.6 per cent, n=46), were most commonly mentioned, followed by 'others' (8.3 per cent, n=26), clients (5.4 per cent, n=17) and clerks (4.8 per cent, n=15). 2.5 per cent (n=8) of respondents preferred not to reveal who was responsible for the bullying, discrimination and/or harassment they experienced.

The findings further revealed that barristers were most likely to face bullying, harassment or discrimination from judges (50.6 per cent, n=87) or peers in the workplace (26.2 per cent, n=45). Solicitors commonly reported senior partners (29.0 per cent, n=29) as perpetrators, as did trainees, pupils, and legal apprentices (25.9 per cent, n=7), caseworkers (33.3 per cent, n=4), directors (42.9 per cent, n=3) and legal executives (40.0 per cent, n=2). Solicitors also commonly reported line managers (23.0 per cent, n=23) as the perpetrator, as did trainees, pupils, and

[53] A further five respondents (1.6%) indicated that they would prefer not to say.

[54] Figure excludes clerks, head of chambers and practice managers as these groups reported no instances of bullying, harassment or discrimination. Total group numbers as follows: head of department (n=9); solicitor (n=128); barrister (n=212); legal executive (n=8); trainee/pupil/paralegal (n=32); caseworker (n=16); director (n=12); billing clerk (n=5); other (n=6).

[55] Practitioner Respondent Number 662.

[56] Practitioner Respondent Number 978.

[57] Practitioner Respondent Number 944.

[58] Practitioner Respondent Number 1200.

[59] Newman and Dehaghani (n 1).

Figure 4.1 Rates of bullying, harassment and/or discrimination by current legal aid practitioner role (n=428)

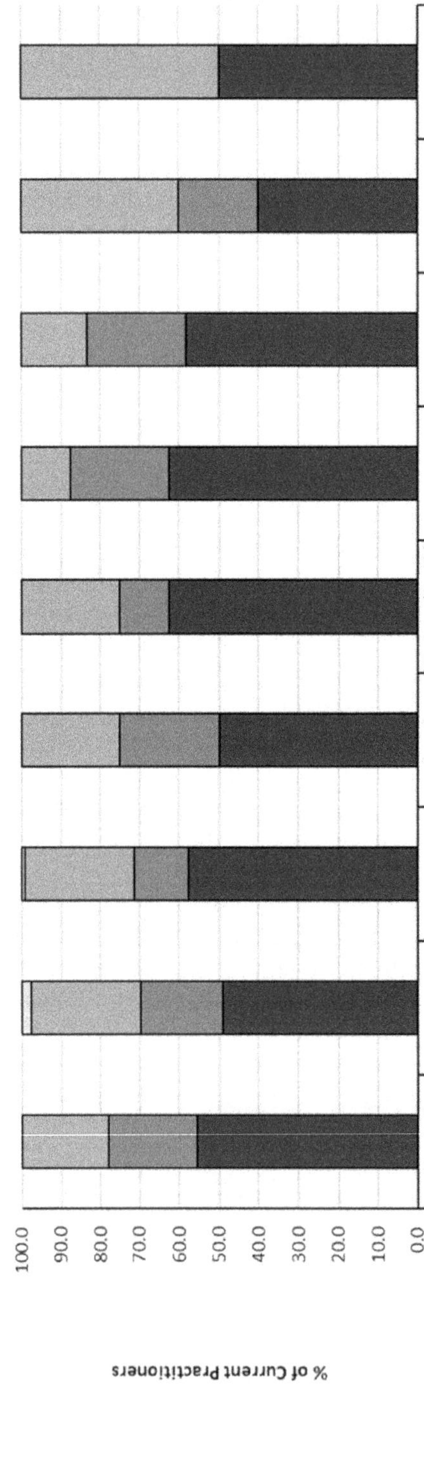

	Head of Department	Solicitor	Barrister	Legal Executive	Trainee/Pupil/ Paralegal	Caseworker	Director	Billing Clerk	Other
Prefer not to say	0.0	2.3	0.9	0.0	0.0	0.0	0.0	0.0	0.0
Discrimination	22.2	28.1	27.8	25.0	25.0	12.5	16.7	40.0	50.0
Harassment	22.2	20.3	13.7	25.0	12.5	25.0	25.0	20.0	0.0
Bullying	55.6	49.2	57.5	50.0	62.5	62.5	58.3	40.0	50.0

legal apprentices (22.2 per cent, n=6), caseworkers (33.3 per cent, n=4), billing clerks (50.0 per cent, n=2), paralegals (60.0 per cent, n=3) and directors (28.6 per cent, n=2). Heads of departments most often identified peers in the workplace as perpetrators (60.0 per cent, n=3).

There appeared to be toxic working cultures at some of the organisations respondents worked in: 'I had a supervisor who … constantly harassed me about how I was not doing enough work and should have 100+ cases and eventually caused a nervous breakdown and a suicide attempt'.[60] The problems of bullying, harassment and discrimination, then, appeared to go hand-in-hand with some of the well-being issues described in the previous chapter, especially with regards to burn-out. If practitioners did not push themselves hard enough, they could be subject to bullying as captured by this response:

> In a previous role my manager bullied/forced me and others into taking more cases then we could manage and would give paralegals cases that were too complex/had no experience on under no supervision; if targets not met we would be shouted at, told off or would not be allowed to work from home during the pandemic; a lot of pressure and expectation that needed to work late everyday.[61]

What seems to emerge is a sector where junior staff are indoctrinated into high-stress working environments and pressured into taking on unrealistic workloads. This comes across in how one respondent talked of their experience as a paralegal where 'my first supervisor was very stressful to work for because of the pressure she put on [herself] which transferred to me … she was bullying and manipulative'.

The seniority of the perpetrators seemed to have a knock-on effect in how many of the accounts included discussion around the lack of action taken, as found in experiences such as a respondent who faced racism from a colleague then 'when I went to the equity partner who managed us both was told to ignore it'.[62] A similar situation was shown in the following example:

> At my previous firm (also legal aid), I experienced bullying by several member of staff including a partner and my line manager. I also experienced sexual harassment by my line manager. The culture of the firm was such that no action was taken against senior members of staff who bullied junior members of staff. Because of this, I knew no action would be taken regarding the sexual harassment, so did not report it.[63]

Research has shown that even though lawyering and especially legal aid work is becoming more diverse, change in attitudes and assumptions has been slow to follow. Thus, it is understandable that the senior members of the sector – and their attendant bad practices – may exert considerable sway and make it hard for what Sommerlad terms 'outsider lawyers' to challenge these behaviours.[64]

[60] Practitioner Respondent Number 865.
[61] Practitioner Respondent Number 885.
[62] Practitioner Respondent Number 887.
[63] Practitioner Respondent Number 446.
[64] Hilary Sommerlad, 'Researching and Theorising the Process of Professional Identity Formation' (2007) 34 *Journal of Law and Society* 190.

Of those respondents who identified a protected characteristic as relevant to their experience of bullying, harassment or discrimination (n=291), 29.2 per cent (n=85) cited their sex as a factor and 13.7 per cent cited their race (n=40). This accords with existing scholarship that shows the broader legal profession as gendered and raced in its organisation.[65] A considerable proportion also indicated that they would prefer not to say (28.9 per cent, n=84). These results are further elucidated in Figure 4.2 below.

Figure 4.2 Rate at which current legal aid practitioners attributed their experience of bullying, harassment and/or discrimination to a protected characteristic (n=291)

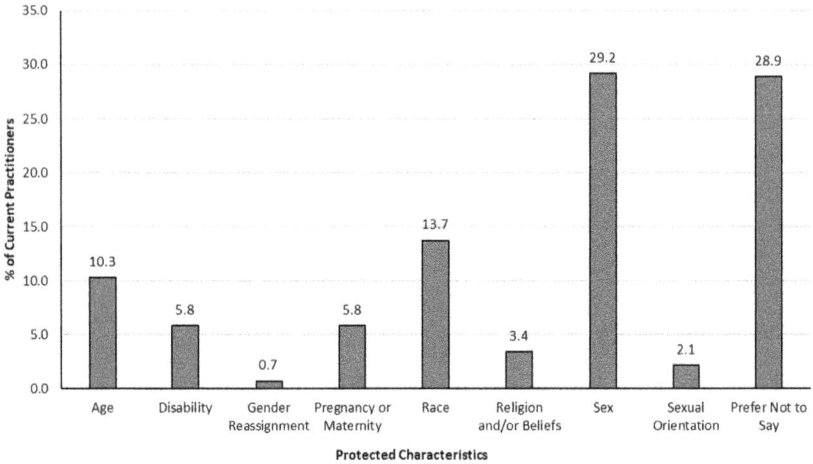

Further insight was revealed by open-ended responses to the Census where there were significant problems around gender, which could occur at court or in the organisations. As an example of the former, 'when I was a pupil barrister [a] member of security staff said I was just at court to provide the older[male] barristers with tea and coffee all day',[66] while the latter is shown by statements such as 'I was paid less than a male colleague for the same work'.[67] The Census included numerous comments around the impact of pregnancy, as in the following: 'Maternity discrimination. I was demoted from a head of dept role whilst on maternity leave. I was a co-head of dept with a colleague who was promoted to partner. The firm then demoted me from head of dept.'[68]

Gender discrimination thus appears as a major problem in this sector. This is reflective of the wider legal profession. Sommerlad and Sanderson have documented the prevalence of sexual harassment, and how women are reluctant to

[65] Dermot Feenan et al, 'Life, Work and Capital in Legal Practice' (2016) 23 *International Journal of the Legal Profession* 1.

[66] Practitioner Respondent Number 500.

[67] Practitioner Respondent Number 622.

[68] Practitioner Respondent Number 660.

report unsavoury behaviour from partners, colleagues and clients.[69] The Bar Standards Board has shown the high levels of discrimination amongst woman barristers,[70] while the Law Society has documented the adverse impact of bias for women solicitors.[71] Sommerlad has already described the work culture of the legal profession as 'hyper-masculine', and her research shows the way that the legal profession can be an inhospitable climate for women including some specific issues at work in the legal aid sector such as the pressures caused by the financial precarity of legal aid work.[72]

Racism was also a prominent problem that came out in the open-ended responses: 'I have experienced racism at all levels … lots of racist microaggressions over the years'.[73] This racism could happen at court, where on practitioner noted an incident where someone 'commented on how I needed to get a British accent',[74] while another told how someone 'assumed I was the defendant at court'.[75] The racism could also happen in the organisations they worked for. One practitioner discussed their firm where 'speaking with the only other person of colour … we are both referred the most difficult clients, and little else, pushing us both towards state and charity grants, whilst others (including less-senior colleagues) flourish'.[76] One respondent explained the issues they faced had at their law centre: 'A colleague … asked me if I did kung fu. I told him that's not an appropriate question and he didn't understand the point. He later asked me for the inside track on [C]OVID because I must have family in China.'[77]

These results align with work done by professional bodies that show the impact of racism in the broader legal profession. For example, the Law Society has conducted research that clearly demonstrates existing problems with organisational culture in law firms as minority ethnic solicitors frequently report feeling like outsiders, and almost all participants in their study had experienced racist microaggressions in their work.[78] Ethnic minority solicitors in their research duly report lower levels of workplace well-being compared to white solicitors. Further, according to Bar Council research, barristers from ethnic minority backgrounds can feel hyper-visible and marginalised at work.[79] These barristers report far higher

[69] Hilary Sommerlad and Peter J Sanderson, *Gender, Choice and Commitment: Women Solicitors in England and Wales and the Struggle for Equal Status* (Routledge, 1998).

[70] Bar Standards Board, 'Women at the Bar' (Bar Standards Board, 2016).

[71] The Law Society of England and Wales, 'Women in Leadership in Law' (The Law Society, 2019).

[72] Hilary Sommerlad, 'Women Solicitors in a Fractured Profession: Intersections of Gender and Professionalism in England and Wales' (2002) 9 *International Journal of the Legal Profession* 213.

[73] Practitioner Respondent Number 887.

[74] Practitioner Respondent Number 570.

[75] Practitioner Respondent Number 627.

[76] Practitioner Respondent Number 1181.

[77] Practitioner Respondent Number 1139.

[78] The Law Society of England and Wales, 'Race for Inclusion: The Experiences of Black, Asian and Minority Ethnic Solicitors' (The Law Society, 2020), available at www.lawsociety.org.uk/topics/research/race-for-inclusion-the-experiences-of-black-asian-and-minority-ethnic-solicitors.

[79] The Bar Council, 'Race at the Bar: A Snapshot Report' (The Bar Council, 2021), available at www.barcouncil.org.uk/uploads/assets/d821c952-ec38-41b2-a41ebeea362b28e5/Race-at-the-Bar-Report-2021.pdf.

levels of bullying than their white peers. What emerges among both solicitors and barristers is a lack of representation and structural problems that adversely impact practitioners. Rowan and Vaughan have conducted research into law student choice of firms, which shows that students will often factor in whether they feel represented at a firm through issues such as gender and race.[80] Lack of diversity is identified as an issue across law firms and while some students will avoid firms where they do not feel they fit in, other students will apply to those firms in the hope of adding something complementary. What our Census worryingly suggests is that increased diversity in these ways may not be alleviating unacceptable practices towards women, minority ethnic groups and others who do not conform to traditional lawyer stereotypes. There appears to be a gap wherein increased participation in the profession, especially in the legal aid sector, is not having the knock-on effect of improving working conditions for these groups.

The experience of bullying, harassment and/or discrimination on the basis of a protected characteristic aligned with practitioners' view of broader issues across the profession. 324 practitioners provided further detail when asked to indicate – in an open-ended response – what they thought the most prevalent forms of bullying, harassment and/or discrimination were within the legal aid sector. Coding these responses into common themes, as shown in Table 4.2 below, demonstrates that sexism and sexual harassment were viewed as leading problems and were mentioned by 28.1 per cent (n=91) of practitioners in their open-ended responses. This was followed by bullying, harassment and/or discrimination based on cultural background, skin colour and/or race (23.1 per cent, n=75). In line with the response of those who experienced bullying, harassment and/or discrimination, a fifth of practitioners acknowledged that ill-treatment from judges and magistrates (20.4 per cent, n=66), and from colleagues, opposing counsel and managers (19.8 per cent, n=64) were prominent problems. Over a tenth of respondents identified age (14.8 per cent, n=48) and target pressures/financial bullying (12.3 per cent, n=40) as prevalent, with a further 14.5 per cent (n=47) indicating that they were not sure.

Table 4.2 Current legal aid practitioners' views on the most prevalent forms of bullying, harassment and/or discrimination in the legal aid sector (n=324)

	N	%
Sexism/sexual harassment	91	28.1
Cultural background/skin colour/race	75	23.1
Judges/magistrates bullying lawyers	66	20.4
Colleagues/opposing counsel/managers	64	19.8

(continued)

[80] Eleanor Rowan and Steven Vaughan, 'Fitting in and "Opting out": Exploring How Law Students Self Select Law Firm Employers' (2018) 52 *Law Teacher* 216.

Table 4.2 ***(Continued)***

	N	%
Age	48	14.8
Unsure	47	14.5
Target pressures/financial bullying	40	12.3
Parental status/caring responsibilities	21	6.5
Disability	17	5.2
Class/Socio-economic background	12	3.7
Clients bullying practitioners	10	3.1
Transphobia(mainly)/LGBTIQ+	6	1.9
Creed	4	1.2

This data suggests that bullying, harassment and discrimination are not infrequently experienced within the sector. Problematically, at least some of the bullying, harassment and/or discrimination that occurs is attributed by victims to protected characteristics. That the perpetrators of bullying, harassment and/or discrimination also appear to hold positions of authority relative to the victim (such as judges, line managers and supervisors) magnifies the difficulties associated with addressing the behaviour. Reassuringly, however, the majority of respondents (61.0 per cent of 1,082) stated that they agreed or strongly agreed that they feel 'well supported by line management' in their place of employment, with only 10.9 per cent disagreeing or strongly disagreeing (n=118) and 28.1 per cent (n=304) indicating they neither agreed nor disagreed.

D. Salaries and Working Hours

When it comes to challenges, remuneration is a prominent issue for legal aid lawyers considering the problems around pay, which will be explored further in the following chapter. For example, Newman identified salary as the major talking point amongst the criminal legal aid lawyers he studied:

> The lawyers in my study were acutely aware of this financial situation. Throughout the research, I was privy to seemingly boundless levels of griping and grumbling concerning the lawyers' lesser levels of remuneration compared with their peers. During the participant observation, I often recorded in my notebooks that this was the main subject of conversation. Lawyers bemoaned these circumstances with such frequency to anyone who would listen.[81]

Questions around salary thus formed an important part of the Legal Aid Census and respondents were understandably keen to engage. When it came to

[81] Daniel Newman, *Legal Aid Lawyers and the Quest for Justice* (Hart, 2013) 56.

practitioner's perspectives on their salary and working arrangements, more than half of 1,128 current practitioner respondents either disagreed (33.2 per cent, n=375) or strongly disagreed (22.8 per cent, n=257) with the proposition that the salary and working arrangements for their role were fair, with just over a quarter either strongly agreeing (6.3 per cent, n=71) or agreeing (20.7 per cent, n=234) and 16.9 per cent (n=191) neither agreeing nor disagreeing.

When asked to express in their own words why they agreed or disagreed that their salary and working arrangements were fair, coding of open-ended responses revealed that practitioners most often indicated that remuneration was unfair given the difficulty of legal aid work. This was further expanded upon in the open-ended responses provided by practitioners. Table 4.3 shows the 10 most common reasons that emerged in the open-ended responses provided by practitioners. It reveals that 31.4 per cent (n=164) of responses alluded to the level of remuneration as being unacceptable or insulting; 17.6 per cent (n=92) indicated that 'remuneration does not factor in the difficulties/stress of the job, including difficult clients, unsociable hours or being on stand-by';15.7 per cent (n=82) stated that their 'remuneration is inadequate or some work is unpaid' or that the 'remuneration does not reflect how hard we work'; and 13.8 per cent (n=72) indicated that their remuneration is less compared to similar roles in the private sector.

Table 4.3 Top 10 reasons current legal aid practitioners agreed/disagreed that their salary/working conditions are fair (n=523)

	N	%
The level of remuneration is unacceptable/insulting	164	31.4
Remuneration does not factor in the difficulties/stress of the job, including difficult clients, unsociable hours, being on stand-by	92	17.6
Remuneration is inadequate or some work is unpaid	82	15.7
Remuneration does not reflect how hard we work	82	15.7
Compared to other similar roles in the private sector my remuneration is less	72	13.8
The level of remuneration makes my life very difficult	70	13.4
Remuneration does not reflect my qualifications/experience	52	9.9
My remuneration is acceptable	40	7.6
Remuneration has not kept in line with inflation	37	7.1
The work I undertake is paid well	26	5.0

Respondents were often frank about what they thought of the pay. For some, 'the salary is shit',[82] while for others, 'the pay is crap'.[83] Regardless of how they described it, across the nearly one-third of respondents who discussed the unacceptable

[82] Practitioner Respondent Number 746.
[83] Practitioner Respondent Number 561.

and insulting nature of the pay, there was often great frustration that 'we have no option but to accept the derisory rates of payment'.[84] Legal aid lawyers, as Newman has previously shown, will often consider their wage relative to other occupations, such as plumbing, where on the face of it one would expect the lawyer to receive higher remuneration.[85] This was also the case in the census, with one respondent explaining that 'I am paid less than a McDonald's Manager and have fewer rights, despite working twice the hours of a McDonalds [sic] Manager'.[86] Some respondents gave insight into why they believed their situation was so unfair given the relative sums of money involved: 'I earn next to nothing, I am responsible for a turnover of one million and I earnt 5 thousand last year and 25 thousand the year before'.[87] As a result, some respondents talked with a sense of hopelessness about how they could only afford to work in the legal aid sector due to effectively being subsidised by their partners:

> Were I the principal breadwinner I would have had no option but to leave the profession some years ago. Fortunately my wife works in the private sector and supports my continued involvement with legally aided work and appreciates the importance of such a role in a civilised society.[88]

The situation appears starker still considering the accounts of the one-fifth of respondents that suggested the pay did not meet the demands of the job. A common theme here was for respondents to contextualise the pay in terms of the well-being problems such as anxiety and burn-out discussed earlier in this chapter, which practitioners believe make the wage even more desultory. For some this was about the amount of work, 'due to the hours worked, including overtime most days, the stress and pressure of the job, the salary is low'.[89] Others noted how pay does not reflect the difficulty of the work, and 'is never in line with the effort and complexity required to assist clients'.[90] Another common complaint related to the impact of the type of work: 'the nature of and mentally injurious nature of the work that we do is not rewarded or compensated in any reasonable way'.[91] Fundamentally, respondents did not believe their pay matched the kind of work done in the sector: 'Extremely underpaid for the mental load we are expected to manage. Legal aid is offered for the most vulnerable clients, in extremely difficult situations, and the practitioners assisting these individuals are not compensated for the service we provide.'[92]

As explored further in chapter five, practitioners considered that they were underpaid but also sometimes *unpaid*. This is evident in responses that discuss

[84] Practitioner Respondent Number 719.
[85] Newman (n 81).
[86] Practitioner Respondent Number 364.
[87] Practitioner Respondent Number 592.
[88] Practitioner Respondent Number 376.
[89] Practitioner Respondent Number 96.
[90] Practitioner Respondent Number 352.
[91] Practitioner Respondent Number 819.
[92] Practitioner Respondent Number 386.

pay in terms of the additional work they had to do on top of that accounted for through legal aid or describe how hard they work for the wage. One respondent explained the situation lawyers faced in the sector: 'we all routinely work outside of our contracted hours, most evenings and weekends just to try to keep on top of work demands including the key parts of the role and all non-chargeable aspects of it too'.[93] It was not uncommon for practitioners to tell how they 'put in many hours of unremunerated work'.[94] A point frequently made by respondents was that the salary might be appropriate for the hypothetical job that lawyers are perceived to do, but not for the practical reality of their work. As one respondent explained:

> I agree that they are fair if I work the hours that I am contracted to. But I don't. I work evenings, weekends and snatched moments during my non-working days when I am meant to be with my children. I begrudge receiving a part-time wage when I am effectively working nearly full time hours across the 7 day week as a whole.[95]

A common point of contrast raised within these complaints was the disparity that also exists between the salaries for legal aid work as compared with salaries that are seen within other parts of the legal system – especially the private sector. Newly qualified solicitors in commercial firms could be earning over £100,000 per year, which engulfs the average starting salary in the legal aid sector, as will be explored in chapter five.[96] The comparison is not surprising when all law students – including those who go into legal aid – are presented with the same images of what a law career represents: generally the glamorous and privileged quality of life promised by corporate practice.[97] Corporate fees topping £100,000 are an extreme example, but Newman has shown how, even more than other occupations, legal aid lawyers consider themselves in relation to their peers across other areas of law with an acute awareness of how those working in legal aid lag behind.[98] Respondents spoke of how 'compared to colleagues in private practice the remuneration rates are low',[99] while 'law centre salary just doesn't compare to other legal sectors'.[100] Some respondents working in criminal defence specifically drew comparisons with prosecution fees; 'in the CPS [Crown Prosecution Service] … I would be earning 50,000 more plus'.[101] Generally, practitioners across the sector compared their private fees to their legal aid fees, with legal aid always coming out poorly. As one respondent explained, 'my hourly rate

[93] Practitioner Respondent Number 833.
[94] Practitioner Respondent Number 418.
[95] Practitioner Respondent Number 660.
[96] Jonathan Ames, 'Linklaters Offers £107,000 Starting Salary For 24 Year Old Solicitors' (*The Times*, 25 September 2021), available at www.thetimes.co.uk/article/linklaters-offers-107-000-starting-salary-for-24-year-old-solicitors-vt0dsg76n.
[97] "Richard Collier, '"Be Smart, Be Successful, Be Yourself …"?: Representations of the Training Contract and Trainee Solicitor in Advertising by Large Law Firms' (2005) 12 *International Journal of the Legal Profession* 51.
[98] Newman (n 81).
[99] Practitioner Respondent Number 1038.
[100] Practitioner Respondent Number 1124.
[101] Practitioner Respondent Number 289.

on legal aid is less than half my private rate'.[102] When comparing their salaries to those elsewhere, it was the social agenda that legal aid lawyers interviewed by Newman reported kept them in this sector,[103] such was reflected here also: 'if I had any good sense, and did not have such a strong sense of calling to the work that I do, I would leave the publicly funded criminal bar tomorrow, and work in other better remunerated areas of practice'.[104]

Invariably, concerns about salaries were linked with concerns about the volume of work and the hours that were required to make ends meet. Current legal aid professionals provided mixed responses when asked to reflect on the issues they faced around working hours and the extent to which they felt they had an effective work–life balance. As detailed in Table 2.3 (see chapter two), most practitioners (66.3 per cent, n=795) worked full time in their roles, with 21.9 per cent (n=262) working variable hours, 10.1 per cent (n=121) working part time, 1.7 per cent (n=20) working condensed hours and 0.1 per cent (n=1) reporting an 'other' form of working schedule.

When asked about the extent to which their working hours fit with their family and/or social commitments outside of work, of the 1,190 practitioners who responded to the question, 11.1 per cent (n=132) of practitioners responded 'very well', with 38.2 per cent (n=455) saying that their working hours fit 'well'. However, just over half of the respondents indicated that their working hours fit 'not very well' (40.9 per cent, n=487) or 'not at all' (9.7 per cent, n=116). Such findings reflect scholarship showing how work–life balance is a myth in the legal profession.[105] While present approaches to work hours clearly have an adverse impact on the work–life balance of all practitioners, it is important to recognise that certain marginalised groups, such as women, will be disproportionately and most obviously affected. This is demonstrated, for instance, by Webley and Duff's argument that women's experiences of legal practice can serve as an indicative barometer for wider problems relating to working conditions in the profession.[106]

As shown in Figure 4.3 below, this tended to vary by the role of the practitioner, with barristers, directors and head of chambers more often reporting that their working hours fit 'not very well' or 'not at all' with their family and/or social commitments outside of work.[107,108]

[102] Practitioner Respondent Number 1076.

[103] Newman (n 81).

[104] Practitioner Respondent Number 918.

[105] Hilary Sommerlad, '"A Pit to Put Women In": Professionalism, Work Intensification, Sexualisation and Work–Life Balance in the Legal Profession in England and Wales' (2016) 23 *International Journal of the Legal Profession* 61.

[106] Lisa Webley and Elizabeth Duff, 'Women Solicitors as a Barometer for Problems Within the Legal Profession – Time to Put Values Before Profits? (2007) 34 *Journal of Law and Society* 374.

[107] Whilst clerks also reported that their working hours fit with their family/social commitments 'not very well' or 'not at all', it should be noted that only two clerks responded to this question, severely limiting the inferences that might be drawn.

[108] Total group numbers as follows: head of department (n=49); solicitor (n=422); barrister (n=403); legal executive (n=24); trainee/pupil/paralegal (n=141); caseworker (n=42); clerk (n=2); practice manager (n=12); director (n=42); head of chambers (n=10); billing clerk (n=24); other (n=17).

Figure 4.3 The extent to which current legal aid practitioners feel their working hours fit with family/social commitments outside of work by principal role (n=1,188)

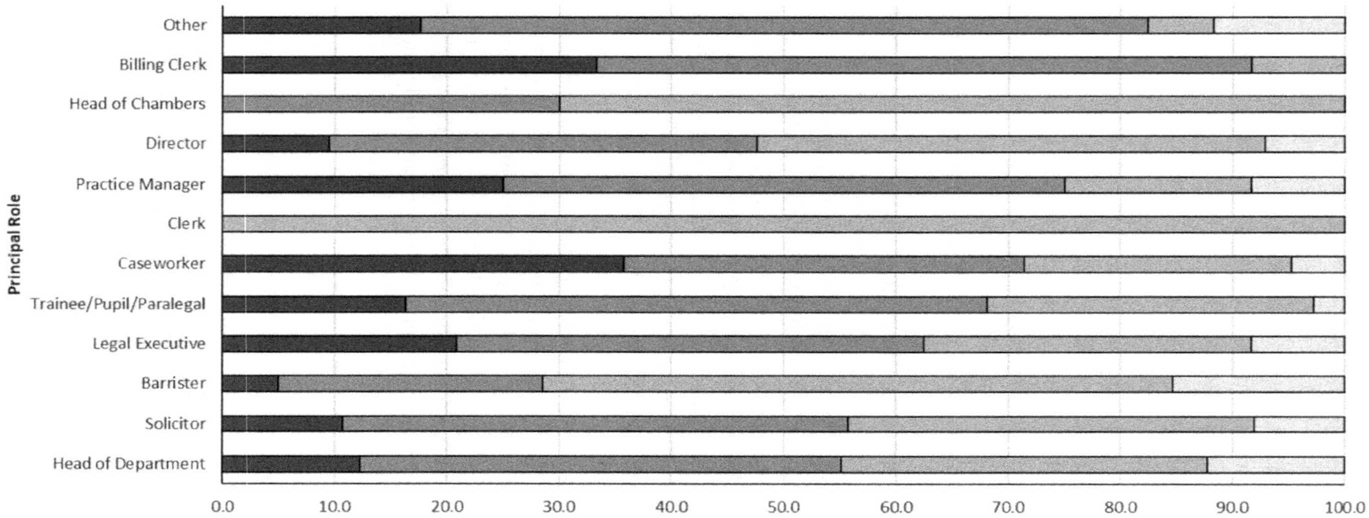

	Head of Department	Solicitor	Barrister	Legal Executive	Trainee/Pupil /Paralegal	Caseworker	Clerk	Practice Manager	Director	Head of Chambers	Billing Clerk	Other
■ Very well	12.2	10.7	5.0	20.8	16.3	35.7	0.0	25.0	9.5	0.0	33.3	17.6
■ Well	42.9	45.0	23.6	41.7	51.8	35.7	0.0	50.0	38.1	30.0	58.3	64.7
□ Not very well	32.7	36.3	56.1	29.2	29.1	23.8	100.0	16.7	45.2	70.0	8.3	5.9
□ Not at all	12.2	8.1	15.4	8.3	2.8	4.8	0.0	8.3	7.1	0.0	0.0	11.8

% of Current Practitioners

Additionally, almost all of the 1,179 practitioners who provided an answer worked in their free time. Only 3.0 per cent (n=35) of those who responded did not work in their free time. Around two-thirds (62.0 per cent, n=731) reported working in their free time every day. Over a quarter (26.8 per cent, n=316) worked in their free time less frequently but still at least one or twice a week, whilst 8.2 per cent (n=97) worked in their free time once or twice a month. As before, the extent to which practitioners worked in their free time varied by role type, with heads of department, barristers, practice managers and heads of chambers more often reporting having to work in their free time nearly every day.[109] Figure 4.4 reflects these results in greater detail.[110]

Taken together, these responses suggest that legal aid work in England and Wales is strongly characterised by a need to work beyond set working hours in order to meet demands and by challenges for many to fit work around their family and/or social commitments. Such findings on the demanding nature of these practices are reflective of international research on lawyer working hours more widely.[111] There have been growing concerns that the increasing digitisation of work in law – meaning work outside traditional office locations and office hours are normalised – could have damaging effects on the ability to achieve a healthy work–life balance.[112] Thus we see the clear links between the earlier negative well-being results and these working practices across the Census. Thornton writes that

> high levels of emotional exhaustion and burnout … includes not only long hours in the office but the spillover of work at home 'always being connected' has exacerbated the problems associated with the long-hours culture as it has caused the boundary between work and home to dissolve, allowing work to colonise the intimate space of the home.[113]

Further, the intrusion of remote working through email, mobile phones and video conferencing is presumably more challenging still since the uptake in usage with the pandemic as shown in research on the legal aid sector.[114]

[109] Whilst clerks also reported having to work in their free time almost daily at higher rates than other practitioners, it should be noted that only two clerks responded to this question, severely limiting the inferences that might be drawn.

[110] Total group numbers as follows: head of department (n=50); solicitor (n=419); barrister (n=399); legal executive (n=24); trainee/pupil/paralegal (n=138); caseworker (n=42); clerk (n=2); practice manager (n=12); director (n=41); head of chambers (n=10); billing clerk (n=25); other (n=17).

[111] For example, Iain Campbell, 'The Elephant in the Room: Working-Time Patterns of Solicitors in Private Practice in Melbourne' (Centre for Employment and Labour Relations Law, 2008); Ingo Forstenlechner and Fiona Lettice, 'Well Paid but Undervalued and Overworked: The Highs and Lows of Being a Junior Lawyer in a Leading Law Firm' (2008) 30 *Employee Relations* 640.

[112] Margaret Thornton, 'The Flexible Cyborg: Work-Life Balance in Legal Practice' (2016) 38 *Sydney Law Review* 1.

[113] Margaret Thornton, 'Squeezing the Life Out of Lawyers: Legal Practice in the Market Embrace' (2016) 25 *Griffith Law Review* 471.

[114] Jessica Mant et al, 'Blended Advice and Access to Justice' (Ministry of Justice and the Access to Justice Foundation, 2022).

Figure 4.4 The average frequency with which current legal aid practitioners have to work in their free time to meet work demands by principal role (n=1,177)

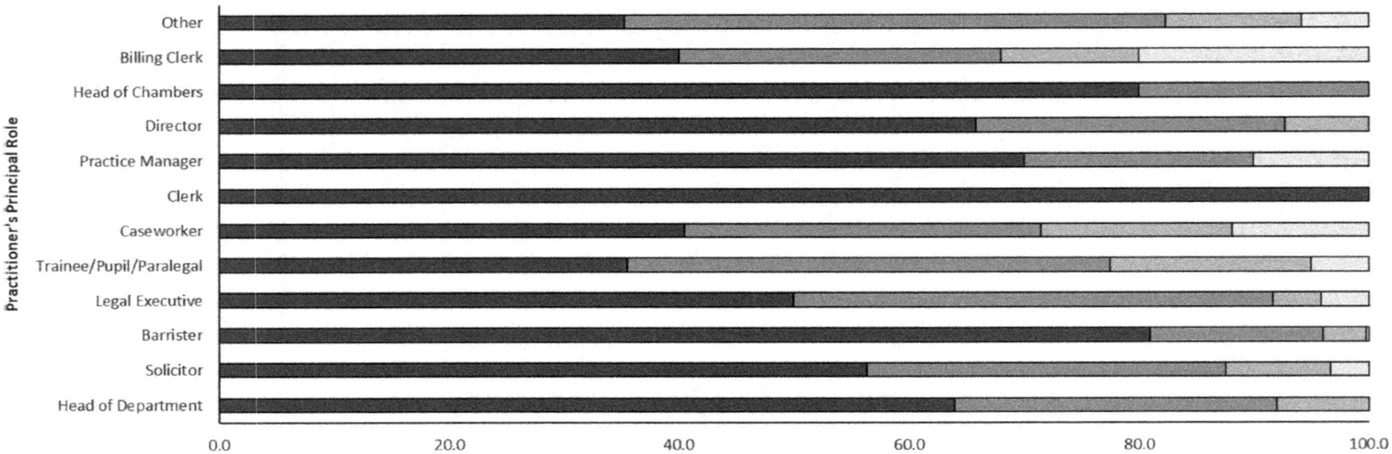

	Head of Department	Solicitor	Barrister	Legal Executive	Trainee/Pupil /Paralegal	Caseworker	Clerk	Practice Manager	Director	Head of Chambers	Billing Clerk	Other
Nearly every day	64.0	56.3	81.0	50.0	35.5	40.5	100.0	70.0	65.9	80.0	40.0	35.3
Once or twice a week	28.0	31.3	15.0	41.7	42.0	31.0	0.0	20.0	26.8	20.0	28.0	47.1
Once or twice a month	8.0	9.1	3.8	4.2	17.4	16.7	0.0	0.0	7.3	0.0	12.0	11.8
I don't work in my free time	0.0	3.3	0.3	4.2	5.1	11.9	0.0	10.0	0.0	0.0	20.0	5.9

% of Current Practitioners

IV. Job Satisfaction

Notwithstanding the degree of concern expressed by practitioners with respect to the issue of their remuneration, the majority of current practitioners expressed satisfaction with their choice of career in legal aid. This apparent paradox between negative well-being and positive job satisfaction has been addressed by Chan's work, which explores stress as an ingrained part of existing legal working cultures – and thus an accepted aspect of lawyer identities.[115] As such, while the foregoing challenges might suggest low job satisfaction, her scholarship shows that 'prevailing assumptions and attitudes in legal practice … can play a part in normalising certain lifestyles and responses to work stress'.[116] Thus, the Census revealed that, in total, of 1,149 practitioners who answered, 22.0 per cent (n=253) were very satisfied and 41.2 per cent (n=473) were satisfied with their choice of career in legal aid, while 18.4 per cent (n=211) were neither satisfied/unsatisfied, 12.3 per cent (n=141) were unsatisfied and 6.2 per cent (n=71) were very unsatisfied.

In particular, there were a number of common responses practitioners gave when asked to identify in their own words what they liked most about working in legal aid. These coded open-ended responses are captured in Table 4.4 below. When drawing out the main themes emerging from the coding of these responses, over half of the 692 practitioners who provided an answer (56.2 per cent, n=389) can be seen to have identified 'making a difference in people's lives/helping vulnerable people' as the aspect of legal aid work they found most gratifying. This view matches the notion of the 'social agenda', which has previously been identified as a major motivator for legal aid lawyers in England and Wales.[117] Indeed, such findings also reflect US research on lawyer happiness, which suggests that money is less important than motivation.[118] Further, they tally with Australian research on the importance of social value as a resource to make lawyering worthwhile work.[119] Making a difference is thus understandably important for promoting positive job satisfaction amongst the practitioners who responded to the census.

Some practitioners cast this idea of making a difference in terms of hierarchies and power dynamics: they are 'standing up for the little person who has usually had a bad deal … winning against a landlord who has not followed the correct procedure'.[120] Respondents often noted how those they help otherwise wouldn't be

[115] Janet Chan, 'Conceptualising Legal Culture and Lawyering Stress' (2015) 21 *International Journal of the Legal Profession* 213.

[116] ibid, 215.

[117] Hilary Sommerlad, 'Criminal Legal Aid Reforms and the Restructuring of Legal Professionalism' in Richard Young and David Wall (eds), *Access to Criminal Justice: Legal Aid Lawyers and the Defence of Liberty* (Blackstone, 1996).

[118] Lawrence S Krieger and Kennin M Sheldon, 'What Makes Lawyers Happy? A Data-Driven Prescription to Redefine Professional Success' (2015) 83 *George Washington Law Review* 554.

[119] Adele J Bergin and Nerina L Jimmieson, 'Australian Lawyer Well-Being: Workplace Demands, Resources and the Impact of Time-Billing Targets' (2014) 21 *Psychiatry, Psychology and Law* 427.

[120] Practitioner Respondent Number 219.

able to get representation ('people who otherwise wouldn't be able to afford representation')[121] and would be priced out of justice ('the very people who would not otherwise have access to justice').[122] Many emphasised their particular satisfaction in 'helping the most vulnerable in society',[123] sometimes going so far as to note how they 'find it a privilege to work with vulnerable clients'.[124] Some practitioners made a point of how they felt pride in helping those clients who had been marginalised by wider society, as in this account:

> Representing people that others have written off. Seeing the humanity in people who have committed horrific crimes. Finding a way to communicate with clients who find it hard to open up, are traumatised or otherwise very vulnerable. Recognising mental health needs and learning disabilities in my clients when others haven't. Managing difficult clients. In short, working with people during the most vulnerable moments of their lives.[125]

There was a sense of importance attached to the work that legal aid lawyers do, as summarised by the respondent who professed that 'I am never in doubt that the work we do matters'.[126]

In addition to the satisfaction derived from helping people, just over a quarter of respondents (29.9 per cent, n=207) claimed to generally enjoy their work. Values and morals were important to many practitioners here. There was a 'sense of purpose and fulfilment that I get from work and the feeling of sharing values with colleagues',[127] and the feeling that 'I don't have to compromise my morals to get the work done'.[128] The shared sense of values and morality with others working across the sector was also significant, with some talking about 'the community – I think legal aid lawyers are wonderful',[129] and others, 'my colleagues are fantastic'.[130]

Meanwhile, just under a quarter (21.8 per cent, n=151) cited the opportunity to work on interesting or challenging cases. As one respondent explained, 'the combination of intellectual challenge and the sense of making a difference to people in need makes it a very rewarding role'.[131] Respondents told that 'every day is different, no case is ever predictable',[132] which partly stems from the nature of legal aid work where 'the variety is endless as social problems are all unique despite common denominators'.[133] Winning such challenging cases

[121] Practitioner Respondent Number 615.
[122] Practitioner Respondent Number 1011.
[123] Practitioner Respondent Number 102.
[124] Practitioner Respondent Number 242.
[125] Practitioner Respondent Number 389.
[126] Practitioner Respondent Number 446.
[127] Practitioner Respondent Number 1158.
[128] Practitioner Respondent Number 887.
[129] Practitioner Respondent Number 350.
[130] Practitioner Respondent Number 270.
[131] Practitioner Respondent Number 632.
[132] Practitioner Respondent Number 1027.
[133] Practitioner Respondent Number 483.

can feel especially rewarding for practitioners: 'the cases can be interesting and complex … raise novel points of law, and the gravity of what is at stake does give a sense of satisfaction if a good outcome is achieved'.[134]

Table 4.4 What current legal aid practitioners like most about working in legal aid (n=692)

	N	%
Making a difference in peoples' lives/helping vulnerable people	389	56.2
Job satisfaction/'I like my job'	207	29.9
Working on interesting/challenging cases	151	21.8
Helping to provide access to justice	113	16.3
Face-to-face client work	99	14.3
Camaraderie with like-minded lawyers	79	11.4
Holding the government/public sector/organisations to account	41	5.9
Nothing/not much	17	2.5
Attending court	7	1.0

It is interesting to note the continuity between why current practitioner respondents entered the profession in the first place and their motivation to stay. Indeed, the sentiment expressed here parallels the findings set out in chapter two, wherein a majority of respondents indicated that they were most attracted to legal aid work due to a desire to 'help those facing economic, cultural or social disadvantage', 'make access to justice more equitable', 'have a positive impact on society', 'improve access to justice', and/or 'apply my skills to help others'. These findings suggest that it is possible for practitioners to achieve the ambitions within the sector that had originally motivated them to pursue a career in legal aid, though not without making significant sacrifices and/or balancing a number of other difficult issues.

Indeed, many of the responses to the question of what practitioners liked about working in legal aid were bittersweet and tinged with bittersweet sadness at the attendant problems considered previously. For example, one respondent evoked the idea of burn-out: 'I love the complexity of the work, the challenges and the capacity to make change but I am realising that I am near to burn out and this makes me feel disappointed in myself'.[135] Another respondent raised the issue of funding, writing: 'I enjoy the work, helping clients and the nature of proceedings but the underfunding and low pay with high stress and demand makes the role unattractive'.[136]

[134] Practitioner Respondent Number 523.
[135] Practitioner Respondent Number 260.
[136] Practitioner Respondent Number 815.

These negative issues were explored in greater depth via open-ended responses provided by practitioners in response to the question 'What do you like least about working in legal aid?' and are demonstrated in Table 4.5 below:

Table 4.5 What current legal aid practitioners like least about working in legal aid (n=726)

	N	%
Poor remuneration/for the complexity of work	305	42.0
Too many audits/administrative work/battling LAA for payment	232	32.0
Unsustainably large workload/'burn-out'/long hours	110	15.2
The Legal Aid Agency/Ministry of Justice/Client and Cost Management System (CCMS)	95	13.1
Lack of resources/funding for LA and related bodies (inadequately resourced CCMS, courts, etc)	94	12.9
Poor fees/amount of work needed to do to get paid a decent salary	80	11.0
Impact on mental health, eg stress, anxiety, vicarious trauma	78	10.7
Feeling undervalued/poor public perception of legal aid work	74	10.2
Lack of client eligibility/scope of legal aid too narrow	45	6.2
No work–life balance/impacts on personal time	44	6.1
Complex client personal issues (non-law related)/difficult clients	28	3.9
No career progression/very slow career progression/no up-skilling	27	3.7
No future in Legal aid/unsustainable	22	3.0

Perhaps unsurprisingly given the number of practitioners who expressed concerns regarding the fairness of their remuneration, nearly half of the 726 practitioners who gave an open-ended response (42.0 per cent, n=305) identified poor remuneration as a factor they least liked about working in legal aid. For example, respondents complained about 'the fact that the legal aid rates do not properly reflect the quality and the amount of work undertaken',[137] and that 'fees are not commensurate with the work needed to be done'.[138] One respondent highlighted their frustration at 'having to work 3 jobs to have a reasonable standard of living',[139] as their reason for disliking legal aid work, which tallies with the respondent reflect on how 'we are overqualified and underpaid'.[140] Newman and Welsh have highlighted how undervalued such legal aid lawyers feel, with their findings for criminal lawyers reflected across the sector in this Census.[141]

[137] Practitioner Respondent Number 138.
[138] Practitioner Respondent Number 486.
[139] Practitioner Respondent Number 1176.
[140] Practitioner Respondent Number 760.
[141] Daniel Newman and Lucy Welsh, 'The Practices of Modern Criminal Defence Lawyers: Alienation and Its Implications for Access to Justice' (2019) 48 *Common Law World Review* 64.

A further 32 per cent (n=232) of respondents highlighted excessive auditing by the LAA, too much administrative work required to obtain payment, and constant battles with the LAA for payment. Forbess and James have demonstrated the increasing complexity of working in and around the sector, and the way having to act as intermediaries across different organisations was frustrating practitioners.[142] For respondents to the Legal Aid Census, working to obtain legal aid reimbursement was the most burdensome of all. A large number of respondents suggested they were deterred from legal aid work by 'all the administration that goes along with it and hoops to jump through',[143] and 'the bureaucracy of the legal aid agency where most of the time is spent making sure we are compliant'.[144] There were particular frustrations about 'spending time that should be spent helping my vulnerable clients fighting with the Legal Aid Agency to accurately apply their own rules'.[145] Practitioners complained about the 'sheer complexity involved in every day applications for legal aid … a specialist subject in itself',[146] to the extent that some respondents even suggested that the 'bureaucracy feels designed to wear down the practitioner'.[147]

These financial and administrative issues had obvious knock-on effects to workload, with 15.2 per cent of practitioners (n=110) citing an unsustainably large workload, burn-out and/or long hours, as was discussed earlier in this chapter. These included concerns about the impact of workload on their practice, such as 'not [being] able to run cases to the quality I would like due to having too many cases',[148] and 'the feeling that I do not have enough time to do the work as well as possible'.[149] Some of these accounts even expressed this as a lack of hope in legal aid work, a concerning theme that is explored further in chapter six: 'It is unrelenting and a depressing job to be in. I feel undervalued and abandoned, and it is just getting worse. If I could leave I would.'[150]

These factors of dissatisfaction align closely with the extensive work that Sommerlad has conducted on the reconfiguration of access to justice under neoliberalism, trends which only seem to have been exacerbated by the pandemic.[151] Underlining these negative feelings was the extra pressure that came from being a legal aid lawyer in what is generally seen as a vocation, which carried with it 'the expectation that you will not moan about it because working in legal aid is

[142] Alice Forbess and Deborah James, 'Acts of Assistance: Navigating the Interstices of the British State with the Help of Non-Profit Legal Advisers' (2014) 58 *Social Analysis* 73.

[143] Practitioner Respondent Number 1163.

[144] Practitioner Respondent Number 1116.

[145] Practitioner Respondent Number 554.

[146] Practitioner Respondent Number 864.

[147] Practitioner Respondent Number 349.

[148] Practitioner Respondent Number 664.

[149] Practitioner Respondent Number 403.

[150] Practitioner Respondent Number 754.

[151] Hilary Sommerlad, 'Some Reflections on the Relationship between Citizenship, Access to Justice and the Reform of Legal Aid' (2004) 31 *Journal of Law and Society* 345. See also, Newman and Welsh (n 141).

a "privilege".[152] In research conducted in the United States, there has been the suggestion that the decline in working conditions for lawyers in this sector is leading to disengagement and detachment, a decline from the social justice ideals expressed earlier.[153] Concerns must be raised that such circumstances could also develop here considering these results despite the current positive job satisfaction that exists – there may be a limit for legal aid lawyers that we need to be alert to for its implications for the sector and access to justice.[154]

V. Professional Networks, Training and Development

Professional networks offer a potential means for working through some of the challenges faced by lawyers in the sector. While professional networks in law can be understood as the kind of practical courtroom user groups recently explored by Welsh in terms of criminal justice, the Census focused on them as broader member organisations.[155] The former involve immediate solutions to everyday issues, such as defence lawyers and prosecutors discussing how to proceed with a case as they come up in a local court. The usage in this Census refers to wider groups that work across groups of practitioners, and can offer support, solidarity and mobilisation at a range of levels. The Law Society, for example, strongly advocates for the importance of networks, in part for helping practitioners deal with the kind of bullying, harassment and discrimination that minority groups can experience.[156] In terms of engagement with the broader profession, the practitioner Census found a high degree of participation and membership within professional networks among practitioners with 1,073 practitioners indicating they belonged to one or more professional network. The top five groups included the Law Society (33.5 per cent, n=359), the Bar Council (24.4 per cent, n=262), the Legal Aid Practitioners Group (20.9 per cent, n=224), Young Legal Aid Lawyers (18.2 per cent, n=195) and the Family Law Barristers Association (17.2 per cent, n=186).

Most current practitioners felt professional networks were useful, with 49.4 per cent (n=557) finding them quite useful, and 25.0 per cent (n=282) finding them very useful from a total of 1,127 practitioners.[157] When asked to explain why they did or did not find professional networks useful, a number of themes

[152] Practitioner Respondent Number 978.

[153] Marina Zaloznaya, 'Mechanisms and Consequences of Professional Marginality: The Case of Poverty Lawyers Revisited' (2011) 36 *Law & Social Inquiry* 919.

[154] Newman (n 18).

[155] Lucy Welsh, *Access to Justice in Magistrates' Courts: A Study of Defendant Marginalisation* (Hart, 2022).

[156] The Law Society of England and Wales, 'Networking Tips For LGBT+ Lawyers' (The Law Society, 18 April 2019), available at www.lawsociety.org.uk/topics/lgbt-lawyers/networking-tips-for-lgbt-lawyers.

[157] Nine respondents provided more than one answer to this question. Six respondents selected both 'quite useful' and 'not very useful', two selected 'very useful' and 'quite useful' and one respondent selected 'not very useful' and 'not at all useful'. In order to translate this to a single response variable, the most favourable response was taken and the second response was excluded. It is noted that the

were identified from the 309 open-ended responses given by practitioners. These answers are set out in Table 4.6 below.

Table 4.6 Why current legal aid practitioners did/did not find professional networks useful (n=309)

	N	%
Gathering niche knowledge/updates/training for my area of practice	135	43.7
I don't like them/can't afford more memberships/don't have time	100	32.4
In general networks fulfil their purpose	69	22.3
Collegiate support	63	20.4
Collaborative meetings/seminars/events share knowledge and group action	55	17.8
Jobs/career contacts	16	5.2
Represent my interests/advocate for lawyers	11	3.6

Most commonly (43.7 per cent, n=135), respondents indicated in their open-ended responses that professional networks were useful for gathering niche knowledge, updates and training for the practitioner's area of practice. Some described how professional networks 'help keep you in the loop with what is going on within the profession and provide you with practical updates'.[158] As an example of why professional networks could be useful for developing such knowledge, some respondents explained that they were 'supportive of questions about legal aid or casework'.[159] In terms of how professional networks could best promote such knowledge, it was said that they are 'most useful at a micro level i.e. being able to share issues and good practice with others within the organisation or at similar grades in other organisations'.[160]

However, despite the apparent value for gaining knowledge, a further 32.4 per cent (n=100) of practitioners indicated that they did not find them useful, did not like them, could not afford the membership fees or did not have time to engage with the network. Some responded that they 'don't have time to attend and don't get much out of them';[161] others reported that they 'cannot join more because of the personal cost.'[162] Another view was that 'talkshops achieve little – other than self perpetuating how badly off we all feel'.[163] More informal personal networks were sometimes considered of greater value than formal professional networks:

> As a wider entity, 'legal aid lawyers' are too diverse a group to have enough in common to want the same things. Where they might be useful is in dealings with government,

number of practitioners who reported finding professional networks useful exceeded the number who indicated which professional networks they belonged to.

[158] Practitioner Respondent Number 965.
[159] Practitioner Respondent Number 679.
[160] Practitioner Respondent Number 632.
[161] Practitioner Respondent Number 1187.
[162] Practitioner Respondent Number 331.
[163] Practitioner Respondent Number 355.

> but government has no interest in engaging. Personal networks are more useful in my view.[164]

Nevertheless, 22.3 per cent (n=69) suggested that in general, networks fulfilled their purpose.

Alongside professional networks, the Census also sought to capture the extent to which respondents considered training and development as mechanisms that could help lawyers work through some of the issues they face (or, conversely, add to them). When it came to training and development, only 14.6 per cent (n=168) of the 1,150 practitioners who answered felt that their professional development needs were being met in full. Nearly half (47.3 per cent, n=544) of practitioners indicated that their needs were mostly being met, while just over a quarter (28.7 per cent, n=330) indicated that their training and development needs were partly being met. 7.4 per cent (n=85) indicated their needs were not being met at all, whilst 0.9 per cent (n=10) indicated that they did not feel they needed training, and 1.1 per cent (n=13) responded that training and development was not applicable to them. Practitioners have long been shown as frustrated that training can be inadequate.[165] Law Society research has shown that training is important to practitioners, while employers cited lack of funding and time could get in the way of practitioners accessing the training they want.[166]

As shown in Table 4.7 below, of those practitioners who detailed their training priorities (n=974), most indicated that they would like training on work-life balance (42.1 per cent, n=410) and personal well-being and stress management (41.2 per cent, n=401) when given the opportunity to identify their training needs in their own words. Respondents also indicated that they would like training on dealing with vicarious trauma (31.9 per cent, n=311), advocacy (31.7 per cent, n=309) and updates on legislative changes (31.3 per cent, n=305).

Table 4.7 The training priorities of current legal aid practitioners (n=974)

	N	%
Work–life balance	410	42.1
Personal well-being and stress management	401	41.2
Dealing with vicarious trauma	311	31.9
Advocacy	309	31.7
Updates on legislative changes	305	31.3
Dealing with complex clients	287	29.5

(continued)

164 Practitioner Respondent Number 61.

165 Richard Moorhead and Fiona Boyle, 'Work in Progress: Quality of Life and Trainee Solicitors: A Survey' (1995) 2 *International Journal of the Legal Profession* 217.

166 Matthew Williams et al, 'Research to Inform Workforce Planning and Career Development in Legal Services Employment: Trends, Workforce Projections and Solicitor Firm Perspectives' (Institute of Employment Studies, 2019).

Table 4.7 ***(Continued)***

	N	%
Legal aid contract management	266	27.3
Cultural awareness	198	20.3
Management and leadership skills	197	20.2
Staff supervision	189	19.4
Partnering and collaborating with other organisations	135	13.9
Communication skills	93	9.5
Monitoring and evaluation of services	77	7.9
Grant writing	48	4.9
Other	21	2.2

Of those who suggested an 'other' topic on which they required training, 18 respondents provided further details and suggested areas such as billing, complex legal aid claims, scope and eligibility, business development, career development, public speaking and knowledge of relevant areas of law, among others.

VI. Implications of Findings

Experiences of working in legal aid from across the surveys comprising the Census reveal several significant issues faced by those in the sector, all of which highlight the vulnerability of the legal aid sector and those working within it. In assessing working conditions, we have seen the cumulative day-to-day challenges experienced by legal aid practitioners. The difficulties encountered in doing this work should be understood within the vulnerability frame – legal aid lawyers and the institution of legal aid itself should be considered vulnerable.

It is clear from the findings of the Legal Aid Census that working in legal aid takes a toll on the mental well-being of practitioners. The pressures as well as the nature of legal aid work in some areas of practice meant that almost half of practitioners felt that legal aid work had an overall negative effect on their mental well-being. They faced a range of stressors that explained and exacerbated this negative well-being, which the chapter has examined in greater detail. Workplace bullying, harassment, and/or discrimination is also not infrequently experienced within the sector. Problematically, at least some of the bullying, harassment and/or discrimination that occurs is attributed by victims as being related to protected characteristics and as being perpetrated by authority figures (such as judges, line managers, and supervisors, among others) in the sector.

Remuneration was also a significant concern for practitioners as will be developed in the following chapter, with the majority indicating that they felt their salary and working arrangements for their role was unfair, frequently needed to work beyond set hours to meet demands, and often struggled to fit work around their family life and personal commitments. Notwithstanding the degree of concern expressed by practitioners with respect to their remuneration and working conditions, the majority of current practitioners expressed satisfaction with their choice of career in legal aid. Satisfaction with legal aid work was attributed to the ability to help people and make a difference to people's lives through legal aid, as well as to an enjoyment of the actual work involved with legal aid practice. In terms of training and development, only a minority of practitioners felt that their professional development needs were being met in full, with training on work–life balance, personal well-being and stress management all frequently identified as training needs within the sector. More positively, the Census did find evidence of a high degree of engagement with the broader profession, as many practitioners reported that they participated in professional networks. Although membership fees and time constraints prevented such networks from being beneficial for everyone, networks were cited as useful for gathering niche knowledge, updates and training for different areas of practice.

Overall, this chapter has depicted a sector in which practitioners fundamentally lack resilience despite their ostensibly privileged position as lawyers. Drawing directly on the experiences and perceptions of legal aid practitioners currently working in the sector, the Legal Aid Census has demonstrated that there are several significant concerns as to the working conditions in the legal aid sector; many of these are underpinned by challenges relating to financial insecurity and unsustainability. This theme will therefore be further explored in the next chapter, which examines in detail the implications of fees, hourly rates, and financial sustainability of those working within the legal aid sector.

5

Remuneration and Fees

I. Introduction

In designing the legal aid system for England and Wales, the Rushcliffe Committee stressed the importance of lawyers receiving adequate remuneration for their services.[1] Nonetheless, there has long been a tendency to equate overall legal aid spending with misguided assumptions about the rates of pay and related working conditions of legal aid lawyers. As discussed in chapter one, high rates of pay for a small minority have fuelled an anti-legal aid lawyer rhetoric which collectively presents them as 'fat cats' in policy debates and in the media.[2] Against this background, repeated spending cuts and wider reforms have been justified as 'maintaining public confidence' in the system.[3] As Moses LJ noted in his judgment in relation to a judicial review challenge to the residence test for legal aid, public confidence has in practice been 'little more than reliance on public prejudice'.[4] In fact, a number of independent inquiries have recently demonstrated the fallacy of the assumptions upon which legal aid reforms have rested and the inadequacy of current rates of pay.[5] As discussed in the last chapter, legal aid lawyers express frustration and dismay at the low rates of remuneration and challenging working conditions. These conditions are hardly consistent with images of legal aid lawyers as 'fat cats', especially given that they work in an increasingly industrialised and standardised way within a wider justice system in crisis.[6]

Over the last four decades, both internal and external forces have brought significant change to the legal aid profession. As discussed in chapter one, the marketisation and increased bureaucratisation of the system from the 1980s

[1] The Rushcliffe Committee, 'Rushcliffe Committee Report on Legal Aid and Legal Advice in England and Wales' (CM6641, 1945) Recommendation 6.

[2] Helen O'Nions, '"Fat Cat" Lawyers and "Illegal" Migrants: The Impact of Intersecting Hostilities and Toxic Narrative on Access to Justice' (2020) 42 *Journal of Social Welfare and Family Law* 319.

[3] Ministry of Justice, 'Transforming Legal Aid: Delivering a More Credible and Efficient System' (CP14/2013, HMSO, 2013) 3.

[4] *Public Law Project v Secretary of State for Justice* [2014] EWHC 2365 (Admin) [84].

[5] The Westminster Commission on Legal Aid, 'Inquiry into the Sustainability and Recovery of the Legal Aid Sector' (All-Party Parliamentary Group on Legal Aid, 2021); House of Commons Justice Committee, 'The Future of Legal Aid: Third Report of Session 2021–22' (Her Majesty's Stationery Office, 2021).

[6] Avrom Sherr, 'Of Superheroes and Slaves: Images and Work of the Legal Professional' (1995) 48 *Current Legal Problems* 327.

onwards created highly complex fee arrangements. Hanlon observed that policymakers were 'engaged in trying to redefine professionalism so that it becomes more commercially aware, budget-focused, managerial, entrepreneurial',[7] which brought about change in the relationship between legal aid lawyers and the state. Others point to the individualistic approach of the state to legal aid, which some assert had long been focused on 'providing economic and administrative support for a system which should operate at arm's length' and therefore limits 'concepts of partnership, participation and active citizenship',[8] and consequently the appreciation of legal aid as a public good which should be adequately funded.

Changes to service provision were also common outside of legal aid practice in the 1990s, as Sherr observes, because the industrialisation of the legal sector significantly changed both the overall performance and management of professional legal work.[9] By the turn of the millennium, tasks were 'deskilled and broken up into different activities' which had the knock-on impact of long hours and the repetitive nature of the work creating increased levels of stress.[10] Importantly, Sherr also noted the extent to which relationships with clients changed during this time:

> Lawyers, even those in small high street communities, could not behave like a general practice doctor with long-term information about the client and the client's family to back up decisions made and follow through with any necessary care or treatment. Instead, the lawyer would be involved in crisis intervention without thinking further of the person saved or the situation remedied.[11]

These more limited forms of client communication and interaction represented a move away from lawyers as generalist practitioners to more specialist technicians.[12] Therefore, whereas lawyers used to be perceived as playing an important role in public life and had a longstanding professional role across separate but related areas of law, they now began to be relied upon only during times of crisis. The legal aid system was increasingly thereafter shaped and designed to function much in the same way, with packaged-up fee arrangements demanding that lawyers work less holistically in their problem-solving for clients. There is a continuing tension therefore between the values that underpin the system, to which most legal aid lawyers subscribe as outlined in chapter two, and the reality of rigid fee arrangements which fail to promote those values in practice.

We can trace the alarm sounded about legal aid remuneration to the early years of this century. Moorhead notes that the then Lord Chancellor observed that there

[7] Gerard Hanlon, *Lawyers, the State and the Market, Professionalism Revisited* (Macmillan, 1999) 121.

[8] Maureen Spencer, 'Public Subsidies without Strings – Labour and the Lawyers at the Birth of Legal Aid' (2002) 9 *International Journal of the Legal Profession* 251, 277.

[9] Sherr (n 6).

[10] Avrom Sherr, 'Professional Work, Professional Careers and Legal Education: Educating the Lawyer for 2010' (2000) 7 *International Journal of the Legal Profession* 325, 326.

[11] ibid, 327.

[12] Alan Paterson, 'Specialisation and the legal profession' (1986) *New Law Journal* 697.

was a 'weakening of the supply base' due to the 'rates [the Government] can afford to pay' following the implementation of legal aid contracting and related forms of audit and control.[13] Nonetheless, as Moorhead observed, the political rhetoric even then was 'broadly hostile' to both the legal aid scheme and to lawyers.[14] He points to the 'significant cumulative growth in the legal aid budget' throughout the 1990s and notes that despite a marked increase in the overall budget, the levels of remuneration in terms of hourly rates and fixed fees for work 'only increased broadly in line with public spending, GDP and inflation until 1992/93 but thereafter remuneration rates remained static'.[15] Other explanations offered for the growth in overall spending include the recession during this time, which resulted in a 'coalition of the real needs of the public, and the desire (of the profession) to supply' as well as a 'one off spike in the levels of claims' in response to the 'deregulation of the conveyancing market'.[16] Nonetheless, contrary to public opinion, overall legal aid spending at the turn of the century, as now, did not result in significantly increased rates of pay for lawyers themselves. This, coupled with some parts of legal aid diminishing while others showed 'above trend increases in cost' caused Moorhead to predict that the judicare model might not be sustainable due to the simple economics of private practice:

> With static hourly rates, and the pressure to do more work for the same pay, the ability of legal aid departments to keep pace with their private practice client colleagues is diminishing, particularly if they have now wrung any efficiency gains out of working harder and recording more time.[17]

Further cuts in more recent austerity times, as set out in chapter one, have further exacerbated sustainability pressures. While sustainability relates to the feasibility of different models of legal aid, it also concerns the determination of what an 'adequate' rate of remuneration might be, as envisaged by the Rushcliffe Committee. This involves multifaceted considerations, and what is clear from the discussion in the last chapter is that the majority of legal aid practitioners perceive their pay to be inadequate. This is supported by the wealth of evidence we have about problems with recruitment and retention in the sector more generally, which we consider in chapter seven. The definition of sustainability put forward by the Westminster Commission on Legal Aid is informative as it is underpinned by the need to 'make a profit and to provide an income to the business owner that is commensurate with their skills and seniority as a lawyer and a reasonable commercial return on the business'.[18] For the wider advice sector (ie not-for-profit providers) sustainability should 'enable them to generate a surplus that ensures they can operate

[13] Richard Moorhead, 'Legal Aid and the Decline of Private Practice: Blue Murder or Toxic Job?' (2004) 11 *International Journal of the Legal Profession* 159, 160.

[14] ibid.

[15] ibid, 163.

[16] ibid, 167.

[17] ibid, 179.

[18] The Westminster Commission on Legal Aid (n 5), 84.

with sufficient reserves to satisfy guidance provided by the Charity Commission' while salaries must be 'competitive within the legal market and provide employees with a reasonable standard of living' and they should enable recruitment of lawyers from a 'wide range of socio-economic backgrounds' and offer 'realistic career progression'.[19]

Despite considerable systemic reforms and wider forces of change impacting upon legal aid, it is clear that rates of remuneration remain static. A body of work has sought to better understand the impact this has had on lawyers themselves and their relationship to their professional responsibilities.[20] As outlined in chapter one, problems have exacerbated over the last 20 years in the austerity era for legal aid and have brought issues of sustainability to the forefront of practitioners' minds. It is well documented that low rates of pay alongside negative perceptions in the public sphere have led to low morale and diminishing professional self-worth. As set out in the last chapter, poor working conditions have heightened vulnerability and had adverse impacts upon well-being. Likewise, the relationship between economic insecurity and mental ill health, including low self-esteem, is well established.[21] Further, our data analysis suggests that legal aid fee regimes fail to promote efficiency and risk undermining access to justice. This chapter therefore sets out Census findings in relation to fixed fees and hourly rates of pay in order to better understand legal aid working practices. In doing so, we can shed light on the ways in which remuneration influences professional decision-making, as well as more accurately typify lawyers in terms of professional self-identification.[22] The chapter also seeks to interrogate the ways in which lawyers attempt to mitigate loss in their day-to-day work, in order to ensure their organisations, and their own jobs, survive in an increasingly challenging landscape.

II. Salaries of Current Practitioners

The Census provides an interesting picture of the salaries of legal aid practitioners. As shown in Figure 5.1 below, legal aid practitioners reported wide-ranging salaries in categorised from under £9,999 to over £240,000. Most practitioners, however, indicated a salary level of £30,000–£39,999 (19.3 per cent, n=228), followed by £20,000–£29,999 (16.3 per cent, n=194) and £40,000–£49,999 (13.8 per cent,

[19] ibid.

[20] Hilary Sommerlad, 'I've Lost the Plot: An Everyday Story of Legal Aid Lawyers' (2001) 28 *Journal of Law and Society* 335; Jacqueline Kinghan, Lawyers, *Networks and Progressive Social Change: Lawyers Changing Lives* (Hart, 2021); Daniel Newman and Jon Robins, *Justice in a Time of Austerity: Stories of a System in Crisis* (Bristol University Press, 2021).

[21] See eg, Donald Gardener et al, 'The Effects of Pay Level on Organization-Based Self-Esteem and Performance: A Field Study' (2004) 77 *Journal of Occupational and Organizational Psychology* 307.

[22] Sherr (n 6) 327.

n=163). In total, 7.1 per cent of respondents received £9,999–£19,999 (n=84) and 1.1 per cent (n= 13) received less than £9,999. Taken together, more than half of legal aid practitioners (57.6 per cent, n=682) earn £49,999 or less.

Figure 5.1 Annual salary of current legal aid practitioners (n=1,185)

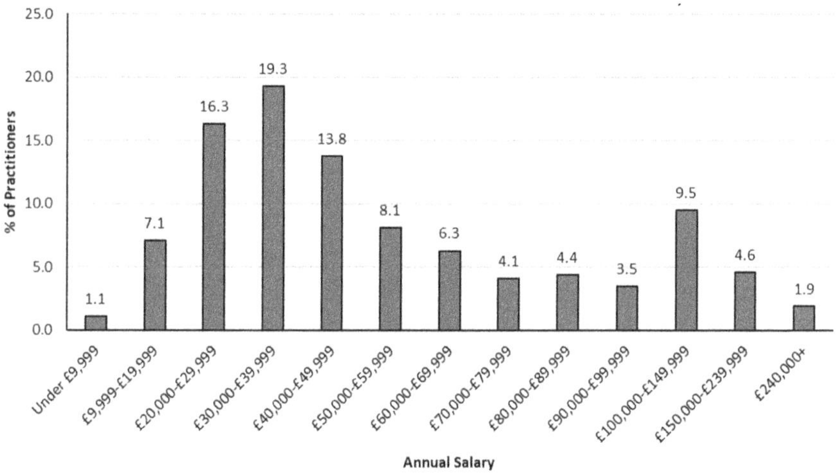

It is notable that 8.2 per cent (n=97) of practitioners earn less than £19,999. This salary falls below the current minimum trainee salary recommended by the Law Society, which is set at £23,703 in London and £21,024 outside of London.[23] It is perhaps surprising that of those earning less than £19,999, at least 17 (17.5 per cent) are fully qualified solicitors and several act as heads of department (see Figure 5.2 below).

A total of 42.4 per cent of practitioners (n=503) earn more than £50,000. The most common salaries in the upper range were £50,000–£59,999 (8.1 per cent, n=96) and £100,000–£149,999 (9.5 per cent, n=112). Figure 5.2 breaks down salary information by principal role of practitioners. A small number of practitioners (1.9 per cent, n=23) reported earning £240,000 or more. Of these, 87.0 per cent (n =20) reported their principal role as 'barrister' with 8.7 per cent (n=2) indicating they were 'head of chambers' and only one respondent (4.3 per cent) holding the role of solicitor. Notably, of those earning £100,000–£149,999 only four practitioners provided only legal aid services. There were no practitioners earning £150,000–£239,999 providing only legal aid services, whilst just one practitioner earning in excess of £240,000 provided only legal aid services. All these practitioners nominated their principal role as 'barrister'. Therefore, out of the

[23] The Law Society of England and Wales, 'Recommended Minimum Salary for Trainees and SQE Candidates' (The Law Society, 25 July 2022), available at www.lawsociety.org.uk/topics/hr-and-people-management/recommended-minimum-salary-for-trainee-solicitors-and-sqe-candidates.

188 practitioners earning more than £100,000, only five (2.7 per cent) provided legal aid services in isolation, and all were barristers.[24]

Figure 5.2 Annual salary of current legal aid practitioners by principal role (n=1,184)

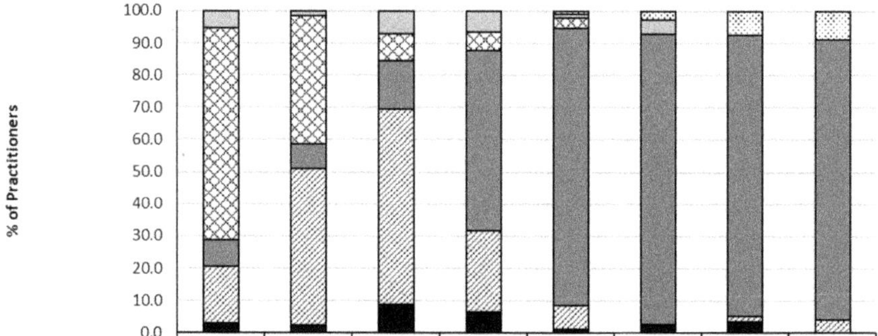

	Under £19,999	£20,000- £39,999	£40,000- £59,999	£60,000- £79,999	£80,000- £99,999	£100,000- £149,999	£150,000- £239,999	£240,000+
Head of Chambers	0.0	0.0	0.0	0.0	1.1	2.7	7.3	8.7
Director	5.2	1.4	7.0	6.5	1.1	4.5	0.0	0.0
Other	66.0	39.8	8.5	5.7	3.2	0.0	0.0	0.0
Barrister	8.2	7.8	15.1	56.1	86.2	90.2	87.3	87.0
Solicitor	17.5	48.6	60.5	25.2	7.4	0.0	1.8	4.3
Head of Department	3.1	2.4	8.9	6.5	1.1	2.7	3.6	0.0

Annual Salary

The gap between commercial and legal aid salaries is arguably the largest it has ever been, with most legal aid salaries for solicitors, regardless of the number of years in practice, being significantly less than newly qualified lawyers in the corporate legal sector. As discussed in the last chapter, most practitioners report that they do not think the salary and working conditions for their roles are fair. The threat this poses to the socio-economic diversity of the profession has been explored in chapter two. Many practitioners noted the stagnant rates of pay (see Table 4.3 in chapter four), where fees have not risen in line with inflation:

> I received a 10 per cent pay cut in 2013–14 and it took 5 years to finally get that back. I have then only had a small remuneration since then. Therefore, it is not in line with the cost of living and I have not had an increment since 2019. It is unlikely I will have one in the next few years. We should receive cost of living rises every year. It is appalling. Every year we are told it is due to legal aid cuts and no increase in fees.[25]

> No pay rise since September 2006. My bills go up. I'm robbing Peter to pay Paul. When I started, salaried partners/senior lawyers of my experience earned the same as GPs/

[24] We note that barristers' rates of pay are subject to a reduction in earnings by way of rent payable to chambers. Of 392 barrister respondents who supplied rent information, the average proportion of salary payable to chambers was 16.6% of earnings. At the top end, the maximum amount of chambers rent paid was 30% of earnings.

[25] Practitioner Respondent Number 27.

> dentists/MPs/head teachers. Now we earn maybe half their salaries when our work is even more onerous. I didn't expect the riches of commercial work. But I did expect fair pay.[26]

This strongly aligns with evidence submitted to the Justice Committee on the Future of Legal Aid. For example, Welsh noted in her evidence to the Justice Committee that in criminal legal aid the 8.75 per cent fee cut to the Litigator Graduated Fee Scheme in 2014 and the lack of fee increases for over 20 years 'has led to market contraction and reduced firms' capacity to conduct legal aid work and reduced capacity for training contracts and pupillages.'[27] Likewise, it is clear that the relationship between the fee arrangements and the overall remuneration practitioners receive by way of salary or any additional profit-sharing is complex. One respondent noted that they would rather have a 'graded salary system', as exists for other public sector workers such as doctors or teachers, but that the 'entire construction of the costs regime appears to hold the sector hostage to thinking in these terms.'[28] This relates to the point elucidated by Moorhead, and explored above, as to whether the judicare model is itself sustainable or alternatives require closer consideration.

III. Fixed Fees

A. Working under Fixed Fees

The 2006 Carter review of legal aid had recommended 'moving away from a system which simply rewards hours worked, and towards one that rewards the case as a whole.'[29] Fixed fees were therefore introduced and intended to 'encourage efficiency and innovation.'[30] Despite some opposition from the sector, the Government expressed its 'firm view' that it was the right course in order to 'encourage a focus on the work required' and promote 'best value'.[31] The fee arrangements were part of a wider gradual shift towards price competitive tendering (known as best-value tendering) for legal aid contracts.[32] According to Census responses, fixed fees now comprise the most common form of arrangement under which individual practitioners are remunerated for their work. A total of 70.1 per cent (n=829) of 1182 practitioner respondents worked under fixed-fee arrangements, compared to 29.9 per cent (n=353) who did not. The most common areas for fixed fees were crime (33.5 per cent, n=273),

[26] Practitioner Respondent Number 840.
[27] House of Commons Justice Committee (n 5) para 33.
[28] Practitioner Respondent Number 1181.
[29] Department for Constitutional Affairs, 'Legal Aid: The Way Ahead' (Cmd 6993) (HMSO, 2006) 7.
[30] ibid, 6.
[31] ibid, 11.
[32] This form of tendering no longer exists in the way it was originally envisaged.

public family law (25.9 per cent, n=211) and private family law (24.3 per cent, n=198).

The magnitude of the shift towards bureaucracy and managerialism described above is well evidenced by Census findings in relation to fixed fee arrangements. Despite the efficiency aims of the fixed-fee regime, practitioners observe that they present a variety of challenges in practice. We also note that a high number of respondents were unclear about the fees that applied to their area of practice, for example, because others took care of billing or because of the complexity of the fee arrangements. Consistent with findings explored in the last chapter – wherein practitioners reported having to work beyond set or designated hours – respondents provided additional concerning details regarding the extent to which they engaged in unpaid work under fixed fees. Excluding those who did not provide a clear indication of which fixed fees applied to their work in their response,[33] a very high proportion of responses given by practitioners (94.1 per cent, n=333 of 354) overall indicated that the fixed fees did not adequately cover the number of hours actually worked to complete a fixed-fee task. A far smaller proportion of responses indicated that it took less time to complete a fixed-fee case than the number of hours afforded under the fixed-fee regime (2.8 per cent, n=10) whilst 3.1 per cent of responses (n=11) indicated that the number of hours covered under the fixed fee matched the number of hours it took to complete the work.

In total, the responses provided by practitioners indicated that 100 per cent of the fixed-fee work conducted in the areas of public family law, welfare benefits, prison law, discrimination, education and actions against the police took more hours to complete than was paid. Areas where responses indicated that fixed-fee work took less or the same number of hours as was paid are listed in Table 5.1.[34] There were only a small number of responses which pointed to practitioners being paid for longer than they worked.[35] Given the anomalous nature of these responses, it is worth looking at them in greater depth. Of the 10 responses provided by six respondents, one referred to the time taken to complete a straightforward divorce (three to four minutes) versus the number of hours afforded under a fixed fee for legal help in respect of a divorce petition (£146 + VAT). Two responses provided by a single respondent indicated that with regards to the asylum legal help fixed

[33] In total, 1,208 respondents gave 1391 responses when asked to indicate the specific fixed fees they worked under, the number of hours of work the fixed fee was intended to cover and the number of hours of work that the fixed-fee case actually took. Percentages are calculated excluding 1,037 responses because they either provided (i) no answer to the number of hours taken and/or the number of hours paid by the LAA, (ii) responses that were unclear, (iii) indicated that each case varied and an average could not be produced or (iv) indicated that they didn't know. The total number of useable responses relied upon to produce these statistics equalled 354.

[34] There were 21 responses that could not be linked to a specific practice area and are excluded from this analysis.

[35] These were in crime, private family law, immigration and asylum, and housing. There were some responses in relation to crime, immigration and asylum, community care, mental health and public law which indicated that the time paid was equivalent to the time worked. Data was not available in respect of debt, mediation, clinical negligence, claims against public authorities, and Court of Protection work.

fee and the asylum-controlled representation fixed fee at Stage 1, the fixed fee covered between eight and nine hours whilst the work under the fixed fee could be completed in eight hours.

Table 5.1 Practice areas where responses indicated current legal aid practitioners were being paid for a longer period of hours than was worked, or for the same number of hours as worked

	Work longer than paid		**Paid for longer than worked**		**Paid for the same time as worked**	
	N	%	N	%	N	%
Crime	36	81.8	3	6.8	5	11.4
Family (private)	19	90.5	2	9.5	0	0.0
Immigration and asylum	50	90.9	4	7.3	1	1.8
Housing	64	98.5	1	1.5	0	0.0
Community care	18	94.7	0	0.0	1	5.3
Mental health	10	83.3	0	0.0	2	16.7
Public law	33	97.1	0	0.0	1	2.9

A response provided by a different practitioner relating to the same Stage 1 fixed-fee work estimated that the fixed fee covers 10–15 hours of work; however, the work itself can take approximately seven to eight hours. Another response – one of three provided by the practitioner – referred to fees for a magistrates' court trial as covering five hours although the work could be completed in four to five hours. It is notable that this was the only one of the three responses provided by this practitioner which was seen as being capable of completion in fewer hours than afforded under the fixed fees. Of the other fees referred to by this practitioner, the magistrate's court guilty plea fixed fee was deemed to take a greater number of hours to complete than was paid, whilst the police station attendance fee took the same number of hours to complete as was paid. Therefore, for a small minority of practitioners across different practice areas, fixed fees achieved their stated goal of efficiency in terms of either being able to work within the designated time. However, this was not the case for the vast majority of practitioners (94.1 per cent, n=333 of 354 as cited above).

Table 5.2 (with outliers removed) shows the differences between hours worked and hours remunerated under the fixed-fee scheme.[36] The data in the table reflects

[36] Outliers were removed using the 1.5 +/− Interquartile Range (IQR) method. In addition to removing outliers, these statistics also exclude those who did not provide answers in respect of both (i) the number of hours covered by the fixed fee and the (ii) number of hours taken on average to complete that fixed-fee work. 224 refers to the number of responses not the number of unique respondents (n=163), recognising that a single practitioner may provide information in respect of more than one fixed fee.

the responses which indicated that the number of hours taken to complete work under the fixed fee exceeded the number of hours paid (n=224). Relying on the median, the data revealed the fixed-fee amount as covering 4.5 hours of work, with the work performed under that fixed fee actually amounting to 10 hours. With a ratio of number of hours worked for every hour paid at 2.1:1, only 57 minutes of every two hours of work performed is remunerated under the fixed-fee regime.[37] Alternatively, this can be understood as requiring 106 minutes of work for every 60 minutes of remuneration.

Table 5.2 Summary statistics in relation to current legal aid practitioners hours worked and hours remunerated under the fixed-fee scheme (outliers removed) (n=224)

	Number of hours paid for under the fixed fee	**Number of hours taken to complete work under the fixed fee**	**Number of hours worked for every hour paid**
Mean (SD)	5.1 (2.6)	12.0 (7.2)	2.5 (1.1)
Median	4.5	10.0	2.1
Mode	3.0	10.0	2.0

Breaking these statistics down by practice area revealed which areas attracted a discrepancy well above the norm of 2.1:1. As detailed in Table 5.3, these included welfare benefits work (which attracted a ratio of 4.3 hours worked for every one hour remunerated), community care work (which attracted a ratio of 2.5 hours worked for every one hour remunerated), and public law work (where the ratio was 2.3 hours of work for every one hour remunerated). Private family immigration and asylum, and housing work attracted a ratio of 2.2:1, or only slightly above the overall median of 2.1:1. Only education was associated with a ratio that was more than 0.1 below the overall ratio at 1.8; however, the veracity of this discrepancy is constrained by the low number of responses provided for this practice area.

These findings align with wider research highlighting the disparity between hours worked and hours paid under the fixed-fee regime across different areas of legal aid practice. For example, it has been noted that remuneration in the field of immigration and asylum is insufficient to cover the work high-quality practitioners and organisations actually do.[38] In Wilding's study of the immigration legal aid market, she found that costs were 'two to three times the standard fee' for solicitors and they were in fact paid for 'only a half or two fifths of the work done'.[39]

[37] When leaving outliers in (n=283), the medians for the 'Number of hours paid under the fixed fee', the 'Number of hours worked under the fixed fee' and the number of hours worked for every hour paid were 5.0, 12.5 and 2.2 respectively, the modes remained unchanged and the means were higher at 7.6 (8.9), 19.1 (18.1) and 3.3 (3.3) respectively.

[38] Jo Wilding, 'Droughts and Deserts: A Report on the Immigration Legal Aid Market' (University of Brighton, 2019), 25.

[39] ibid, 26.

For barristers, the simplest case involved costs of 1.5 times the fee paid for doing the work.[40] Wilding observes that the result was that lawyers lose money on every case they deal with under fixed fees, which has a number of important knock-on impacts. Firstly, organisations have to subsidise the loss from other areas including grant funding, charitable funding or by undertaking other non-legal work.[41] Secondly, practitioners and organisations are incentivised to adopt questionable working practices to cut costs, for example, 'cherry-picking' cases such as those that might be paid on hourly rates and turning away 'walk-in' enquiries.[42] Wilding also argues that in this environment, poor-quality providers are more likely to thrive because they have 'chosen to reconcile financial viability and client access by reducing quality' by, for example, using less qualified staff to complete work.[43] It has also been argued that the incentives towards delivering poorer quality work has been further exacerbated by the Civil Legal Aid (Remuneration) Coronavirus Regulations 2020, which increased hourly rates but significantly reduced costs recoverable in complex cases.[44]

In crime, the impact of fee arrangements on case management and the quality of service provision has been widely explored.[45] The research tends to suggest that criminal legal aid lawyers are in fact influenced by financial incentives in their decision-making around cases, especially where finance is one of several competing considerations.[46] Thornton also asserts that fee conditions encourage poor working practices and concludes that policymakers should be mindful of the 'risks of financial self-interest focussed practice' and 'inefficient working' in implementing reforms.[47] The incentivisation and considerations at play vary widely across the many types of fee arrangements at different levels of criminal proceedings for solicitors and barristers. The discrepancy between hours worked and hours paid is well set out in the Independent Review of Criminal Legal Aid's discussion of the graduated fee scheme. It is acknowledged that the calculations are highly complex but that the 'main driver of the litigators' fee is the PPE [pages of prosecution evidence] irrespective of the work actually done on the case'.[48] Again, this has resulted in a system which encourages perverse

[40] ibid, 25.
[41] ibid, 26.
[42] ibid.
[43] ibid, 27.
[44] O'Nions (n 2) 329.
[45] See eg Daniel Newman, *Legal Aid Lawyers and the Quest for Justice* (Hart, 2013); Peter Tague, 'Barristers' Selfish Incentives in Counselling Clients' (2008) *Criminal Law Review* 3; Hilary Sommerlad, 'Criminal Legal Aid Reforms and the Restructuring of Legal Professionalism' in Richard Young and David Wall (eds), *Access to Criminal Justice: Legal Aid Lawyers and the Defence of Liberty* (Blackstone, 1996) 307.
[46] Cyrus Tata, 'In the Interests of Clients or Commerce? Legal Aid, Supply, Demand and "Ethical Indeterminacy" in Criminal Defence Work' (2007) 34 *Journal of Law and Society* 489, 496.
[47] James Thornton, 'The Way in Which Fee Reductions Influence Legal Aid Criminal Defence Lawyer Work: Insights from a Qualitative Study' (2019) 46 *Journal of Law and Society* 559, 585.
[48] ibid, 94.

incentives and fails to prioritise high-quality legal representation. As Bellamy notes in the review:

> In my view the central weakness of the LGFS [Litigators' Graduated Fee Scheme] is that it is based very largely on the pages served, not on work done or even on whether the pages are read or not. This does not incentivise providers to do the actual work they are supposed to do but rather incentivises firms to try to obtain cases with a large amount of served material, and then delay the outcome until the trial begins.[49]

The problems presented by the fee regime in the context of criminal defence work are extensive. For example, the time-consuming nature of deciding what constitutes PPE diverts focus and attention away from simply deciding 'whether a litigator's work was reasonably done'.[50] The Review also found evidence of firms being incentivised to use cases with higher PPE to cross subsidise other work, to make applications to the Court to transfer a legal aid certificate simply to gain revenue, to make applications for further disclosure made with a view to increasing the PPE; or changing a plea to guilty shortly after the start of the trial, thus triggering an increased fee than would have been payable in the case of an earlier guilty plea.[51] The incentives to engage in practices of this nature raise obvious access to justice concerns, as they are not being driven by the needs of clients and may well be in conflict with them. As Bellamy notes, 'a fee scheme should minimise the possibility of conflict between the client's best interests and the interests of the provider'; however, the criminal defence graduated fee scheme has largely failed to do so.[52] He argues that the misaligned incentives of the scheme can be alleviated by introducing a fee regime similar to that used in the Magistrates' Court in Crown Court cases and would allow for exceptional fees in non-standard cases.

Table 5.3 Median number of hours worked, hours remunerated, and the median ratio given between the two under the fixed-fee scheme by area of law reported by current legal aid practitioners (outliers removed) (n=224)

	Responses provided	**Number of hours paid for under the fixed fee**	**Number of hours taken to complete work under the fixed fee**	**Number of hours worked for every hour paid**
	N	**Median**	**Median**	**Median**
Family (public)	7	6.0	9.0	2.0
Crime	30	4.0	8.5	2.0
Family (private)	12	3.0	10.0	2.2
Welfare benefits	3	3.5	15.0	4.3

(continued)

[49] ibid, 95.
[50] ibid, 96.
[51] ibid, 97.
[52] ibid.

Table 5.3 ***(Continued)***

	Responses provided	Number of hours paid for under the fixed fee	Number of hours taken to complete work under the fixed fee	Number of hours worked for every hour paid
	N	Median	Median	Median
Immigration and asylum	33	8.0	20.0	2.2
Housing	57	3.0	7.5	2.2
Prison law	7	5.0	10.0	2.0
Community care	13	5.0	10.0	2.5
Mental health	9	7.0	15.0	2.0
Public law	26	5.0	13.5	2.3
Education	1	5.5	10.0	1.8
AATP	5	6.0	15.0	2.1

It is also notable that the discrepancy between hours worked and those paid in the area of welfare benefits is high, at 4.3 hours worked for every hour paid. Legal aid is only in scope for welfare benefits for cases to the Upper Tribunal and higher courts. However, the area of welfare benefits is one where clustering of legal problems tends to be high and it can be time-consuming dealing with the complex medical and wider circumstances of a client's case. Gathering the wealth of evidence needed in such cases can be particularly time-consuming[53] and can lead to large amounts of unpaid labour, as explored further below.[54]

B. The Viability of Fixed Fees

Census responses indicate that current practitioners perceive there to be a wide range of issues and challenges inherent in the fixed-fee regime. In total, 85.8 per cent (n=659) of the 768 practitioners who responded did not think the fixed-fee regime was sustainable. A smaller number of respondents said they did not know (8.5 per cent, n=65) and 6.1 per cent (n=47) thought that the regime was sustainable.[55]

[53] See eg Lisa Vanhala and Jacqueline Kinghan, 'The "madness" of accessing justice: legal mobilisation, welfare benefits and empowerment' (2022) 44 *Journal of Social Welfare and Family Law* 22.

[54] Data was not available in respect of debt, mediation, clinical negligence, claims against public authorities, and Court of Protection work. 21 responses that could not be linked to a practice area were not included in this table.

[55] Three practitioners answered yes and no to this question, and then qualified their response in an open-ended follow-up question by indicating that they were referring to two separate areas of law.

Practitioners elaborated on their responses in their own words and a number of common themes were identified. Table 5.4 below details the top 10 substantive explanations given by practitioners to explain their view on the sustainability of fixed fees. A majority of respondents identified that the levels of pay were simply too low or were not sufficiently motivating (28.0 per cent, n=115) and a further 20.4 per cent (n=84) commented that cases took much longer than provided for by the fixed-fee regime. In total, 18.2 per cent (n=75) referenced that the rates had not been increased in some time, 13.6 per cent (n=56) said they could not break even or otherwise had concerns in relation to profit and loss and 9.5 per cent (n=39) set out challenges in relation to how several different types of costs had to be subtracted from fixed fee rates. As one practitioner notes, 'The level of work required per case is not reflected in the fee. In order to earn sufficiently, we need to take on more and more work which is unsustainable and crippling.'[56]

Other responses included concerns about how to sustain the profession in view of poor rates of pay under fixed-fee arrangements (17.0 per cent, n=70) as well as concerns that the structure of the fee system did not adequately ensure that legal aid practitioners could meet client needs (5.8 per cent, n=24). Many respondents highlighted the extent to which legal aid clients required increased levels of support which is not accommodated by the fee regime – for instance, due to mental or physical ill-health conditions. Practitioners explained further:

> A domestic abuse case is £507. This kind of work includes meeting an extremely vulnerable client for the first time, seek[ing] their confidence to open up about traumatic abuse, prepar[ing] a detailed statement and application, serv[ing] papers, attend[ing] potentially two hearings, liais[ing] with [them,] etc. I would say these cases generally require around 25–30 hours of work.[57]

However, 'The fee paid per hour is not reflective of the experience required to conduct cases that are complex. The clients can often be very demanding with mental and physical illnesses.'[58]

A fixed fee of £507 for 25 hours' work, for example, would equate to £20.28 per hour, which falls far short of the 'competitive' rates of pay envisaged by the sustainability proposals made by the Westminster Commission on Legal Aid set out above. Relatedly, it is notable that, whilst not appearing in the top 10 detailed in Table 5.4 below, 1.2 per cent of practitioners (n=5) reported that the rates of pay forced reliance on family members for financial support.[59]

[56] Practitioner Respondent Number 514.

[57] Practitioner Respondent Number 1037.

[58] Practitioner Respondent Number 1159.

[59] Responses not listed in Table 5.4 include: reduces service offered to clients (5.4%, n=22); does not reflect practitioner expertise or experience (3.6%, n=15); it is sustainable/fair in some examples but not necessarily all (3.6%, n=15); legal aid work is a vocation, not a profit-making enterprise (3.4%, n=14); leads to overwork (3.4%, n=14); can't answer (2.9%, n=12); high-costs cases are a problem (1.5%, n=6); forces reliance on family (1.2%, n=5); other (1.02%, n=5).

Especially in light of the wider evidence in relation to adverse impacts upon service provision, a notable response (again, not detailed in Table 5.4) included the view of 5.4 per cent (n=22) of practitioners that rates forced a reduced service or quality offering. One respondent commented, for example, that the fee regime 'incentivises low quality work' and further notes the relationship between inadequate pay, poor quality and experiences of burn-out.[60] Another said the low fees meant prioritisation of 'easy low risk work and shirking attempts to break new ground.'[61] Others elaborate, saying that: 'The fixed fees do not provide adequate time to complete the work required to give a good level of service. We have to go over the fixed fee to meet even the absolute minimum criteria to pass peer review.'[62] Another respondent asserted that 'In crime they encourage poor preparation as they are too low by such a proportion that they are not likely to be changed to reflect a reasonable level of remuneration.'[63] One respondent observed that 'Fees have not increased over the years. Many good advocates refuse to do legal aid work or at least certain legal aid work once they are senior. The result is very junior people handling complex cases which are beyond their capabilities.'[64]

Several respondents also highlight that in order to provide a good quality, professional service they simply have to work beyond the hours they are paid: 'It is difficult to say exactly how long a case will take to prepare but the continuing cuts means that in order to properly fulfil our legal obligations to our clients, we will always be working at a loss.'[65] Another respondent stated: 'I am a professional. I will spend as long as it takes to prepare a case.'[66]

Table 5.4 Top 10 responses given by current legal aid practitioners as to why fixed fees were not sustainable (n=411)

	N	%
Poor rates of pay	115	28.0
Cases take longer than fixed regime suggests	84	20.4
Lack of increase in rates	75	18.2
Practitioners leaving/refusing to do legal aid work	70	17.0
Cannot break even/cases make a loss	56	13.6
Ignores other costs (eg tax, waiting, rent, admin, hiring other practitioners)	39	9.5
Problems with escape fee/claims procedures	32	7.8

(continued)

[60] Practitioner Respondent Number 1071.
[61] Practitioner Respondent Number 1181.
[62] Practitioner Respondent Number 1148.
[63] Practitioner Respondent Number 45.
[64] Practitioner Respondent Number 416.
[65] Practitioner Respondent Number 766.
[66] Practitioner Respondent Number 719.

Table 5.4 ***(Continued)***

	N	%
Needing to subsidise with other work	31	7.5
Needing to work long hours for volume/must work hard to make it work	26	6.3
Cannot attend to needs of clients	24	5.8

A majority of practitioners generally expressed a sense of exasperation in terms of what is expected of them under the fixed-fee regime; for instance, one practitioner observed that 'Nobody else would be expected to work for the fixed fee work. The work is complicated, the clients are vulnerable and it can often take significant time going through documents and dealing with the issues.'[67]

In the criminal legal aid context, many respondents noted the problem of time spent waiting – often due to delays in the system – which are unremunerated. Several referenced that even within the context of remote hearings, these 'delays' are still challenging:

> Fixed fee for a police station attendance varies due to day and time. Travel time and cost is only occasionally chargeable. Delays out of my control, i.e. no interpreter/appropriate adult/nurse practitioner/mental health assessment available, increase the hours I am required in attendance … I may spend hours waiting around, unable to deal with anything. Equate the time spent to the fixed fee and it is very little.[68]

Another respondent stated that with 'regard to waiting, wasted time due to inefficiencies in the criminal justice system endemic across the board [I] probably average about £25 per hour.'[69]

Several barrister respondents pointed to the problem of wasted preparation on cases that may be 'returned' to other barristers should they, for example, have a diary clash as a result of repeated adjournments.[70] The returns system has largely relied on the goodwill of barristers for some time, but it is taking its toll amidst other challenges and pressures. The Criminal Bar Association highlights in particular that having lost almost a quarter of full-time criminal barristers since 2017, there are a high number of court adjournments due to a lack of available barristers to prosecute and defend.[71] At the time of writing, criminal barristers in England and Wales have been engaged in industrial action involving a 'no returns' policy in order to push for an uplift on rates of pay by

[67] Practitioner Respondent Number 205.

[68] Practitioner Respondent Number 123.

[69] Practitioner Respondent Number 290.

[70] The Criminal Bar Association defines 'return' in the Crown Court as 'any instruction to appear in any hearing, in relation to any case, in which another advocate is, or was, instructed as the trial advocate'. See The Criminal Bar Association of England and Wales, '"No Returns" Guidance 2022' (The Criminal Bar Association of England and Wales, 18 March 2022), available at www.criminalbar.com/wp-content/uploads/2022/03/CBA-No-Returns-Guidance-18th-March-2022-.pdf.

[71] ibid, 1.

25 per cent. The following respondent highlights the impact of adjournments on remuneration:

> We are expected to do a huge amount of preparation work on a case which one would ordinarily do. However, when courts unilaterally change trial dates and move it to a date that is not convenient, who pays me for the wasted hours of preparation? The wasted prep payment facility is paltry and is an affront to what we actually have to do. It would be far preferable if there was an hourly rate paid for preparation on a case. That way if the case had to be returned to another barrister at least you will be able to claim for the work done on it.[72]

A further challenge highlighted by respondents (7.8 per cent, n=32) is the time-consuming nature of claiming for legal aid or dealing with the LAA. Several respondents elaborated on this point with reference to Legal Help in particular:

> The reality is the time spent on the paperwork signing someone up for Legal Help and then reporting on it to the LAA exceeds the costs recoverable under the fixed fees. So essentially all work is carried out at a loss. It is worth taking this risk if we think that there is a viable chance of the matter proceeding to litigation but we have to limit the advice and assistance we offer to ensure that we have a viable practice. Often we don't even bother signing a client up for Legal Help and just do the initial work 'at risk' because it saves time and expense.[73]

More generally, some senior practitioners expressed concern that rates of pay are 'a fraction' of that which is paid privately and will as such 'drain' the profession in future. As evidenced by discussion in other chapters, this is a recurring theme across different parts of the Census. In a similar vein, others expressed lament at the lack of progression given stagnant rates of pay alongside the hours that need to be worked:

> I am a very experienced QC in practice for nearly 35 years. I love the work I do but have to work extremely hard. I am fortunate to have been able to supplement the legal aid work I have done with privately paid work. That is not always possible. I am conscious that many people would consider I earn a lot of money but would be horrified by the number of hours I have to work to do so ...[74]
>
> Pay rates have remained the same for the last 20 years or so. Our income has not kept pace with inflation & increases in the cost of living. Staff wages & overheads have continued to increase but our income has not kept up with increases outlined earlier. As a 64 year old solicitor who qualified in 1981 I earn less now than I earned 15 years ago for the same return.[75]

As shown in Table 5.5 below, the majority of respondents indicated that they did not think fixed fees were sustainable; however, a higher proportion of 'I don't

[72] Practitioner Respondent Number 474.
[73] Practitioner Respondent Number 1066.
[74] Practitioner Respondent Number 259.
[75] Practitioner Respondent Number 51.

know' responses was noted in relation to public and private family law, education and court of protection work relative to the number of respondents saying 'yes' or 'no'. A higher proportion of respondents in family law and undertaking inquest work also considered that fixed fees were sustainable as compared to other areas. This may be explained by the fact that family law practitioners are perhaps more likely to take on private work in order to subsidise their legal aid work. Whilst 100 per cent of respondents indicated that the fixed fees for employment law were sustainable, the low number of respondents (n=1) limits the inferences that can be drawn in relation to the practice area.

Table 5.5 Whether current legal aid practitioners viewed fixed fees as sustainable by practice area (n=765)

	Yes		**No**		**Don't know**	
	N	**Row %**	**N**	**Row %**	**N**	**Row %**
Crime	11	4.1	247	91.5	14	5.2
Prison law	3	7.3	36	87.8	2	4.9
Claims against public authorities	3	4.5	61	91.0	4	6.0
Community care	1	1.4	64	92.8	4	5.8
Debt	0	0.0	8	100.0	0	0.0
Discrimination	2	5.9	32	94.1	0	0.0
Education	1	6.3	13	81.3	2	12.5
Mediation	0	0.0	8	100.0	0	0.0
Housing	2	1.6	117	91.4	9	7.0
Immigration and asylum	3	3.0	91	91.0	6	6.0
Family (public)	26	11.6	169	75.4	31	13.8
Family (private)	20	9.7	156	75.4	32	15.5
Clinical negligence	0	0.0	3	100.0	0	0.0
Mental health	4	7.1	46	82.1	6	10.7
Public law	6	3.5	153	88.4	14	8.1
Welfare benefits	0	0.0	23	95.8	1	4.2
Court of Protection	2	3.1	53	81.5	10	15.4
Inquests	1	25.0	3	75.0	0	0.0
AATP	0	0.0	1	100.0	0	0.0
Employment	1	100.0	0	0.0	0	0.0

Notably, no respondents holding positions as heads of department, directors or practice managers considered the fixed-fee arrangements to be sustainable. Across practitioner roles, a majority of solicitors (86.6 per cent, n=258), barristers

(84.2 per cent, n=192) and caseworkers (100.0 per cent, n=30) found the fixed fee arrangements to be unsustainable.

C. Mitigating Losses under Fixed Fees

Practitioners were explicitly asked how they mitigate loss under the fixed-fee regime. While some practitioners acknowledged that they engaged in a variety of activities to try to mitigate loss, most did not think it was possible to do so. Responses given by 321 practitioners revealed that the majority did not think anything could be done to mitigate loss because clients' needs had to be met and/or the best interests of clients had to be served (34.0 per cent, n=109). A number of respondents also indicated the need to take on private work as a way of compensating for loss (18.4 per cent, n=59), or to work longer hours or otherwise increase the volume of work in order to mitigate the loss (13.1 per cent, n=42). For example, one practitioner commented: 'I have to work longer hours and take less annual leave than my privately funded counterparts. I sacrifice my weekends and evenings regularly. I cannot afford to take prep days unless I really have to.'[76]

A total of 11.5 per cent of respondents (n=37) said they tried to change the fee type in some way, with the majority of responses within this group saying they would try to 'break the escape limit'. One respondent said they would always try to do so 'whenever justified and possible.'[77] Others said breaking the escape limit sometimes involved 'artificially increasing costs' such as 'drafting case summaries'[78] or 'drafting long orders'.[79] Others noted, however, that it was sometimes simply not possible to meet the escape threshold:

> Most cases I take on just by their nature will require substantial amounts of work, and that usually takes the case 3× over the fixed fee. That means in most cases I am paid for the actual work done, albeit it at very low hourly rates. However, it is impossible to avoid the possibility of a case concluding with costs well above the fixed fee but not 3× over the fixed fee, in which cases there is a loss.[80]

Legal help in particular was mentioned in relation to escape fees; for instance, 'We try to make legal help case[s] go beyond the escape fee threshold, [and] adjust which cases you take on. Not really worth doing negative advice legal help as it will be loss leading.'[81] Relatedly, some responses are indicative of a 'swings and roundabouts'[82] approach to legal aid casework where loss is mitigated across

[76] Practitioner Respondent Number 870.
[77] Practitioner Respondent Number 842.
[78] Practitioner Respondent Number 335.
[79] Practitioner Respondent Number 1005.
[80] Practitioner Respondent Number 624.
[81] Practitioner Respondent Number 1139.
[82] Practitioner Respondent Number 119.

different cases. For example, one respondent noted that while they will work to escape the limit in some cases, they 'do less work than the fixed fee in other cases'[83] and another observed that it 'all balances out between cases.'[84] In relation to criminal casework, the role of PPE in mitigating loss was also acknowledged in this context: 'Within crime, the small number of high page count Crown Court cases subsidise the 95 [per cent] of break even or loss making cases.'[85]

Whilst the fixed-fee regime was introduced with the intention of removing the incentive for practitioners to accumulate hours unnecessarily on hourly paid work, it is notable that so few respondents (5.9 per cent, n=19) identified efficiency or time management as feasible mitigation strategies. Troublingly, almost double the number of respondents (11.2 per cent, n=36) indicated that they limited the fixed-fee cases they took on or elected not to undertake fixed-fee cases likely to lose money. For example, one respondent asserted that '[We] take on fewer legal aid cases [and] avoid cases where we think they will be unprofitable because of the fixed fee.'[86] Another acknowledged that 'I specifically try to take on cases I won't lose money by staying on circuit etc.'[87] Other respondents concur:

> We have had to stop accepting some legal help work because the fixed fees were even lower and we would make a loss on our time and they are heavily audited. It is not worth the time doing the work for money and with an expectation of exceptional service.[88]
>
> To mitigate these losses we minimise the number of cases we take on which involve early stage advice. We have to ensure that the bulk of our work is actual litigation (in a costs shifting regime) to have any chance of viability.[89]

Another respondent specifically mentioned *inter partes* costs orders – the costs orders made against an opposing party in a case – as a way to recover costs in relation to unpaid work. However, they also highlighted the difficulty in adopting a strategy of selecting cases on this basis:

> We aim to take on primarily fixed fee cases which are likely to lead to an inter partes costs order against the defendant; however, it is difficult to make this assessment, and on many cases we therefore make a (significant) loss. It also means that cases which are meritorious but unlikely to result in inter partes costs being recovered are unlikely to be taken on, meaning those prospective clients do not get access to advice and representation due to the low level of fixed fees for Legal Help work.[90]

[83] Practitioner Respondent Number 844.
[84] Practitioner Respondent Number 1193.
[85] Practitioner Respondent Number 61.
[86] Practitioner Respondent Number 249.
[87] Practitioner Respondent Number 547.
[88] Practitioner Respondent Number 1054.
[89] Practitioner Respondent Number 1066.
[90] Practitioner Respondent Number 465.

A total of 4.7 per cent (n=15) of respondents – those predominantly working in law centres and charities – indicated that they were able to mitigate losses by having different forms of grant funding to supplement their work. For example:

> As a Law Centre we have been lucky to be able to secure non LAA funding. My last legal aid high street private practice firm closed as it was not possible to mitigate against such losses (together with other problems surviving on [legal aid] income.[91]

Another law centre respondent said they always make sure they have 'other funded projects' running alongside their casework.[92]

Table 5.6 Top 10 responses given by current legal aid practitioners to improve the viability of the fixed-fee regime (n=458)

	N	%
Increase fees	237	51.7
Return to hourly rates	61	13.3
Abandon fixed fees	60	13.1
Wider reforms (eg lower threshold for hourly rates, easier to access escape fee cases, less complexity)	58	12.7
Remunerate additional work (eg administration, preparation, travel, meetings)	44	9.6
Increase pay	41	9.0
Annual increases tracking inflation	39	8.5
Increase hourly rates	37	8.1
Increase rates for serious or complex cases and / or more flexibility	28	6.1
Other (eg change time periods, criticism of LAA, belief legal aid practice is unsustainable)	20	4.4

In response to an open-ended question, practitioners offered a number of suggestions for how to improve the viability of the fixed-fee regime (n=458), which were thematically coded. Table 5.6 highlights the top 10 responses provided by practitioners. Over half of these suggestions (51.7 per cent, n=237) involved a general comment on the need to raise fees: 'Increase in fees to reflect the work actually done'[93] and 'Increase fees dramatically after decades of stagnation and neglect'.[94]

Practitioners also commonly suggested a return to hourly rates (13.3 per cent, n=61) or abandoning fixed fees altogether (13.1 per cent, n=60) as in the following examples: 'Increase hourly rates to certificated level and scrap fixed fees,'[95]

[91] Practitioner Respondent Number 849.
[92] Practitioner Respondent Number 1118.
[93] Practitioner Respondent Number 571.
[94] Practitioner Respondent Number 402.
[95] Practitioner Respondent Number 1207.

'Scrap them and return to hourly rates,'[96] and 'Removal of fixed fee work so that all legal aid work is on legal aid certificates where the payment reflects the hours worked by the legal representative.'[97]

This was followed by making a range of suggestions for reform designed to increase accessibility including lower thresholds, making it easier to access the escape or generally reducing complexity in the system (12.7 per cent, n=58). Some practitioners (8.5 per cent, n=39) explicitly referenced the need for fixed fees to be subject to annual increases or to track rates of inflation. Others commented on the need for fixed-fee arrangements to be more flexible or to increase rates for serious or complex cases (6.1 per cent, n=28).[98] It is notable that while a large number of respondents suggested abolishing the fixed-fee regime, only a negligible number of respondents suggested more radical reforms involving institutional change:

> Get rid of the LAA. Give the power back to the court clerks who are actually in court and know what is going on. The LAA asks the court for the court clerk's log anyway so it makes perfect sense. The LAA has, I'm afraid, a reputation for being slow, useless, inefficient, wrong and – sorry to say – on a mission to pay people less.[99]

Another argued in favour of 'Salary[ing] legal aid lawyers. Pay them at grades and accredit them. The fees and costs regimes are monstrosities.'[100]

Overall, then, the Census shows that the discontent with fixed fees was high.

IV. Hourly Rates

A. Working under Hourly Rates

The operation of hourly rates is both complex and variable depending on the area of legal aid practice and type of work being undertaken. Notably, when it came to hourly rates, a large number of practitioners either did not know the applicable hourly rates relevant to their area of legal aid practice[101] or asserted that there were too many applicable rates to list in response to the Census question. When asked how many hours the average case takes under hourly rates and how many hours they are paid (excluding those who did not provide a clear

[96] Practitioner Respondent Number 1092.

[97] Practitioner Respondent Number 55.

[98] Reasons that did not appear in the 10 most common suggestions provided in Table 5.6 include: review fees (3.5%, n=16); improvements to application/payment process (3.1%, n=14); government should invest in legal aid/change attitude towards it (2.6%, n=12); recognise the experience of lawyers (1.7%, n=8), change rates to align with the market/commercial rates or CPS fees (1.5%, n=7); bring back legal aid into certain areas (1.3%, n=6); provide more pay for out-of-hours work (0.9%, n=4); introduce salaried lawyers/block funding of firms (0.7%, n=3).

[99] Practitioner Respondent Number 999.

[100] Practitioner Respondent Number 1181.

[101] Some respondents indicated this was because others (eg clerks or practice managers) dealt with billing.

indication in their response), the vast majority of the 271 current practitioners who answered[102] indicated that they worked more hours than they were paid by the LAA (85.2 per cent, n=231). A far smaller proportion (13.3 per cent, n=36) of practitioners indicated that they claimed the hours worked yet recognised that the claim might ultimately be rejected by the LAA (1.5 per cent, n=4).

Table 5.7 (outliers removed) shows the differences between hours worked and hours claimed under the hourly rates scheme for those practitioners who indicated that the number of hours taken on the average case exceeded the number of hours claimed and who provided clear indications of what those hours were (n=173).[103] Relying again on the median as the best measure of central tendency, the number of hours claimed on the average case was 10, while the number of hours taken on the average case was 20. With the median number of hours spent to hours claimed 1.5:1, the data showed that for every 90 minutes worked, practitioners can claim for only 60 of those minutes.[104]

Table 5.7 Summary statistics in relation to hours worked and hours remunerated under the hourly rate scheme (n=173)

	Number of hours claimed from LAA on average case	**Number of hours spent on average case**	**Number of hours worked for every hour claimed**
Mean (SD)	19.3 (18.7)	28.1 (25)	1.6 (0.4)
Median	10.0	20.0	1.5
Mode	10.0	15.00	1.5

Unlike the fixed fee data, it was not possible to link the hourly rate data to a particular area of law. As such, differences across practice areas could not be identified.

B. Unpaid Work

Table 5.8 below sets out the most significant costs that go unremunerated under hourly rates according to the coded open-ended responses of 682 practitioners.

[102] Percentages are calculated excluding 937 respondents (from the original cohort of 1,208 practitioners). Excluded respondents either provided (i) no answer to either the number of hours taken and/or the number of hours paid by the LAA, (ii) responses that were unclear, (iii) simply indicated that they could not provide an estimate as it was too hard to say, (iv) indicated that they didn't know, or (v) referred to private rates of pay, rather than hourly rates under the legal aid scheme.

[103] Outliers were removed using the 1.5 +/– Interquartile Range (IQR) method. In addition to removing outliers, these statistics also exclude those who did not indicate that the number of hours worked exceeded the number of hours paid, and who did not provide answers for both (i) the number of hours claimed from the LAA on the average case and the (ii) number of hours spent on the average case.

[104] When leaving outliers in (n=206), the medians for the 'Number of hours claimed from the LAA on the average case', the 'Number of hours worked on the average case' and the number of hours worked for every hour paid were 12.5, 20.0 and 1.5 respectively, the modes remained unchanged and the means were higher at 32.4 (53.9), 54.5(128.7) and 1.8(1.1) respectively.

Most practitioners (39.3 per cent, n=268) indicated that case preparation – including time spent preparing documents, conducting legal research and bundle preparation – was the most significant unremunerated cost. One referenced in particular time spent 'reading 1000s of pages of medical evidence and reports'[105] and another noted the hours of 'free written and oral advice' to solicitors and the CPS to 'ensure cases run smoothly.'[106] Notably, the impact of LASPO 2012 reforms is evidenced across many of the responses. Some highlight having to provide unremunerated advice in areas that are no longer in scope for legal aid, such as welfare benefits. This was particularly the case in the area of housing: 'welfare benefits advice for rent arrears possession cases or advice about compensation in disrepair claims.'[107] Another respondent described related 'add-on work' no longer being done elsewhere such as 'ensuring the client is on the housing register, making referrals to social services and ensuring benefits are in place.' They note that all of these tasks are necessary in order to ensure 'the housing work we do is not wasted.'[108]

The burden of unpaid general administration is noted by 14.8 per cent (n=101) of respondents as the most significant unremunerated cost. The extent to which lawyers engage in administration has been said to correlate to their diminishing sense of professional self-worth and risks undermining autonomy.[109] Other practitioners also referenced the time it takes to make applications to the LAA and deal with compliance issues (19.1 per cent, n=130). A number of practitioners referenced the time-consuming nature of conferences and dealing with clients that could not be remunerated (15.8 per cent, n=108) and time spent travelling or waiting at court (13.6 per cent, n=93). Some practitioners (2.6 per cent, n=18) said that supervising trainees was the most significant unremunerated cost. A small number of respondents (1.3 per cent, n=9) highlighted levels of unpaid work when cases did not proceed. For example, in relation to judicial review, which is pertinent given that it is another area which was restricted under LASPO where pre-permission stage work was limited: 'We have sometimes lost on permission which has meant all of the work has been unremunerated, sometimes £8–10,000 work, including counsel's fees,'[110] and 'We do not get paid if permission is not granted therefore we lose out completely.'[111]

The general under-remuneration of legal aid work in certain types of cases (such as immigration cases) as well as specific concerns about unpaid work related to liaising with individuals (such as experts or interpreters) and dealing with complaints were also noted.

[105] Practitioner Respondent Number 630.
[106] Practitioner Respondent Number 426.
[107] Practitioner Respondent Number 254.
[108] Practitioner Respondent Number 59.
[109] Hilary Sommerlad, 'The Implementation of Quality Initiatives and the New Public Management in the Legal Aid Sector in England and Wales: Bureaucratisation, Stratification and Surveillance' (1999) 6 *International Journal of the Legal Profession* 311.
[110] Practitioner Respondent Number 1067.
[111] Practitioner Respondent Number 1203.

Table 5.8 Most significant cost not remunerated (n=682)

	N	%
Case preparation/documents/research/bundles	268	39.3
Legal aid application and compliance issues	130	19.1
Dealing with clients/conferences	108	15.8
Administration	101	14.8
Travel and waiting/wasted time at court	93	13.6
Additional advice above the fee/out of scope work/signposting	91	13.3
General under-remuneration of legal aid work	90	13.2
Correspondence/chasing other parties	47	6.9
Other (eg being on call, experts, interpreters, complaints, damages, Crown Court cases, IT, problems with solicitor)	24	3.5
Supervision/training	18	2.6
Cases not going ahead/missed cases	9	1.3

In addition, a high proportion of practitioners acknowledged that often they did not claim for legal aid work because it was too time-consuming to do so. In total, 43.0 per cent of respondents (n=441) said they avoided claiming for certain work as compared to 38.6 per cent (n=394) who said they did not, and 18.9 per cent (n=193) who said they were unsure. The likelihood of carrying out work that was not claimed for was particularly high in the areas of clinical negligence (57.1 per cent, n=8), immigration and asylum (54.3 per cent, n=57), prison law (53.8 per cent, n=28), crime (53.9 per cent, n=166) and mental health (50.0 per cent, n=39). In addition, a slightly higher proportion of solicitors (49.9 per cent, n=182) than barristers (39.5 per cent, n=137) reported being likely to work but not receive pay for that work under the hourly rates of pay. Those at more senior levels (such as heads of department and directors) were also more likely to report working without pay than those in more junior positions, such as caseworkers and paralegals. Similarly, there is a steady rise in the number of respondents likely to undertake work they do not claim for commensurate with the number of years in practice.

The types of unremunerated work referenced by practitioners are extensive. Aside from the most significant unremunerated work, practitioners also noted other general tasks undertaken but not claimed for under hourly rates. The 10 most commonly described tasks are captured in Table 5.9 below.[112] As with the most significant costs not remunerated, several practitioners revealed that tasks

[112] Responses not detailed in Table 5.9 include: Travel and Waiting (1.9%, n=6); Judicial Review (1.6%, n=5); Appeals (1.0%, n=3); Training/Supervision (0.6%, n=2).

relevant to making applications for legal aid again made up a large proportion of unremunerated work (40.3 per cent, n=124). For example, one practitioner noted:

> Sometimes I will help a client but not apply for funding as the process is too arduous with legal aid or because the rules are so difficult to meet that it is not worth the risk that you may not be able to tick all the boxes.[113]

Here we are told that the rules are hard to follow. Another practitioner commented to explain the extra work involved chasing details for a claim: 'We can only claim 48 mins for a legal aid application when in reality it can take all day chasing clients and having to re-enter information. Plus amending rejected applications is even worse.'[114]

Some practitioners (29.9 per cent, n=92) also noted the unpaid nature of different forms of case preparation, including drafting, legal research or considering evidence. For example, 'Telephone calls often aren't charged as it is administratively too cumbersome to record every discussion – a synopsis is produced instead of multiple calls. As this is not evidence of itemised work it becomes non chargeable.'[115]

Others referenced dealing with correspondence or chasing clients (10.4 per cent, n=32), or described 'other' work including dealing with specific individuals (such as special guardians or hospital managers) or issues relevant to cases including committals, prison matters or civil breaches (8.8 per cent, n=27). This was followed by investigative work on cases before legal aid is granted (8.4 per cent, n=26). Some practitioners referenced the unremunerated work in particular areas of practice, including family law (specifically divorce cases and domestic violence), judicial review and police station attendance.

Table 5.9 Ten most commonly mentioned forms of work carried out but not claimed (n=308)

	N	%
Legal aid applications/compliance/escape fees/exceptional case funding	124	40.3
Preparation/drafting/legal research/considering evidence	92	29.9
Correspondence/chasing other parties/responding to clients	32	10.4
Other (eg dealing with specific individuals or issues)	27	8.8
Investigative work prior to legal aid application	26	8.4
Legal help	25	8.1
Meetings with other practitioners/experts/conferences	20	6.5
Police station pre and post matters/client forms/telephone advice	19	6.2
Family/divorce/domestic violence	16	5.2
Specific housing/welfare benefit/debt/visa assistance	14	4.5

[113] Practitioner Respondent Number 1054.
[114] Practitioner Respondent Number 723.
[115] Practitioner Respondent Number 1075.

Practitioners provided more detail on other types of non-billable work in relation to hourly rates in an open-ended format. Quantitative coding of these responses for general themes revealed that the most prevalent non-billable work was providing support to clients (41.1 per cent, n=209). Many practitioners referenced again the particular needs of legal aid clients, while others (32.1 per cent, n=163) commented on the nature of legal aid applications and other wider tasks in relation to billing:

> Any legal aid lawyer knows that we are dealing with disadvantaged people – and we are probably the only professionals they come into contact with who might give them some time – so one becomes a part time social worker … it's the myriad of things people ask us to do that we cannot get paid for.[116]

Another respondent noted:

> It is very time consuming [to claim for work]. When you have clients who may lose their home, liberty or rights imminently, then the legal work has to take priority. This means time recording will take a back seat and tasks or time will be missed.[117]

A third respondent pointed out that 'If a case goes three times the value, you can bill it on hourly rates but the forms and sorting out the file is time consuming and I don't have anyone to assist me.'[118]

Quantitative coding of open-ended responses regarding other examples of non-billable work was completed and is relayed via Table 5.10 below. Practitioners often cited legal research and case preparation (27.8 per cent, n=141) and correspondence (14.6 per cent, n=74); this was followed by references to other non-billable work such as general administration (14.4 per cent, n=73), training and supervision duties (5.9 per cent, n=30), travel and waiting (5.1 per cent, n=26), work not going ahead or being delayed (5.1 per cent, n=26), work after a police station attendance or court hearing (4.5 per cent, n=23), other types of duties (3.3 per cent, n=17) (such as attending forums, being on call, responding to complaints or engaging with professional bodies) and dealing with a client's family (1.2 per cent, n=6).[119]

Table 5.10 Ten most common 'other' examples of non-billable work (n=516)

	N	%
Client support/advice before or after claim/conferences/free advice	209	41.1
Legal aid applications/compliance/billing	163	32.1
Preparation/drafting/bundles/legal research/going through evidence	141	27.8

(continued)

[116] Practitioner Respondent Number 355.
[117] Practitioner Respondent Number 1177.
[118] Practitioner Respondent Number 169.
[119] Responses not detailed in Table 5.10 include: Dealing with families of clients (1.2%, n=6).

Table 5.10 ***(Continued)***

	N	%
Correspondence/dealing with and assisting different parties/practitioner meetings	74	14.6
General administration	73	14.4
Training/supervision/supporting colleagues/managerial responsibilities	30	5.9
Travel/waiting	26	5.1
Work that does not go ahead/delayed	26	5.1
Work before and after court hearing/police station attendance	23	4.5
Other	17	3.3

C. The Viability of Hourly Rates

As with fixed fees, a large number of current practitioners thought that hourly legal aid rates were unsustainable. In total, 78.5 per cent of respondents (n=822) considered hourly rates to be unsustainable, while 15 per cent indicated they 'didn't know' (n=157) and 7.6 per cent (n=80) considered that they were sustainable. It is notable that a higher percentage of practitioners considered that fixed fees were unsustainable (85.8 per cent, n=659 of 786) as compared to hourly rates.

In analysing findings by practice area, practitioners were more likely to find hourly rates unsustainable in the areas of housing (86.7 per cent, n=26) and education (86.7 per cent, n=26), followed by debt (85.7 per cent, n=12) and crime (85.1 per cent, n=257). Whilst 50 per cent of respondents indicated that the hourly rates for actions against police were sustainable and 100 per cent for employment, the low number of respondents (n=1) limits the inferences that can be drawn in relation to these practice areas. Aside from these areas, practitioners were more likely to find hourly rates sustainable in immigration and asylum (17.0 per cent, n=18), mediation (16.7 per cent, n=2) and debt (14.3 per cent, n=2), though lower response rates with respect to the latter two categories again limits the extent of inferences drawn. As with fixed fees, it is interesting to note the highest proportion of 'I don't know' responses were in relation to private (24.7 per cent, n=74) and public (24.0 per cent, n=77) family law.

As with fixed fees, higher proportions of senior practitioners found the rates to be unsustainable. For example, 95.7 per cent (n=44) of heads of department and 90.0 per cent (n=36) of directors of organisations thought hourly rates were not viable as compared to 69.6 per cent (n=78) of trainees, legal apprentices and pupils and 70.0 per cent (n=14) of paralegals. A higher proportion of barristers (10.9 per cent, n=37) than solicitors (3.9 per cent, n=15) considered that hourly rates were sustainable.

V. Exceptional Case Funding

Practitioners have the option to make applications for exceptional case funding for clients where an issue is otherwise not in scope for legal aid. Exceptional case funding should be available in cases where there is a potential breach of human rights or European Union law.[120] The question to be considered is whether the client would be able to present their case effectively and without unfairness if they did not have legal aid. Since the scheme was introduced, it has been widely criticised for its inaccessibility.[121] Several legal challenges resulted in changes to the guidance and an amendment to the test in relation to prospects of success.[122] The LASPO post-implementation review recommended changes including simplifying the application process, improving timelines for decision-making and introducing a procedure for urgent applications.[123] Evidence suggests that problems persist with the scheme and points to the need for systemic reform. For example, addressing the high number of applications for Article 8 immigration cases by bringing them back into scope for legal aid or giving powers to legal aid providers to grant exceptional case funding for controlled work to resolve accessibility issues.[124] However, of the 236 practitioners who indicated whether they had made an application for exceptional case funding, most had only made one application (35.6 per cent, n = 84). Of those who indicated the number of applications they made and the number that were successful (n=138), 23.2 per cent (n=32) had no successful applications, 21.7 per cent (n=30) has less successful applications than the number they made, and 55.1 per cent (n=76) had the same number of applications successful as they made. Table 5.11 details the rate of successful applications for those who reported having less applications successful than made with outliers removed (n=23).[125]

[120] Exceptional case funding was introduced by LASPO, s 10.

[121] See eg The Bar Council, 'The Legal Aid, Sentencing and Punishment of Offenders Act 2012 (LASPO): One Year On – Final Report' (The Bar Council, 2014); Rights of Women, 'Accessible or Beyond Reach? Navigating the Exceptional Case Funding Scheme without a Lawyer' (Rights of Women, 2019); Shazia Choudhry and Jonathan Herring, 'A Human Right to Legal Aid? – The Implications of Changes to the Legal Aid Scheme for Victims of Domestic Abuse' (2017) 39 *Journal of Social Welfare and Family Law* 152; Nigel Balmer and Pascoe Pleasence, 'Mental Health, Legal Problems and the Impact of Changes to the Legal Aid Scheme: Secondary Analysis of 2014–15 Legal Problem Resolution Survey Data' (PPSR, 2018).

[122] *Gudanaviciene and Ors v Director of Legal Aid Casework and the Lord Chancellor* [2014] EWCA Civ 1622; *IS v Director of Legal Aid Casework and the Lord Chancellor* [2015] EWHC 1965 (Admin) and [2016] EWCA Civ 464.

[123] Lord Chancellor and Secretary of State for Justice, 'Post-Implementation Review of Part 1 of the Legal Aid, Sentencing and Punishment of Offenders Act 2012 (LASPO)' (His Majesty's Stationery Office, 2019) [568].

[124] Joe Tomlinson and Emma Marshall, 'Improving Exceptional Case Funding: Providers' Perspectives' (Public Law Project, 2020).

[125] This question asked respondents to indicate how many exceptional case funding applications they had made and how many were successful. Instances where respondents did not clearly demarcate the number applied for and the number of successful applications were removed from analysis. Where an

As shown in Table 5.11, relying again on the median, showed that two applications had to be made for every one application that was successful.

Table 5.11 Summary statistics in relation to the number of exceptional funding applications made and the number of exceptional funding applications successful (outliers removed) (n=23)

	Number of applications of exceptional funding made	**Number of applications for exceptional funding that are successful**	**Number of applications made for every one successful application**
Mean (SD)	3.9 (1.6)	2.1 (1.0)	2.0 (0.8)
Median	4.0	2.0	2.0
Mode	2.0*	1.0*	2.0

*denotes that multiple modes existed. The smallest value is shown.

Although respondents were not asked to indicate what area of law these applications were made in, a small number (n=6) noted that they were in the area of inquests. Of these, 66.7 per cent (n=4) reported that all of the applications they made were successful, with the remaining 33.3 per cent (n=2) unsuccessful, suggesting a slightly higher rate of successful applications in respect of inquests. This is perhaps unsurprising given that the guidelines and criterion for inquest-related cases are different to other cases.[126]

The demanding nature of exceptional case funding applications was also noted by some respondents when asked which types of work were most time-consuming and went unremunerated. For example, one practitioner noted that applications were 'very time-consuming and [you] can only charge £30.'[127] Another practitioner commented that 'Applying for exceptional funding [is] not worth the risk.'[128]

application outcome was still pending, the application was removed from the calculation of application success, but retained when calculating the overall number of applications made. Where individuals provided a ratio of success but not an estimate of the number of applications made, the ratio was used in calculating the average success ratio but not in calculating the number of applications made or the number of successful applications. Outliers were removed using the 1.5 +/− Interquartile Range (IQR) method. In addition to removing outliers, these statistics also exclude those who did not indicate that the number of applications made exceeded the number of applications that were successful, and those who did not provide answers for both (i) the number of exceptional funding applications made, and (ii) the number of exceptional funding applications that were successful.

[126] Ministry of Justice, 'Lord Chancellor's Exceptional Funding Guidance (Inquests)' (Ministry of Justice), available at assets.publishing.service.gov.uk/government/uploads/system/uploads/attachment_data/file/1045704/legal-aid-chancellor-inquests.pdf.

[127] Practitioner Respondent Number 236.

[128] Practitioner Respondent Number 1170.

VI. Other Income Sources

It is important to acknowledge the different funding landscape for those organisations working in the not-for-profit sector. Organisations specified in their responses whether they had other income sources aside from legal aid or private legal aid work. What emerged from these responses was that most organisations did not receive any other form of funding (76.4 per cent, n=272 of 356). A total of 21.3 per cent (n=76) received other forms of grant funding from trusts and foundations, 14.6 per cent (n=52) received local government funding and a small proportion (7.0 per cent, n=25) received central government funding. Ministry of Justice research shows that almost half of not-for-profit providers surveyed in 2014/15 received additional income from local government, with charitable sources as the second most common funding source.[129] The Census findings therefore demonstrate a shift in more recent years, with local government funding being much more constrained. More recent research from the Access to Justice Foundation aligns with these findings. In analysing the income of 432 registered charities delivering specialist legal advice, the Foundation found that only 18 per cent came from central or local government funding.[130] The research also demonstrates that Citizens Advice Bureaux are comparatively in a stronger position than law centres and other charitable providers. Whereas major charities, other charities and law centres have seen slow funding growth since 2016, Citizens Advice Bureaux have experienced a 30 per cent growth in cash terms.[131]

Grant funding is an important source of funding for smaller not-for-profit providers, especially law centres. The wider research shows that grant funding constitutes 20 per cent of law centre income, as compared to six per cent of the income of charities more widely (such as Citizens Advice Bureaux and larger charities).[132] An obvious challenge with grant funding is the short-term nature of grant-making and the risk posed by the strategic direction changing to no longer support the area in which a particular organisation might work. Of the 76 organisations that reported receiving other forms of grant funding from trusts and foundations, only a small number (7.9 per cent, n=6) reported that the sources of funding were quite certain for the future. Most organisations reported that the funding was either quite uncertain (38.2 per cent, n=29) or very uncertain (25.0 per cent, n=19) with a further 28.9 per cent (n=22) indicating that they were neither certain or uncertain.

[129] Ashley Ames et al, 'Survey of Not for Profit Legal Advice Providers in England and Wales' (Ministry of Justice Analytical Series, 2015) 25.

[130] Access to Justice Foundation, 'Specialist Legal Advice Providers: Sector Profile Reports' (Access to Justice Foundation, 2022).

[131] ibid, 4.

[132] ibid, 11.

For those organisations supported by charitable grants in addition to legal aid funding, organisations listed 80 different sources from charitable trusts and foundations. Of 71 organisations, the National Lottery (50.7 per cent, n=36) funded the highest number followed by the Legal Education Foundation (40.8 per cent, n=29). The Access to Justice Foundation (22.5 per cent, n=16), the Community Justice Fund (22.5 per cent, n=16), Trust for London (21.1 per cent, n=15) and AB Charitable Trust (19.7 per cent, n=14) also funded higher numbers of organisations. The next most commonly identified sources of funding were City Bridge Trust, the London Legal Support, the charitable foundations of corporate law firms and the Baring Foundation.[133]

VII. Implications of Findings

The rates of remuneration, coupled with the rigidity and complexity of legal aid fee arrangements, pose considerable challenges for legal aid practitioners. The findings set out in this chapter strongly align with those in chapter four, wherein practitioners reported frequently needing to work beyond set hours to meet demand and struggling to fit work around their family life and personal commitments. Here, we have seen the extent to which legal aid practitioners engage in unpaid work and the frustrations created by fee arrangements, which depict an image quite distinct from that of so-called fat cat lawyers.

Wilding points to the disconnect between the way in which legal aid is funded and administered and the reality of legal aid practice on the ground. Whereas the system assumes that legal aid practitioners are 'rational economic actors' they are in fact motivated by a complex range of concerns related to the access to justice needs of their clients.[134] They also share a strong sense of collective identity with other practitioners, evidenced by the range of professional networks we explore in chapter four. Drawing upon Thaler and Sunstein's work, Wilding highlights the risks associated with imposing 'econ-like initiatives' on 'humans engaged in fundamentally human activity'.[135] She notes that 'even the most committed workers' experience pressure within 'an incentive-responsive business model.'[136] As such, the quality of service provision is adversely impacted and while practitioners maintain their sense of solidarity to one another, and to their clients, they have little faith in the system.

[133] Other identified sources of funding (in order of frequency) included the Tudor Trust, Children in Need, Comic Relief, British Gas Energy Trust, Garfield Weston Foundation, Lloyds Bank Foundation, Henry Smith Foundation, Therium Access, Steve Morgan Foundation, Paul Hamlyn Foundation, Oak Foundation, Money and Pensions Service, Nationwide Foundation, Esmee Fairbairn Foundation, Matrix Chambers and the Walcott Foundation.

[134] Jo Wilding, *The Legal Aid Market: Challenges for Publicly Funded Immigration and Asylum Legal Representation* (Policy Press, 2021) 26.

[135] ibid.

[136] ibid, 162.

As we explore elsewhere in this book, this financial instability has led to high rates of attrition in the profession and a failure to incentivise new practitioners into many areas of legal aid practice. The pressures that lawyers describe in relation to both fixed fees and hourly rates are expressed with frustration, exasperation and at times a sense of real despair. A clear majority of practitioners think both fixed fees and hourly rates are unsustainable. Notably, when asked how they mitigated losses under the fixed-fee regime, most practitioners said they did not think anything could be done as the best interests of clients had to be met, so they simply accepted the loss of the unpaid work. A large proportion of practitioners also said they worked longer hours or took on private work to try to mitigate the loss. Neither of these practices will ensure the long-term viability of legal aid.

It is notable that the solutions offered do not seem to meet the scale of the problems identified. For example, Bellamy rejected wholescale reform in the independent review of criminal legal aid. While noting the existence of a small-scale Public Defender Service of salaried lawyers already in operation in some parts of the UK, there was little engagement with the apparent success or failure of that model. Without any comprehensive analysis, it was concluded that its expansion – or indeed any 'radically different alternative' to the status quo – would be 'unlikely to improve upon what we have in terms of cost, quality and efficiency'.[137]

Given the scale of the structural problems with respect to remuneration, it seems unlikely that short-term injections of further funding will do anything other than allow failings to persist. Further research is needed to carefully scope a range of alternatives. There have been numerous calls for more radical reforms, including system-wide approaches,[138] funding arrangements that better take the clustering of legal problems into account[139] and closer engagement with salaried lawyer models rather than tinkering around the edges of the judicare system.[140] These reforms prioritise access to justice, the best interests of clients and quality service provision. The mistake of policymakers to date has been to divorce these interests from cost efficiency; and from the voices and experiences of lawyers trying to deliver advice and representation within a broken system.

[137] ibid, 8.
[138] ibid.
[139] Luke Clements, *Clustered Injustice and the Level Green* (Legal Action Group, 2020).
[140] See eg Tom Cornford, 'The Meaning of Access to Justice' in Ellie Plamer et al (eds), *Access to Justice: Beyond the Policies and Politics of Austerity* (Hart, 2016).

6

Responding to COVID-19

I. Introduction

The March 2020 outbreak of the COVID-19 pandemic marked what many commentators termed 'unprecedented' times which fundamentally altered the ways that people live, work and interact with each other in their daily lives. Across the globe, it appears that *no one* has been left unaffected by this event as citizens invariably felt the effects of either the pandemic itself or global governments' associated responses which sought to minimise the threat to public health. However, it is crucial to acknowledge that experiences of the pandemic have been far from homogenous. In reality, the impact of the COVID-19 pandemic has been disproportionately borne by marginalised groups who were already feeling the effects of disadvantage within society. Those who were already contending with precarious financial circumstances, unpredictable employment arrangements or caring responsibilities found themselves in perilous situations such as being unable to go to work because their industries were closed during lockdowns, or having no choice but to go to work and potentially expose themselves and their families to the virus. These challenges are compounded because the pandemic forced the dissolution of caring arrangements for children and vulnerable relatives. In other words, many who were already on the cusp of insecurity were unable to continue relying on the strategies that they would typically take to keep themselves and their households afloat. As a consequence, many individuals began to require legal advice for the first time during the pandemic, concerning issues such as their employment, social welfare benefits, family breakdown or housing. At the same time, populations who were already typically reliant on legal advice services before March 2020 found that their existing difficulties were intensely exacerbated, with serious risks to safety and well-being manifesting during this time.

The pandemic can therefore be understood as inducing a range of new legal needs as well as worsening existing problems. Both had to be met by services that were already operating under the strain of several organisational challenges discussed so far in this book. High workloads, limitations on remuneration and fees, as well as various stressors for professional well-being are just some examples of the concerns that already framed the working environments of legal aid organisations before the pandemic. After March 2020, these challenges were compounded by the need to assist a broader range of clients presenting from an even more diverse range of circumstances, all whilst shifting their services to a new dynamic of remote advice provision and adapting to new virtual processes – such as virtual and hybrid court hearings – within the justice system.

This chapter will provide much-needed insight into how legal aid lawyers and organisations have responded to the unique circumstances of the COVID-19 pandemic. It will articulate how these circumstances have, on the one hand, exacerbated many existing challenges within the legal aid sector, and on the other hand, initiated a new era for this sector by transforming the incidence and nature of legal problems as well as the ways that organisations are able to provide support to those experiencing legal needs. In terms of structure, the chapter begins by setting out how legal needs have fluctuated and changed during the pandemic. It then explores the ways that legal aid lawyers have sought to meet these needs and situates those responses within the broader organisational challenges that emerged during this period, including workload implications of new ways of working and the associated financial and practical pressures on both organisations and individual lawyers. Finally, the chapter reflects on how the pandemic has transformed the working environments and professional practices of legal aid lawyers. It emphasises that, in many ways, legal aid lawyers have risen to the challenge of adapting to the new world of remote and hybrid support. In fact, the pandemic has provided specific opportunities for the sector to become more innovative and efficient and has facilitated the use of a broader range of tools in order to support an even wider and more complex range of clients. However, these practices are unlikely to be sustainable as we move into a post-pandemic era due to existing, systemic problems that characterised the sector long before the pandemic.

II. The Impact of COVID-19

When the COVID-19 virus was declared a pandemic in March 2020, governments across the globe were forced to impose restrictions on our interpersonal interactions and use of public services to limit the spread of the virus.[1] Beyond obvious concerns for public health and the importance of protecting vulnerable individuals, this also had serious consequences for the ways that the public began interacting with law and legal institutions. The closure of several industries and necessitated social isolation meant that many individuals began experiencing financial precarity for the first time in their lives, and with this came an increase in the level of legal need related to issues like employment, housing, and social welfare entitlements.[2]

[1] World Health Organization, 'Timeline of WHO's Covid-19 Response' (World Health Organization, 2020), available at www.who.int/emergencies/diseases/novel-coronavirus-2019/interactive-timeline.

[2] Law Centres Network, 'Law For All: Our New 50th Anniversary Campaign and Report' (Law Centres Network, 2020), available at www.lawcentres.org.uk/policy/news/news/law-for-all-our-new-50th-anniversary-campaign-and-report; Naomi Creutzfeldt and Diane Sechi, 'Social Welfare [Law] Advice Provision During the Pandemic in England and Wales: A Conceptual Framework' (2021) 43 *Journal of Social Welfare and Family Law* 153; Daniel Newman et al, 'Vulnerability, Legal Need and

Research conducted with advice organisations providing social welfare advice indicated a change in typical client profiles, with greater proportions of younger, employed people seeking advice for the first time and presenting with different needs than usual clients who would typically seek support due to being unable to find work.[3] The relative unfamiliarity of social welfare systems and processes to these new clients, combined with their higher level of capability and confidence, means that they require different kinds of support from services. For example, anecdotal evidence suggests that many of these new clients present at an earlier stage, when they are not quite ready to take legal action but rather require clarity about whether they have a legal problem. Such clients require prospective advice relating to how such a problem might progress, escalate to the point where advice is required, or be avoided entirely.[4] For several organisations, this increased demand outstripped their capacity, with some *pro bono* organisations reporting that they had to turn people away during the pandemic.[5]

This required organisations to adapt the ways in which they provide advice, adding another dimension to the challenge of responding to an increased demand for advice. One of the respondents to a survey of 133 such organisations conducted on behalf of the Administrative Justice Council reported that the biggest change for their organisation during the pandemic was the

> sheer numbers of a 'COVID cohort' of younger, more IT confident clients who found themselves [with issues] in employment, income or debt … and reached out to our services in the immediate aftermath of the lockdown.[6]

Although the evidence base is still developing, the pandemic can therefore be associated with an emergence of legal need among certain population groups who had not previously sought assistance from advice organisations. Importantly, this has required organisations to adapt the format and nature of the assistance they provide, so as to effectively respond to the circumstances and needs of these new client groups.

What is less clear, however, is how this affected population groups that were already relying on these services. For instance, 12 per cent of respondents to the Administrative Justice Council survey indicated that at the same time that they were responding to the emergence of the 'COVID cohort', they noticed a disturbing absence of their typical clients who had usually relied on their assistance on a regular or recurring basis. These client groups are typically those with limited

Technology' (2021) 23 *International Journal of Discrimination and the Law* 230; James Organ et al, 'How Legal Advice Can Ameliorate the Unequal Health Impact of Covid-19' (2021) 28 *Journal of Social Security Law* 54.

[3] Administrative Justice Council, 'Welfare Benefit Advice During the Pandemic' (Administrative Justice Council, 2021) 11.

[4] Patricia Ng, 'Delivering a Pro Bono Clinic During the Pandemic: Some Thoughts on Access to Justice, Everyday Problems and the Current Legal Landscape' (2021) 3 *Amicus Curiae* 76, 86.

[5] ibid.

[6] Administrative Justice Council (n 3) 9.

resources who are reliant on social welfare benefits and social housing. They would have previously presented in person at advice services as and when they needed assistance relating to these arrangements, either because they had used the service before or because they had been referred to the organisation by other services like foodbanks, medical services or social workers.

The absence of these clients can be explained by two factors. The first is the fact that advice organisations had to rapidly adapt their services so as to provide assistance remotely once the first lockdown was announced. These traditional client groups are those most likely to struggle to maintain contact via email or telephone because they often have inconsistent access to technology, unpredictable or chaotic schedules, or require additional support with translation.[7] In such circumstances, advice services are most effective when it is possible to engage these clients face-to-face at the point they present. Without this option, it became very difficult for services to reach clients who either could not access technology or telephones, or were not comfortable using them to discuss their personal matters with people they could not see in person.[8]

The 'digital divide' in England and Wales is steadily declining, in alignment with the global progression towards an increasingly digitised world that was already occurring even before COVID-19. However, access to technology has become a growing marker of inequality. While there are fewer and fewer non-Internet users each year, they still comprise approximately eight per cent of the UK population.[9] Further, even among those who have access to the Internet, the Local Government Association estimates that 11.7 million people in the UK (22 per cent of the population) lack the digital skills needed for everyday life, and nine million (16 per cent of the population) are unable to use the Internet and their device by themselves.[10] Moreover, these statistics are disproportionately represented by those who are already contending with social exclusion, deprivation and poverty.[11] In addition to the ways that lockdowns and social distancing restrictions transformed the ways that such client groups could engage with advice services, it also closed off options such as public libraries, which might have gone some way towards providing people with facilities and support to use technology when they needed to seek advice.

[7] Newman et al (n 2).

[8] Jessica Mant et al, 'Blended Advice and Access to Justice' (Ministry of Justice and the Access to Justice Foundation 2022).

[9] Office for National Statistics, 'Exploring the UK's Digital Divide' (Office for National Statistics, 2019), available at www.ons.gov.uk/peoplepopulationandcommunity/householdcharacteristics/homeinternetandsocialmediausage/articles/exploringtheuksdigitaldivide/2019-03-04#the-scale-of-digital-exclusion-in-the-uk.

[10] Local Government Association, 'Tackling the Digital Divide' (House of Commons, 2021), available at www.local.gov.uk/parliament/briefings-and-responses/tackling-digital-divide-house-commons-4-november-2021.

[11] Hannah Homes and Gemma Burgess, 'Coronavirus has Highlighted the UK's Digital Divide' (Cambridge Centre for Housing and Planning Research: University of Cambridge, 2021), available at www.cchpr.landecon.cam.ac.uk/Research/Start-Year/2017/building_better_opportunities_new_horizons/digital_divide.

Relatedly, the second factor in the absence of traditional client groups from advice organisations can be attributed to the impact of the pandemic on various public services through which these clients would normally be referred to advice organisations. For instance, an evaluation of services conducted in Liverpool during the pandemic revealed that during earlier lockdowns, doctors' surgeries were unable to continue their usual practice of referring patients to welfare support services due to holding consultations online and facing a lack of clarity over whether and how other services were operating during these periods. To some extent, this was mitigated through local outreach activities, whereby some advice organisations would approach GP surgeries for lists of particularly vulnerable individuals for them to contact so that they were able to identify issues and provide assistance. While innovative, this approach undoubtedly was accompanied by concerns over data protection, and ultimately only enabled organisations to reach a certain proportion of those who would normally have been referred to their services.[12] In this study, a similar problem was identified in relation to food banks; there was an increased demand for food parcels from a wider population during the pandemic, which is likely to include the 'COVID cohort' described above. Combined with social distancing requirements and staff shortages due to isolation requirements, this phenomenon reduced the capacity of volunteers working in these services to continue asking questions, ascertain information from service users, and refer people to advice organisations for support in relation to their social welfare benefits, housing arrangements or legal rights.[13]

While these examples relate to just one geographic area, they are nevertheless indicative of how certain populations were left with very few places to turn during the pandemic. After the first lockdown was announced in March 2020, the public services on which they would typically rely were suddenly overwhelmed by a new wave of demand from new client groups while services were simultaneously transformed into remote formats so as to comply with the lockdown restrictions. While some organisations strived to instigate outreach measures so as to reach their vulnerable clients, this was invariably challenging due to the increased demand and organisational uncertainty they were facing at this time. These difficulties led some respondents to the Administrative Justice Council survey to acknowledge that, at least for certain periods, several organisations were resigned to the fact that many of their clients who require face-to-face contact would be excluded from their services.[14]

These constraints on advice organisations were somewhat mitigated during the later stages of the pandemic, as easing restrictions were accompanied by the gradual reintroduction of face-to-face advice. Nevertheless, the pandemic-related increase in legal need is unlikely to be temporary. In reality, many legal problems are likely to come to light once we reach a moment of increased social stability.

[12] Organ et al (n 2).
[13] ibid.
[14] Administrative Justice Council (n 3) 11.

In the initial wake of the pandemic, the Government introduced several initiatives which were intended to provide a safety net during lockdowns. For instance, it implemented a moratorium on housing evictions and a furlough scheme in order to provide financial support to those who could not continue working during the pandemic and to incentivise employers to retain their staff during lockdowns. Whilst providing a vital lifeline for many people, these schemes are in practice likely to have delayed experiences of financial and employment precarity among recipients. These realities will only emerge once the true impact of the pandemic on businesses and housing providers is ascertained.

At the same time, people themselves may refrain from making major life changes when they are already under conditions of stress and uncertainty. Consequently, an increase in the number of legal problems post-pandemic is likely, since people delay their decisions to take action in response to the challenges they face. In family law, for example, the pandemic has created a unique set of circumstances whereby many couples were pressured into making major relationship commitments. With lockdowns and strict limits on socialising across household bubbles, many couples decided to accelerate decisions to begin cohabiting together to avoid the alternative of not being able to see each other or living alone in isolation. Feeling rushed into isolating together as a household may strain some relationships and cause more disputes to emerge later down the line.[15]

Finally, the incidence and nature of legal need has also been shaped by the pandemic's effect on other components of the justice system. As with other services that were reliant on in-person processes, the pandemic impacted the operations of courts and forced Her Majesty's Courts and Tribunals Service to facilitate a shift to digital hearings across several areas of law. This change had a considerable impact upon those working in the justice system, who were required to negotiate these new dynamics and processes. In several areas, this caused delays, disruption and uncertainty as many hearings were postponed while the system came to terms with this 'new normal'.[16] In turn, this created a ripple effect for advice organisations, who noted that a number of clients were presenting at their services with escalated problems that had become more complex while they were awaiting their court hearings.[17]

Taken together, the relationship between the pandemic and legal need is far from straightforward. The reality of how this event has transformed the practices, requirements and challenges for legal advice services is still unfolding. Nevertheless, some of the indicative understandings outlined above can be elucidated and deepened by the data collected through the Legal Aid Census. Despite only forming one topic within the surveys that comprised the Census, the pandemic was a recurring theme throughout several responses. Practitioners and

[15] Graeme Fraser, 'Reflections on Changing Family Law Practice During the COVID-19 Lockdown' (2020) 4 *Family Law* 1115.

[16] Law Centres Network (n 2); House of Commons Justice Committee, 'The Future of Legal Aid: Third Report of Session 2021–22' (Her Majesty's Stationery Office, 2021).

[17] Ng (n 4) 86.

organisations have contributed first-hand insight into how the pandemic has, in many ways, restructured the nature and format of the work that they do.

III. Meeting Legal Need During the Pandemic

In order to determine the impact of the pandemic on the work of current legal aid practitioners, the Census collected initial baseline data on what a typical month in practice looked like prior to the pandemic. This baseline data took the form of how many new matters practitioners would have opened or how many new instructions they would have received. This information was coupled with data collected on what a typical month in practice looked like after March 2020, which marked the commencement of the first lockdown in England and Wales. Collecting this information separately allowed for a comparison between the amount of new work commenced before and after March 2020.

As Figure 6.1 below indicates, one major impact of the COVID-19 pandemic was a decrease in the number of new matters or instructions being taken on by practitioners.

Figure 6.1 Number of new matters/instructions opened per month by current legal aid practitioners before and after the COVID-19 pandemic

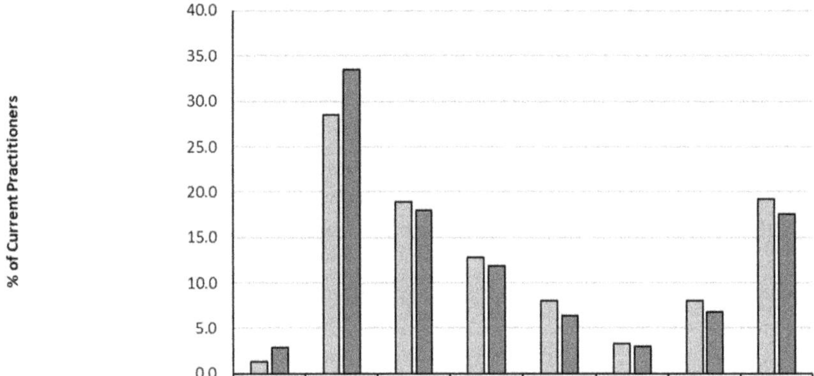

	None	1 to 5	6 to 10	11 to 15	16 to 20	21 to 25	26+	Unsure
Prior to Covid-19 (n=1159) %	1.3	28.5	18.9	12.8	8.0	3.3	8.0	19.2
Since Covid-19 (n=1157) %	2.9	33.5	18.0	11.9	6.4	3.0	6.8	17.5

New Matters/Instructions Opened per Month

The number of matters taken on at any time inevitably varies by area of law and the size of a practitioner's organisation, and the picture drawn of a typical month for practitioners before the pandemic reflects this diversity. The pre-March 2020 data indicates that most practitioners would typically have taken on somewhere between one and 15 new instructions per month, with the majority taking on between one and five per month. However, a significant minority of practitioners took on many more matters than this, with eight per cent taking on more than 26 per month.

After March 2020, this distribution shifted. Across the board, the number of practitioners taking on more than six matters per month decreased, with the most notable decrease occurring among the minority of practitioners who would have typically taken on high numbers (more than 26) of new matters. At the same time, the category of practitioners taking on the lowest numbers of new matters per month (one to five) has increased. Additionally, the number of practitioners who reported that they would not take on any new instructions in a typical month has more than doubled after March 2020. This suggests that, on the whole, practitioners during the pandemic were typically starting fewer matters per month than they did before the outbreak of the pandemic, and that after March 2020, there are more practitioners taking on no new matters at all in a typical month.

At first view, this decrease in new matters starts appears to starkly contrast with the increased legal need depicted by emerging research studies. However, a temporary drop in formal new matter starts is in practice unsurprising due to the nature of the demand described earlier. For instance, it is possible that these figures do not reflect the scale of demand from the 'COVID cohort' due to the fact that this cohort was frequently seeking clarificatory assistance and information ahead of being ready to take legal action. At the same time, the enforced closures of advice organisations meant that the advice network was rendered far less accessible to traditional client groups who would typically approach organisations at the point that action needed to be taken. At the same time, there was also a pause in official mechanisms that would usually prompt clients to seek advice from these services, such as welfare benefit decisions, evictions and debt collections.[18]

To appreciate the impact of the pandemic on legal need, it is therefore important to distinguish between the number of new matter starts and the number of people making enquiries at advice organisations. These are not necessarily the same thing. The distinction between these two groups is clearly demonstrated by the fact that nearly two-thirds of practitioners (62.3 per cent, n=706 of 1,133) indicated that they were seeing an increased demand for legal services as compared to one third who were not (37.7 per cent, n=427). As shown in Figure 6.2, practitioners especially emphasised increased demand for public (38.2 per cent, n=264) and private (36.6 per cent, n=253) family legal aid, followed by crime (24.7 per cent, n=171) and housing (23.2 per cent, n=160).

Despite the fall in new matter starts, practitioners nevertheless reported that levels of client demand had increased significantly during the pandemic. In response to an open-ended question about the impact of COVID-19 on their work, practitioners referenced this increase in public enquiries, demand

[18] Organ et al (n 2).

Figure 6.2 Increased demand for legal aid services observed by current legal aid practitioners over the last 12 months by area of law (n=691)

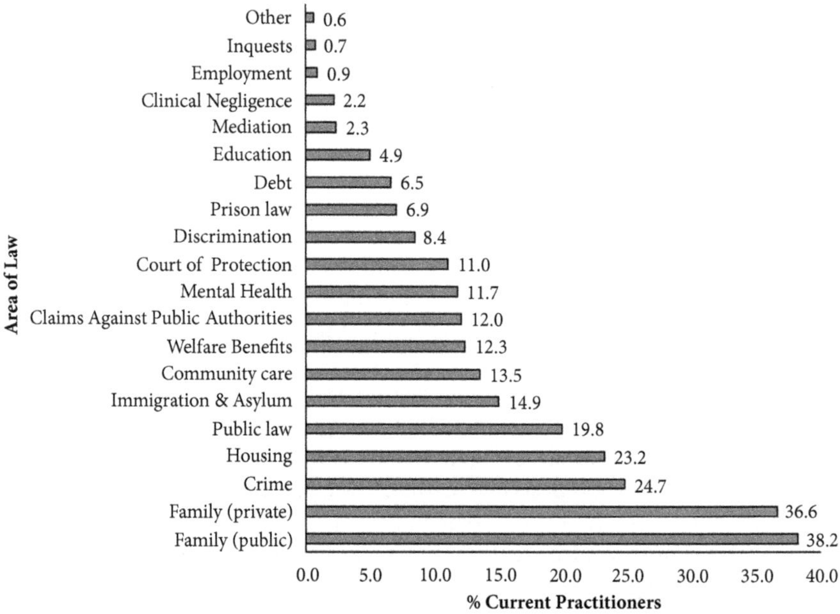

for services and/or the complexity of client needs frequently enough such that it became the fifth most commonly raised issue (15.5 per cent, n=136).[19] This suggests that although the pandemic has resulted in fewer matter starts for practitioners, it has in fact led to an influx of people who are experiencing legal need. As indicated in response to other survey questions, many of these individuals are seeking legal assistance for the first time.

Initial enquiries themselves require a great deal of work from practitioners relating to collecting relevant information, narrowing down issues, identifying any urgent matters and assessing eligibility for legal aid. This additional work is rendered invisible by the apparent decrease in new matter starts as in the following quotes from respondents:

> It has increased demands from clients and led to new clients coming in, while adding an extra layer of complexity to each matter given the vulnerabilities of most clients and the logistics involved with staying Covid secure. The time spent on these issues has not always been billable, meaning there is additional pressure to put more hours in on top.[20]

[19] Derived from quantitative coding of the responses provided by 875 practitioners in response to the following open-ended questions: 'How would you describe the impact Covid-19 has had on your work?' and 'Is there anything else you would like to add about the impact of Covid-19 on legal aid work more generally?'. As similar themes arose across both questions, responses were coded jointly.

[20] Practitioner Respondent Number 864.

> There was an overwhelming burden of homelessness assistance, an entirely overwhelming burden of work around suitability of homelessness placement, a very high volume of benefits work synced to pandemic problems, a large volume of domestic violence linked immigration cases … Staff went above and beyond contractual duty but I anticipate a fallout.[21]

This distinction between new matter starts and initial enquiries is also evident in wider data across England and Wales. For instance, it is useful to consider these findings alongside statistical data produced by the Legal Services Board, which continues to track the number of *enquiries* (not matter starts) across different areas of law throughout the pandemic.[22] This data firstly demonstrates the scale of the pandemic-induced increase in legal need. For example, this data indicates that the number of people seeking information about Universal Credit hitting a record increase of 520 per cent in April 2020, compared with April 2019. Second, this data reinforces concerns about the extent to which the pandemic may mean that people have delayed taking legal action in response to their problems. Debt-related enquiries, for example, were 39 per cent lower in December 2020 than a year earlier, but at the same time, organisations were responding to an increased number of general enquiries about employment and financial services. This may be indicative of looming debt issues that will emerge later, as the true economic implications of the pandemic are determined for businesses and individuals alike.[23]

Broadly speaking, legal need has increased since March 2020 due to the consequences that necessitated social distancing and lockdown measures have had on people's lives. This has led to a greater number of people seeking assistance from legal aid practitioners, but also a concerning absence of traditional clients, who may be unable to rely on services that are provided in remote formats or which are already overwhelmed by a complex range of enquiries. This change in client profile has necessitated advice organisations to rise to the challenge of adapting their strategies and practices for meeting legal need in the post-COVID landscape.

IV. Methods of Working During the Pandemic

Although much of the emerging research concerning the impact of COVID-19 on legal advice is focused upon the ways that services were forced to rapidly shift towards remote service provision, it is important to acknowledge that the legal profession and justice system were already undergoing a great deal of

[21] Organisation Respondent Number 259.

[22] Legal Services Board, 'Covid Dashboard Gives Clearest Picture Yet of Pandemic Impact on Legal Services' (Legal Services Board, 2021), available at legalservicesboard.org.uk/news/covid-dashboard-gives-clearest-picture-yet-of-pandemics-impact-on-legal-services-february-2021-update.

[23] ibid.

change. Over the previous two decades in particular, developments in technology have transformed the ways that lawyers communicate with each other, their clients, and other components of the justice system.[24] The emergence of email, the Internet, cloud storage and case management software have facilitated mass alterations to the mechanisms by which procedures are followed, documents are provided and evidence is assessed.[25] Even before the pandemic, there was a gradual shift towards increasingly digitised justice systems occurring across the globe.[26] As such, researchers and practitioners were already grappling with the potential ethical and legal implications of incorporating automation and artificial intelligence into the processes that underpin legal advice or court hearings.[27] Debates about the role that technology could and should play within legal advice and legal systems have typically been centred around two opposing arguments. The first is that making greater use of such technology provides opportunities to improve access to justice by making the justice system and the legal profession more efficient and cost-effective. The second is that increased reliance on technology may in practice impair access to justice by creating additional barriers for marginalised groups who may be excluded from its use.

Regarding the first argument, there is some evidence to suggest that incorporating virtual or remote methods of advice provision may broaden the accessibility of legal information and advice, especially for certain client groups. For instance, these groups include people who struggle to travel to an advice service due to mobility-related disabilities or because they live in rural areas. Communicating via instant messaging and email can also be useful and easier for clients who do not speak English as a first language, who may find it easier to digest and translate information provided in writing, or who are younger and therefore who may be more comfortable seeking advice online.[28] Additionally, research conducted with advice organisations themselves indicates that some advisors viewed the pandemic-related shift to remote provision as having many positive implications for their service and clients. For many organisations, remote working provided the

[24] Richard Susskind, *The Future of Law* (Oxford University Press, 1996); Richard Susskind, *Tomorrow's Lawyers: An Introduction to Your Future* (Oxford University Press, 2013); Hilary Sommerlad et al (eds), *The Futures of Legal Education and the Legal Profession* (Bloomsbury Publishing, 2015).

[25] Erin Murphy, 'Databases, Doctrine, and Constitutional Criminal Procedure' (2010) 37 *Fordham Urban Law Journal* 803.

[26] Naomi Creudzfeldt, 'Towards a Digital Legal Consciousness?' (2021) 12 *European Journal of Law and Technology*.

[27] Meredith Rossner, 'Remote Rituals in Online Courts' (2021) 48 *Journal of Law and Society* 334; Jane Donoghue, 'The Rise of Digital Justice: Courtroom Technology, Public Participation and Access to Justice' (2017) 80 *MLR* 995, 996; Roger Brownsword, *Rights, Regulation and the Technological Revolution* (Oxford University Press, 2006); Catrina Denvir and Amanda D Selvarajah, 'Safeguarding Access to Justice in the Age of the Online Court' (2021) 85 *MLR* 25.

[28] Elizabeth Cain and JE Goldring, 'WhatsApp as a Debt Advice Channel: Reaching People Other Advice Channels Do Not Reach' (Manchester Metropolitan University, 2018); Sam Fennell, *Disability Benefits During the Pandemic* (Citizens Advice, 2018); Mant et al (n 8).

opportunity to work more efficiently by removing the need to travel to face-to-face appointments and increasing their availability for their clients.[29]

Prior to the pandemic, scholars, practitioners and policymakers were also beginning to emphasise the benefits of digitalisation for court processes. The incorporation of video links and e-filing into procedures meant that courts were increasingly capable of facilitating participation among people who might otherwise be unable to travel to court or who would be uncomfortable attending in person, such as victims of crime or survivors of domestic abuse. Digital tools, including case management systems, the capability to record or transcribe hearings and the use of wireless technology such as laptops or tablets in the courtroom all also have the potential to make the legal system more efficient. Through these tools, courts may be able to expedite processes which, in turn, creates greater capacity among judges, lawyers and court staff.[30] Consequently, although the development of court-based technology has been relatively slow in England and Wales compared to other jurisdictions, there has nevertheless been an increasingly accelerated journey towards digitised justice systems.[31] For several decades, the courts and tribunals service has long relied upon resource-intensive paper-based processes, operating on only limited or basic information technology systems. However, initial trials of virtual hearings in 2009 were quickly followed by large-scale commitments to increase the use of technology, such as the introduction of Wi-Fi in court buildings, television screens in courtrooms and hand-held tablets for judges working in magistrates' courts. By 2016, the courts and tribunals service was undergoing an ambitious programme of reform, including the automation of routine administrative tasks, widespread establishment of video link services and even a pilot scheme for an online system capable of processing online convictions and fines for summary offences.[32]

In many ways, this suggests that the justice system and legal profession were already highly modernised in terms of advice provision and court processes, and that increasing digitisation was overwhelmingly positive for access to justice. However, it is important to acknowledge the ways that such progress has been significantly shaped by neoliberal policy concerns. Donoghue, for instance, points to the 'pervasiveness of economic rationalism' that underpinned the court reform programme.[33] Donoghue asserts that policymakers are keen to maximise the cost–saving benefits that digital tools can have for court systems, even when there is a risk that this may contravene other goals which are more central to the purpose of the justice system such as ensuring quality of case outcomes or facilitating

[29] Administrative Justice Council (n 3); Mant et al (n 8).

[30] Donoghue (n 27) 997.

[31] Joe Tomlinson, *Justice in the Digital State* (Policy Press, 2019); Penny Darbyshire, *Sitting in Judgment: The Working Lives of Judges* (Bloomsbury Publishing, 2011).

[32] Ministry of Justice, 'Transforming Our Justice System' (Ministry of Justice, 2016); Donoghue (n 27) 1000–01.

[33] Donoghue (n 27) 998.

meaningful participation in hearings.[34] Increased digitisation has, for instance, been described as a 'gamble' due to the way that governments have invested public funds into improving court-based technology while at the same time closing a significant number of court buildings, making approximately 5,000 court staff redundant and removing legal aid eligibility for entire areas of law where there was scope for some issues to be dealt with online.[35] In other words, before the pandemic, the government was 'anticipating that digital technologies [would] provide the "transformative" panacea for improving efficiency and access to justice that will 'liberate tens of thousands of individuals from injustice'.[36] Technology and digital tools were imagined to provide a way for public services to provide improved access to justice with far fewer resources.

This 'gamble' is central to the second, opposing argument that underpins the digitisation debate. While increased reliance on technology certainly appears to provide the opportunity for legal professionals and court systems to work more efficiently, there is also a significant body of evidence to suggest that many vulnerable people may be left behind or excluded from law altogether if face-to-face or traditional options for legal participation are not retained. Studies have emphasised that certain client and litigant populations are likely to be digitally excluded, meaning they lack access to appropriate technology that is increasingly required in order to participate in digitised justice systems or that they lack capability and confidence needed to use such technology effectively.[37] These obstacles are disproportionately likely to affect those who require legal support or intervention in order to secure access to social welfare benefits or to dispute proposed eviction from their homes; this is due to the fact that these clients are likely to have access to few resources.[38]

There is also some evidence to suggest that virtual advice may be less effective, even if such client groups are able to access it. Centralised telephone advice gateways, for instance, have been found to provide lower-quality advice due to the fact that advice does not incorporate knowledge of 'local legal culture' that is the familiarity and knowledge of local geographical areas, local policies and procedures and how clients may have intersecting relationships with different departments within local authorities.[39] For those who find themselves subject to an eviction order or those who need to challenge a decision concerning their social welfare benefits advisors, meeting face-to-face with advisors is an essential starting point for building trust and sharing personal information especially where there may already

[34] ibid.
[35] Tomlinson (n 31) 3.
[36] Donoghue (n 27) 1025.
[37] Creudzfeldt (n 26).
[38] Newman et al (n 2); Creudzfeldt (n 26); Marie Burton, 'Justice on the Line? A Comparison of Telephone and Face-to-Face Advice in Social Welfare Legal Aid' (2018) 40 *Journal of Social Welfare and Family Law* 195.
[39] Marie Burton, 'Lost in Space: The Role of Place in the Delivery of Social Welfare Law Advice Over the Phone and Face-to-Face' (2020) 42 *Journal of Social Welfare and Family Law* 341.

be mistrust of public services.[40] In criminal justice, for example, defence lawyers have complained about the inadequacies of 'live link' technology – appearances from prison – for communicating and discussing the complex matters of a case.[41] Concerns have also been raised with regards to increasingly digitised court hearings; for example, research has identified that video hearings are likely to involve fewer opportunities for judges to assist defendants with cognitive impairments or mental health issues.[42] Additionally, scholars have emphasised the potential impact of virtual hearings on the material factors that contribute to perceived legitimacy and authenticity of the court process, such as physical locations or the way that this format may transform the cultural context and attitudes within hearings.[43] The reality is, as Gibbs has found, that we do not yet fully understand the impact of remote access on access to justice – nevertheless, enough concerns have been raised that we need to be cautious.[44]

In sum, there is evidence to suggest that digitised justice – whether it be advice provision or participation in court hearings – requires different legal and digital capabilities from users of the justice system; furthermore, this reality appears to have been underexplored within cost-driven policy initiatives.[45] The lack of robust understanding as to the efficacy and accessibility of remote legal services was therefore already the subject of various concerns before March 2020. Since the outbreak of the pandemic, these concerns have rapidly come to the fore. Responses to the Legal Aid Census revealed a great deal of anxiety among practitioners in terms of how well they have been able to provide advice and support their clients since the pandemic-induced shift to remote advice and virtual court hearings. The pandemic has not simply affected the quantity of practitioners' work, but has also impacted the ways in which practitioners are working. For instance, when asked generally about the impact of COVID-19 on their work, 27.3 per cent (n=239) of current practitioner respondents stated that a major challenge they faced during the pandemic was accessing or using technology to do their work.[46] At the same time, 29.1 per cent (n=92)[47] of organisations and 23.8 per cent (n=5)[48] of chambers

[40] Burton (n 38).

[41] Daniel Newman and Roxanna Dehaghani, *Experiences of Criminal Justice* (Bristol University Press, 2022).

[42] Equality and Human Rights Commission, 'Inclusive Justice: A System Designed for All' (EHRC, 2020).

[43] Linda Mulcahy, 'The Unbearable Lightness of Being? Shifts Towards the Virtual Trial' (2008) 35 *Journal of Law and Society* 464; Tomlinson (n 31) 4.

[44] Penelope Gibbs, *Defendants on Video – Conveyor Belt Justice or a Revolution in Access?* (Transform Justice, 2017).

[45] Creudzfeldt (n 26); Tomlinson (n 31) 8.

[46] See n 19.

[47] Derived from coding of responses given by 316 organisations in relation to the open-ended question 'What has been the most significant challenge in managing your organisation during the Covid-19 pandemic?'.

[48] Derived from coding of open-ended responses provided by 21 chambers in response to the question 'What has been the most significant challenge in managing your set of Chambers during the Covid-19 pandemic?'.

reported that the need to source equipment and adapt to the new role of technology had the most significant impact of COVID-19 on their capacity to manage staff during the pandemic.

Even once 'work from home' practices had become more routine, several practitioners still found it difficult to give effective advice without being able to meet their clients face-to-face. In the following examples, respondents explained some of the difficulties in remote advice:

> Remote advising can be inefficient, can miss the point or be partial, without sight of all relevant documents, so the problems might compound rather than be allayed … It is hard to get to grips with complex problems requiring concentration when the phone/email/WhatsApp never stops ringing.[49]

> It has to be realised that [remote working] can be much more time consuming for bits of work e.g. it is much easier to view physical bank statements than to piece together pictures sent by a client on their phone.[50]

Practitioners frequently reported that conducting client consultations remotely made it more difficult to gain a full view of the relevant circumstances. This issue was compounded by the fact that practitioners could not gain an understanding of their client's situation by looking through relevant documents or letters that would usually have been brought by their clients to meetings. They additionally noted that it was much more arduous to fill out relevant paperwork with a client when they were not able to physically guide them through the required forms.

The challenge of ascertaining information about a clients' circumstances during remote advice sessions has also been identified within other studies conducted during the pandemic. While younger client groups may typically be able to share documents by sending photographs or screenshots through to advisors by email or instant messaging services, this has been recognised to be far more difficult when trying to support clients who are less confident or able to use these tools, and may only be reached by telephone, if at all.[51] For these clients, studies have identified a range of contingency measures including asking clients to read their documents aloud over the telephone, to visit other locations to ask someone else to scan in copies, or to send these items through the post. In some instances, there are simply no other options available, and advisors have reported putting themselves at personal risk during the pandemic by organising door-step collections or meeting clients in public places in order to gather hard copy documents from clients.[52] Remote advice provision therefore comes with several delays, as advice sessions are truncated by requests for documents and increased questioning to try and elicit information from clients. As the first quote suggests, where contextual information or potentially important facts are omitted due to the remote nature of

[49] Practitioner Respondent Number 135.
[50] Organisation Respondent Number 259.
[51] Ng (n 4) 84; Administrative Justice Council (n 3).
[52] Administrative Justice Council (n 3) 10.

the session, there is a real concern that legal problems may be compounded rather than allayed.

Challenges associated with technology also caused complexity for practitioners representing their clients at remote hearings. Given the unexpected and rapidly changing context of the pandemic, judicial guidance was frequent, uncertain and inconsistently implemented by different courts across England and Wales. In some areas, hearings were adjourned for any case involving a contested application or the need for parties to give evidence or participate in cross-examination; in other areas, all such cases continued.[53] For hearings that did go ahead, legal professionals, court staff and the judiciary were faced with the challenge of trying to make court hearings work effectively without the familiar rhythms of the courtroom. As Byrom et al note, a chronic lack of investment in the courts and tribunals service over the years preceding the outbreak of COVID-19 meant that the court system was poorly prepared for the sudden demand to conduct large-scale remote hearings.[54] Evaluations of court proceedings during the pandemic report that the initial shift to remote hearings required legal professionals to source appropriate equipment, such as a second screen that would allow them to view relevant documents and court bundles at the same time as the other participants in the hearing. These evaluations also indicate that there was initially a lack of centralised planning for the platforms that should be used for remote hearings and who should bear responsibility for inviting participants to hearings meant that the roles and responsibilities of hearing participants was often inconsistent, with lawyers themselves sometimes having to host video calls and manage participants because courts in some regions did not have access to the appropriate technology or administrative support.[55] These logistical issues meant that lawyers needed to find technological workarounds to meet their obligations during proceedings, such as communicating with their clients via instant messaging or text instead of relying on the ability to pass messages or have a quiet word that comes with physical proximity in the courtroom.

The open-ended responses practitioners gave to two questions seeking to capture the impact of COVID-19 on their work revealed that the task of representing a client in court remotely is challenging for multiple reasons.[56] Firstly, practitioners are often faced with managing the expectations of both clients and the courts. Clients require guidance on relevant court procedure as well as an understanding of how important it is that these processes are replicated through a telephone or video call. Alternately, courts themselves require contextual information about

[53] Natalie Byrom, 'What We Know About the Impact of Remote Hearings on Access to Justice: A Rapid Evidence Review' (Nuffield Family Justice Observatory and the Legal Education Foundation, 2020); Natalie Byrom et al, 'The Impact of COVID-19 Measures on the Civil Justice System' (Civil Justice Council, 2020).

[54] Byrom et al (n 53) 24.

[55] Mary Ryan, 'Remote Hearings in the Family Justice System: A Rapid Consultation' (Nuffield Family Justice Observatory, 2020).

[56] See n 19.

vulnerable clients and their participation needs. Practitioners reported that the onus was frequently placed on them to ensure that services remained accessible to clients, with 22.4 per cent (n=196) indicating that this had an impact upon their work.[57] These reported concerns related to the accessibility of services broadly, but often specifically related to concerns about ensuring that remote or hybrid hearings ran smoothly. Practitioners reported that they were frequently required to go above and beyond their usual roles to find 'workaround' solutions, such as providing technology or a quiet space for clients to join hearings:

> I feel as if one of the essential tools I need to do my job has been taken away by remote working. Many of my lay clients have cognitive disabilities. Wherever possible I have tried to meet them in person and had hybrid hearings but this has not always been possible. Most people, myself included, rely on non-verbal clues to gauge responses to questions or information. It is an essential tool not available in remote working.[58]

Secondly, some practitioners reported concerns about their ability to support clients during remote hearings when they are not physically together, with 3.4 per cent (n=30) indicating that concerns about safeguarding clients during remote hearings impacted on their work during COVID-19.[59] Before the pandemic, sitting beside the client would allow practitioners to pass notes, have quiet words and read non-verbal cues to understand when their client might need assistance, explanation or a break. Without this physical proximity, practitioners are resigned to using messaging tools like WhatsApp to communicate with their clients and reading non-verbal cues as best they can via video feeds during the hearing. Of course, these tools are contingent on individuals having access to multiple forms of technology that allow them to use video calling as well as a messaging service, which is far from realistic for many legal aid clients.

While several of the challenges reported by practitioners appear to be largely logistical, they have nonetheless had a notable effect on the kinds of relationships that practitioners have established with their clients and the extent to which practitioners feel able to meet the legal need which has emerged since March 2020. Effectiveness of advice is, for instance, about more than just the ability of a practitioner to gain information. In their responses, practitioners also raised several concerns regarding their ability to build sufficient rapport with clients, and the consequences arising from an inability to rely on non-verbal cues to determine whether a client is comfortable, holding back, or fully understanding the advice being given:

> I can do my job on a laptop but my client's struggle with telephone calls and Zoom, sometimes you need the cup of tea and the face-to-face. I don't think the pandemic has made me a better lawyer, but I think I have become less supportive to my clients as a result of not being able to see them.[60]

[57] See n 19.
[58] Practitioner Respondent Number 715.
[59] See n 19.
[60] Practitioner Respondent Number 760.

The value of emotional support and 'being there' for clients was expressed by several practitioners as a casualty of the move to remote working, especially as many legal aid practitioners are used to supporting clients who are coping with legal problems that involve significant disruption to their personal lives such as family breakdowns, housing issues, and problems with social security and benefits. This foundational component of advice-giving is not only important to ensure that clients feel comfortable enough to share potentially relevant information about their situation, but also to ensure that clients feel empowered to implement the advice they receive within sessions and to take action in response to their legal problems.

Census responses from practitioners therefore frequently expressed concerns about how remote advice provision had impacted the effectiveness of advice for clients. This was deemed particularly relevant for certain client groups who were at risk of struggling to access services remotely because they faced barriers in securing consistent access to technology and demonstrating the capacity necessary to use it. Many practitioners explained the problems clients faced as in the following examples:

> It's really difficult with my clients who are already vulnerable due to physical and mental health problems. They have little IT skills so signing documents is hard. I have had to meet clients in the park (depending on Covid rules at the time). Clients also take out their frustration more on you as a solicitor to improve their living conditions during the pandemic.[61]

> Remote working with a client base that has little money and limited access to technology or free WiFi has been a challenge. I know some clients have given up trying to fight their case purely because they did not have the technical experience or equipment to present their case or prove legal help eligibility.[62]

> It has made things much more difficult working with vulnerable individuals in terms of obtaining instructions, which is much easier to do in person. It has also been much more difficult to obtain relevant documents. Most clients do not have computers and cannot scan and email relevant documents. This means most documents are provided by taking photos of documents and then sending in via email from phones. This is difficult to collate. Alternatively clients have to post or drop off documents, which is time consuming. Being able to meet in person and decide what documents are relevant and obtain copies at the first meeting is very helpful in a case.[63]

Access to a computer, smartphone, or tablet is by no means widespread, especially among the traditional client base for some legal aid firms. However, it became a prerequisite for accessing advice during the pandemic. Practitioners suggested that although they were dealing with additional work involved with advising clients remotely, they were also concerned about those vulnerable client groups who were not contacting their services at all. This aligns with the reflections of other practitioners, such as Ng from the Mary Ward Legal Centre, who reflected on her experience of the pandemic:

> The reality was that only a limited service could be provided, which essentially meant that the pro bono clinic could only assist those who could receive telephone calls and

[61] Practitioner Respondent Number 205.
[62] Practitioner Respondent Number 285.
[63] Practitioner Respondent Number 624.

would be able to email us relevant documents prior to their appointment. In addition, clients who faced a language barrier while shielding at the same time, and who did not have anybody at home who could assist were in effect excluded from the clinic.[64]

For those that did manage to make contact, practitioners struggled to advise effectively given the limitations of online advice giving, clients' inconsistent access to technology, or the fact that clients with certain characteristics struggled to make contact digitally. This was especially prevalent among those living in institutionalised settings such as mental health units, care homes or prisons, where many clients were left without advice whilst lawyers were unable to visit in person.[65] Further, practitioners were keenly aware that barriers to remote advice were only the beginning of the problem for these client groups. Rather, they observed that difficulties with using technology to access advice was also likely to affect clients' abilities to engage with subsequent parts of the process, such as establishing eligibility for legal aid or participating in court hearings.

As Figure 6.3 demonstrates, although difficulties were not unanimously experienced, almost half of practitioners reported strongly agreeing (13.7 per cent, n=158 of 1,157) or agreeing (32.9 per cent, n=381) that they had 'struggled to meet the demands of clients since the beginning of the Covid-19 pandemic in March 2020'. This compared to 22.7 per cent (n=263) who neither agreed nor disagreed, 21.4 per cent (n=248) who disagreed and 9.2 per cent (n=107) who strongly disagreed.

Figure 6.3 Extent to which current legal aid practitioners agreed or disagreed with the statement 'I have struggled to meet the demands of clients since the beginning of the COVID-19 pandemic in March 2020' (n=1,157)

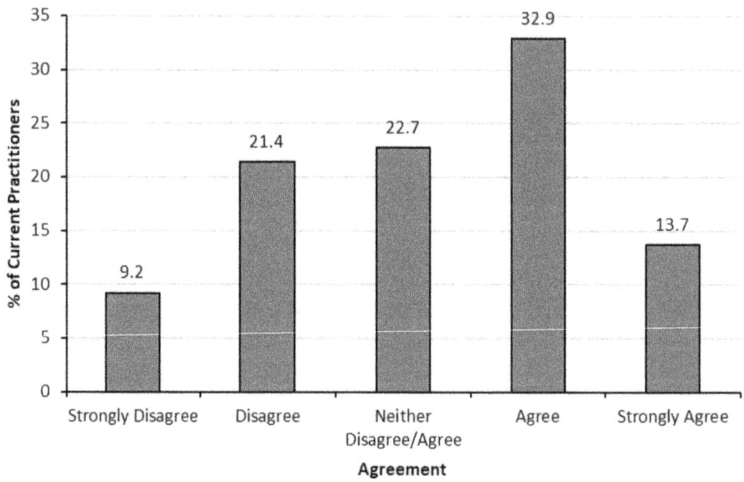

[64] Ng (n 4) 84.

[65] The Law Society, 'Law Under Lockdown: The Impact of COVID-19 Measures on Access to Justice and Vulnerable People' (The Law Society, 2020).

Meeting clients in person, especially for the first point of contact, was perceived as important for *establishing* a positive and productive ongoing client relationship. It was noted earlier that practitioners were challenged in their ability to ascertain information during remote advice sessions. In contrast, a face-to-face meeting often allows for a more pragmatic approach to quickly identifying relevant information and evidence, especially when dealing with vulnerable clients. At the same time, practitioners also reported that it has also been more difficult to *maintain* positive client relationships since the beginning of the pandemic. Several respondents felt that since March 2020, their clients had higher expectations of the time that practitioners should invest in their cases as well as what could realistically be achieved in the context of court delays and the challenges of remote working. For instance, one practitioner observed that 'clients have become more demanding. Since I am working from home and therefore [at] all hours, clients think they can contact me at anytime.'[66] Another practitioner noted observed that:

> The work has increased and the time taken to end a case increased too. That means more demanding clients yet less scope for the cases to end. It has led to less time to do anything and more expectation[s] that things will be done.[67]

Taken together, practitioners in the Census revealed several challenges associated with meeting legal need during the pandemic. Crucially, these can be traced back to several concerns that already characterised political emphasis on the increasing role of technology within advice provision and the justice system. The pandemic has exposed the fragilities inherent in processes that rely heavily on digital tools and brought to bear concerns about how these methods may in practice facilitate the exclusion of vulnerable client groups. Given the extent to which it has supported these clients, the legal aid sector has felt significant pressure to mitigate these challenges. This, in turn, has created additional obstacles for practitioners and organisations who were already facing adversity in relation to the pre-pandemic funding landscape.

V. Workloads and Financial Pressures During the Pandemic

As discussed earlier, the shift to remote working has created several challenges for practitioners in terms of providing advice and attending hearings remotely, with cases and inquiries taking longer and becoming more varied in the context of the pandemic. Although practitioners reported a lower number of new matter starts after the outbreak of COVID-19, there was an overwhelming consensus that actual *workloads* had significantly increased since the beginning of the pandemic.

[66] Practitioner Respondent Number 246.
[67] Practitioner Respondent Number 1193.

In addition to facing an increased number of enquiries, several practitioners reported that the communications they received from clients were more demanding during the pandemic.

This can partially be attributed to the increased variety of demand that organisations sought to meet during the pandemic. On one hand, practitioners were faced with a significant increase in the number of new enquiries from the 'COVID cohort' who, as discussed earlier, are likely to be those with higher levels of capability, digital literacy and confidence in seeking support from organisations. At the same time, practitioners were going to extreme lengths in attempts to maintain contact with their traditional clients, contending with the challenge of reaching out to vulnerable clients remotely. In order to respond appropriately to this newly diverse range of clients, research indicates that practitioners have introduced a range of strategies, such as increasing their availability through offering a greater range of appointment options, including weekends and evenings, or investing a greater amount of time preparing for remote advice sessions to ensure that telephone calls are as effective as possible, to mitigate the potentially high risk of disengagement among certain client groups.[68] Research conducted by the Administrative Justice Council indicates that practitioners are well attuned to the reality that remote advice is most effective when it involves flexibility on the part of the advice organisation. For instance, this might involve adapting communication methods for each client, undertaking additional follow-up contact, and even liaising with clients' social workers, relatives and care co-ordinators to maximise quality of advice and ensure that it has been adequately understood.[69]

Advising during the pandemic was therefore far more demanding in terms of workload. However, the diversity of client needs was just one factor contributing to the pressures felt by advice organisations. Additionally, practitioners reported that this task of responding to enquiries was often more complex and time-consuming than before the pandemic due to the ways that different components of the justice system have been forced to adapt:

> It has increased the pressure – volume of work has increased, court timescales have increased, [there is] no extra support. Working from home has inevitably increased working hours. Work-life balance [has] changed.[70]
>
> Dealing with the increase in work as a result of remote working. We are now expected to be available 24/7 and to move between hearings during the day seamlessly, whereas in the past travel time at least had to be allowed for. It is now relentless with meetings from 8am and back to back hearings during the day. There is a serious risk of burn out and exhaustion.[71]

Practitioners are, of course, not alone in having adapted their services and pivoting to remote working. Court services, the police, social services and relevant

[68] Ng (n 4) 84–85.
[69] Administrative Justice Council (n 3); Mant et al (n 8).
[70] Practitioner Respondent Number 557.
[71] Chamber Respondent Number 16.

government departments have also shifted their working practices in response to the pandemic. For example, the initial stay on possession proceedings and varied approach to hosting court hearings for different case types in the civil and family justice systems meant that practitioners were expected to navigate procedures subject to frequent change during 2020/21. This created additional challenges for practitioners in terms of signposting individuals to relevant services and providing appropriate support to those who enquired about a legal problem, especially when processes were adapted inconsistently or sporadically. Crucially, these left practitioners caught between the dual challenges of trying to support cases to conclusions despite the pandemic and delays in other areas of the justice system, as well as reassuring clients who have increasing demands as a consequence of such delays.

One of the biggest changes to the justice system during the pandemic was the shift to remote court hearings. This has also contributed to the increased sense of pressure and workload reported by practitioners, due to the additional challenges that come with representing a client remotely. The workloads of practitioners have varied based on the way that the court system itself has responded to the pandemic. Practitioners also explained about the extra tasks that were now required in their work:

> Initially, it had a huge impact on workload as the family court switched to remote hearings overnight, without having the infrastructure in place to facilitate the same. It has also caused difficulty with our clients, who by very virtue of being legal aid clients, tend to be on very low incomes and often may have their own vulnerabilities, such as cognitive difficulties, [which makes] the process of remote hearings difficult and stressful for all involved. The Court[s] have seemed to put an onus on solicitors to resolve issues associated with this, for example providing 'spare' electronic devices for clients to attend court hearings which as legal aid firms we do not have. It has also been necessary to prepare hard-copy bundles for clients who are not able to access e-bundles, more often than not because they do not have enough devices to attend the remote hearing as well as to access an e-bundle. We have also had difficulty with Courts stating in some cases that attending remotely using a phone is insufficient and the client needs a laptop or tablet, which often they do not have, nor do they have the resources to obtain such device.[72]

Some practitioners explained the impact of new working practices, noting that the increased rates of case contestation provide another layer to pandemic-related workload challenges:

> The workload in late 2020 and early 2021 has been massive as there has been a surge in contested hearings that were due to take place originally during the first lockdown, as well as cases which have begun since then also coming to contested hearings. I find that the clients are more likely to challenge the outcome of a case when they aren't facing the

[72] Practitioner Respondent Number 123.

> prospect of actually going to a courtroom to give evidence so there are more contested hearings in general, and this has an impact on workload[73]

Many court cases were postponed in the initial response to the COVID-19 outbreak, but in late 2020, remote hearings became more commonplace and the court system began addressing the backlog of cases that had emerged, partly through the establishment of Nightingale Courts around the nation. Since then, hybrid hearings (where some participants attend remotely and others attend in person) have also been used as an option for hearing cases.[74] The variability of these arrangements, however, meant that certain case types were 'bottled up' in the early stage of the pandemic, with practitioners required to manage an increased number of complex hearings at the same time. It is perhaps not surprising that 14.6 per cent (n=128) of practitioners observed that delays due to court backlogs or closures had an impact on their work.[75]

In practice, all of these factors have increased the workload of practitioners despite most taking fewer instructions overall. In some respects, remote working provided the opportunity for practitioners to mitigate these workloads, with 15.9 per cent (n=139) observing that working from home had increased their productivity by negating the need for commuting.[76] In the context of remote hearings specifically, practitioners frequently reported the benefits of being able to spend more time on preparing cases and conducting pre-hearing negotiations with the other side, instead of travelling long distances to hearings in different areas across England and Wales. Some practitioners reflected on how remote methods could have a positive impact on their work, observing that 'the volume of work has increased and I have been able to get to more cases as time is not wasted on travelling which makes legal aid work much more viable',[77] and that 'in some respects, the pandemic has forced the system to reflect on its practice. Remote hearings in many cases are more cost effective and allow more time for advocates to prepare and work.'[78] Another practitioner observed that the pandemic 'had a positive impact on my work practice because most court hearings are now online. I am more efficient because I am not travelling to and from court so have more hours in the day to work on cases.'[79]

The ability to attend multiple hearings in the same day was described by several practitioners as a benefit of the shift to remote hearings because work can be done more efficiently, and unnecessary travel and waiting times at court can be avoided. To some extent, this provides a degree of evidential support for the pre-pandemic goals of improving efficiency within the justice system. However, the increased efficiency reported by practitioners was frequently reported alongside significant

[73] Practitioner Respondent Number 391.
[74] Mant et al (n 8).
[75] See n 19.
[76] See n 19.
[77] Practitioner Respondent Number 1099.
[78] Practitioner Respondent Number 496.
[79] Practitioner Respondent Number 499.

concerns about their ability to support and effectively represent their clients when attending hearings via phone or online, as well as concerns about economic insecurity.

Financial pressures are far from a new feature of the legal aid sector. In reality, practitioners and organisations alike have felt the effect of increased marketisation and austerity measures targeted at the public sector, including the introduction of fixed fees for legal aid work and changes to payment arrangements which meant that legal aid fees are paid in arrears after cases are closed. As explored earlier in this book, LASPO provides perhaps the most dramatic example of such reforms by removing entire areas of law from the scope of legal aid eligibility and diminishing the ability of organisations to sustain cashflow by taking on different kinds of cases whilst waiting for other cases to be closed.[80] The outbreak of the pandemic compounded this economic insecurity because organisations reliant on volunteer support were impaired in their ability to offer services and many organisations were frequently unable to invest in new equipment or software that might have helped them to establish remote services more efficiently.[81] Moreover, many organisations were left with limited income during the pandemic while court hearings were delayed or postponed, due to cases not progressing to the point of closure at which fees could be claimed.[82] Despite the Government's introduction of some temporary funding opportunities for the advice sector in response to COVID-19,[83] scholars and practitioners have criticised the short-term nature of this assistance and argued that due to historic underfunding, the sector was not capable of responding as robustly as was required by the challenges of 2020.[84]

For organisations and chambers, income and cashflow issues were a significant cause for concern. These issues were raised by 52.4 per cent (n=11) of those who responded to the Census on behalf of chambers,[85] and 31.0 per cent (n=98) of those who responded on behalf of organisations.[86] As Table 6.1 indicates, the profit margins reported by organisations during the 12-month period between April 2020 and April 2021 were generally low.[87] While just under a third of organisations reported a comfortable profit margin of at least 11 per cent, 11.6 per cent (n=36) of organisations reported breaking

[80] Jo Wilding, 'Social Welfare and Asylum Legal Aid: A Complex System View of Provider Survival Pre- and Post-Pandemic' (2021) 28 *Journal of Social Security Law* 130.

[81] Administrative Justice Council (n 3) 10.

[82] Wilding (n 80) 132.

[83] 360Giving, 'COVID-19 Grants Tracker' (360Giving, 2022), available at covidtracker.threesixtygiving.org.

[84] Organ et al (n 2); Newman et al (n 2).

[85] See n 48.

[86] See n 47.

[87] Profit margins may include income from different sources aside from legal aid. Four organisations selected more than one response to the question on profit margins. As it was not possible to deduce which choice was correct, these responses were removed from the analysis. Percentages are calculated removing these responses and excluding 55 organisations who did not answer the question.

even or earning only a small profit margin of six to 10 per cent (19.0 per cent, n=59), or one to five per cent (23.9 per cent, n=74). A further 14.2 per cent (n=44) reported running at a loss during this period. This can be contextualised within the broader picture of what profit margins looked like before the pandemic, while removing those who reported having made a loss between April 2020 and April 2021;[88] although 22.3 per cent (n=59) of organisations reported an increased profit margin during this period, the pandemic reduced the profit margin for 44.3 per cent (n=117) organisations compared to the previous year.[89]

Table 6.1 Profit margins of organisations over the last year (April 2020–April 2021) and how this compared to the year before (April 2019–April 2020)

		N	%
The percentage profit margin of organisations during April 2020–April 2021 (n=310)	Running at a loss	44	14.2
	Broke even	36	11.6
	1–5%	74	23.9
	6–10%	59	19.0
	11–20%	48	15.5
	> 21%	49	15.8
How the profit margin during April 2020–April 2021 compares to April 2019–April 2020 (n=264)	Less than	117	44.3
	About the same	76	28.8
	More than	59	22.3
	Not sure	12	4.5

Figure 6.4 below plots the level of profit reported during the year April 2020–April 2021 against the comparison of that profit against April 2019–April 2020.[90] It reveals that there were some winners and losers during the pandemic. Those who reported breaking even in April 2020–April 2021 (with a profit of zero per cent) were more likely to indicate that this was less than the previous year – that is, that their profits had declined. Conversely, those reporting higher profit margins more often indicated that this represented a gain on the year April 2019–April 2020.

[88] Organisations were asked two questions in succession. The first asked 'Can you give an estimate of the percentage profit margin of your organisation in the last 12 months (where applicable)?' and provided the response options of A loss/0%/1–5%/6–10%/11–20%/21%+. The second question asked 'Is this less or more than the 12 months prior to that? (April 2019–April 2020)' with the response options of More than/Less than/About the Same/Not Sure. It is possible that this led to some confusion for those who reported making a loss in relation to the first question. For these organisations, indicating that this loss was greater than April 2019–April 2020 may have led them to select 'More than' in relation to the second question, even although 'Less than' would have been the appropriate choice to indicate a reduction of profits during the April 2020–April 2021 period.

[89] Percentages are calculated removing 52 organisations who did not respond to the question from the original cohort of 369 and a further 53 organisations who reported making a loss in April 2020–April 2021 for the reasons outlined in n 87.

[90] See n 88.

Figure 6.4 Organisations' profit margin for the period April 2020–April 2021 and whether this represented a loss/gain compared to April 2019–April 2020 (n=264)

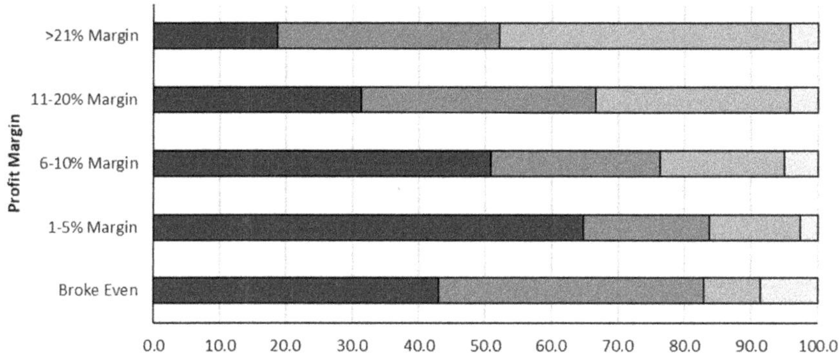

	Broke Even	1-5% Margin	6-10% Margin	11-20% Margin	>21% Margin
Less Than	42.9	64.9	50.8	31.3	18.8
About the Same	40.0	18.9	25.4	35.4	33.3
More Than	8.6	13.5	18.6	29.2	43.8
Not Sure	8.6	2.7	5.1	4.2	4.2

% of Organisations

When it came to explaining their April 2020–April 2021 profits, quantitative coding of the open-ended responses of 248 organisations revealed that over half (55.6 per cent, n=138) attributed a reduction in their profits to the impact of COVID-19. Relatedly, 17.7 per cent (n=44) attributed their shortfall to a reduction in work in specific areas of law affected by the pandemic. Reasons given to explain an increase in profit margins over the year April 2020–2021 included an increase in work in specific areas of law (9.3 per cent, n=23) and reduced expenditure in the form of lower overhead costs due to remote working, limited travel and staff furloughs (12.5 per cent, n=31).[91] As one organisational respondent explained, 'We had a huge fall in profit/revenue when the first lockdown came as our private areas of work could not continue; like conveyancing, which we rely on to keep the firm afloat financially.'[92]

Generally speaking, it therefore appears that most organisations suffered financially as a result of the pandemic. However, experiences varied according to the specific areas of law that were disproportionately affected by the pandemic and the extent to which losses in some areas could be offset by savings

[91] Other reasons included: other (impact of RUI, staff illness, too many suppliers, good management, adapted well, marketing, increased market share (6.9%, n=17); fixed fees/legal aid not profitable (4.8%, n=12); have shrunk/staff redundancies/less fee earners (4.0%, n=10); little difference in volume of work (4.0%, n=10); not for profit (3.6%, n=9); working hard (3.2%, n=8); reduced income unrelated to Covid-19 (3.2%, n=8); grants/funding (2.8%, n=7); problems with LAA (2.8%, n=7), Covid-19 impact would be felt in future years (2.8%, n=7); grant/other funding sources restricted/lack of support (2.0%, n=5);have expanded (1.6%, n=4); chose to reduce amount of legal aid work (1.6%, n=4); and Home Office delays (1.6%, n=4).

[92] Organisation Respondent Number 361.

in respect of overheads, travel and so forth. In response to these economic challenges, organisations and chambers therefore took a range of different actions in order to mitigate the financial impact of COVID-19 on their businesses, including sourcing alternative interim funding, restructuring staff working hours, and reducing staff pay and deferring pupillages and training contracts. Additionally, 22.6 per cent (n=7) of chambers and 20.1 per cent (n=69) of organisations reported being forced to make staff redundant during the pandemic. Overwhelmingly, the most common response to financial difficulties was to place staff on furlough, with 93.5 per cent (n=29) of chambers and 79.1 per cent (n=272) of organisations reporting that they made use of the furlough scheme to sustain their business during the pandemic.

Of those organisations that reported having to place staff on furlough, most commonly between two to five staff members (46.0 per cent, n=115), six to 10 staff members (16.4 per cent, n=41) or one staff member (14.4 per cent, n=36) were furloughed. However just over a fifth of organisations furloughed 11 or more staff members, as shown in Figure 6.5.[93]

Figure 6.5 Number of staff that organisations placed on furlough (n=250)

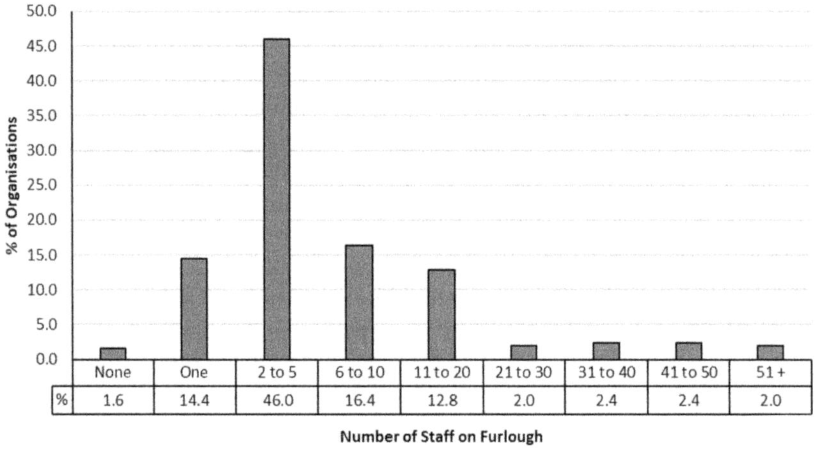

In addition to those who placed staff on furlough, 23.5 per cent (n=85) of organisations reported that they had to make some of their staff redundant between April 2020 and April 2021.[94] In response to a single open-ended question, 38 organisations indicated the staff they had made redundant. Quantitative coding of these open-ended responses revealed that administration and support staff

[93] 272 organisations indicated that they placed staff on furlough in response to COVID-19. Percentages in this table are calculated using the denominator of 250 which represents the number of respondents who provided an answer as to how many staff they placed on furlough.

[94] The impact on staffing within chambers appeared to be much less significant than the impact on organisations, with 61.3 per cent (n=19) of chambers reporting no changes to their staffing levels within the last three years, including the initial year of the pandemic during April 2020–April 2021.

were disproportionately impacted by redundancies, with 73.7 per cent (n=28) of redundancies being of administration and support staff. This compared to 18.4 per cent (n=7) of organisations reporting having made caseworkers, advisors and paralegals redundant, 10.5 per cent (n=4) who made solicitors/legal executives or counsel redundant and 2.6 per cent (n=1) who made other staff redundant. In response to the same question 74 organisations provided a reason for having made redundancies. Of these, 41.9 per cent (n=31) were due to the impact of COVID-19, whilst 37.8 per cent (n=28) were attributed to the impact of finances, 13.5 per cent (n=10) to a lack of work, 4.1 per cent (n=3) to the loss of contracts, teams or offices and 2.7 per cent (n=2) due to business restructure. These findings reveal both COVID-19 and difficult financial conditions precipitating staff redundancies.

For practitioners, the financial pressures characterising their workplaces manifested most prominently within their concerns about job security and economic precarity during the pandemic. These concerns were disproportionately experienced by solicitors and especially respondents at earlier career stages, and varied across different areas of legal practice, with crime and housing disproportionately represented among those experiencing furlough and redundancy. Additionally, several respondents reported concerns about pandemic-related economic insecurity, stemming from large outstanding caseloads subject to delays in the wider justice system as well as pre-existing concerns about the financial viability of legal aid work and economic precarity within the sector.

During the COVID-19 pandemic, 12.0 per cent (n=142 of 1,185) of practitioners reported that they had been furloughed as compared to 88.0 per cent (n=1,043) who had not. A further 1.5 per cent (n=17 of 1,169) of practitioners reported that they had been made redundant, whilst 98.5 per cent (n=1,152) had not. However, as Table 6.2 below indicates, these experiences were not equally distributed across practitioner role types.[95] For example, the proportion of all caseworkers (30.2 per cent, n=13), trainees, pupils, and legal apprentices (27.3 per cent, n=33) and solicitors (18.0 per cent, n=75) furloughed was markedly higher than the proportion of all barristers furloughed (0.5 per cent, n=2). Rates of furlough were also higher amongst those reporting an 'other' role (26.7 per cent, n=4) and legal executives (17.4 per cent, n=4), though the low number of practitioners who identified either of these as their principal role limits the inferences that can be drawn with respect to these practitioner groups. These patterns did not repeat in regard to redundancies, with the proportion of all paralegals made redundant (8.7 per cent, n=2) higher than the proportion of solicitors, heads of department, legal executives, trainees, pupils, and legal apprentices and caseworkers made redundant. Again, however, the small overall number of paralegals responding to the Census urges caution in the interpretation of these findings.

[95] This table excludes responses from clerks, head of chambers and practice managers where no furloughs or redundancies were reported.

Table 6.2 Proportion of current legal aid practitioners from each role-type furloughed and/or made redundant as a result of COVID-19

	Furloughed during COVID-19 (n=142)		**Made redundant as a result of COVID-19** (n=17)	
	N	**Row %**	**N**	**Row %**
Head of Department	3	5.7	1	1.9
Solicitor	75	18.0	8	2.0
Barrister	2	0.5	0	0.0
Legal executive	4	17.4	1	4.3
Trainee/pupil/legal apprentice	33	27.3	4	3.3
Caseworker	13	30.2	1	2.4
Director	2	4.7	0	0.0
Billing clerk	3	12.5	0	0.0
Other	4	26.7	0	0.0
Paralegal	3	13.0	2	8.7

Concerns about job security were also experienced unevenly across areas of legal practice. For instance, although they comprised a minority of practitioner respondents, debt and clinical negligence practitioners were significantly affected. Over a quarter (28.6 per cent, n=4) of debt practitioners who responded reported being furloughed during the pandemic, and 14.3 per cent (n=2) reported being made redundant. Similarly, a fifth (20 per cent, n=3) of clinical negligence practitioners were furloughed. Comprising a larger proportion of practitioner respondents, those practising in housing and crime also frequently reported experiences of job insecurity, with 15.5 per cent (n=34) of housing practitioners and 15.2 per cent (n=53) of crime practitioners being furloughed.

Concerns about job security therefore varied significantly across the sector, with almost half of respondents having no concerns about job security. Of the 30.7 per cent (n= 359) who reported concerns about their job security during the pandemic,[96] the Census data suggests that solicitors and junior practitioners across the areas of crime and housing were most affected, as these respondents were disproportionately represented across those who reported being furloughed or made redundant during the pandemic. However, the findings also suggest that there were disparities across the workforce, with some areas experiencing more furlough than others, and some areas experiencing higher levels of redundancy.

[96] Derived from those who indicated that they agreed (18.5%) or strongly agreed (12.2%) with the statement 'I have concerns about my job security in the legal aid sector as a result of the Covid 19 pandemic.'

In addition to these specific concerns about job security, 15.8 per cent (n=138) of practitioners reported that concerns about general economic insecurity was a major implication of the pandemic on their work.[97] Concerns about economic insecurity (namely a loss of income, reduced cash flow, maintaining overhead costs and new capital expenses required for a shift to working from home) frequently stemmed from pandemic-specific issues, including delays to court hearings and case completions that were caused by the initial postponement of court cases in the justice system, and the subsequent delays as courts adapted to hosting hearings remotely. One practitioner reflected that 'All court hearings were cancelled and I experienced a significant decrease in work from March-May 2020, and the pickup has been slow because solicitors have not been able to see new clients face to face.'[98]

As discussed earlier in this chapter, the shift to remote advice provision meant that many cases were taking longer due to increased difficulties in ascertaining information, supporting vulnerable clients and making progress on cases. This, combined with the delays to court hearings within the justice system, meant that many practitioners were dealing with high levels of incomplete cases. With several outstanding cases for which fees cannot be processed, many practitioners struggled financially.

Some of these practitioners specifically lamented the lack of government support for the legal aid sector during these financial difficulties:

> At the beginning of the pandemic, the closure of the Crown Courts and cessation of trials had a disastrous impact on work. The situation is only just starting to recover now. I lost around half my earnings from trials being cancelled and not proceeding. And I did not qualify for any Government assistance and there was no sector specific support.[99]

> It nearly cost me my relationship, I thought I would lose the house that I had just bought, I thought I would have to leave the profession, all due to the sudden drop in earnings due to courts being shut. The government help for barristers has been derisory.[100]

As indicated above, some practitioners highlighted that they fell into gaps in government assistance and, as a result of there being no comprehensive government support for the legal aid sector, several practitioners suffered significant economic precarity as a result of the pandemic. There were also financial impacts and knock-on effects to the personal lives of these practitioners.

Other practitioners who reported financial difficulties emphasised that economic precarity within the legal aid sector was a pre-existing issue and should

[97] Derived from qualitative coding of the responses provided by 875 practitioners in response to the following two open-ended questions: 'How would you describe the impact Covid-19 has had on your work?' and 'Is there anything else you would like to add about the impact of Covid-19 on legal aid work more generally?'. As similar themes arose across both questions, responses were coded jointly.

[98] Practitioner Respondent Number 479.

[99] Practitioner Respondent Number 942.

[100] Practitioner Respondent Number 696.

not be attributed solely to the repercussions of the pandemic. Indeed, 7.3 per cent (n=64) of practitioners indicated that COVID-19 exacerbated existing problems in the sector or that the problems they faced during COVID-19 had predated the emergence of the pandemic.[101] It was noted earlier that remote attendance at court hearings did, for several practitioners, make legal aid work more efficient and allowed practitioners to conduct more court hearings overall. However, this benefit was frequently related to the fact that legal aid fees themselves are perceived by an overwhelming majority of practitioners as very low. The ability to attend multiple hearings remotely has therefore provided an opportunity for many practitioners to do more work than they would physically have been able to do before the pandemic, which in their view, renders the overall income from legal aid as more sustainable in terms of keeping organisations and individuals financially afloat:

> Two of us had to do the work of 10. Fortunately the use of Videolink court hearings and remote police station hearings made it possible for two people to cover three separate areas. It is essential that remote police station attendances are funded and permitted in the future as well as the courts accepting advocates appearing via video link. It is simply the only way legal aid rates can sustain a practice.[102]

It is also important to note that this 'stacking' of remote hearings was frequently accompanied by concerns about poor or non-existent work–life balance, excessive workloads, and burn-out. While many practitioners expressed that they would like some element of remote or hybrid hearings to continue in the future, this was often rooted in concerns about the sustainability of their practice which predated the pandemic. While some practitioners reported that remote and hybrid hearings were a useful way to increase the efficiency of their working practice, this should therefore be taken alongside significant concerns about the long-term financial security of legal aid work, as well as the impact of 'stacking' hearings on practitioners' well-being and work–life balance.

Furthermore, the high rate of furloughed staff and the prevalence of staff redundancies within organisations and chambers may have reinforced practitioners' concerns about increased workloads during the pandemic. Earlier, it was discussed that administrative and support staff were disproportionately affected by redundancies and furloughing. While this may have provided a way to mitigate some of the economic impact of the pandemic on organisations, this also had negative consequences for other staff members, including individual practitioners who responded to the Census. When asked about the impact of COVID-19 on their work, 12.0 per cent (n=105) of practitioners indicated that they were struggling to cope with the increased level of administration and pressure that resulted from other staff members within their organisations being furloughed or

[101] See n 19.
[102] Practitioner Respondent Number 79.

made redundant.[103] The following quote gives an insight into the organisational experience of furlough:

> We had to furlough a lot of staff which left those left working under extreme pressure. There was very low morale with people working crazy hours to try and service the contract. Resentment built up between those working and those on furlough. The way the media talk about legal aid generally really gets people down and at a time like this it made things far worse.[104]

Another factor which explains the increased workload of practitioners despite overall fewer matter starts is expectation put upon practitioners to manage high caseloads with minimal support. As the above quote illustrates, respondents have contended with increasing numbers of inquiries, greater demand from clients, challenges adapting to remote advice-giving and economic insecurity, all within the same pre-pandemic parameters of legal aid work. These additional pressures have led to a decreased sense of morale and an altered working environment for legal aid practitioners.

In reality, the legal aid sector is no stranger to the need to diversify and strategise in response to financial pressures. The pandemic has been no exception, but it has also posed specific challenges to the usual mechanisms that organisations have historically relied upon to stay afloat such as offsetting and combining different types of work. Delayed fee payments for legal aid work held up during the pandemic, combined with a cataclysmic shift in the level and nature of legal need, means that COVID-19 has posed a new context characterised by limited economic security and spiralling workloads. Given that the true extent of the pandemic is yet to unfold, these are far from temporary problems for the legal aid sector. As Wilding argues, 'continued existence does not equate to sustainability' for organisations providing legal aid, and there is a need for further evaluation to ascertain the additional resource needs that are likely to be needed as we move towards a post-pandemic world of legal advice.[105]

VI. Implications of Findings

This chapter has shown that the pandemic has posed several new challenges for the sector, as well as severely exacerbating several systemic problems that have characterised the sector for decades. The post-pandemic era of legal aid is likely to be underpinned by conflicting narratives which, on the one hand, depict important lessons that have been learned on the sector's frontline about the need for flexibility in ensuring accessibility of advice and legal systems, and, on the other

[103] See n 19.
[104] Organisation Respondent Number 361.
[105] Wilding (n 80).

hand, reinforce policy objectives which continue to promulgate technology and increased digitisation as cost-saving solutions to the economic challenges of the pandemic.

While these contrasting positions are likely to take several years to reconcile at a policy level, practitioner responses to the Census offered indicative insights into how the post-pandemic era is likely to unfold in the meantime. Two key concerns were identified when practitioners were asked about the future: first, the challenge of sustaining well-being and work–life balance in light of these pandemic-induced challenges, and second, the impact of the post-pandemic context on the capacity of the sector to support training and development among junior staff and those entering the legal aid profession.

Despite the potential efficiency gains of working remotely, the intermeshing of work and personal life coupled with the increased demands placed on practitioners by clients may go some way to explaining why 12.8 per cent (n=112) of practitioners reported difficulties with burn-out and work–life balance during COVID-19.[106] One practitioner, for example, stated that 'My workload has increased substantially. I am working longer hours 7 days a week with a couple of days off every month. It is not sustainable and I am concerned that I am going to burn out.'[107]

The long hours discussed in chapter four have thus been exacerbated by the pandemic. Another practitioner asserted that 'Covid-19 has created so much more work, [and I am] working very long hours from home and getting paid very little for it. It has been an absolute burn out.'[108]

This chapter has also detailed various strategies employed across the legal aid sector in an attempt to meet the diverse range of legal need that organisations are now facing, such as making appointments for clients available beyond typical working hours, incorporating flexibility into methods of advice provision and undertaking additional labour associated with increased follow-ups and outreach work. Given the range and extent of these strategies as well as the limited resources on which organisations are relying upon now that opportunities to access temporary pandemic funding have expired, it is unsurprising that work–life balance and well-being is at the forefront of practitioners' minds when they look to the future. Other studies have also noted that during the midst of the pandemic, legal professionals struggled to set effective boundaries with clients when providing advice from home, and found their own mental and physical health deteriorating due to inadequate workspaces in their homes; for instance, some were frequently speaking to clients from their living rooms and bedrooms.[109] One respondent to the Administrative Justice Survey also found 'it difficult mentally to have clients' voices coming into [their] house'.[110]

[106] See n 19.
[107] Practitioner Respondent Number 1162.
[108] Practitioner Respondent Number 342.
[109] Ng (n 4) 84.
[110] Administrative Justice Council (n 3) 10.

Within the Census responses, practitioners were not only concerned about the economic sustainability of legal aid work during the pandemic, but also specifically identified that the working practices which developed over the course of the pandemic were unsustainable. In addition to taking a significant toll on practitioners' well-being and work–life balance, it also appeared to reframe how some practitioners perceived the value of legal aid work:

> It has made it very lonely which was not the case at all before. I have not seen colleagues or clients or counterparts or anyone involved in my work for over a year and that makes it a very different type of role to the one I signed up for. It also means that the work feels very isolated and abstract. I do not feel part of a community of people doing this work at all.[111]

Another respondent wrote that the pandemic 'has made everything feel dislocated and remote, gradually chipping away at the significance of the work and its importance to the people and clients affected by the important decisions being made about their lives.'[112]

Indeed, 1.7 per cent (n=15) of practitioners reported that COVID-19 had actually facilitated their departure from the profession.[113] While this may seem like a small proportion, it should be read alongside data collected from organisations, where respondents were divided on whether their organisations would need to make further redundancies in the future. While 20.4 per cent (n=74 of 363) stated they were very unlikely and 37.7 per cent (n=137) stated they were unlikely to make redundancies in the next 12 months, 17.1 per cent (n=62) of organisations expected it was likely and 9.4 per cent (n=34) expected it was very likely that they would need to make redundancies in the next year. A further 15.7 per cent (n=57) remained unsure. Taken together, this paints a relatively uncertain future for practitioners, who may find themselves in a position of insecurity, either by way of their own career opportunities or the financial stability of the organisation in which they are based.

Further, as these responses illustrate, the shifts that have taken place during the pandemic have influenced the way that some respondents feel about the work they are doing. This indicates that connections with other legal aid professionals as well as full interactions with clients are both perceived as very important by practitioners in terms of deriving value and satisfaction from their work. This may be essential for encouraging junior practitioners to remain within the legal aid sector, as they are likely to be disproportionately disadvantaged by a lack of support and opportunities to learn from their colleagues and fewer positive experiences of assisting clients.

When asked about the impact of the pandemic on their work, 4.6 per cent (n=40) of practitioners specifically stated that the shift to remote working had

[111] Practitioner Respondent Number 261.
[112] Practitioner Respondent Number 448.
[113] See n 19.

created barriers to proper supervision of trainee practitioners.[114] The following quote reflects on the difficulties caused with managing staff in remote working:

> It has also presented a challenge given the need to properly supervise and develop junior members of staff. Our organisation had plans to grow prior to the pandemic which we have continued to implement but onboarding, training, supervision and maintaining culture are all difficult whilst the majority of staff work remotely full time.[115]

These barriers related specifically to the difficulty in maintaining a sense of community and supportive culture within the workplace whilst working remotely, which was an issue separately raised by a further 3.0 per cent (n=26) of practitioners. Some practitioners were themselves junior, and were able to elaborate upon the challenges they had faced to developing their skills and capacities during the pandemic:

> It has made a big difference to my training contract. 3 of my 4 seats have been undertaken during the pandemic. It is harder to access support from colleagues and learn by shadowing colleagues and attending court. It can be isolating working from home.[116]

Connections with others working in legal aid are therefore not only important for maintaining a sense of value and satisfaction among legal aid practitioners. Although only discussed by a minority of practitioners, this suggests that collaborative working styles are also essential for ensuring productive supervision and training opportunities for junior practitioners embarking upon their legal aid careers in the years following the initial outbreak of COVID-19.

It would be short-sighted, therefore, to assume that the impact of the pandemic on the legal aid sector will be restricted to the calendar years in which restrictions were in place. As noted earlier in this chapter, there is likely to be a significant amount of pandemic-induced legal need which is yet to emerge. At the same time, the sector finds itself under-resourced and faced with a host of new challenges to overcome in the immediate term. The lack of resilience within the sector to begin with is likely to have an adverse effect on its ability to address longer-term concerns, such as the future sustainability of its working practices, environments, and decreased opportunities for training and development of its junior members.

Perhaps most concerning is the uncertainty of how this future will play out, given that the Government appears to be staunchly committed to the position that the pre-pandemic shift towards digitised justice has 'enabled us to keep the wheels of justice turning during the pandemic. And it will help us tackle the longer-term impact of the pandemic.'[117] Of course, as discussed throughout

[114] See n 19.
[115] Organisation Respondent Number 33.
[116] Practitioner Respondent Number 627.
[117] Her Majesty's Courts and Tribunals Service, 'The HMCTS Reform Programme' (HMCTS, 2021), available at www.gov.uk/guidance/the-hmcts-reform-programme#reform-in-a-time-of-covid-19.

this chapter, the impact of the COVID-19 pandemic on the legal aid workforce is far from this straightforward. During 2020/21, practitioners adapted to the new world of remote working, providing advice and representing clients virtually and via telephone. While this has its advantages – such as reducing the time spent travelling to hearings and reducing overhead costs for premises – this shift has also come with significant challenges. The tasks of supporting vulnerable groups as well as the new 'COVID cohort' of clients, maintaining a supportive and cohesive workplace community and a healthy work–life balance, and proper supervision and training provision for junior staff have all become more difficult since March 2020.

The pandemic has also brought significant concerns about economic sustainability for organisations, chambers and individuals. Concerns about job security and economic precarity, for instance, were two key consequences of the pandemic reported by practitioners. These concerns were disproportionately experienced by solicitors and respondents at earlier career stages, and varied across different areas of legal practice, with crime and housing disproportionately represented among those experiencing furlough and redundancy. Additionally, several practitioners reported concerns about pandemic-related economic insecurity, stemming from large outstanding caseloads subject to delays in the wider justice system as well as pre-existing concerns about the financial viability of legal aid work and economic precarity within the sector. Taken together, these factors demonstrate that the legal aid sector is facing significant challenges as it moves beyond the immediate repercussions of the pandemic and begins to look towards the post-COVID future of the legal aid workforce.

7

Recruitment and Retention

I. Introduction

In recent years, high numbers of legal aid practitioners in England and Wales have left the profession. In criminal legal aid, the number of barristers practising full time in publicly funded criminal law fell by 10 per cent in 2018/19.[1] As of February 2022, there were just 1,062 law firms with criminal legal aid contracts as compared to 2,010 in 2007.[2] Alarmingly, as many as 130 law firms left the criminal legal aid market in 2018/19 alone.[3] As identified in chapter two, in view of the low numbers of new recruits, the ageing legal aid profession is a matter of concern with respect to longer-term sustainability. For example, the Law Society estimates that only four per cent of criminal legal aid solicitors are under the age of 35 and there is a severe shortage in duty solicitors with, for example, only seven available in some geographic areas meaning each is required to be on duty for a full 24-hour period every week.[4] In civil legal aid, the rates of retention are similarly concerning and well demonstrated by advice deserts in certain areas of law. Community care, education, housing, immigration and social welfare have all been identified as advice deserts with low numbers of legal aid providers. For example, it is estimated that 68 per cent of the population in England and Wales do not have access to a community care legal aid provider.[5] In education, 88 per cent of the population do not have access to a provider and nowhere in England and Wales has access to more than three providers.[6] The Bar Council has also highlighted that

[1] The Bar Council, 'Bar Council Data Analysis Criminal Bar' (The Bar Council, 2022), available at www.barcouncil.org.uk/resource/bar-council-data-analysis-criminal-bar-april-2022.html.

[2] UK Parliament, 'Legal Aid Scheme: Contracts' (Question for the Ministry of Justice tabled by Afzal Kahn, 21 February 2022), available at https://questions-statements.parliament.uk/written-questions/detail/2022-02-09/121917.

[3] Ministry of Justice, 'Data Compendium: Summary Information on Publicly Funded Criminal Legal Services' (Ministry of Justice, February 2021) 19.

[4] The Law Society of England and Wales, 'Defending the Future of Criminal Legal Aid: What We are Doing for Members' (The Law Society, 2022), available at lawsociety.org.uk/topics/legal-aid/defending-the-future-of-criminal-legal-aid.

[5] The Law Society of England and Wales, 'Legal Aid Deserts' (The Law Society, 22 August 2022), available at www.lawsociety.org.uk/campaigns/legal-aid-deserts.

[6] ibid.

civil legal aid is proving to be an unsustainable area of practice for junior members of the Bar for those without independent financial means.[7]

The evidence suggests that the failure to recruit and retain practitioners has been particularly acute in some areas, which tends to align with emerging evidence in relation to advice deserts. For example, recent research in community care law finds that some organisations have simply been unable to recruit lawyers at supervisor level, therefore significantly impacting upon service provision. As such, it is extremely challenging to train new practitioners; as was discussed in chapter three, this matter is already made difficult by the poor awareness of the specialism among students and the failure to teach social care in law schools.[8] In the field of immigration law, problems with the retention of specialist lawyers in the field has led to poor levels of service provision.[9] In social welfare, LASPO reforms and the move to telephone legal advice has reduced the number of regulated practitioners working in the field. Indeed, telephone advice has been linked to poor awareness of relevant local issues such as available support and a narrow understanding of the intersection of issues in the field, again resulting in overall poor service provision.[10]

The 2022 practitioner strikes also brought recruitment and retention issues in relation to criminal defence work into sharp focus. Retention problems with respect to criminal legal aid have been long-standing: as discussed in chapter five, the so-called New Public Management reforms helped create a culture of burn-out, which had an overall impact upon well-being and morale.[11] Kemp's 2010 study of criminal defence solicitors noted high levels of demoralisation within the profession alongside perceived levels of decline in status.[12] Similar to Moorhead's 2004 study, which highlighted the 'escape routes' available for legal aid lawyers meaning they did not stay in the profession long term,[13] Kemp also observed the rising numbers of practitioners moving into other types of government work rather than staying in criminal defence work.[14]

[7] The Bar Council, 'Running on Empty: Civil Legal Aid Research Report' (The Bar Council, 2021) 5.

[8] Karen Ashton et al, 'Community Care Legal Career Pathways' (Access Social Care, 2022), available at static1.squarespace.com/static/5f2160ae3e84ef21653b8190/t/627250a7c95f3e62241f1e2c/1651658921088/Adult+social+care+and+unmet+needs+May+2022.pdf.

[9] Jo Wilding, *The Legal Aid Market: Challenges for Publicly Funded Immigration and Asylum Legal Representation* (Policy Press, 2021).

[10] Marie Burton, 'Lost in Space: The Role of Place in the Delivery of Social Welfare Law Advice Over the Phone and Face-to-Face' (2020) 42 *Journal of Social Welfare and Family Law* 341.

[11] Hilary Sommerlad, 'I've Lost the Plot: An Everyday Story of Legal Aid Lawyers' (2001) 28 *Journal of Law and Society* 335.

[12] Vicky Kemp, *Transforming Legal Aid: Access to Criminal Defence Services* (Legal Services Research Centre, 2010) 107.

[13] Richard Moorhead, 'Legal Aid and the Decline of Private Practice: Blue Murder or Toxic Job?' (2004) 11 *International Journal of the Legal Profession* 159, 180.

[14] Kemp (n 12).

Thornton's more recent study of criminal defence lawyers also suggests significant problems with demoralisation leading to retention issues. He notes, for example, the prevalence of lawyers doing criminal defence work as a secondary area due to the pressures in attempting to maintain a practice in full-time criminal legal aid.[15] While acknowledging that in some respects maintaining a diverse practice can be positive, Thornton points to the empirical evidence that suggests that specialism leads to better-quality work and client service provision.[16] In summary, Thornton asserts that low levels of remuneration in criminal legal aid can have direct effects but also act as 'an indirect driver of morale and frustrations.'[17] Examples of this may include dictating that lawyers and law firms work in particular ways, low levels of remuneration becoming a source of stress and businesses generally becoming unviable.[18] Thornton argues that these frustrations negatively influence morale further such that 'a relatively small increase in funding could have a disproportionately positive effect in terms of lawyer morale.'[19]

Another issue of concern that has served to exacerbate financial pressures in the early years of legal aid practice – and indeed serves as a deterrent – relates to the low levels of funding available for education and training. Unlike many other areas of the public sector, such as healthcare or education, the Government does not currently subsidise the costs of education and training. For not-for-profit providers and law firms struggling with low profit margins, the costs of training and supervision prohibit the provision of training placements. In the past, the Legal Services Commission funded legal aid trainees with grants of £20k per year. This scheme helped to train more than 750 trainees to qualify as legal aid lawyers, but was abolished in 2010. There has been long-standing concern about the costs of training having an impact upon legal aid recruitment and retention, especially with respect to social mobility.[20] As discussed in chapters three and five, high levels of debt combined with low levels of remuneration serve to make legal aid work unsustainable for those from lower socio-economic backgrounds.

The Justice First Fellowship was established by the Legal Education Foundation in 2014 partly in recognition of this problem. Fellows are funded during their

[15] James Thornton, 'Is Publicly Funded Criminal Defence Sustainable? Legal Aid Cuts, Morale, Recruitment and Retention in the English Criminal Law Professions' (2020) 40 *Legal Studies* 230, 242.

[16] See, eg, Richard Moorhead, 'Lawyer Specialisation – Managing the Professional Paradox' (2010) 32 *Law and Policy* 226.

[17] ibid, 251.

[18] ibid, 248.

[19] ibid, 251.

[20] Young Legal Aid Lawyers, 'Young Legal Aid Lawyers: Social Mobility in a Time of Austerity' (Young Legal Aid Lawyers, 2018), available at www.younglegalaidlawyers.org/sites/default/files/Soc Mob Report – edited.pdf.

period of legal training and work predominantly in not-for-profit organisations such as law centres and charitable organisations, although some are also hosted in legal aid law firms and chambers. Out of 88 fellowship graduates to date, the Legal Education Foundation reports that 90 per cent are still working in roles as lawyers in the public interest and 77 per cent are working in specialist not--for-profit providers, law firms or sets of chambers.[21] While these numbers are small, the rates of retention appear positive and arguably provide a framework for the reinstatement of a more comprehensive programme of funding from the Government to bring higher numbers of trainees into the profession. Some progress has also been made to date through the support of corporate law firms and the tenacity of young practitioners determined to resolve recruitment issues in areas of social welfare law.[22] Together with education provider Barbri, the Social Welfare Solicitors Qualification Support Fund identifies and funds SQE preparation and assessment for aspiring social welfare solicitors. However, these cumulative initiatives are still not able to meet the scale of the problem, nor should philanthropy be expected to underwrite such a vital public service. The Westminster Commission on the Sustainability of Legal Aid recommended that the Ministry of Justice fund training placements in legal aid law firms and further support publicly funded sets of chambers as a matter of urgency. As discussed in chapter three, the Commission recommended the inclusion of social welfare modules on the SQE 'to encourage bright and committed individuals to its ranks' and ensure the diversity of the profession in future.[23]

Against this background, this chapter contributes to the evidence base on legal aid recruitment and retention by examining the extent to which organisations are able to find suitable practitioners for legal aid work. Taking a comprehensive sector-wide approach, it also provides an accurate picture of the areas of practice in which practitioners, organisations and sets of chambers no longer work. As such, it highlights the precarious areas of the sector and elucidates how the legal landscape has changed in recent years. It further discusses the reasons that respondents have left legal aid with reference to reasons according to specific areas of practice. Finally, the chapter explores the key concerns reported by current practitioners such as work-life balance, pressure and available support within the sector.

[21] The Legal Education Foundation, 'Justice First Fellowship Retention Monitoring Data 2022' (unpublished, on file at the Legal Education Foundation).

[22] See eg, the Social Welfare Solicitors Qualification Support Fund (SWSQF) run by Young Legal Aid Lawyers, the City of London Law Society and Barbri, which funds SQE preparation courses and assessments: The City of London Law Society, 'Social Welfare Solicitors Qualification Support Fund (SWSQF)' (The City of London Law Society), available at www.citysolicitors.org.uk/clls/social-welfare-solicitor-qualification-fund.

[23] The Westminster Commission on Legal Aid, 'Inquiry into the Sustainability and Recovery of the Legal Aid Sector' (All-Party Parliamentary Group on Legal Aid, 2021) 24.

II. Finding and Retaining Suitably Qualified Practitioners

A. Chambers

It is perhaps surprising given the high numbers of applications for pupillage and tenancy that sets of chambers report difficulties in finding suitably qualified candidates for legal aid work. Yet, as detailed in Figure 7.1, only 7.7 per cent (n=2) of chambers indicated that it was very easy to find suitably qualified legal aid barristers and 30.8 per cent (n=8) indicated that it was easy. A further 30.8 per cent (n=8) stated that finding suitable qualified legal aid barristers was not that easy and the same number (30.8 per cent, n=8) indicated it was not at all easy to do so. In total, the majority of chambers (61.6 per cent, n=16) expressed difficulty finding qualified legal aid barristers. Notably, retention of suitably qualified barristers was also found to be challenging; 34.5 per cent (n=10) of chambers stated that it was not that easy to retain those who were suitably qualified and 31.0 per cent (n=10) stated that it was not at all easy. This contrasted with 17.2 per cent (n=5) of chambers who found it very easy and a further 17.2 per cent (n=5) who also professed to finding it easy.

Figure 7.1 The ease with which chambers can find (n=26) and retain (n=29) suitably qualified legal aid barristers

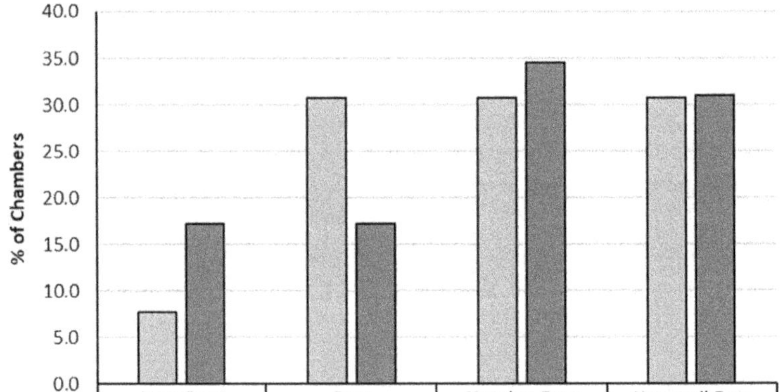

	Very Easy	Easy	Not that Easy	Not at all Easy
Find	7.7	30.8	30.8	30.8
Retain	17.2	17.2	34.5	31.0

When asked to explain why it was easy or difficult to find suitable qualified legal aid barristers, 18 sets of chambers offered further explanations. Coding these open-ended responses for commonalities revealed over 50.0 per cent of chambers (n=9) attributed the difficulty to there being better salaries available for barristers elsewhere. As such, it is difficult to compete with the much more favourable salary and working conditions available in other areas of practice. A smaller number of chambers (11.1 per cent, n=2) attributed the difficulty to the lack of practitioners and high demand for their employment. The same proportion and number of chambers (11.1 per cent, n=2) attributed the challenge to legal aid barristers tending to leave the profession entirely. At least one set of chambers observed each of the following challenges: finding barristers with sufficient experience was difficult; barristers want to work in different locations; barristers do not want to work in legal aid; and barristers do not want to leave where they were currently working. Only one set of chambers (5.6 per cent) out of the respondents indicated that it was not difficult to find suitable qualified barristers because some barristers are committed to working in legal aid and are happy to do so for less remuneration than they might be paid in other areas of work.

The relevance of remuneration was also a factor in the reasons provided by 16 sets of chambers as to why it was easy/difficult to retain suitable qualified barristers, with 50 per cent (n=8) of chambers observing that it was difficult because there are better salaries elsewhere, 25 per cent (n=4) of chambers indicating that barristers leave because they do not want to continue working in legal aid, and at least one set of chambers (6.3 per cent) raising each of the following reasons: there are better working conditions elsewhere; there is poor work–life balance, challenging work and stressful workloads in legal aid; there is less legal aid work available for barristers; and barristers who leave legal aid leave the profession entirely. There were, however, a number of responses which painted a more positive picture. 12.5 per cent (n=2) of chambers indicated that ease of retention depended on the area of practice and 18.8 per cent (n=3) of chambers observing that retention was possible as long as legal aid work is offset by private practice work. Only one set (6.3 per cent) indicated that they had no difficulty with retention, which they attributed to their good working environment.

B. Organisations

Figure 7.2 depicts the ease with which organisations reported being able to find and retain suitably qualified lawyers. 25.0 per cent (n=76) stated that it was not that easy and 68.1 per cent (n=207) found it not at all easy. This compared to 5.6 per cent (n=17) of organisations who found it quite easy and 1.3 per cent (n=4) who found it very easy. Similarly, 38.8 per cent (n=119) indicated that it was not easy and 23.8 per cent (n=73) indicated it was not at all easy to retain suitably qualified lawyers. Only 6.5 per cent (n=20) of organisations found it very easy to retain suitably qualified lawyers, while a higher proportion (30.9 per cent, n=95) indicated that it was quite easy to retain suitably qualified lawyers.

Figure 7.2 The ease with which organisations can find (n=304) and retain (n=307) suitably qualified legal aid lawyers

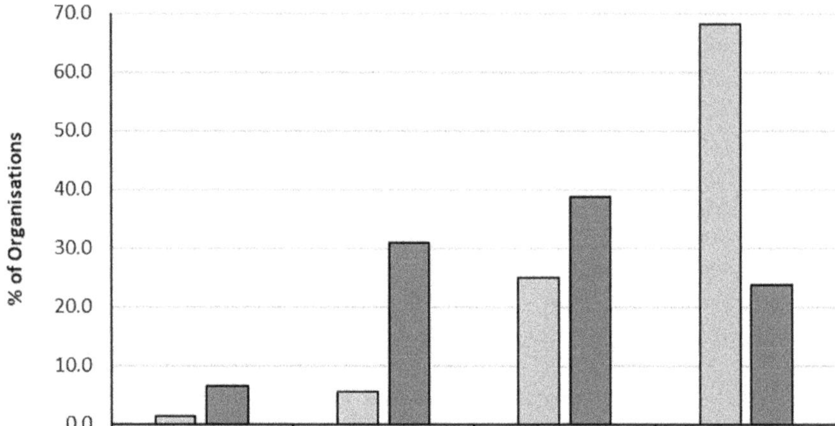

	Very Easy	Easy	Not that Easy	Not at all Easy
Find	1.3	5.6	25.0	68.1
Retain	6.5	30.9	38.8	23.8

When it came to explaining why it was or was not easy to find suitably qualified lawyers, 315 organisations provided open-ended responses. Once coded, a number of key themes emerged. Comparatively low levels of remuneration again dominate as a key issue. As with chambers, a large proportion of organisations (40.0 per cent, n=126) attributed the difficulty of finding suitably qualified legal aid lawyers to the fact that there are better salaries elsewhere. Similarly, 37.1 per cent (n=117) attributed the challenges to a lack of lawyers and the fact they are in demand. Fewer organisations (14.6 per cent, n=46) cited that it was difficult to find lawyers with the requisite experience, with 13.0 per cent (n=41) of organisations observing that lawyers were put off by the prospect of working in legal aid. Better working conditions elsewhere was noted by 8.6 per cent of organisations (n=27). 6.3 per cent (n=20) of organisations observed that younger lawyers were more likely to gravitate towards other employers within the legal profession, and 4.8 per cent (n=15) of organisations observed challenges related to having to compete with the salaries and conditions offered by the Crown Prosecution Service (CPS). Less frequently mentioned reasons included lawyers wanting to work in different locations; an ageing workforce that is close to retirement; the existence of bureaucratic challenges in the sector, which operated as a deterrent for prospective new entrants; a real or perceived lack of opportunities for career progression and security; an inability to retain legal aid contracts; the fact that those leaving their roles tend to leave the profession entirely; the fact that lawyers often did not want to leave their current positions; and finding suitably qualified lawyers was down to luck.

Far fewer responses indicated that the organisation had no challenges with recruitment. Some 8.9 per cent (n=28) of responses indicated that recruitment difficulties were dependent on practice area, and only 1.6 per cent (n=5) of the total responses received stated that the organisation had no trouble recruiting because of the organisation's reputation or the fact that they offered good benefits. A further three organisations (1.0 per cent) reported that it was not difficult for them to recruit because they had contacts within the sector, whilst 0.3 per cent (n=1) of organisations reported at least one of the following: they found lawyers with the help of recruitment agencies; it was not difficult to recruit because some lawyers are committed to working in legal aid and are happy to do so for less; and they had no difficulty recruiting generally.

In addition to providing open-ended responses with respect to why it was easy or difficult to find suitably qualified legal aid lawyers, organisations were also asked the same regarding the *retention* of suitably qualified legal aid lawyers. Of the 256 organisations who provided a response, salaries were described as a key concern. In total, 44.5 per cent (n=114) of organisations cited that the availability of better salaries elsewhere made retention of lawyers challenging. Working conditions were also identified as a significant issue 11.7 per cent (n=30) of organisations suggested that there are better working conditions elsewhere, that the legal aid sector has a poor work–life balance, and that legal aid work is challenging and stressful. In contrast, the CPS was seen as a more favourable employer in terms of salaries and working conditions. Duly, 10.2 per cent (n=26) of organisations responded by discussing how CPS recruitment drives made recruitment into legal aid work difficult. Other responses were given in small numbers, with the most common answers identifying that there is a lack of experienced and qualified practitioners (6.3 per cent, n=16) and that practitioners move on because of lack of security and/or opportunities for progression (6.3 per cent, n=16).

It is worth noting that almost a quarter of these organisations (24.6 per cent, n=63) reported no difficulty in retaining staff. Reasons cited here include that the organisation had a good working environment, there was a firm ethos at the organisation and the organisation rewarded staff well. 3.9 per cent (n=10) of organisations also noted that lawyers stay because they are committed to working in legal aid and are happy to do so for less remuneration than in private work.

Consistent with wider research in relation to the criminal legal aid recruitment, organisations who provided a response in respect of practice areas (n=94), most often referenced crime (26.6 per cent, n=25) as being an area in which they were trying to recruit new practitioners, as shown by Table 7.1. This was followed by public family (19.1 per cent, n=18), and private family (14.9 per cent, n=14). Clinical negligence (1.1 per cent, n=1), employment (4.3 per cent, n=4), and wills and probate (4.3 per cent, n=4) were far less commonly mentioned areas of active recruitment.

Table 7.1 Areas of planned recruitment for organisations (n=94)

	N	%
Crime	25	26.6
Family (public)	18	19.1
Family (private)	14	14.9
Community care	11	11.7
Public law	11	11.7
Prison law	10	10.6
Housing	10	10.6
Immigration and asylum	10	10.6
Mental health	10	10.6
Court of Protection	10	10.6
Claims against public authorities	7	7.4
Education	7	7.4
Debt	6	6.4
Mediation	6	6.4
Discrimination	5	5.3
Welfare benefits	5	5.3
Other	5	5.3
Wills and probate	4	4.3
Employment	4	4.3
Clinical negligence	1	1.1

III. Exiting Practice Areas

A. Practitioners

As reported in Table 7.2, practitioners worked across all areas of legal aid practice, with the majority working in public family law (31.9 per cent, n=384) followed by crime (29.6 per cent, n=357) and private family law (29.0 per cent, n=349). These areas also represented the most populous areas of former practice, albeit in a different order. Notably, of the areas of legal aid current practitioners had stopped practising in, crime (42.6 per cent, n=270) was most common. This was followed by private (30.0 per cent, n=190), and public (20.8 per cent, n=132) family law. Table 7.2 below further details that just over a fifth of respondents had ceased working in housing law (22.4 per cent, n=142) and just under a fifth had ceased working in welfare benefits law (18.1 per cent, n=115).

Table 7.2 The current and former legal aid practice areas of current legal aid practitioners

	Current practice areas (n=1205)		**Areas of previous practice** (n=634)	
	N	%	**N**	%
Crime	357	29.6	270	42.6
Immigration and asylum	123	10.2	91	14.4
Family (public)	384	31.9	132	20.8
Family (private)	349	29.0	190	30.0
Clinical negligence	15	1.2	59	9.3
Mental health	85	7.1	68	10.7
Public law	299	24.8	44	6.9
Welfare benefits	49	4.1	115	18.1
Court of Protection	141	11.7	36	5.7
Other	8	0.7	10	1.6
Inquests	18	1.5	3	0.5
Prison law	59	4.9	101	15.9
AATP	2	0.2	–	–
Employment	3	0.2	18	2.8
Claims against public authorities	147	12.2	64	10.1
Community care	139	11.5	64	10.1
Debt	14	1.2	81	12.8
Discrimination	74	6.1	26	4.1
Education	33	2.7	37	5.8
Mediation	13	1.1	13	2.1
Housing	222	18.4	142	22.4
General civil/litigation	–	–	11	1.7
Personal Injury	–	–	14	2.2

When practitioners were asked why they no longer worked in these areas of legal aid by way of an open-ended question, analysis of the 585 responses provided revealed that the departure from an area of practice was most commonly attributed to the practitioner 'pursuing specialisation in a different area' (56.5 per cent, n=331). A number of wider reasons might underpin a decision to pursue a different specialisation. However, a third of respondents indicated that they exited the area as it was no longer a financially viable area of practice (36.8 per cent, n=215) and just under a quarter reported that they were forced to exit the area as it had been taken out of the scope of legal aid

(24.6 per cent, n=144). A further 12.8 per cent (n=75) indicated that they had changed employers or that their employer had moved away from undertaking legal aid work. An additional 5.5 per cent (n=32) reported that the legal aid contract held was terminated, not renewed, given up or could not be secured, and 4.6 per cent (n=27) cited that they left the area because they were tired of chasing fees from the LAA; could not manage all of the unpaid aspects of performing legal aid work; or could no longer meet the revised supervision requirements set down by their legal aid contract. Some practitioners were motivated strongly by the problems of legal aid administration: 'I hope not to have to deal directly with the [LAA]. Within a year I hope not to be working in law at all. My experiences of legal aid have been highly stressful and off-putting.'[24]

A small proportion (4.6 per cent, n=27) attributed their exit to 'personal preference'. A very slightly higher number (4.8 per cent, n=28) indicated that they found it difficult to sustain balancing family and caring responsibilities with work. There were additional family-related pressures such as the unpredictability of some areas of legal work such as crime: 'Re crime, as a mother I couldn't guarantee being able to pay childcare if a trial didn't go ahead and that happened frequently.'[25]

The remaining reasons provided included the inability to keep up with the law in two different areas of practice (2.7 per cent, n=16); the need to switch area of practice following/during qualification (2.1 per cent, n=12); the emotional toll/stress of work (1.5 per cent, n=9); changing client needs (1.7 per cent, n=10); social/moral/ethical issues, namely the difficulty of only being able to serve those deemed eligible by the LAA (0.9 per cent, n=5); the fact that there was no future in legal aid (0.3 per cent, n=2); and difficulties with recruitment (0.3 per cent, n=2). A further 2.9 per cent (n=17) gave 'other', largely unspecified reasons for their decision.

We note that the reasons provided by practitioners varied by practice area. Whilst pursuing specialisation in a different area remained the most common explanation across nearly all practice areas, it is notable that just under half (49.4 per cent, n=127) of crime practitioners reported leaving this area of practice because it was no longer financially viable. This is consistent with the analysis in chapter five, which speaks to criminal lawyers' concerns about the lack of fee increases for many years. The findings in this respect strongly align with evidence gathered by the Westminster Commission on the Sustainability of Legal Aid.

For example, this practitioner describes problems relevant to low levels of remuneration in criminal legal aid and, as identified by Thornton and described above, increased levels of stress as a result:

> Sometimes the train ticket to court cost more than my fee so I was literally paying to go to court. Crime often involves covering a case for someone because they are not available but the prep work was not being done by the case owner because it wasn't financially

[24] Practitioner Respondent Number 723.
[25] Practitioner Respondent Number 648.

> viable for them to work on a case for a hearing they weren't covering. So virtually every case was a nightmare that hadn't been prepped. I would be spending hours and hours sorting something out for one hearing. I would be paid less than £100 for total out of which I had to get travel, subsistence and chambers fees. The stress was off the scale too. In the end, it just became too much. I only wanted to practise in criminal legal aid when I was qualifying, now I don't do it at all. The stress of the legal aid system and the lack of compensation at any reasonable rate is the reason.[26]

There could also be a domino effect as practitioners leave their original area of legal aid for another but then find similar problems in the new area. Such is the experience of this respondent: '[I] [g]ave up crime to focus on my family practice [and] [g]ave up legal aid private family work due to the appalling rates of pay.'[27]

The effect of LASPO in removing large areas of legal aid from scope can also be seen when looking at those areas of law where 'pursuing specialisation in a different area' was not the response of the majority. For debt, welfare benefits and employment, the area being taken out of legal aid scope was provided as an explanation as frequently as or more frequently than pursuing a different specialisation (53.9 per cent, n=41 for debt; 50.9 per cent, n=55 for welfare benefits; and 52.9 per cent, n=9 for employment). This suggests that myriad factors are at play when practitioners pursue other areas of practice, and the decision to move is not as simple as personal preference but is often dictated by wider factors linked to austerity reforms, instability and low levels of remuneration.

Therefore, for many practitioners, their decisions will have been motivated by a combination of the factors cited above. In this response from a practitioner, a range of reasons are thus identified:

> Legal aid contracting progressively shrank the sector by excluding whole areas from scope; increasingly confining what contractors could do under legal aid contract; expanding unpaid bureaucracy and controls disproportionately; decreasing pay rates to loss-making levels (which gave incentive to cynical working systems); producing a situation where contract supervisor standards could not be met because of the latter controls (e.g, insufficient new matter starts to equate with required volume of experience for supervisors); undermining professionalism and commitment of lawyers as social welfare agents of fairness, amelioration and change by unrealistic confinement to diminishing areas of law (e.g. an immigration practitioner can advise on ECHR article 3 but not article 8); and generally sending us out to bat with half a bat.[28]

What emerges is that there are many reasons why practitioners feel the need to leave legal aid work. These reasons are interrelated to one another, but strongly centre around the 'diminishing' nature of some areas of practice and high levels of stress created by concerns regarding sustainability and viability of the work in future.

[26] Practitioner Respondent Number 499.
[27] Practitioner Respondent Number 523.
[28] Practitioner Respondent Number 135.

B. Organisations

From 362 organisations, 6.9 per cent (n=25) indicated that they did not hold a legal aid contract, whilst 93.1 per cent (n=337) did. All organisations were asked if there were areas of legal aid where they no longer provided legal services. From the responses given, 50.1 per cent (n=183) of organisations indicated that there were areas where they used to but no longer provided legal aid services.[29] Further examination revealed that there were certain areas of practice where the provision of legal aid services was discontinued by organisations. As shown in Table 7.3, the areas of debt (29.8 per cent, n=54), welfare benefits (29.8 per cent, n=54), and housing (23.8 per cent, n=43) were most commonly cited as those where organisations used to provide legal services but no longer did so.

Table 7.3 Areas where organisations used to provide legal aid services (n=181)

	N	%
Debt	54	29.8
Welfare benefits	54	29.8
Housing	43	23.8
Crime	42	23.2
Prison law	34	18.8
Family (private)	25	13.8
Community care	24	13.3
Immigration & asylum	24	13.3
Family (public)	24	13.3
Clinical negligence	18	9.9
Mental health	16	8.8
Education	12	6.6
Claims against public authorities	9	5.0
Public law	8	4.4
Employment	7	3.9
Mediation	6	3.3
Discrimination	5	2.8
Other	5	2.8
Court of Protection	2	1.1
Personal injury	2	1.1

It is unsurprising given that the areas of debt and welfare benefits fell out of scope for legal aid and housing was severely restricted under LASPO reforms. As such, organisations are more likely to move away from holding legal aid contracts in

[29] 46.8% (n=171) said no and 3.0% (n=11) did not know.

these areas and a range of procedural and economic barriers to continuing with these areas of work are presented.

When asked to explain why their organisation had moved away from certain areas of legal aid practice, the open-ended responses given by 164 organisations – when quantitatively coded – reinforced the prominence of financial concerns. These are detailed in Table 7.4. The majority (61 per cent, n=100) explained their exit from certain areas of practice as because it was not profitable or economically viable to undertake the work. The difficulties involved in making the contract work financially was expressed by one organisational representative as follows: 'The solicitors could not generate enough income to cover their salaries, let alone their employment costs and made no contribution to office costs.'[30]

Another organisational respondent drew out the implications for their clients:

> We do very little immigration work now because it is morally wrong to charge our client group for this work and we cannot offer the service free at source. We also do far less family reunion than we would otherwise do because it was put as an immigration application, despite it clearly being a right under the refugee convention. A cruel and life threatening decision for all those family members left languishing in refugee camps and other vulnerable settings.[31]

In terms of specifically referencing the impact of reforms or contract changes, over a third (37.2 per cent, n=61) of organisations reported that they were not working in areas of legal aid because they had their contract terminated or the area had moved out of scope following LASPO.

Table 7.4 Why organisations were no longer working/did not retain contracts in certain areas of legal aid (n=164)

	N	%
Not profitable/economically viable to undertake this work	100	61.0
LA contract terminated/not renewed/given up/not awarded/area of law out of scope following LASPO	61	37.2
Contract requirements changed and could no longer meet new conditions/requirements	40	24.4
Couldn't recruit sufficiently qualified staff/staff left	31	18.9
LAA repeatedly refused to pay us/didn't pay on time/too much red tape/too many audits	9	5.5
Organisation changed focus away from legal aid	3	1.8
Not possible to manage caseload across different areas of practice	2	1.2
Organisation changed speciality or specialised	1	0.6

In addition to those organisations discussed above who reported explicitly having exited certain practice areas, the data revealed that some organisations

[30] Organisation Respondent Number 143.
[31] Organisation Respondent Number 313.

remained in practice areas by continuing to hold a contract in that area; in reality, however, they found it difficult to provide services under the contract due to concerns around financial viability. Of the organisations holding a legal aid contract, 27.5 per cent (n=91 of 331) said that there were types of work under their legal aid contract(s) where they do not routinely offer services and/or refer clients elsewhere because it is not cost-effective to undertake the work, compared to 72.5 per cent (n=240) who said that they did not experience this problem.

When asked to indicate the type of work they do not routinely offer because it is not cost effective to do so, 73 organisations elaborated by providing an open-ended response. These were quantitatively coded and are summarised in Table 7.5. As the table shows, the most common response was 'private family law or family legal help work' (27.1 per cent, n=19). As the answer provided by one organisation made clear, organisations were discerning with the number of cases of a certain type they were able to take on: 'We take on a small number of private law children cases, but send the rest away. We could probably have 6 fee earners at least doing private law family full time to meet demand we turn away, but it is not economic to do so.'[32]

The number of organisations indicating that they did not routinely offer services and/or they referred clients elsewhere because it was not cost-effective for them to undertake the work was also higher in relation to appeals (18.6 per cent, n=13), housing (11.4 per cent, n=8) and civil/non-family legal help (11.4 per cent, n=8). A number of organisations also referenced 'other' work which included education, confiscation, costs, debt and financial relief (18.6 per cent, n=13). While responses generally focused on the problems of specific areas not being cost-effective, some highlighted broader issues such that it was now 'impossible to provide quality due to cost in some areas.'[33] Others mentioned that legal aid's cost inefficiency means that 'most legal aid work is now referred elsewhere.'[34] These findings obviously have concerning access to justice implications given the restrictions described both in initial service provision and continuing care, for example, being unable to pursue appeals.

Table 7.5 Areas where legal aid contract-holding organisations do not routinely offer services and/or refer clients elsewhere because it is not cost effective to undertake the work (n=70)

	N	%
Private family law/legal help	19	27.1
Other (including adjudication, confiscation, education, financial relief, debt, damages, meditation, mortgages)	13	18.6
Appeals	13	18.6

(continued)

[32] Organisation Respondent Number 85.
[33] Organisation Respondent Number 118.
[34] Organisation Respondent Number 363.

Table 7.5 ***(Continued)***

	N	%
Prison law	7	10.0
Housing	8	11.4
Civil/non-family legal help	8	11.4
Exceptional case funding applications	7	10.0
Immigration	5	7.1
Broader criminal legal aid	4	5.7
Welfare benefits	3	4.3
All legal aid work	1	1.4

Organisations who held a contract were also asked to indicate – in the form of an open-ended response – whether they found work under that contract cost-effective. As shown in Table 7.6, quantitative coding of the responses given by 64 organisations revealed that the majority reported rates of legal aid pay were simply too low (60.9 per cent, n=39) or, similarly, that the profit margins were too low (39.1 per cent, n=25). Others referenced the problem of administrative burdens being too high (28.1 per cent, n=18) or being unable to claim work because it is not in scope (28.1 per cent, n=18). Other organisations referenced issues such as the impact of the COVID-19 pandemic or problems associated with delay in the justice system such as court listings or clients failing to attend.

Table 7.6 Reasons organisations provided for why legal aid contract work was not cost-effective (n=64)

	N	%
Rates of pay too low	39	60.9
Low profit margin/not economical	25	39.1
Administrative burdens too high	18	28.1
Some work cannot be claimed/areas not in scope	18	28.1
Court listing/defendant attending problems	6	9.4
Other (including police station/court closures, payment regime, too complicated to add extra work, used as a loss leader)	6	9.4
Travel/time out of office	5	7.8
Impact of Covid-19	5	7.8
Must subsidise fees	3	4.7
Fees do not make sense	3	4.7

Practitioners spoke about their concerns regarding contracts: 'This contract is run at a loss and is subsidised by other funds but we have continued it for the benefit of the clients.'[35] This pattern of cross-subsidising work was a strategy observed in respect of changes introduced by LASPO as early as 2012, meaning that this has been a necessary survival mechanism for over a decade.[36] As discussed in chapter six, the impact of COVID-19 could prove a final tipping point for some organisations, considering how difficult it was to justify holding contracts already: 'Profit margins [are] so slim, the financial impact of Covid (and disappearance of almost all Crown Court trial work) means [that the] only way to continue is through personal debt. LAA contractual demands are burdensome and expensive.'[37] The feeling that comes across from the practitioners is that many may soon get to a point where they might have to relinquish their contracts.

What emerges from the data, then, are three cohorts: those who have exited certain areas, those who have exited in practice but not in principle and those who are at risk of exiting. It is clear that financial inadequacy of legal aid work in its many forms – most notably relating to rates of pay, profit margins and the removal of areas from scope – alongside the excessive burdens of legal aid administration result in organisations not providing services or being at risk of exiting. While these issues are experienced heavily in criminal law they are shared widely across the sector, thus demanding a comprehensive solution across both civil and criminal legal aid.

C. Chambers

As with practitioners and organisations, chambers reported a retreat from service provision in certain areas of legal aid practice. Their responses are set out in Table 7.7 below.[38] When asked which areas of legal aid chambers found it challenging to accept instructions (as a result of a reduction or lack of instructions, or due to the area being removed from scope), crime was most again commonly identified (39.3 per cent, n=11) followed by private family work (32.1 per cent, n=9) and public family work (28.6 per cent, n=8). A quarter of chambers indicated challenges in housing (25.0 per cent, n=7) and just over a fifth noted challenges relating to immigration and asylum (21.4 per cent, n=6) and claims against public authorities (21.4 per cent, n=6).

[35] Organisation Respondent Number 31.

[36] Pascoe Pleasence et al, 'A Time of Change: Solicitors' Firms in England and Wales' (The Law Society, Legal Services Board, Ministry of Justice, 2012) 6.

[37] Organisation Respondent Number 171.

[38] Mediation was removed from this table as there were zero chambers nominating this area of law.

Table 7.7 Practice areas chambers reported finding it challenging to accept instructions (n=28)

	N	%
Crime	11	39.3
Family (private)	9	32.1
Family (public)	8	28.6
Housing	7	25.0
Claims against public authorities	6	21.4
Immigration and asylum	6	21.4
None	5	17.9
Public law	5	17.9
Prison law	4	14.3
Community care	4	14.3
Education	4	14.3
Employment	4	14.3
Clinical negligence	3	10.7
Welfare benefits	3	10.7
Court of Protection	3	10.7
Inquests and public inquiries	3	10.7
Discrimination	2	7.1
Mental health	2	7.1
Debt	1	3.6
Other	1	3.6
Exceptional funding	1	3.6

When asked to explain in their own words why it was particularly challenging to accept instructions in these areas, 16 sets of chambers provided a response and three-quarters (75.0 per cent, n=12) cited financial issues. Here, financial issues did not simply relate to income, but also pertained to chambers' ability to recruit and train junior staff. As explained by one chambers, 'The fees are so low that it is very difficult for us to recruit sufficient junior members to undertake the work.'[39] Another noted that:

> The fees level for private children act work are such that only our most junior practitioners would accept it as proper remuneration. There is a wealth of public law work available at a better paid level, and practitioners are attracted to that. The other area is matrimonial finance. There used to be junior level work at legal aid rates for practitioners to establish an expertise in before moving onto privately paying work, but that legal

[39] Chamber Respondent Number 32.

> aid is no longer available. That means that we cannot grow the area in the way we used to, as practitioners do not have the more junior level cases to build on.[40]

In addition to financial issues, the availability of legal aid in certain areas was identified as the cause of challenges for 43.8 per cent (n=7 of chambers). An additional 12.5 per cent (n=2) observed a reduced volume of work and/or greater competition for work, whilst 6.3 per cent (n=1) identified the pandemic as a factor.

IV. Exiting the Sector

A. Former Practitioners

For those practitioners who had completely exited legal aid as opposed to simply exiting a particular area of legal aid practice, a broad range of justifications were advanced to substantiate their decision. Table 7.8 below sets out the responses given by former practitioners and includes both pre-defined, prompted explanations as well as popular reasons that emerged unprompted when respondents were asked to elaborate upon their reasoning.

Consistent with wider evidence on legal aid 'escape routes', practitioners tended to leave the profession for better prospects in other sectors. The most common reason for leaving legal aid – selected by over half (58.5 per cent, n=145) of respondents from the prompted explanations – was for better pay, working conditions or entitlements. A total of 39.9 per cent (n=99) left to advance career opportunities or prospects, and 31.9 per cent (n=79) left for an easier or less stressful position. This leaver summed up the position of many: 'Absolutely no prospects, earning potential or work-life balance.'[41]

It can thus be understood that working conditions therefore played a big part in the decisions of most former legal aid practitioners who had left the sector. This is perhaps unsurprising in view of discussion as to perceptions of working conditions analysed in chapter four: most former practitioners summarise their decision to leave as being related to the hope of better conditions elsewhere. The unprompted responses also pointed towards issues of working conditions: 11.7 per cent (n=29) were frustrated by LAA bureaucracy; 8.9 per cent (n=22) emphasised hours and workload; 8.1 per cent (n=20) felt emotionally burnt out; and 7.7 per cent (n=19) felt motivated by work–life balance.

The importance of these working conditions meant that other considerations tended to outweigh enjoyment of one's work:

> I enjoyed the work and helping those in need. Unfortunately the career prospects and the salary levels were just not manageable in London. I had to take a pay cut to become a trainee solicitor at a legal aid firm and in the end couldn't stay in legal aid after qualification. As an independent person with no partner I had to earn enough for myself.[42]

[40] Chamber Respondent Number 16.
[41] Leaver Respondent Number 201.
[42] Leaver Respondent Number 1.

It is also significant to note that a quarter (25.4 per cent, n=63) of former legal aid practitioners suggested that they left because their area of practice fell out of scope for legal aid, while 8.5 per cent (n=21) left because their firm closed or lost their contract. Such was the experience of this leaver: 'Our large social welfare law dept closed down when it no longer came under the scope of legal help.'[43] It is not inconceivable that this latter group may have otherwise carried on working in the sector despite the challenges they faced.

Table 7.8 Reasons given as to why former legal aid practitioners left legal aid (n=248)

		N	%
Prompted reasons selected	Better pay, working conditions and entitlements	145	58.5
	To advance career opportunities or prospects	99	39.9
	I wanted an easier / less stressful position	79	31.9
	Area of practice fell out of scope for legal aid	63	25.4
	It was time to move on	45	18.1
	I wanted to seek new challenges	41	16.5
	I wanted to spend more time with family/friends	41	16.5
	I was unhappy with my role	31	12.5
	I did not get on with management	26	10.5
	Other (digitisation, solicitors doing more work themselves, quality of instruction from solicitors often poor, LASPO, career change, not specified)	19	7.7
	I wanted to retire	13	5.2
	I did not get on with colleagues	3	1.2
Unprompted reasons provided	LAA bureaucracy	29	11.7
	Hours/workload required to work to keep firm/me solvent	22	8.9
	Firm closed/firm lost contract or funding/current firm does not have contract	21	8.5
	Emotional toll of work/burn-out	20	8.1
	Work–life balance	19	7.7
	Pressure from firm about doing LA-funded work/work targets imposed by employer	16	6.5
	Inability to do the work well within current payment regime	15	6.0
	No future in LA	14	5.6
	Inability to support a family/start a family or balance work with starting a family	13	5.2
	Health issues	11	4.4
	Lack of respect/thanklessness of LA work	10	4.0
	Inability to afford housing	7	2.8

[43] Leaver Respondent Number 21.

B. Current Practitioners

Notwithstanding the issues identified by current legal aid practitioners above, the majority of practitioners who responded (n=1146) indicated that they were likely (29.0 per cent, n=332) or very likely (40.7 per cent, n=466) to remain in legal aid in the next three years, compared to 11.0 per cent (n=126) reporting that they were unlikely to remain, 7.3 per cent (n=84) who were very unlikely to remain and 12.0 per cent (n=138) indicating that they were neither likely nor unlikely to remain.

Those current practitioners planning to leave legal aid practice were invited to select one or more reasons for their desire to leave from a set of 15 pre-defined, prompted reasons. These reasons – along with the most common unprompted reasons provided by respondents in a follow-up open-ended question – are listed in Table 7.9. It should be noted that whilst these questions were directed at those who had indicated they planned to leave legal aid, the questions attracted responses from some of those who indicated they were unlikely to.

Looking at the responses of all practitioners (those who indicated that they were planning to leave and those who indicated that they were not planning to leave), 'better pay, working conditions or entitlement' was the single most motivating factor as selected by 60.7 per cent (n=321) of practitioners. This was followed by 'the desire for an easier or less stressful position' (34.2 per cent, n=181), and the desire 'to advance career opportunities or prospects' (25.3 per cent, n=134). These were the same three reasons which were also foremost amongst former legal aid practitioners. The issues raised by the cohorts are thus similar, suggesting that people thinking of leaving legal aid for these reasons seem likely to also become 'former' legal aid practitioners in the future.

Practitioners were open to talking in more detail about all these reasons and a cross-section of the reasons is offered in the following quote:

> I have been in practice for 31 years and during that time I have seen my role be increasingly unappreciated and my remuneration effectively reduced significantly. The levels of stress are increasing as the cases and clients are more complex. I feel that this is causing me more damage and I don't really enjoy the job any more. It's not all about money, but with current levels of remuneration I can't take 'breathing space', whether to prepare cases within reasonable wording hours or to have sufficient time for a reasonable work-life balance. There are many more initiatives readily available to assist our wellbeing but that raises 2 questions – why do we need such initiatives? Surely if we had decent working arrangements then we would not need so much intervention? Secondly, when am I supposed to find the time to engage with all these 'wellbeing' initiatives? If legal aid work was properly resourced & respected, we wouldn't be in this position.[44]

[44] Practitioner Respondent Number 924.

Table 7.9 also breaks responses down based on how likely practitioners were to remain. Amongst both those who will likely remain and those who are unlikely to remain, better pay, working conditions or entitlements was the most popular choice; 51.1 per cent (n=97) of the former and 63.1 per cent (n=130) of the latter selected this option. More of those unlikely to remain (41.7 per cent, n=86) selected that they wanted an easier or less stressful position – the second most popular choice for this group – compared to those likely to remain (22.1 per cent, n=42) for whom it was the third most popular choice. Advancing career opportunities or prospects was the second most popular choice for those likely to remain, though there was a similar proportion of this group and those unlikely to remain who selected this option (25.3 per cent, n=48 versus 26.2 per cent, n=54).

Of the unprompted reasons, retirement or reaching retirement age was the most popular choice overall (11.3 per cent, n=60) amongst both those likely to remain and those unlikely to remain (10.0 per cent, n=19 and 14.6 per cent, n=30 respectively). As discussed above, this highlights the importance of education and training new recruits, considering a significant number of practitioners in the sector are looking towards retirement. The unprompted reasons generally expand upon and provide more depth to the prompted reasons, thus underpinning the sense that the financial situation and working conditions of the sector are a prominent concern. For example, mental health problems, exhaustion and other health reasons comprised the second most common unprompted response overall (5.7 per cent, n=30) and legal aid not being sustainable was the third most popular unprompted response (5.1 per cent, n=27). It is also important to note that 2.1 per cent (n=11) of the overall total were still considering whether to move on and have not yet finalised this decision.

The significance of concerns about financial sustainability can be seen in the open-ended responses provided, which illustrate the extent to which legal aid practitioners are determined to stay in legal aid but are nevertheless struggling to stay afloat and retain a sense of well-being:

> I am the finance manager of the firm and have been with the partners since they opened the firm in 1999 (and previously worked with them at another legal aid firm for five years before that). I am committed to the work we do and will only leave the sector if the firm does not survive. It has evidently become more difficult to be financially viable as a legal aid firm – even before the pandemic we only just about managed to balance the books. A loss was made in the last financial year due to the pandemic. If we continue to make a loss in the coming 3 to 6 months, the firm will have to close.[45]

For some respondents, these pressures amounted to a perception of powerlessness within the sector and a sense that they would inevitably be forced to leave legal aid in the near future. Such concern is expressed in the following quote: 'Now aged 66 and my employers will be looking to replace me with a cheaper newly

[45] Practitioner Respondent Number 5.

Table 7.9 Reasons provided by current legal aid practitioners as to why they would leave legal aid by whether likely or not to remain in legal aid for the next three years

		All (n=529)		**Very/likely to remain** (n=190)		**Neither likely nor unlikely** (n=113)		**Very/unlikely to remain** (n=206)	
		N	**%**	**N**	**%**	**N**	**%**	**N**	**%**
Prompted Reasons Selected	Advance career opportunities or prospects	134	25.3	48	25.3	28	24.8	54	26.2
	A permanent or longer-term position	41	7.8	14	7.4	8	7.1	17	8.3
	Better pay, working conditions or entitlements	321	60.7	97	51.1	80	70.8	130	63.1
	Want clients who are easier to work with	49	9.3	9	4.7	12	10.6	28	13.6
	I am just unhappy in my role	55	10.4	9	4.7	11	9.7	33	16.0
	I don't get on with management	20	3.8	2	1.1	4	3.5	12	5.8
	I don't get on with my colleagues	6	1.1	1	0.5	0	0.0	5	2.4
	It's time to move on	70	13.2	13	6.8	14	12.4	41	19.9
	I want an easier or less stressful position	181	34.2	42	22.1	44	38.9	86	41.7
	My partner has taken or is looking for another job	6	1.1	2	1.1	1	0.9	3	1.5
	My position will end soon	16	3.0	6	3.2	2	1.8	7	3.4
	Seek new challenges	87	16.4	27	14.2	20	17.7	37	18.0
	To be closer to family or friends	54	10.2	13	6.8	10	8.8	29	14.1
	No reason	16	3.0	13	6.8	2	1.8	1	0.5
	Other	4	0.8	2	1.1	1	0.9	1	0.5

Unprompted Reasons Given	Reducing the amount of LA work I take on	22	4.2	7	3.7	5	4.4	10	4.9
	Inability to afford a house/start family	11	2.1	2	1.1	1	0.9	7	3.4
	Mental health/exhaustion/health problems	30	5.7	8	4.2	6	5.3	16	7.8
	Lack of pensions	6	1.1	2	1.1	1	0.9	2	1.0
	Lack of respect	6	1.1	1	0.5	1	0.9	4	1.9
	Want to work in areas of law not funded by LA	2	0.4	0	0.0	1	0.9	1	0.5
	Firm/department at risk of closing	6	1.1	3	1.6	1	0.9	2	1.0
	LA not sustainable	27	5.1	7	3.7	8	7.1	12	5.8
	Having to fight the LAA	6	1.1	1	0.5	1	0.9	4	1.9
	Work–life balance	24	4.5	9	4.7	6	5.3	7	3.4
	Retirement or reaching retirement age	60	11.3	19	10.0	10	8.8	30	14.6
	Still considering whether to move on	11	2.1	7	3.7	3	2.7	1	0.5
	Would like to exit but I have no other options	14	2.6	10	5.3	1	0.9	3	1.5

qualified model due to the limited rates of legal aid.'[46] Others were clearly already past the point of feeling incentivised to leave legal aid and were instead reflecting on the difficulty of finding somewhere else to go: 'I am looking for an escape route. I feel devalued, unloved and discriminated against.'[47] Such practitioners, feeling unappreciated and worn down, would leave if they could. Other practitioners felt compelled to stay due to a lack of alternative options. The starkness of feeling stuck in the work was expressed evocatively by this practitioner: 'I am aged 68. I feel that my mental health has collapsed but cannot leave the business at present. I only have a state pension and the local food bank.'[48]

C. Organisations

As outlined above, only 25 organisations (6.9 per cent) reported that they did not hold legal aid contracts. When asked why they did not hold legal aid contracts, 21 organisations elaborated via an open-ended question. Quantitative coding of these responses revealed nine key explanations. Whilst for at least one organisation a contract was not held due to retirement of staff (4.8 per cent, n=1), the remaining organisations cited difficulties associated with viability/revenue in legal aid (19.0 per cent, n=4), areas moving out of scope (14.3 per cent, n=3), contract administration or standards being too arduous (19.0 per cent, n=4) and/or issues with working with the LAA (4.8 per cent, n=1). As one organisation reported, 'We chose not to bid for the renewal of our housing contract as the revenue was so small and the quality standards too arduous.'[49]

Another attributed their exit from service provision to financial considerations: 'I specialise in [w]hite [c]ollar crime. I am a qualified [duty solicitor] but I will not work for low legal aid rates and a system that does not allow the work required to properly represent defendants.'[50]

For the remaining half, the reasons provided indicated that most had never been involved in the provision of contracted services. For example, 42.9 per cent (n=9 of 21) of these organisations did not hold legal aid contracts due to their role as cost lawyers or agents, 14.2 per cent (n=3) reported another reason including that they offered mediation services, 4.8 per cent (n=1) indicated that they provided free services not funded by legal aid, and 4.8 per cent (n=1) stated that they relied on grants. Even among those organisations which had never held legal aid contracts, it appears that any work in the legal aid sector was avoided for some organisations. One respondent explained:

> We are a firm of costs lawyers and as such never did hold any contracts with the LAA nor provide services to the public via legal aid. However, we did for many years provide

[46] Practitioner Respondent Number 139.
[47] Practitioner Respondent Number 696.
[48] Practitioner Respondent Number 1207.
[49] Organisation Respondent Number 238.
[50] Organisation Respondent Number 288.

> costing services to law firms that provided services under legal aid contracts / certificates. We no longer offer costing services in respect of legal aid funded matters owing to the very poor rates of pay and ever-increasing bureaucracy.[51]

Notwithstanding the fact that some of the organisations had never held legal aid contracts and as such could not be taken to have 'exited the sector', the responses overall highlight that legal aid policy regarding fees, eligibility and the bureaucratisation of claiming and billing procedures have all had an impact on organisations' decisions to continue to provide legal aid services.

When asked an open-ended question whether they had closed any offices or departments in the last 12 months or were planning to, several organisations gave responses suggestive of an exit from legal aid work. As shown in Table 7.10, quantitative coding of responses that directly addressed the issue of office/department closures revealed that 35 organisations (47.9 per cent) were planning to stop offering services in certain practice areas; 24 organisations (32.9 per cent) had or were reducing/selling or otherwise winding down areas of practice or departments; 18 organisations (24.7 per cent) had closed offices; and 11 organisations (15.1 per cent) had given up legal aid contracts or were intending to refuse to undertake further legal aid work.[52] Importantly, whilst 21 organisations (28.8 per cent) did not attribute these changes to a specific cause, 29 organisations (39.7 per cent) indicated that the changes were a reflection of their general financial situation, four organisations (5.4 per cent) attributed the changes to non-payment of over auditing by the LAA and 12 organisations (16.4 per cent) attributed the changes to their inability to recruit into sector or the retirement of existing practitioners. A further seven organisations (9.6 per cent) cited the impact of COVID-19, as discussed in chapter six.

Table 7.10 Coded open-ended responses given by organisations in relation to whether they had closed offices or departments in the last 12 months or planned to (n=73)

	N	%
Getting rid of practice areas	35	47.9
Reduction/sale/winding down of departments/areas of practice	24	32.9
Offices closed	18	24.7
Permanent changes to the size/number of premises are planned/likely	13	16.8
Giving up LA contracts/refusing further LA work	11	15.1
Reductions in staff/members	10	13.7
General overhead reductions	4	5.5
Likely closure of firm	3	4.1

[51] Organisation Respondent Number 274.

[52] In total 275 organisations provided an open-ended response in relation to this question. Percentages presented in this table are calculated having removed the responses of 179 organisations who indicated that they could not answer the question and a further 23 organisations who provided open-ended answers which did not directly address the issue of office/department closures.

Unlike practitioners, organisations were not asked specifically whether they intended to continue providing legal aid services. However, the responses of practitioners relating to office and department closures provide some insight into the number of organisations who may be intending to leave the sector.

In addition, a question directed at assessing whether organisations could be sustained on legal aid funding alone – coupled with a follow-up, open-ended question which allowed organisations to provide further details – revealed a number of factors that could be perceived as putting organisations at risk of exiting legal aid. Overall, the vast majority of respondents (83 per cent, n=302 of 364) indicated that they did not believe their organisations would be sustainable solely on legal aid as compared to 17.0 per cent (n=62) who did. Quantitative coding of a subsequent open-ended question yielded relevant responses from 266 organisations. The 10 most common reasons given are provided in Table 7.11 below. Unsurprisingly, given the themes raised in the data and reported on to date, most explanations pointed to the impact of fees, funding and the bureaucracy of the legal aid process. A total of 56.8 per cent (n=151) of respondents referenced challenges with the legal aid fee regime (for instance, fees were too low or did not meet overheads; fees did not keep pace with inflation rates; or practitioners were ultimately working at a loss); 40.2 per cent (n=107) of respondents noted that legal aid work required subsidisation through other work or grant funding; and 21.1 per cent (n=56) of respondents referenced issues with the legal aid application process, contract requirements, and/or delays in funding.[53]

Table 7.11 Top 10 reasons organisations provided as to why it was not sustainable for them to rely solely on legal aid income (n= 266)

	N	%
Fees are too low/do not meet overheads/not kept up with inflation/working at a loss	151	56.8
Subsiding with other work/requires grant funding	107	40.2
Problems with legal aid application process/delays in funding/contract requirements	56	21.1
It can be sustainable	32	12.0
Needs a high volume/a lot of hard work to make it work/overwork/worries about too little work	31	11.7

(continued)

[53] Reasons that did not appear in the ten most common explanations provided in the table include: that legal aid work involved a lot of risk (3.6%, n=10); the impact of COVID-19 (3.6%, n=10); reduced income unrelated to COVID-19 (3.2%, n=8); grants/funding (2.8%, n=7); problems with LAA (2.8%, n=7), Covid-19 impact would be felt in future years (2.8%, n=7); grant/other funding sources restricted/lack of support (2.0%, n=5); have expanded (1.6%, n=4); chose to reduce amount of legal aid work (1.6%, n=4), and; Home Office delays (1.6%, n=4).

Table 7.11 ***(Continued)***

	N	%
Stopped legal aid/considering stopping legal aid work/concerns about the future	22	8.3
Areas out of scope/need to do *pro bono*	21	7.9
Hard to recruit at legal aid rates/staff leaving	21	7.9
Comparisons with pay in other areas/private work	14	5.3
Need to rely on small number of big cases	11	4.1

These organisational responses indicate that there are significant concerns about the sustainability of legal aid practice, as many organisations reported working at a loss if they attempted to sustain their practice on legal aid contracts alone. These assertions echo the doubts about the sustainability of current funding structures raised by practitioners in chapter five. The issues raised by organisations feed into a broader narrative that has emerged in the responses of former legal aid practitioners, current practitioners and chambers around financial concerns and onerous administration. Cumulatively, they paint a worrying picture about the sustainability of legal aid work for those who provide it.

V. Attracting New Entrants

A. Deterrents

As explored in chapter two, prospective practitioners identified several motivations underpinning their desire to pursue a career in legal aid. Importantly, a number of factors continue to dissuade new entrants to the profession, even among those who specifically express a desire to pursue a career in legal aid. The factors identified by students illuminate the potential barriers the legal aid sector faces in attracting a new generation of practitioners to its ranks.

When asked what deters them the most from a career in legal aid, prospective practitioners (comprising all students, not just those undertaking qualifying degrees) commonly referenced insufficient pay. These responses are summarised in Table 7.12 below. Notably, insufficient pay was referenced across both those students who indicated that they were considering a career in legal aid (63.1 per cent, n=113) and those who were not (71.2 per cent, n=126). Similarly, both sets of respondents referenced a belief that they lacked the financial resources to work in legal aid (39.7 per cent, n=71 and 42.4 per cent, n=75 for those considering and not considering a legal aid career respectively). Students also referenced a lack of information regarding legal aid as a career across both the 'considering' and 'not considering' groups (40.2 per cent, n=72 and 49.2 per cent, n=87 respectively).

However, those who *were not* considering a career in legal aid more often indicated that the nature of the work did not appeal (28.8 per cent, n=51); the pay was insufficient (71.2 per cent, n=126); they had a preference to work with different client groups (21.5 per cent, n=38); there was a lack of opportunities for career development in legal aid (43.5 per cent, n=77); or that they didn't know much about legal aid (33.3 per cent, n=59). Alternately, those who *were* considering a career in legal aid more often cited the unpredictable hours (30.2 per cent, n=54); the lack of training contracts (53.6 per cent, n=96); and pressure from families (7.8 per cent, n=14) or their law school (15.1 per cent, n=27) to pursue different options. The number of respondents giving 'other' reasons was similar across both the 'considering' and 'not considering' groups (2.8 per cent, n= 5 and 3.4 per cent, n=6 respectively). Of these, only one respondent (who was not considering a career in legal aid) provided further detail, explaining that they did not have an LLB.

Table 7.12 Factors deterring students from pursuing a career in legal aid

	Considering a career in legal aid?			
	Yes (n=179)		**No** (n=177)	
	N	%	**N**	%
The nature of the work does not appeal to me	2	1.1	51	28.8
The pay is insufficient	113	63.1	126	71.2
The hours are unpredictable	54	30.2	37	20.9
I would prefer to work with different client groups	4	2.2	38	21.5
Lack of legal aid training contracts	96	53.6	54	30.5
Lack of opportunities for career development in legal aid	60	33.5	77	43.5
Legal aid lawyers I have spoken to have put me off	21	11.7	33	18.6
Pressure from family to pursue different options to legal aid	14	7.8	9	5.1
I do not have the financial resources to work in legal aid	71	39.7	75	42.4
Pressure from law school to pursue different options to legal aid	27	15.1	15	8.5
Lack of information on legal aid as a career choice	72	40.2	87	49.2
I generally don't know much about legal aid	37	20.7	59	33.3
Other	5	2.8	6	3.4

When respondents were subsequently asked to identify a factor that deterred them from a career in legal aid the most, insufficient pay was a key issue for both those considering a career in legal aid (37.1 per cent, n=65) and those not (39.5 per cent, n=70). As one respondent who was considering a career in legal aid explained:

> Becoming a skilled legal aid lawyer requires financial and time investment that simply isn't reflected in the pay provided. While I will always accept that public service isn't necessarily well-paid, the discrepancy between the high standards of work needed to support those in vulnerable legal situations and the financial remuneration is significant.[54]

This assertion mirrors the concerns about financial sustainability expressed by current and former legal aid practitioners reported in the other surveys comprising the Census. Furthermore, concerns about pay may be preventing young lawyers from pursuing a career in legal aid in the first place, especially given the widespread perception among student respondents that they would not have the financial resources required to offset the financial costs of working in legal aid.

For those considering a career in legal aid, 21.7 per cent (n=38) cited the 'lack of legal aid training contracts,' as the main factor discouraging them from pursuing a career in legal aid. One respondent explained the predicament:

> Competition for training contracts is high so it can be disheartening to get rejected multiple times. It is a shame the sector is able to train so few people. There needs to be more skilled and qualified lawyers in this sector, not less. However, I understand why it is difficult for firms who do this kind of work to take many trainees.[55]

For those not considering a career in legal aid, a lack of knowledge about legal aid was the second largest deterrent (13.6 per cent, n=24). This seemed to be the case even for those who had had some exposure to the sector, as one respondent acknowledged that 'I have experience volunteering in a pro bono law clinic which includes a significant amount of legal aid eligibility work but I do not know much at all about pursuing legal aid work as a career.'[56]

This suggests that although students may be deterred by what they know of the sector and the working conditions within it, a lack of knowledge of the sector is also a determinant. This phenomenon may be the result of the insufficient exposure of students to legal aid during their legal education, as discussed in chapter three.

B. Preferred Practice Areas and Locations

In addition to the specific dimensions mentioned above, an exploration of the preferred work locations and practice areas specified by students considering a career in legal aid reveal a tendency to favour certain types of work and locations.

[54] Student Respondent Number 285.
[55] Student Respondent Number 283.
[56] Student Respondent Number 122.

Prospective practitioners (all students) who responded (n=194) indicated a strong preference for gaining employment in London, with 45.4 per cent (n=88) nominating it as their preferred location. This was followed by 11.9 per cent preferring to work in the North West of England (n=23) and South East England, and 10.8 per cent (n=21) preferring to work in the English Midlands. Fewer respondents indicated a preference for North East England (9.8 per cent, n=19), South West England (4.6 per cent, n=9), South Wales (3.6 per cent, n=7) and North Wales (2.1 per cent, n=4). No respondents indicated a preference for West Wales and Mid Wales. When asked to explain this preference, the majority of those who provided an open-ended response (n=96 total) indicated that they already lived in this area or had established personal relationships in the region (63.5 per cent, n=61). A further 36.5 per cent (n=35) of respondents answered that the legal aid offered in their preferred region was more strongly aligned with their interests or that they thought there were more job opportunities in that location with 62.9 per cent (n=22) of these 35 respondents indicating a preference for London. A total of 27.1 per cent (n=26) were flexible with their preferred location, stating that whilst they lived in their preferred region they would be prepared to relocate if their personal circumstances changed or an opportunity arose elsewhere. Some 2.1 per cent (n=2) of respondents noted the existence of family commitments in their preferred location.

There is also some evidence that the preferred areas of work for prospective practitioners do not align with the areas of work where recruitment more commonly occurs. Specifically, the top five preferred areas of work for prospective practitioners were crime (56.3 per cent, n=111), immigration and asylum (55.3 per cent, n=109) claims against public authorities (54.3 per cent, n=107), discrimination (50.3 per cent, n=99) and mental health (49.7 per cent, n=98), while the top five areas of work where recruitment was planned (as per Table 7.1) were crime (29.6, n=25), public family law (19.1 per cent, n=18), private family law (14.9 per cent, n=14), public law (11.7 per cent, n=11), and community care (11.7 per cent, n=11). As discussed in chapter three, the relative lack of availability of careers advice in legal aid may go some way in explaining these discrepancies. Students generally report that the focus tends to rest upon corporate opportunities, with information on legal aid being poor by comparison. This may suggest a need for a more concerted effort to widely share opportunities, including related funding options that currently exist such as the Justice First Fellowship scheme and the Social Welfare Solicitors Qualification Fund discussed above. Likewise, law schools rarely offer courses in areas such as community care, education, housing and mental health, which can restrict the likelihood of students being afforded the opportunity to develop interests in these areas. In any event, there is always the possibility that students may be less likely to develop interests in some areas over others, leading to discrepancies in areas where students prefer to work and those areas where recruitment occurs. Further research is needed in order to more adequately understand preferred areas of practice and the extent to which these preferences change and develop over the course of a legal career, including both the personal and professional factors that impact upon such changes. It is positive to note, however, that crime was both the most common area of interest for prospective practitioners and the most common area where recruitment was planned by organisations.

VI. Implication of Findings

It is clear that issues relevant to recruitment and retention, while more prevalent in some areas than others, are nonetheless shared across the breadth of legal aid practice. As scholars have argued, moving beyond traditionally rigid understandings of legal aid to a better understanding of how values and experiences are shared across the sector is critical to comprehensively understanding the issues faced by the profession and to resolving those issues in future.[57] The Census findings show that retention issues are not unique to solicitors but have also adversely impacted upon legal aid practice at the Bar: both chambers and organisations reported that it was difficult to find legal aid practitioners and highlighted that better salaries in other areas was the key reason behind this difficulty. Furthermore, practitioners, organisations and chambers all reported having exited certain areas of legal aid; additionally, a third of practitioners, over half of organisations and three-quarters of chambers cited financial reasons as a motivation behind such decisions.

Findings detailed in this chapter also revealed the reasons that respondents leave the legal aid sector altogether. A number of 'escape routes' were identified: practitioners who left, for instance, tended to do so for better prospects in other sectors, while those still practising identified their desire for better pay, working conditions or entitlements than those offered in the legal aid sector. Similarly, organisations who cease to provide legal aid services cited problems with viability and revenue in legal aid work, which are issues that have also been discussed by currently operating legal aid organisations.

Relatedly, in examining the reasons that deter students from pursuing careers in legal aid, findings reveal that large proportions of students referenced the poor pay, lack of legal aid contracts, and difficulty in affording to work in legal aid as significant drawbacks. Notably, as discussed in chapter three, they also identified the lack of information provided regarding legal aid as a career as a barrier. These factors have long-term implications for the viability of the legal aid sector and together with the allocation of government funding for legal aid education and training must be addressed as a matter of urgency. As we explore further in chapter eight, the sustainability of the profession cannot withstand the current practitioner exit rates alongside such low levels of entry for new trainees. A holistic, sector-wide approach that is alive to both the direct and indirect impacts of low remuneration coupled with high levels of student debt, and seeks to remedy them, is needed to ensure the sustainability of the profession for the future.

[57] See, eg Emma Cooke, The Working Culture of Legal Aid Lawyers, developing a 'Shared Orientation Model (2021) 31 *Social and Legal Studies* 704; Jacqueline Kinghan, *Lawyers, Networks and Progressive Social Change: Lawyers Changing Lives* (Hart, 2021).

8

Facing the Future of Legal Aid

The findings of the Legal Aid Census presented in this book are of vital importance for understanding the challenges, pressures and barriers that have the potential to impede access to justice in both the immediate and longer term. The purpose of this final chapter is to articulate how these findings reveal a deeper understanding about the challenges that have underpinned the legal aid sector in the past, as well as those that are likely to characterise the future. In doing so, it explores proposals and recommendations for policy change and future research in order to set a foundation for how to secure the sector for those that will need to rely upon it in future.

I. The Challenges for Legal Aid

As set out in chapter one, the Census sought to provide a comprehensive view of the legal aid sector as it exists within its current political, social and financial context. Throughout this book, we have articulated a baseline demographic profile of legal aid practitioners, as well as their experiences of education and training, salaries, fee arrangements and job satisfaction. In direct contrast to media representations of 'fat cat lawyers', the Census reveals a legal aid profession which comprises a largely state-schooled cohort, many of whom were first-generation students at university and the first person to qualify as a lawyer in their immediate family. Moreover, responses provided by current, former and prospective practitioners indicate that motivations to pursue careers in legal aid are firmly grounded in concerns about widening access to justice and serving those who have experienced disadvantage. In reality, legal aid practitioners are often motivated by experiences in their personal lives and past employment, which inspired them to pursue careers fighting for social justice even despite their own difficulties and financial hardships.

The book also sets out several of the key challenges facing legal aid lawyers across different areas of law. Financial challenges, for instance, are a consistent feature of being a legal aid practitioner. The Census indicates that the majority of practitioners currently working in legal aid faced financial barriers to entering the legal aid sector in the first place, and financial concerns continue to operate as a significant disincentive for students pursuing careers in legal aid. The reality of this economic precarity challenges some narratives of privilege that surround wider assumptions about the legal profession and reveals the need for financial support for those preparing for a career in legal aid. However, it also reveals a need for broader support at these early stages. Although opportunities to study courses relevant to legal aid improved at the conversion or vocational stage, less than half of practitioners reported having had the opportunity to take courses relevant to legal aid at an undergraduate level. The responses indicate only a small number of educational opportunities available in areas of immigration, housing, welfare benefits, education and community care at the undergraduate stage. Key challenges facing the legal aid sector therefore include not only the retention of current lawyers, but also the continued attraction and recruitment of new lawyers; this is increasingly difficult when law students have few opportunities to explore this career path, and those that do are frequently concerned about the economic prospects of doing so.

Relatedly, the book explores several aspects of the current working conditions in the legal aid sector and how these are inextricably shaped by these financial and recruitment challenges. Remuneration is a significant concern for practitioners, with the majority indicating that their salary and working arrangements for their role are unfair, that they frequently need to work beyond set hours to meet demands and that they often struggle to fit work around their family life and personal commitments. Working in legal aid also takes a toll on the mental well-being of practitioners. The pressures of legal aid work as well as the nature of the work in some areas of practice means that almost half of practitioners feel that legal aid work has an overall negative effect on their mental well-being. Compounding this, workplace bullying is also not infrequently experienced within the sector. Problematically, at least some of the bullying, harassment or discrimination that occurs is attributed by victims as related to protected characteristics. That the perpetrators of bullying, harassment and discrimination also appear to be in a position of authority over the victim – including judges, line managers and supervisors – magnifies the challenges associated with addressing the behaviour. In terms of training and development, only a minority of practitioners feel that their professional development needs are met in full, with training on work–life balance, personal well-being and stress management all frequently identified as needed within the sector.

There are therefore several significant concerns raised by this research about the working conditions in the legal aid sector, which are largely underpinned by financial insecurity and unsustainability. Legal aid practitioners have strong concerns about existing fee arrangements with the majority, who work under fixed fees, not believing that these fees are sustainable. On average, practitioners work an average of 106 minutes for every 60 minutes of remuneration, requiring many to work longer hours or take on private work in attempts to mitigate their losses. Even those still working under hourly rates work longer hours than they are paid for; an average of 90 minutes for every 60 minutes of remuneration. Organisations also highlighted problems with the sustainability of their present funding situation, with most not receiving other forms of income aside from legal aid funding and others relying on trusts, foundations and local government funding where ongoing availability is not guaranteed.

Notwithstanding the degree of concern expressed by practitioners in respect of their remuneration and working conditions, the majority of current practitioners are satisfied with their choice of career in legal aid. Satisfaction with legal aid work was attributed to the ability to help people and make a difference to people's lives through legal aid, as well as an enjoyment of the work involved with legal aid practice. The Census also found evidence of a high degree of engagement with the broader profession, as many practitioners reported that they participated in professional networks. Although membership fees and time constraints prevented such networks from being beneficial for everyone, networks were cited as useful for gathering niche knowledge, updates and training for different areas of practice.

The challenges and concerns that have typically characterised legal aid were starkly intersected by the outbreak of the COVID-19 pandemic and its subsequent impact on all aspects of the justice system as well as the public institutions on which legal aid clients typically rely. While this impact is far from straightforward, it has clearly compounded and exacerbated these existing financial pressures within the legal aid sector. While the new world of remote working and reduced travel to court hearings during pandemic-related restrictions has its advantages – such as allowing practitioners to manage their time more efficiently and reducing overhead costs for premises – this shift has also come with significant and novel economic and practical challenges. One of these is the requirement to support an entire new 'COVID cohort' of pandemic-induced legal need along with traditional client groups who may be less able to engage with services that are provided remotely. Another pandemic-related challenge is the difficulty of maintaining a supportive and cohesive workplace community and a healthy work–life balance, as well as adequate supervision and training provision for junior staff. These difficulties have significant implications for the post-pandemic future of the sector.

The pandemic has also raised substantial concerns about economic sustainability for organisations, chambers and individual practitioners, who all reported concerns about job security and economic precarity. These concerns were most frequently experienced by solicitors and respondents at earlier career stages, and varied across different areas of legal practice, with crime and housing disproportionately represented among those experiencing furlough and redundancy. There is also evidence to suggest that there is additional pandemic-related economic insecurity stemming from large outstanding caseloads subject to delays in the wider justice system, which intersect with pre-existing concerns about the financial viability of legal aid work and general economic precarity within the sector.

Given the complex and intersecting web of both old and new challenges outlined in this book, it is unsurprising that a proportion of the legal aid sector is motivated to leave the profession. Importantly, it is possible to draw parallels between the financial sustainability issues cited as reasons for leaving legal aid by former legal aid practitioners and the challenges that continue to be faced by current legal aid practitioners. Practitioners who had left tended to do so for better prospects in other sectors, while those still practising identified their desire for better pay, working conditions or entitlement than those offered in the legal aid sector. Organisations that had left cited problems with viability and revenue in legal aid work.

There are significant similarities between the challenges and stressors identified by practitioners currently working in legal aid and the reasons given by those who have already left the sector, as well as the reasons that students are deterred from pursuing careers in legal aid; for all these groups, financial issues were at the fore. Chambers and organisations alike have found it difficult to recruit and retain practitioners in legal aid work, chiefly due to the salaries that are available in other areas and especially in criminal law. In terms of organisations, Census responses suggest that legal aid contracts for debt, welfare benefits and housing law were most commonly given up by organisations, and that chambers were most likely to have abandoned work in family law. Taken together, this reinforces the finding that the overwhelming challenge facing the legal aid sector is that of financial insecurity, and all the associated implications that this has – and is likely to continue having – for workload, well-being, and working environments.

II. Giving Voice to the Legal Aid Sector

An underlying goal of the Legal Aid Census was to provide a platform through which those working in legal aid may step back from the detail of their busy and varied schedules in order to reflect upon the significant achievements and challenges that are shared across different areas of the sector. In other words, the Census was an opportunity to give voice to those working at the frontline of legal aid, bringing their perspectives and lived experiences to the fore of debates about access to justice and legal services. In doing so, we have created a vital space within these debates for practitioners themselves to define the scope and scale of the challenges facing the sector, and what kind of future they anticipate for legal aid.

In the current practitioner survey, 836 practitioners did so through responding to an open-ended question. Quantitative coding of these responses, as detailed in Table 8.1, revealed that financial challenges were at the forefront of practitioners' minds; practitioners were most concerned with chronic austerity measures and funding cuts at 40.6 per cent (n=339) and poor remuneration (36.8 per cent, n=308). This is unsurprising given the prominence of financial security as a theme that has characterised each of the chapters in this book; financial matters are pressing, significant concerns for respondents across the Census. It therefore makes sense that the practitioners were motivated to emphasise these concerns again in response to this question. We are confident that they would also think it both appropriate and important for us to emphasise them again here in the conclusion of the book as we reflect on the future of legal aid.

Table 8.1 The most significant challenges facing the legal aid profession identified by current legal aid practitioners (n=836)

	N	%
Austerity measures/funding cuts	339	40.6
Poor remuneration	308	36.8
Recruiting lawyers/staff	177	21.2
Lack of resources/support from the Government	153	18.3
Retaining lawyers	117	14.0
Unsustainably large workload/'burn-out'	86	10.3
Unsustainability of legal aid practice	76	9.1
Administrative issues related to other components of the justice system (including Legal Aid Agency and HMCTS)	57	6.8
Negative public/media attitudes towards the profession	46	5.5
Remuneration not commensurate with inflation	37	4.4
The threshold requirements are too high for clients to access justice/concerns about accessibility of justice	36	4.3
Lack of diversity in the legal aid sector	23	2.8

These financial concerns were frequently expressed in the form of high-level observations about the impact of austerity ('cuts to funding by the government and effects of previous cuts'),[1] which were both specific to legal aid as well as related to underfunding of the wider justice system, which was amplified by the demands of the COVID-19 pandemic ('lack of legal aid funding and the under-resourced justice system').[2] Underpinning these observations was a perception that legal aid lawyers were particularly undervalued compared to others working in the justice system:

> Financial sustainability. As stated above the [LAA] has to increase the rates it pays if the supplier base is to survive. All other people working in the justice system have salary increases annually, and have had since the 1990s, whereas our rates have been reduced in cash terms never mind real terms.[3]

These were not limited to observations about their own precarity. Rather, practitioners saw the plight of legal aid lawyers and legal aid clients as two interwoven dimensions of the same crisis: 'the repeated cuts to the legal aid budget, including

[1] Practitioner Respondent Number 515.
[2] Practitioner Respondent Number 537.
[3] Practitioner Respondent Number 604.

both the reduced access to legal aid for the clients as well as the low fees paid for the work we do.'[4] Practitioners were frustrated that 'so many areas are not eligible for legal aid, and those that are, are vastly underpaid'.[5]

In other words, there was genuine concern among practitioners about where their clients would go for help if their advice organisations are unable to sustain themselves: 'Low hourly and fixed fee rates leading to closure of legal aid firms. The financial pressures prove too much for even large organisations leading to closure of some offices.'[6] This was a common sentiment, frequently expressed as fear about 'survival in the medium to long term – the funding just isn't there.'[7] As one practitioner explained, the biggest challenge facing anyone working in the sector now was 'staying afloat after decades of financial neglect.'[8] There were also broader observations about how this was facilitating a steady transformation from legal aid to private practice as firms struggle to make ends meet:

> Cuts to legal aid mea[n] that the work is unsustainable without undertaking private work, which means that the limited number of specialist legal aid providers have less and less time to take on legal aid cases and will eventually decide to work only for private clients.[9]

While the two most commonly identified challenges in Table 8.1 were explicitly financial in nature, the three that followed – recruiting lawyers and staff (21.2 per cent, n=177), lack of resources or support from the Government (18.3 per cent, n=153), and retaining lawyers (14 per cent, n=117) – were nevertheless implicitly financial. Specifically, an inability to recruit and retain practitioners is likely to be a direct consequence of the precarious financial position of so many legal aid organisations as well as the economic prospects of practitioners working in legal aid. This, inevitably, indicates that the future of legal aid will be characterised by challenges to the sustainability of the sector as a whole.

Despite the fact that many respondents emphasised specific challenges, many practitioners recognised the interwoven nature of these challenges, and expressed these connections in their longer, qualitative responses:

> Pay. No young people are coming into the profession. Older middle aged solicitors do not want to buy into partnerships and older solicitors cannot afford to retire. Many young people who would have made excellent lawyers are not joining the profession. The chance for a training contract is now less than ever. The only people I know who have training contracts have come from very privileged backgrounds where their fathers [*sic*] company did work with the firm.[10]

[4] Practitioner Respondent Number 441.
[5] Practitioner Respondent Number 1156.
[6] Practitioner Respondent Number 614.
[7] Practitioner Respondent Number 987.
[8] Practitioner Respondent Number 402.
[9] Practitioner Respondent Number 554.
[10] Practitioner Respondent Number 272.

For practitioners, therefore, the sector is facing an uncertain future, due to the challenges they face '[retaining] the most skilled and experienced in the sector',[11] especially as the sector becomes 'economically unviable as a whole and especially for younger people with huge student debts so we won't get the talent and also sector becomes even less diverse.'[12] Senior practitioners reflected on their experiences of how this sector has changed over the past few decades, lamenting that 'young lawyers are not choosing it as a career path because the level of remuneration is so poor.'[13] One pronounced anxiety was that the sector was becoming ever more the domain of the privileged due to the financial situation:

> Sustainability of the profession given the low rates of pay. This puts people off from joining and as most legal aid firms cannot afford to support their staff with college fees etc there is a risk that future trainees and young staff members will be drawn from less diverse backgrounds, dominated by people who have family support. This perpetuates inherent inequality in the legal system. It should not be the preserve of those with money. Also the underfunding of the entire justice system is having a profound effect on the legal aid profession. Court closures, significant delays in hearings, etc.[14]

> Cuts to rates which make the future unsustainable. The worst thing is that it affects women and BAME practitioners the most. We have made huge strides to make the professions more equal and diverse. We will lose those gains, to the detriment of society.[15]

As this book has demonstrated, the legal aid sector is not a cohort of 'fat cat lawyers'. Yet, those working in the sector are already expressing concern about how this may change in the future, in light of such increasing pressure and precarity of the profession. The diversity implications of these changes are clearly a concern of current practitioners as they look to how this may shape the future of their sector.

Looking beyond the responses of individual practitioners, financial concerns were also a significant challenge reported by those who responded on behalf of organisations, albeit these concerns lagged behind a concern with administration. When asked to select the five main challenges facing their organisations (the 10 most frequently selected of which appear in Table 8.2 below), issues pertaining to the LAA administration (75.8 per cent, n=273), funding and resources (58.3 per cent, n=210), staff recruitment (42.2 per cent, n=152), budgeting (27.5 per cent, n=99), and capacity of service providers to meet community and client needs (27.2 per cent, n=98) dominated.[16]

[11] Practitioner Respondent Number 667.
[12] Practitioner Respondent Number 41.
[13] Practitioner Respondent Number 86.
[14] Practitioner Respondent Number 624.
[15] Practitioner Respondent Number 911.
[16] Challenges that did not appear in the 10 most frequently selected provided in Table 8.2 include: reporting requirements (11.7%, n=42); client intake and triage (10.3%, n=37); technology (eg suitability of hardware/software) (9.4%, n=34); lack of referral options (9.2%, n=33); fundraising (7.2%, n=26); meeting service targets (6.9%, n=25); staff performance (6.4%, n=23); staff supervision (6.1%, n=22); governance (4.4%, n=16); maintaining policies (3.9%, n=14); engaging the community (3.1%, n=11); systemic work (2.8%, n=10); measuring client need (2.2%, n=8); service planning (2.2%, n=8);

Table 8.2 The 10 organisational challenges most frequently selected by organisations (n=360)

	N	%
Legal Aid Agency administration	273	75.8
Funding and resources	210	58.3
Staff recruitment	152	42.2
Budgeting	99	27.5
Capacity of service to meet community/client needs	98	27.2
Staff retention	84	23.3
Managing staff health and well-being	81	22.5
Political environment	66	18.3
Accommodations and premises	50	13.9
Strategic planning	45	12.5

In a follow-up open-ended question, 207 organisational respondents elaborated on the factors underpinning these challenges. Coding of these responses revealed that the challenges were largely attributed by organisations to funding, profitability and sustainability at 59.4 per cent (n=133), followed by legal aid contract and claim issues (39.7 per cent, n=89) and issues with recruitment and retention (26.3 per cent, n=59).[17] These findings therefore reinforce that financial precarity is at the core of concerns for the future of the sector, not only for individual practitioners but also the organisations within which they work.

By exploring and emphasising the scope and scale of the concerns that practitioners expressed within the Census, we have underscored the central importance of resourcing commitments to the future sustainability of legal aid. Financial challenges and issues related to the administrative burden of working in legal aid were both identified as sector-wide concerns which are likely to shape how legal aid is valued and performed in years to come.

III. Addressing the Crisis

In concluding a monograph, it is customary for authors to compile a set of recommendations for the future. In alignment with our commitment to giving voice to

engaging priority client groups (1.9%, n=7); measuring outcomes (1.9%, n=7); stakeholder relationships (1.9%, n=7); volunteer recruitment (1.9%, n=7); partnership and collaboration (1.7%, n=6); volunteer retention (1.7%, n=6); evaluating services (1.4%, n=5); volunteer training (1.4%, n=5); and filling board or management committee positions (1.1%, n=4).

[17] Other explanations given included: political climate (19.3%, n=40); administration/bureaucracy (10.1%, n=21); well-being/pressure on staff (10.1%, n=21); premises (8.7%, n=18); lack of other local services/areas out of scope (8.2%, n=17); COVID-19 (5.3%, n=11); vulnerable/demanding clients (3.9%, n=8), other (including police station and court closures and unpredictable case volumes) (1.0%, n=2).

those working within the sector, it is appropriate that we start with the suggestions and recommendations of those who responded to the Census. Building upon these responses, we will set out an agenda for policy and future research necessary to address the crisis of legal aid that has been depicted throughout this book.

While responses were similar across the various groups who responded to the Census, we will focus specifically on the responses from current practitioners so as to provide a consistent basis for our policy and research agendas. When asked 'What would make the system more effective?' and 'What recommendations do you have to address these or to otherwise improve the sector?' practitioners had clear views on how these challenges might be addressed to ensure the future sustainability of legal aid. These responses are detailed in Table 8.3.[18] Quantitative coding of open-ended responses to these questions revealed that over three quarters (75.7 per cent, n=608) of practitioner respondents suggested that 'more funding/investment to allow for fairer fees/wages' would improve the legal aid system.

Table 8.3 The 10 most frequent suggestions for improving the legal aid system given by current legal aid practitioners (n=803)

	N	%
More funding/investment to allow for fairer fees/wages	608	75.7
More flexibility/less bureaucracy and red tape from the LAA	149	18.6
Better understanding of the amount of work that is actually carried out compared to that which is remunerated	141	17.6
Abolish LASPO changes/expand eligibility/improve accessibility of legal aid	137	17.1
More positive portrayal of lawyers in the media/by the Government and more appreciation generally	106	13.2
Need for more good-quality lawyers	55	6.8
More streamlined claiming processes/simpler fee structures	50	6.2
Better IT systems/infrastructure (eg improving/replacing CCMS)	46	5.7
Better training for professionals	40	5.0
Greater efficiency/better communication within the courts	38	4.7

[18] Other responses not listed in Table 8.3 included: more trust in legal professionals (4.1%, n=33); better work–life balance (3.2%, n=26); more diversity within the sector (2.5%, n=20); taking authority away from LAA (either giving it to neutral body or back to the profession) (2.4%, n=19); continuation of remote hearings/working and more digitalisation (2.1%, n=17); alternative funding models to provide security to the sector, eg diverse funding streams or early intervention (1.9%, n=15); I don't know/it is too late for these problems to be addressed (1.9%, n=15); better collaboration between the sector as a whole to address problems, including campaign work (1.6%, n=13); less delay in receiving payments for legal aid work (1.2%, n=10); better communication/relationships between lawyers and the CPS/police (1.1%, n=9); complete overhaul of the system/sector (1.1%, n=9); more non-financial support for professionals eg mental health (1.0%, n=8); better working relationships between solicitors/barristers (0.9%, n=7); more equity internally within firms/chambers/organisations (0.7%, n=6);

The overwhelming calls for funding-related change were frequently expressed in simple yet powerful terms, which communicated both how foundational and obvious such solutions were perceived to be. For example, 'funding'[19] and 'money'[20] were common responses. Similarly, responses also included phrases such as 'proper rates of pay',[21] 'better funding',[22] or 'adequate financial remuneration – a pay increase after nearly 30 years'.[23] Frequently, practitioners answered using the language of sustainability, such as asking for 'a sustainable level of remuneration'[24] or demanding 'sustainable rates of pay, whether fixed fees or hourly rates'.[25] Practitioners also sometimes explicitly connected the need for improved funding and the viability of legal aid's future: 'We need to increase fees to make the future of legal aid viable. If we don't, we will lose young lawyers and lose firms who love this area of work because it is financially viable.'[26]

In considering the potential of improved resourcing as a solution for the future, many responses clarified that this would need to be more than a one-off injection of funding, and rather a longer-term funding model that appropriately responded to economic realities, such as by factoring in inflation ('the system would need to take account of inflation'),[27] or committing to a yearly review of fees ('an annual increase and upgrade that as a minimum [keeps] up with inflation').[28] Aligned with this, many responses asserted that legal aid fees should be adapted so that they are capable of more accurately representing the work actually involved in a case. As explored in chapter five, both fixed or hourly fees were criticised for falling short of the work required because 'legal aid fees should be increased and more accurately reflect the work undertaken'.[29] Another recommendation for the re-evaluation of the fee system was evident in several responses that called for greater simplicity in funding ('make rules less complex')[30] and more efficient payment processes to ensure cash flow ('legal aid work would be much easier if payment was prompt').[31]

doesn't need improving (0.6%, n=5); better functioning of government bodies across society so fewer cases need to be brought in the first place (0.5%, n=4); other (including more holistic solutions, more focus on clients, fewer private tenders) (0.5%, n=4); larger cap allowed for legal aid certificates (0.4%, n=3); LAA should pay experts/interpreters directly rather than providers (0.4%, n=3); legal aid is too accessible (0.2%, n=2).

[19] Practitioner Respondent Number 1124.
[20] Practitioner Respondent Number 238.
[21] Practitioner Respondent Number 269.
[22] Practitioner Respondent Number 249.
[23] Practitioner Respondent Number 292.
[24] Practitioner Respondent Number 1155.
[25] Practitioner Respondent Number 740.
[26] Practitioner Respondent Number 1037.
[27] Practitioner Respondent Number 1203.
[28] Practitioner Respondent Number 862.
[29] Practitioner Respondent Number 1035.
[30] Practitioner Respondent Number 1118.
[31] Practitioner Respondent Number 75.

Across these suggestions, there was also hope that those designing the legal aid system might have more knowledge of the sector ('it appears that public funding decisions are not always made by people with legal training').[32] This was also recognised as a shortcoming of those responsible assessing claims ('a cost assessor who has done the job').[33] Underpinning these assertions is a clear desire for increased recognition of the value of legal aid work. For instance, in alignment with the ways that they described the challenges facing the sector, several respondents to the current practitioner survey suggested that what is needed was a simple alignment of legal aid lawyers with professionals working in other areas of the justice system ('fair remuneration that recognises that [l]egal aid lawyers are professionals just like other lawyers'),[34] or those who source their income from private fees ('the system would be more effective if it paid more than 25 per cent of typical private fees').[35] There was often comparison to other traditionally comparable professions ('salaries like doctors, graded'),[36] as in this example:

> Compare the expertise of qualified legal professionals with other professionals with similar training and expertise and compare the level of remuneration and make legal aid fees the same as the fees the government pays to other similar experts given that legal [aid] is ultimately paid by the government.[37]

Taken together, these suggestions were united in their desire for an improved funding model, with many practitioners explicitly explaining how such a model would improve the future of legal aid. For instance, responses indicated that these sorts of mechanisms would enable practitioners to not only work under less pressure, but also provide a better service to their clients because they would not feel forced to balance huge caseloads in order to make ends meet: 'Better remuneration would unburden practitioners from feeling like they have to take on huge amounts of work. Clients would receive a better service and practitioners would feel pressured.'[38] Practitioners were hopeful for a future where they would be able to focus more on supporting their clients than contending with anxieties around profitability and sustainability. Implicit within this future are improvements to lawyers' wellbeing, with practitioners suggesting that 'higher paid cases [would mean] we would be able to do fewer and maybe have a life as well.'[39]

Improved remuneration was therefore perceived as a solution that would not only improve the lives and practices of lawyers already working in the sector, but also the quality of the legal aid profession in the future: 'Pay us better – will lead to

[32] Practitioner Respondent Number 958.
[33] Practitioner Respondent Number 289.
[34] Practitioner Respondent Number 1.
[35] Practitioner Respondent Number 574.
[36] Practitioner Respondent Number 1181.
[37] Practitioner Respondent Number 667.
[38] Practitioner Respondent Number 1109.
[39] Practitioner Respondent Number 888.

higher standards and also attract lawyers to the profession by active choice instead of default.'[40]

With clearer and more accurate funding models, practitioners clearly felt that the talent pool in the sector would improve as it became a more attractive destination for all lawyers. At the same time, some practitioners called on the Government to recognise the wider cost savings that can come with properly resourced early legal advice. For example: 'To factor in public savings brought about by access to legal services, so that the legal aid budget is not seen as purely a drain on the public purse but an investment on savings in other areas.'[41]

Unsurprisingly, given the altruistic motivations for entering the legal aid profession discussed in chapter two, suggestions for improved funding models were frequently rooted in how these changes would improve access to justice. In other words, calls for increased remuneration were about more than just lawyer fees – they were perceived as an essential opportunity to advocate for vulnerable communities that have been excluded from legal aid over the past few decades. For instance, several responses cited the need to bring more matters into scope, recognising the clustered reality of many legal problems: 'bringing more matters within scope, [it is] often difficult to advise on housing if debt is not included'.[42]

Looking beyond the responses that explicitly called for funding improvements, nearly a fifth of current practitioner respondents suggested that 'more flexibility/less bureaucracy and red tape from the LAA' (18.6 per cent, n=149), 'better understanding[s] of the amount of work that is actually carried out compared to that which is remunerated for' (17.6 per cent, n=141), and 'abolish[ing] LASPO changes/expand[ing] eligibility/improv[ing] accessibility of legal aid' (17.1 per cent, n=137) would improve the existing legal aid system. There is obvious overlap between these responses and the explicit calls for changes to funding models, and the extent of the responses in relation to these issues only goes to reinforce the central importance of appropriate funding for addressing the challenges that form the fabric of practitioners' experiences of working in the sector. These responses point to several themes that have underpinned the chapters of this book, namely the insufficiency of the existing fee regime, challenges relating to the LAA, discrepancies between remuneration and work responsibilities and the negative effects of the LASPO changes. While there are clearly myriad problems facing the sector, the bottom-line recommendation from practitioners remains: 'increase legal aid fees – it's not rocket science.'[43]

[40] Practitioner Respondent Number 1075.
[41] Practitioner Respondent Number 759.
[42] Practitioner Respondent Number 387.
[43] Practitioner Respondent Number 445.

IV. Time for Change

As explored throughout this book, the challenges facing the legal aid sector are far from new. Why, therefore, is it so significant for addressing these problems at this moment in time? The answer to this question is clearly articulated in the responses of those who have left legal aid or who are considering a departure from the sector in the near future. Both the current and former practitioner surveys concluded with a final open-ended question, asking respondents if they had anything to add to the detail they had already provided; it is here that respondents clearly conveyed their sense of desperation for this research to finally prompt solutions to these problems.

Within responses to this question, there was a clear tension between heart and head and between a drive to stay and fight, and creeping doubts that it might be time to give up the battle to remain part of the sector. Although responses were comparable across respondents to the different surveys comprising the Census, we will chiefly consider responses from those who responded on behalf of their organisations (n=118) in order to provide insight from those at the helm of trying to sustain legal aid practice.

The two most common responses to this final question restated the overwhelming financial challenges facing the sector, with quantitative coding revealing that 47.5 per cent (n=56) of organisations stated that the profession required better funding and 43.2 per cent (n=51) reported that current funding arrangements served as a disincentive from engaging in legal aid work in the future. By examining responses in more detail, we were able to draw out more specific responses that ranged from complaints about the wider system ('the system is underfunded and has been for a significant period of time')[44] and personal experience ('We don't get paid enough').[45] They revealed that organisations find it difficult to attract people to legal aid ('the rates and bureaucracy make legal aid … impossible to recruit')[46] and that the culmination of challenges are likely to mean that organisations are on the precipice of leaving the sector ('if legal aid is cut any further it would be difficult to see how the practice would be able to continue').[47] Invariably, responses indicated that current practitioners are already leaving the sector, and organisations are going to struggle to replace them, because 'without increases to the charging rates across the board … the supplier base will further reduce as older owners decide to retire.'[48]

Some respondents used this question as another opportunity to plead for change within the sector, for example by restating that 'an increase in the basic remuneration rate for legal aid is long overdue and is essential to the future viability

[44] Organisation Respondent Number 161.
[45] Organisation Respondent Number 88.
[46] Organisation Respondent Number 332.
[47] Organisation Respondent Number 158.
[48] Organisation Respondent Number 215.

of the sector.'[49] Others used the question to remind us that the sector only continues to function due to the extent of goodwill among its practitioners:

> We are committed to it and will always do it. And that is our problem – the government knows it can get away with freezing the rates for over a decade because they know we don't do it for the money.[50]

Indeed, over a quarter (26.3 per cent, n=31) of those responding on behalf of organisations responded in a manner that sought to reinforce the importance of legal aid work and demonstrate their commitment to social justice, even despite an awareness of how this goodwill is being capitalised upon by those that determine the legal aid budget. This was the third most popular comment and provided a vital explanation as to why these practitioners remained in the sector despite the challenges they faced. At times, there was a sense of defiance among the responses to this question: 'We remain committed to providing legal aid to service the community. We have been providing legal aid since it started and will continue to do so.'[51]

Among these responses, it was clear that practitioners felt strongly about the importance of the work that they do. This sense of purpose is likely to have been a key factor in sustaining the sector to date. However, respondents also indicated that they had to be realistic and, as such, these sentiments were often expressed alongside anxiety about just how difficult it was to stay in the sector. Many recognised that they were nearing the point of giving up, stating that 'legal aid is essential for our clients but could tip us over the edge'.[52]

The urgency for change was clear within several poignant, powerful examples provided by those respondents who are enduring hardship in order to sustain access to justice. For many, the pride that they take in carrying out legal aid work can only go so far:

> We are proud to carry out legal aid work to a very high standard and accept fees are always going to be lower than other private client work but it is genuinely approaching the point where it is no longer sustainable. Something has to give.[53]

Respondents were therefore well aware of the limits of their goodwill, and conscious of how quickly they were approaching. Many articulated the present moment as something of a tipping point for their organisations:

> I am so very proud of this work and it would really be a loss to society if we could no longer undertake it. This remains a distinct possibility however given the continuing rates and schemes for payment.[54]

[49] Organisation Respondent Number 281.
[50] Organisation Respondent Number 367.
[51] Organisation Respondent Number 360.
[52] Organisation Respondent Number 257.
[53] Organisation Respondent Number 365.
[54] Organisation Respondent Number 361.

> The constraints in funding and limits on fees make us feel that the legal aid clients are second class citizens. We do everything in our power to overcome this but it is constantly pedalling uphill through treacle.[55]

The idea of 'pedalling uphill through treacle' co-opts a phrase sometimes used by cyclists to describe the feeling where their legs are no longer responding in the way they wish; the cyclist can push themselves as hard as they can but it still feels like they are barely moving. This is how many of these practitioners perceived the task of advocating for the importance of their organisations in the wider context of access to justice. As with the risk of the cyclist causing themselves an injury if they continue to ignore the protestations of their body, these practitioners foresaw personal cost in their continuing to pedal indefinitely:

> We continue to work in this field as we believe in the importance of representation as an integral part of a justice system. However it is at great personal cost and feels undervalued and under appreciated by the [LAA] and government. We will endeavour to continue performing to the highest standards we can but it is becoming very hard.[56]

While the significance of the present moment as a time for change was obvious to respondents, they were conscious that the Government did not necessarily grasp the urgency of the situation.

A clear feature of responses was an understanding that meaningful change will be impossible without such recognition from the Government. Further, this recognition is unlikely within a political context where there is little popular support for access to justice:

> We are a multi-award winning organisation who have taken many cases to the higher courts which have changed the law to the benefit of the poor and those in housing need. Our work is universally recognised as being excellent. Our clients and the wider housing legal world will miss us when we are gone. The government clearly won't.[57]

> We believe everyone should have a fair crack of the whip more commonly known as access to justice. There are no votes in legal aid and this is reflected in the lack of political will to do something about it. We are proud we are able to help those that need it most but are now actively considering a life away from public funding.[58]

Amongst those still in the sector, there are many who are actively considering leaving despite this strong sense of social justice that motivates them to stay. This shows how insurmountable the problems of legal aid practice feel to even the most committed. Further, this demonstrates that calls for increased remuneration and sustainable funding models are fundamentally made by a cohort of driven workers who are willing to earn perpetually less than lawyers working in other areas – in reality, respondents in the sector are calling for funding arrangements to be such that they can remain within the sector, instead of being forced to abandon it.

[55] Organisation Respondent Number 197.
[56] Organisation Respondent Number 106.
[57] Organisation Respondent Number 322.
[58] Organisation Respondent Number 168.

Of course, the Census also included the voices of those who have already left the sector. These responses came from those who had reached this tipping point where social justice motivations could no longer outweigh the problems they faced. A total of 79 former legal aid practitioners provided an answer when they were asked if they had anything else to add to their Census responses, and the most common responses (44.3 per cent, n=35) were those that emphasised there were too many associated problems in the sector that take time away from legal work. These responses focused upon how the vital aspects of their work – helping their clients and facilitating access to justice – were simply too difficult to achieve considering all the problems that characterised the sector. For example, these former practitioner respondents stated that the 'current system [is] not sustainable',[59] and that 'the system also involved excessive paperwork and bureaucracy'.[60] These are common factors that continue to undermine access to justice for current practitioners, and they are clearly also important enough to be emphasised here as factors that finally push people to leave.

Some former practitioners took this question as an opportunity to highlight that leaving the sector was not for want of trying, and that clients and colleagues alike often helped make working in legal aid as sustainable as possible while they were still there. For example, one explained 'it was not the fault of the lawyers or the clients but dealing with [the LAA] and forms was thankless',[61] while another explained that 'colleagues were supportive but similarly overworked and stressed so only able to offer limited support'.[62] Another practitioner asserted that 'For me the move out of legal aid and private practice was not about financial benefits, I found the working environment very stressful … It requires resilience to work in legal aid.'[63] This underscores the reality that there is a tipping point at which the satisfaction of helping clients and the support of colleagues could no longer sustain their work:

> I had wanted to be a criminal barrister since I was a child, I worked incredibly hard and invested a huge amount of time and money; my debt from qualifying is huge. I feel a deep sense of loss and regret for not having been able to make it a financially viable career or to have much of a personal life from working such long hours. I hope one day I will be able to return to it.[64]

The reasons that practitioners leave legal aid can therefore be understood largely as a response to problems in the sector rather than due to the appeal of other areas of work. This sentiment is reinforced by a quarter of respondents to the former legal aid practitioners survey (25.3 per cent, n=20) who reported that they had enjoyed working in legal aid and would return to the sector if it was possible.

[59] Lever Respondent Number 37.
[60] Leaver Respondent Number 103.
[61] Leaver Respondent Number 198.
[62] Leaver Respondent Number 136.
[63] Leaver Respondent Number 65.
[64] Leaver Respondent Number 48.

Taken together, responses to the Census indicate the urgency of taking action in relation to the legal aid sector. By examining the experiences of those who are torn between remaining in the sector and abandoning legal aid, as well as those who have already had to make this difficult choice, it is clear that social justice motivations can only go so far in a sector that is so inhospitable and hostile to its members. The sector as a whole is facing a tipping point from which it may be unable to recover if action is not imminently taken. Despite the demoralising nature of many of these responses, the optimistic hope of these respondents that they might one day return to legal aid combined with the scale of engagement with our questions regarding change needed in the sector, is nevertheless indicative that this tipping point has not yet surpassed us. Rather, there remains an opportunity to facilitate improvements that may restore the sector and its contributions to access to justice from being entirely diminished.

V. Recommendations for Policy

We now turn to policy recommendations that would address the crisis facing legal aid. These recommendations are invariably informed by the frontline experiences of Census respondents across all five surveys. As detailed throughout this chapter, respondents to all surveys bar the student survey were united in the view that action must be taken if we are to ensure that the legal aid sector continues to exist, let alone flourishes in the way that respondent practitioners hoped that it might. Of course, as our respondents have emphasised, reforms to the funding arrangements for legal aid are imperative. Any combination of the proposals put forward by our respondents – increasing fee levels, introducing flexibility and clarity to payment schedules, more accurately recognising the work required to complete a legal matter or reducing the administrative burdens associated with legal aid work – would all be welcome and vital reforms that would go some way towards building a legal aid sector that is somewhat more sustainable. However, it is also crucial to recognise that this fundamental issue of remuneration is, in reality, inextricably rooted in a broader crisis that afflicts access to justice in England and Wales.

As discussed at the beginning of this book, the provision of legal aid plays a key role in facilitating access to justice, helping to meet legal needs and enabling individuals to establish or enforce their rights across various areas of law. Legal aid practitioners assist clients with a wide range of issues, including but not limited to those relating to criminal defence, family matters, education, housing, immigration, discrimination, debt, community care and employment. Nevertheless, the legal aid system is experiencing unprecedented pressures and challenges.[65]

[65] The Westminster Commission on Legal Aid, 'Inquiry into the Sustainability and Recovery of the Legal Aid Sector' (All-Party Parliamentary Group on Legal Aid, 2021).

The COVID-19 pandemic,[66] changes brought about by the LASPO reforms,[67] fee arrangements,[68] court closures[69] and wider attempts to reduce legal aid spending[70] have all contributed to the increasingly unviable nature of the sector. In order to adequately respond to the crisis facing the legal aid sector, we therefore support more wholesale policy recommendations for legal aid that have been set out by the Bach Commission on access to justice.[71]

The Bach Commission was established in 2015 for the purpose of undertaking a comprehensive review of legal aid after the implementation of LASPO. Since its formation, its scope expanded to consider the wider crises affecting the justice system. The Commission has recognised that the scale of these problems requires a deep-rooted, bold and holistic solution: the creation of a new Right to Justice Act. As such, the Commission called for policy reform that goes beyond reversing specific government decisions that the Commission deemed to be regressive or damaging to access to justice. Importantly, this proposal also does more than call for an increase to funding. Rather, the proposed development of such important primary legislation represents deeper, structural reform. In their final report, the Commission justifies the radical rationale behind this proposal:

> An effective legal system in which all can access justice fairly is the cornerstone of a free society. The law is not something that lawyers and judges impose on criminals but a common inheritance to which everybody in society has an equal right. The law guarantees our rights, underlines our duties, and provides an equitable and orderly means of resolving disputes.
>
> There are few principles that so clearly cross party political lines: a properly functioning legal system that maintains the rule of law is, along with democracy, the basis of our political settlement. While big picture political issues like the jurisdiction of the European court of justice dominate discussion, the granular, everyday workings of our justice system are less explored, but at least as important …
>
> The Commission has heard, over the course of nearly two years, striking testimony from many sources about the multiple failures of the justice system. This has led us to conclude that the problems are so deep-rooted, commonplace and various that piecemeal reforms alone would simply be papering over the cracks. We have therefore concluded that what is needed is a new Right to Justice Act which codifies and extends our right to justice.[72]

[66] The Law Society of England and Wales, 'Law Under Lockdown: The Impact of Covid-19 Measures on Access to Justice and Vulnerable People' (The Law Society, September 2020).

[67] James Organ and Jennifer Sigafoos, 'The Impact of LASPO on Routes to Justice' (Equality and Human Rights Commission, 2018).

[68] House of Commons Justice Committee, 'The Future of Legal Aid: Third Report of Session 2021–22' (Her Majesty's Stationery Office, 2021).

[69] Jack S Caird, 'Court and Tribunal Closures' (House of Commons Library, 21 March 2016).

[70] James Thornton, 'Is Publicly Funded Criminal Defence Sustainable? Legal Aid Cuts, Morale, Recruitment and Retention in the English Criminal Law Professions' (2020) 40 *Legal Studies* 230.

[71] Fabian Society, 'The Right to Justice: Final Report of the Bach Commission' (Fabians, 2017).

[72] ibid, 15.

The new Act would codify and supplement the existing framework of legal rights in England and Wales, and establish a new right for individuals to receive reasonable legal assistance without costs they cannot afford. What this entails is the concept of minimum standards for access to justice:

> Such minimum standards [are] neither new, nor without existing legal and international precedent. But the current legal framework and its infrastructure allow too many people to forgo justice. And there is too much ambiguity and therefore too much discretion about what our right to justice means in practice, as the supreme court judgment on employment tribunal fees recently acknowledged. We believe that a single, statute-based right to justice will bring the clarity necessary to reset our justice system and ensure that everyone can access justice.[73]

For the Commission, there are three main benefits that this Act would bring: clarity, political consensus and a broader onceptualization of access to justice.[74] Clarity helps to redress the ambiguity of existing laws around access to justice, as shown in *R (Unison) v Lord Chancellor*, where judges noted that there is currently 'wide discretion conferred upon the Lord Chancellor by the relevant statutory provision' in determining what constitutes reasonable access to the courts.[75] Political consensus would seek to detach access to justice from party politics by making it more difficult for a lord chancellor to propose new legislation that overrides our human rights or the common law principle of unrestricted access to the courts. A broader conception, as is proposed under the Act, would move beyond the idea that mere access to the courts can be a determinant of access to justice. Furthermore, it would recognise the dangers that stem from a lack of knowledge or information about the law or legal processes, and how these can facilitate experiences of injustice for individuals who find themselves with legal problems.

As per the Commission's recommendations, this would also involve establishing a new, independent body called the Justice Commission whose administrative role would include interpreting, monitoring and enforcing the right to justice enshrined in the Act.[76] The Bach Commission recognises that it would take time to change the justice system, and that the new right to justice would not provide an immediately effective solution to the challenges facing legal aid. Considering the inevitable lag, the Justice Commission would help to instigate the transformation in access to justice by taking a proactive role in defining precisely what access to justice should mean going forward. The Justice Commission would be a non-departmental public body led by a chief commissioner, with a board of legal practitioners, public champions and other relevant experts, replacing the LAA. As an independent body operating at arm's length from the Government, the new body would overcome many of the problems of the LAA Agency cited

[73] ibid, 14.
[74] ibid, 15–16.
[75] *R (Unison) v Lord Chancellor* [2017] UKSC 51.
[76] ibid, 19.

throughout this book, which currently sits within the Ministry of Justice and is therefore subject to political party pressures. As such, the Justice Commission would be empowered to challenge government decisions, conduct inquiries and intervene in individual litigation to support implementation of the new right. It would work closely with other relevant bodies, such as the Equality and Human Rights Commission.

The vision of the Bach Commission is for the Right to Justice Act to develop a system of universally accessible advice.[77] Its reasoning behind this significant commitment is that proper functioning of the legal aid system is an essential part of ensuring that such a right can work in practice. At the heart of the concerns reported by all respondents to the Legal Aid Census is the idea that without a sustainable legal aid sector, vulnerable communities will be excluded from advice and support when they experience legal problems. The Bach Commission's policy proposal has emerged from a recognition of many of the same barriers that have been reported throughout this book:

> It is the work of legal aid professionals that props up the legal aid system and ensures that those who are eligible for legal aid can secure justice. It has never been the most lucrative branch of the legal profession. But the legal aid sector must be able to sustain itself, with providers continuing to carry out legally aided work and new recruits bolstering the profession. Yet with downward pressures on legal aid fees, cuts to bursaries for aspiring legal aid lawyers and low morale in the profession, many are turning away from legal aid work altogether. In the medium and long-term, such a shrinkage of the legal aid profession will inevitably have consequences on the quality and quantity of legal aid provision, and therefore people's ability to access justice on a fair footing.[78]

As such, the Bach Commission calls for an independent review of legal aid, the state of the sector and its longer-term viability. In essence, this is precisely what the Legal Aid Census has undertaken. In analysing its response, we have uncovered a variety of complex barriers which mean that the Right to Justice Act proposed by the Commission would be difficult to realise without immediate, substantial support for the legal aid sector. Thus, while our findings support the need for this policy intervention, we also advocate that an essential part of this must be urgent remedial action to protect, preserve and enhance the legal aid sector to make this right something that moves beyond the statute book and into everyday life, so that it may also be felt by the tenant disputing their eviction notice as well as the claimant trying to navigate the procedures of the Department for Work and Pensions.

Fundamentally, creating a statutory right to justice would provide a new conceptualisation of access to justice. Informed by relevant international legal

[77] ibid, 42–43.
[78] ibid, 37.

frameworks,[79] it would provide an opportunity to specifically define what access to justice should mean in both principle and practice. Crucially, it would locate access to justice at the centre of the relationship between citizens and state, highlighting the importance of the legal aid sector which, as we have demonstrated, has been so diminished. Building on the findings of the Legal Aid Census, we argue that the creation of a Right to Justice Act would be an appropriate starting point for overcoming both past and future challenges that have been documented throughout this book. Indeed, such change would facilitate a new era of access to justice, characterised by a simpler, more generous legal aid scheme, reduced administrative burden on suppliers, which addresses the sustainability of the legal aid profession and increases social mobility for legal aid lawyers.

In light of the largest ever engagement of the legal aid sector in England and Wales, our chief proposal is therefore that the time for piecemeal policy reform has come and gone. Rather, in recognition of the reality that the legal aid sector is at a crucial tipping point, we purport that there is a need for more radical and foundational change. As such, we argue that the notion of a right to justice must be taken seriously; if and when it is implemented, it can be the basis of a comprehensive policy platform through which to offer the kind of meaningful access to justice that is under threat for all and is increasingly a myth for so many.

VI. Recommendations for Future Research

The success of any future policy development will inevitably hinge on the quality and breadth of available data and knowledge about the accessibility of justice and the efficacy of the legal aid system. Rigorous studies on the current state of the justice system as well as ongoing evaluations and research to monitor the impact of the pandemic on this system are all required in order to build on the foundational knowledge base that we have established through the Legal Aid Census. Thankfully, there is no shortage of capabilities, skills and willingness among researchers working in this field. Socio-legal researchers, for instance, are frequently motivated by social justice concerns, which means there is significant scope for collaboration between academia and legal practitioners on research projects that seek to test innovations that may improve access to justice.

[79] While outside the scope of discussion in this book, it is worth noting the relevance to access to justice – and subsequently to any new legislation in this area – of international obligations in treaties the UK has signed and ratified including: the International Covenant on Economic, Social and Cultural Rights; the United Nations Convention on the Rights of the Child; the Convention on the Elimination of All Forms of Discrimination Against Women; and the Convention on the Elimination of All Forms of Racial Discrimination. We note developments in Scotland to incorporate each of these treaties into Scottish law in relation to devolved matters and the different position for Wales with respect to giving further effect to the UNCRC in domestic law (Child and Young Persons (Wales) Measure 2011).

There are a number of established access to justice scholars who have already made significant contributions to developing understanding of legal aid's role in pursuing access to justice across a number of fields in England and Wales over recent decades.[80] In fact, access to justice scholarship is emerging as a burgeoning field in its own right, with an array of exciting, inspiring mid- and early-career scholars examining different areas of legal aid.[81] As such, there is a growing recognition that socio-legal researchers are capable of exploring legal aid issues to produce significant, interesting and impactful research that works to forward an agenda for access to justice. Given the vast complexities of the legal aid sector and the variable context in which it operates, the importance of this research has never been clearer. By providing a comprehensive foundation for such research, the Legal Aid Census provides an opportunity for established and emerging access to justice scholars to forge new directions and trial new methodological innovations in this area.

First and foremost, there is a continued need for a robust, all-encompassing, up-to-date dataset that depicts the demographics, trends and challenges characterising the legal aid sector. There is therefore a tangible need for researchers to conduct subsequent surveys or even another Census to build a continuing understanding of the sector so that comparisons can be drawn with that which is provided here. Having established the utility of such a Census for England and Wales as well as showing that it is practically possible to survey such large numbers of practitioners, it is important to build on this success through both replication as well as the adaptation of this Census to incorporate new research perspectives, innovative methodological strategies, and different topics explored. While annual surveys are unlikely to be practicable for the sector, a snapshot of the sector every three to five years would provide baseline data through which the impact of changes and reforms could be monitored and evaluated.

In conducting the first Legal Aid Census, we have been able to identify areas in which we would recommend improvements and changes for the researchers who may take forward these future iterations. Capturing, ordering and analysing the financial data in particular was especially challenging, considering the array of different areas of legal aid with varying remuneration, the range of organisational models in place, as well as the various patterns of work undertaken by legal aid

[80] Hilary Sommerlad, 'Some Reflections on the Relationship between Citizenship, Access to Justice and the Reform of Legal Aid' (2004) 31 *Journal of Law and Society* 345; Vicky Kemp, 'Transforming Legal Aid: Access to Criminal Defence Services' (Legal Services Research Centre, 2010); Richard Moorhead, 'Legal Aid and the Decline of Private Practice: Blue Murder or Toxic Job?' (2004) 11 *International Journal of the Legal Profession* 159.

[81] Daniel Newman and Roxanna Dehaghani, *Experiences of Criminal Justice: Perspectives from Wales on a System in Crisis* (Bristol University Press, 2022); Emma Cooke, 'The Working Culture of Legal Aid Lawyers, Developing a "Shared Orientation Model"' (2021) 31 *Social and Legal Studies* 704; Thornton (n 70); Jo Wilding, *The Legal Aid Market: Challenges for Publicly Funded Immigration and Asylum Legal Representation* (Policy Press, 2021); Lucy Welsh, *Access to Justice in Magistrates' Courts: A Study of Defendant Marginalisation* (Hart, 2022); Jessica Mant, *Litigants in Person and the Family Justice System* (Hart, 2022).

practitioners. There is therefore a compromise to be made between the level of detail that can be obtained and the functionality of the survey instruments, which themselves should not be too arduous so as to avoid discouraging responses. On this basis, we would encourage future researchers embarking on a census of this scale to consider simplifying these details to capture a more generalised picture on remuneration. In turn, this allows space for respondents to discuss other important issues which we would have liked to examine further, such as bullying, harassment and discrimination. Alternatively, there may also be scope for researchers to focus entirely on the issue of remuneration, by reducing the overall breadth of their survey scope to delve into more granular detail on the financial concerns that were so crucial to respondents' experiences in this Census.

We would also encourage future researchers to consider the potential value of a Legal Aid Census within and beyond the jurisdiction of England and Wales. There is a compelling argument to be made for separate evaluations of the two countries that make up the England and Wales jurisdiction. Clear differences between the legal aid sector in different areas of England and Wales, for instance, is evidenced in recent research that has started to challenge the long-accepted assumption that research conducted in England alone can sufficiently document the challenges faced across England and Wales.[82] In reality, there are different approaches to justice within the governments based at Cardiff Bay and Westminster that are likely to have different impacts on the legal aid sector.[83] The Commission on Justice in Wales has, for example, highlighted the paucity of disaggregated Wales-specific data despite the apparently different challenges being faced by access to justice in that half of the jurisdiction.[84] While justice persists as a reserved matter for Westminster, the Welsh Government has recently launched a Justice Commission to investigate how justice could be devolved to Wales. A Wales-only census would therefore remedy the lack of knowledge on access to justice in Wales, and provide an evidence base capable of informing these changes. Justice is already devolved in Scotland, which means that there is likely to be a significant need for a Scottish census to understand the state of legal aid across Scotland, especially given disparate legal aid provision in some regions and concerns as to working conditions and rates of pay, which have resulted in threatened strikes in relation to criminal legal aid.[85] Such data would allow researchers to draw comparisons across the border to capture the impacts of different policy directions within the UK context.

[82] Daniel Newman and Jon Robins, *Justice in a Time of Austerity: Stories of a System in Crisis* (Bristol University Press, 2021); Newman and Dehaghani (n 81).

[83] Anneka Owens, 'Securing Equality Rights and Access to Justice in Wales' (MSc Thesis, Cardiff University, 2020).

[84] Commission on Justice in Wales, 'Justice in Wales for the People of Wales' (Commission on Justice in Wales, 2019).

[85] See eg Mike Wade, 'Scottish defence lawyers threaten strikes over legal aid fees' (*The Times*, 20 June 2022), available at www.thetimes.co.uk/article/scottish-defence-lawyers-threaten-strikes-over-legal-aid-fees-95vp06gp7.

Looking beyond the UK, it would also be useful to identify countries with similar and dissimilar legal aid schemes to England and Wales in order to undertake comparisons of different justice innovations and policies. For example, a census undertaken in Australia, New Zealand, Canada, South Africa or the United States could provide an evidence base from which to draw out the synergies and divergences between alike and contrasting legal aid systems within jurisdictions that are broadly comparable due to their colonial development.

There are many other kinds of research that could deepen the knowledge base provided by the Legal Aid Census. Interview and observation studies are commonly undertaken across legal aid, and there is a stark need for further, contemporary studies of this type to capture the cumulative effect of austerity and COVID-19. With the benefit of the Census's foundational insights, such research might include larger-scale interviews and observational studies exploring the diversity present across geographical areas and organisational types. While we have emphasised the importance of examining sectoral trends over time through future iterations of the Census, we also emphasise the potential value of developing longitudinal studies that follow groups of individuals for specific periods. For instance, given the findings presented in this book that concern barriers to entering the legal aid profession, we would recommend a study that specifically examines the choices made by law students throughout the early stages of their careers. Such a study would be capable of exploring questions such as who chooses or avoids a career in legal aid and why, as well as students' preparedness for legal aid, opportunities to undertake work experience in legal aid and social mobility in legal aid. With respect to recruitment and retention, we consider that there is a pressing need for a longitudinal study of a national cross-section of law graduates, such as the 'After the JD' study in the US,[86] to better inform developments in legal education, track changes following the implementation of the SQE and provide systemic data on the changing nature of legal careers thus deepening our understanding of the paths pursued by graduates. There is also much to be gained from developing larger-scale, experimental pilots such as randomised control trials in order to look at the real-world effects of different approaches to legal aid. For example, looking at the community-level impact of reintroducing a version of the green form scheme, delving further into the potential of more holistic models as pioneered in the US or the effect of introducing legal services innovation into what was previously an advice desert.

Beyond specific types of research, a theme that we believe to be especially important in light of the Legal Aid Census is for scholarship to begin to examine different areas of legal aid together. There are differences between, for example, criminal and debt, which range from the differing levels of availability to the varying models of delivery. While we have drawn out some of this variation as it

[86] See eg Bryant Garth and Ronit Dinovitzer, 'After the JD: First Results of a National Study of Legal Careers' (American Bar Foundation, 2004).

emerged within the Census, legal aid scholarship as a whole – including our own previous work – has often tended towards treating different areas of law as discrete and unique.[87] For example, one scholar may look at criminal justice and establish an academic career doing research on the criminal justice system. In another example, a scholar in immigration might establish themselves as an expert in that area alone. While both are interested in access to justice, and forwarding understandings of access to justice, there is a risk that their siloed expertise may omit several commonalities and interactions between their areas that could help inform specific knowledge on each field, as well as broaden knowledge of access to justice as a concept.

During the course of conducting the Legal Aid Census, we have personally seen the benefits of bringing different areas of law that are or have been funded by legal aid together into one comprehensive investigation. Such collaboration allows us to capture wider trends, enables us to trace the impact of varying developments and makes it easier to understand the role of policy in leading change within our respective areas of expertise. Fundamentally, examining areas of law together has enabled us to begin viewing the sector as a collective cohort of social justice lawyers. Siloed in our various areas of legal scholarship, we might not have otherwise become attuned to the important connections between the practitioners who responded to the Census. While differences are important, recognising these connections provides a potentially powerful analytical and organisational device through which lawyers and academics alike may work purposefully in pursuit of improved access to justice. Working with social justice lawyers across their different areas of practice has certainly influenced the way we will conduct our own research in the future. Their collective challenges, perspectives and experiences have encouraged us to remain open to exploring the wider sector beyond our traditional specialisms and to be more alert to the ways that trends may be experienced more broadly across the profession.

VII. What Next for Legal Aid?

This book has documented the inaugural Legal Aid Census and offered the first comprehensive snapshot into the legal aid sector and those who comprise the legal aid workforce in England and Wales. It has provided the strongest evidence base to date on how those in the sector perceive the challenges they face and has provided the most informed view from the frontline of access to justice. In doing so, it has challenged several narratives which are commonly used in relation to legal professionals, such as the assumption that practitioners only come from privileged

[87] A notable exception is the work of Cooke (n 81) which combines criminal and social welfare lawyers.

socio-economic backgrounds and circumstances, that legal professionals tend to earn significant salaries or even that the main reason that people pursue careers in legal aid is because they are motivated to increase their own personal wealth. In reality, this Census reveals a very different picture. It demonstrates that the legal aid sector is characterised by significant financial insecurity, which in turn has led to risks, problems and constraints. These factors pose significant and tangible threats to the ability of legal aid organisations and chambers to operate, the sustainability of the current workforce, the possibilities for recruiting and retaining the future generation of legal aid practitioners and the accessibility of justice for the individuals and communities that rely upon legal aid services. The challenges facing the sector are also far from new. While it may be tempting to attribute several of the current problems to the unforeseen circumstances that came with the outbreak of the COVID-19 pandemic, many of these challenges pre-existed this crisis. In fact, the insecurity and threats that were already being faced across the sector, meant that the organisations, chambers and practitioners were less resilient in their ability to withstand the economic, practical, and emotional impact of COVID-19. The pandemic merely raised the stakes.

Notwithstanding the scale of the problems identified, the findings from this Census reinforce the resilience, commitment and dedication of those within the legal aid sector and those who intend to pursue a career in it. Findings reveal a widespread sense of commitment to legal aid and understanding of the importance of this work for society. The majority of practitioners were in fact satisfied with their choice of career in legal aid, citing the importance of being able to help people and the enjoyment derived from the actual work involved in legal aid practice. There were also very few stakeholders who did not have a view on how these problems should be addressed. Whilst it is clear that these issues were prevalent before the COVID-19, recent events have only served to exacerbate existing fragilities and problems such that a comprehensive and holistic consideration of what is needed to ensure the future sustainability of this sector must now be brought to bear.

The recurring message arising from this Census is the dire need for investment in the legal aid sector, so that those charged with representing the interests of the most vulnerable in society and upholding the rule of law are provided with adequate pay, progression and support to enable them to perform that job effectively. Functioning access to justice requires a viable legal aid sector as a minimum. However, it is also important to aspire beyond this minimum standard and hold higher aspirations for a more sustainable legal aid sector. Achieving longer-term security will require large-scale, radical reform which goes beyond piecemeal change and makes wider commitments in relation to the way that justice is conceptualised in our society and regarded within our political system. One unavoidable reality is that the legal aid system requires further and greater levels of resourcing: legal aid needs to be properly funded if access to justice is to be realised.

We hope that readers of this book have come away with a clear grasp of both the importance of the legal aid sector and the fragility of access to justice when it is undermined. We are firm in our conviction that the legal aid sector should be given more credit than it has traditionally been granted and that it should be celebrated for the crucial role it plays in empowering citizens across England and Wales. That the sector is still populated by a cadre of passionate, knowledgeable practitioners who will fight for their clients' rights is something to be cherished, but also something for which we should be grateful. A complacent reading of the Census might lead us to suppose that despite all the challenges the sector has faced, there will always be practitioners willing and able to work for justice because they are driven by values of social justice. This stance would not only be unfair, but also myopic; the Census ultimately demonstrates that the current situation is precarious and unsustainable, with practitioners and organisations leaving the sector in swathes. The sector as a whole is facing a tipping point from which it may be unable to recover if action is not imminently taken. Despite the demoralising nature of many of the responses given within the Census, the scale of engagement with our questions regarding change needed in the sector is indicative that this tipping point has not yet passed. There remains a small window of opportunity to facilitate improvements that may restore the sector and prevents its contributions to access to justice from being entirely diminished. This action is urgently required and long overdue.

AFTERWORD

There was a time when associating legal aid with national health and other post-war innovations was a smart move by those wishing to explain the civic importance of the service. There is no doubt that legal aid is one of the pillars of the welfare state developed in the wake of WW2 as a part of the post-war settlement. While it has always been a junior partner to health, social security and education, it nevertheless has played a vital role in the struggle to achieve social justice for those not endowed with sufficient wealth to take legal security in the civil and criminal spheres for granted.

The analogy with health, in particular, is apposite. There are emergency legal procedures, elective legal procedures, general legal practitioners and specialists. Some procedures can transform people's lives, while some legal work is palliative.

However, even the senior partners of the pillars of the welfare state have for some time been under attack by forces we have learned to call neoliberalism. How are we to defend legal aid when even the NHS is traduced with impunity by some in government and many without? And what future can there be for social justice when the Labour Party, eyeing up a relatively clear path to government, cannot bring itself to express full-throated support even for underpaid nurses?

By carefully collating and analysing data, along with accounts of experience and sentiment of those previously and currently in practice in legal aid, this book and the project that gave rise to it has sought to provide some answers to these questions.

It would not be right to consider that what you hold in your hands is merely a snapshot of the sector at a particular moment – that of the pandemic. Beyond the immense and profound human tragedy, one of the many baleful effects of the pandemic crisis is the fact that it has drawn a veil over years of underfunding and mismanagement of public services and decades of increasing structural inequality.

Some vested interests are actively leaning into the narrative that COVID-19, along with other international events, are responsible for the ongoing crises faced by ordinary people. The pandemic has become a convenient 'trash barge' on which the forces of conservatism hope to jettison (at least for the time being) the signifiers of failing neoliberalism.

This book rightly emphasises the fact that structural problems that beset access to justice through the pandemic and ongoing, have been in place for decades. At the same time, there are pandemic-specific phenomena which the project and book have usefully recorded.

So, for the purposes of campaigning for legal aid and access to justice this book informs us that we need to stress the underlying structural problems in the justice and social welfare systems.

But what are these 'access to justice' problems? They arise, in my view, in the following categories; court reforms; domestic law-making; issues around broader international and rights based legislative provisions; legal and civics education; the interface between the justice and social welfare systems; the consumerfication of (what should be) fundamental rights; and, finally, legal aid.

The book also makes clear that it would be wrong to consider only the last of these issues to be the paramount concern of legal aid practitioners. In fact, the point of listing these issues is to thank the authors for (inter alia) helping me to organise my thoughts about the work that we do, beyond the everyday concerns of litigation, advice and assistance. And my peers and colleagues seem to feel the same way. In the last chapter the authors report that, 'practitioners saw the plight of legal aid lawyers and legal aid clients as two interwoven dimensions of the same crisis.'

Admirable. But helpful?

Chris Minnoch, CEO of LAPG, likes to mock-chide legal aid lawyers by wryly pointing out that his job of negotiating and consulting with ministers and civil servants is made much harder when legal aid lawyers continue to show up and carry on regardless of the depredation of the service. Of course, Chris knows implicitly (because he has personal experience) that the sector is served by vocational professionals whose motivations go well beyond financial reward. As this book shows, the rewards are meagre and the public service of legal aid has for many years been effectively subsidised by the moral imperatives heeded by legal aid lawyers.

If I may be allowed to exasperate the authors and make a late addition to the evidence base, I was approached at the Reblaw Conference 2019 by a law student who wanted to know how she could do work in legal aid when she qualified. Her point was that she is a working-class person with no hinterland of financial support whatsoever. She wants to provide legal services to her community once she has incurred all the debts of education and qualifications. But she could not see a route to her own financial security if she were to pursue a career in legal aid. At risk of overstating the point, a large part of the tragedy of this example in my view is that public appreciation of the legal aid sector would be greatly enhanced if users of the service were not habitually confronted by people with whom they cannot readily relate.

But, of course, the difficulties faced by entrants to, and *habitués* of, the legal aid sector go beyond personal finances. Where legal aid lawyers are powered by empathy, they are vulnerable to the psychological effects of trying to help a client group that has been increasingly neglected and abused by government policy. This has been well documented in recent literature.

The implementation of LASPO was intended to focus legal aid on the most needful of issues. So practitioners now face all the most desperate of problems, all of the time. But the most desperate of problems are now commonplace and so demand for these services has not reduced by limiting legal aid. That gives rise to one of the most dissonant issues in legal aid. In most other industries, demand for services is a cause for celebration. Many legal aid lawyers are campaigners for measures to reduce the need for their services. In the project to erase legal aid lawyers, practitioners appear to be in league with the Government, albeit with very different motivations.

But we face new challenges and policy directions which threaten legal aid, including fixed recoverable costs (FRCs). The progenitors of these threats are not primarily the Government or civil service on this occasion, and for once don't relate directly to funding cuts. In fact, FRCs were first proposed by the judiciary in the person of Sir Rupert Jackson and are currently being stewarded into force by judges and barrister and the Civil Justice Council.

The problems of FRCs in relation to legal aid are many and various and not to be aired here. But this is worth noting. There has been no increase in legal aid rates since 1994 and part of the flawed rationale as to why this was acceptable has been that legal aid lawyers could achieve market rates by winning cases and securing costs from the opponent. On that basis, legal rates have been pegged back to 1994 when a pound was worth £2.54.

Now the authorities are content to see that historical rationale for low rates broken. They are either ignorant of the effect on the legal aid sector or unconcerned as to its demise. The judiciary, as a collective, appears to have adopted or internalised the demoralisation of the legal aid sector and may find itself as the agent, witting or otherwise, of successive governments' project to eradicate public funded access to justice. It is hard to celebrate the so-called independence of the judiciary in these circumstances.

Nevertheless, the Government is committed to Sir Rupert's programme. Fixed Recoverable Costs tell us that the authorities' hostility to legal aid goes beyond the cost of legal aid to the treasury. The judiciary (at least the higher echelons) are as enthusiastic about mediation as they are about FRCs. ADR – alternative dispute resolution – has been renamed amongst decision-makers as DR (nothing 'alternative' about this form of 'justice', runs the schtick). Recall, however, that the enthusiasm for both FRCs and mediation does not extend to higher-value claims which do not involve ordinary people.

And now it can be ascertained why so many elements of access to justice are in crisis or managed decline (or both). We are *en route* to a destination where the rule of law exists primarily for the well-off and the corporate world.

This book is an important intervention in the fight that must be waged to resist the disenfranchisement of ordinary people from access to the courts and rule of law. It provides a valuable evidence base of the contemporary legal aid scene from a front-line perspective.

Campaigners will need all the evidence they can obtain. The Government is aware that there is a sustainability problem in legal aid. It is in the middle of a review of exactly that issue. The cause is obvious: LASPO. A major part of the remedy is obvious: reverse LASPO. And yet it is proposed to land FRCs before the review is completed. Unless the case for social justice is made and accepted by government (of whichever flavour holds the ball from 2024), the review may end up being the opening stage of an inquest.

Simon Mullings
January 2023

BIBLIOGRAPHY

360Giving, 'COVID-19 Grants Tracker' (360Giving, 2022).

Access to Justice Foundation, 'Specialist Legal Advice Providers: Sector Profile Reports' (Access to Justice Foundation, 2022).

Administrative Justice Council, 'Welfare Benefit Advice During the Pandemic' (Administrative Justice Council, 2021).

Alston, P, 'Statement on Visit to the United Kingdom, by Professor Philip Alston, United Nations Special Rapporteur on extreme poverty and human rights' (United Nations Human Rights Office of the High Commissioner, 2018).

—— 'Visit to the United Kingdom of Great Britain and Northern Ireland: report of the Special Rapporteur on Extreme Poverty and Human Rights' (United Nations Human Rights Office of the High Commissioner, 2019).

Ames, A et al, 'Survey of Not for Profit Legal Advice Providers in England and Wales' (Ministry of Justice Analytical Series, 2015).

Ames, J, 'Linklaters Offers £107,000 Starting Salary For 24 Year Old Solicitors' (*The Times*, 25 September 2021).

Amnesty International, 'Cuts that Hurt: The Impact of Legal Aid Cuts on Access to Justice in England and Wales' (Amnesty International UK, 2016).

APPG on Legal Aid, 'MP Casework Survey Findings' (APPG on Legal Aid, 2018).

Ashton, K et al, 'Community Care Legal Career Pathways' (Access Social Care, 2022).

Balmer, N and Pleasence, P, 'Mental Health, Legal Problems and the Impact of Changes to the Legal Aid Scheme: Secondary Analysis of 2014–15 Legal Problem Resolution Survey Data' (PPSR, 2018).

The Bar Council, 'Bar Council Data Analysis Criminal Bar' (The Bar Council, 2022).

——'Bar Survey Summary Findings April 2020' (The Bar Council, 2020).

——'Bar Survey Summary Findings July 2020' (The Bar Council, 2020).

——'Barrister's Working Lives Survey: Barrister Wellbeing (BWB) Analysis' (The Bar Council, 2021).

——'Diversity At the Bar 2020: A Summary of the Latest Available Diversity for the Bar' (Bar Standards Board, 2021).

——'Diversity At the Bar 2021: A Summary of the Latest Available Diversity for the Bar' (Bar Standards Board, 2022).

——'Race at the Bar: A Snapshot Report' (The Bar Council, 2021).

——'Running on Empty: Civil Legal Aid Research Report' (The Bar Council, 2021).

——'The Legal Aid, Sentencing and Punishment of Offenders Act 2012 (LASPO): One Year On – Final Report' (The Bar Council, 2014).

Bar Standards Board, 'Statistics on Practising Barristers' (2022, Bar Standards Board).

——'Women at the Bar' (Bar Standards Board, 2016).

Barlow, A et al, *Mapping Paths to Family Justice: Resolving Family Disputes in Neoliberal Times* (Palgrave MacMilan, 2017).

BBC News, *Thousands of Barristers Take Action Over Legal Aid* (BBC, 11 April 2022).

Bellamy, C, 'Independent Review of Criminal Legal Aid' (Ministry of Justice, 2021).

Bergin, AJ and Jimmieson, NL, 'Australian Lawyer Well-Being: Workplace Demands, Resources and the Impact of Time-Billing Targets' (2014) 21 *Psychiatry, Psychology and Law* 427.

Beveridge, W, 'Social Insurance and Allied Services' (His Majesty's Stationery Office, 1942).

BPP, 'Complete SQE 1 and 2 Training' (2020 BPP).

——'Should I do the LPC or SQE?' (BPP, 9 December 2021).

The Bridge Group, 'Socio-Economic Background and Progression to Partner in the Law' (The Bridge Group, 2020).
Brooke, H, 'The History of Legal Aid 1945–2010' (Henry Brooke, 2016).
Bonsignore, JJ, 'Elite Law Practice and Anti-Social Corporate Behavior' (1997) 21 *Legal Studies Forum* 333.
Boon, A, 'From Public Service to Service Industry: The Impact of Socialisation and Work on the Motivation and Values of Lawyers' (2005) 12 *International Journal of the Legal Profession* 229.
Bourdieu, P, *The Logic of Practice* (Stanford University Press, 1990).
Boyce, S, 'Civil Legal Aid is Under Threat: It's Time to Act' (The Law Society, 2022).
Boyd, SB, 'Corporatism and Legal Education in Canada' (2005) 14 *Social and Legal Studies* 287.
Brownsword, R, *Rights, Regulation and the Technological Revolution* (Oxford University Press, 2006).
Burdon Kemp, B, 'Inequality within Britain's Legal Aid Funding System' (Bolt Burdon Kemp, 2022).
Burns, J, 'Barristers Start Indefinite Strike Action Over Pay in England and Wales' (BBC News, 1 September 2022).
Burridge, R, and Webb, J, 'The Values of Common Law Legal Education Reprised' (2010) 42 *The Law Teacher* 263.
Burton, M, 'Justice on the Line? A Comparison of Telephone and Face-to-Face Advice in Social Welfare Legal Aid' (2018) 40 *Journal of Social Welfare and Family Law* 195.
——'Lost in Space: The Role of Place in the Delivery of Social Welfare Law Advice Over the Phone and Face-to-Face' (2020) 42 *Journal of Social Welfare and Family Law* 341.
Byfield Consultancy, 'Opening Up of Shutting Out' (Byfield Consultancy, 2015).
Byrom, N, 'The State of the Sector: The Impact of Cuts to Civil Legal Aid on Practitioners and their Clients' (The University of Warwick, 2022).
——'What We Know About the Impact of Remote Hearings on Access to Justice: A Rapid Evidence Review' (Nuffield Family Justice Observatory and the Legal Education Foundation, 2022).
Byrom, N et al, 'The Impact of COVID-19 Measures on the Civil Justice System' (Civil Justice Council, 2020).
Cain, C, and Goldring, JE, 'WhatsApp as a Debt Advice Channel: Reaching People Other Advice Channels Do Not Reach' (Manchester Metropolitan University, 2018).
Caird, JS, 'Court and Tribunal Closures' (House of Commons Library, 21 March 2016).
Lord Carter of Coles, 'Legal Aid: A Market-Based Approach to Reform' (Ministry of Justice, 2006).
House of Commons Justice Committee, 'The Future of Legal Aid: Third Report of Session 2021–22' (Her Majesty's Stationery Office, 2021).
Campbell, I, 'The Elephant in the Room: Working-Time Patterns of Solicitors in Private Practice in Melbourne' (Centre for Employment and Labour Relations Law, 2008).
Campbell, RW, 'The End of Law Schools: Legal Education in the Era of Legal Service Businesses' (2016) 85 *Mississippi Law Journal* 1.
Cantatore, F, 'The Impact of Pro Bono Law Clinics on Employability and Work Readiness in Law Students' (2018) 28 *International Journal of Clinical Legal Education* 147.
Cantatore, F et al, 'A Comparative Study into Legal Education and Graduate Employability Skills in Law Students through pro Bono Law Clinics' (2021) 55 *Law Teacher* 314.
Chalk, A, 'Written Questions: Legal Aid Scheme: Contracts' (UIN 166396, 16 March 2021).
Chan, J, 'Conceptualising Legal Culture and Lawyering Stress' (2015) 21 *International Journal of the Legal Profession* 213.
Chartered Institute of Legal Executives, 'Facts, Figures, Statistics' (Chartered Institute of Legal Executives, 2022).
Choudhry, S and Herring, J, 'A Human Right to Legal Aid? – The Implications of Changes to the Legal Aid Scheme for Victims of Domestic Abuse' (2017) 39 *Journal of Social Welfare and Family Law* 152.
The City of London Law Society, 'Social Welfare Solicitors Qualification Support Fund (SWSQF)' (The City of London Law Society, 2022).
Clements, L, 'Clustered Injustice and the Level Green' (Legal Action Group, 2020).

Collier, R, '"Be Smart, Be Successful, Be Yourself …"?: Representations of the Training Contract and Trainee Solicitor in Advertising by Large Law Firms' (2005) 12 *International Journal of the Legal Profession* 51.

Commission on Justice in Wales, 'Justice in Wales for the People of Wales' (Commission on Justice in Wales, 2019).

Cooke, E, 'The Working Culture of Legal Aid Lawyers, Developing a "Shared Orientation Model"' (2021) 31 *Social and Legal Studies* 704.

Cornford, T, 'The Meaning of Access to Justice' in E Plamer et al (eds), *Access to Justice: Beyond the Policies and Politics of Austerity* (Hart, 2016).

Creutzfeldt, N, 'Towards a Digital Legal Consciousness?' (2021) 12 *European Journal of Law and Technology*.

Creutzfeldt, N and Sechi, D, 'Social Welfare [Law] Advice Provision During the Pandemic in England and Wales: A Conceptual Framework' (2021) 43 *Journal of Social Welfare and Family Law* 153.

The Criminal Bar Association of England and Wales, 'No Returns' Guidance 2022 (The Criminal Bar Association of England and Wales, 18 March 2022).

Cross, M, 'Legal Aid's Founding Text Turns 70' (*The Law Society Gazette*, 2015).

Darbyshire, P, *Sitting in Judgment: The Working Lives of Judges* (Bloomsbury Publishing, 2011).

Deardon, L, 'Government Attacks on Lawyers "Undermine Rule of Law"' says Lord Chief Justice (*The Independent*, 10 November 2020).

Dehaghani, R, *Vulnerability and Police Custody: Police Decision Making and the Appropriate Adult Safeguard*, 1st edn (Routledge, 2019).

Dehaghani, R and Newman, D, 'The Crisis in Legally Aided Defence in Wales: Bringing Wales into Discussions of England and Wales' (2021) 41 *Legal Studies* 234.

——'"We're Vulnerable Too": An (Alternative) Analysis of Vulnerability within English Criminal Legal Aid and Police Custody' (2017) 7 *Onati Socio-Legal Series* 1199.

Denvir, C and Selvarajah, AD, 'Safeguarding Access to Justice in the Age of the Online Court' (2021) 85 *MLR* 25.

Denvir, C et al, 'We Are Legal Aid: Findings From the 2021 Legal Aid Census' (Legal Aid Practitioners Group, 2021).

Department for Constitutional Affairs, 'Legal Aid: The Way Ahead' (Cmd 6993) (HMSO, 2006).

Dinovitzer, R and Garth, B, 'The New Place of Corporate Law Firms in the Structuring of Elite Legal Careers' (2020) 45 *Law and Social Inquiry* 339.

Donoghue, J, 'The Rise of Digital Justice: Courtroom Technology, Public Participation and Access to Justice' (2017) 80 *MLR* 995.

Dyer, C, 'Legal Aid "Crisis" as Poor Pay Deters Trainees' (*The Guardian*, 22 March 2004).

—— 'Solicitors Shunning Legal Aid Work as Pay Rates Fall, Survey Reveals' (*The Guardian*, 7 January 2008).

Edwards, H, 'The Growing Disjunction between Legal Education and the Legal Profession' (1992) 91 *Michigan Law Review* 34.

Elkins, JR, 'Thinking Like a Lawyer: Second Thoughts' (1996) 47 *Mercer Law Review* 511.

Elson, A, 'The Rushcliffe Report' (1946) 13 *University of Chicago Law Review* 131.

Erlanger, HS et al, 'Law Student Idealism and Job Choice: Some New Data on an Old Question' (1996) 30 *Law and Society Review* 851.

Equality and Human Rights Commission, 'Inclusive Justice: A System Designed for All' (EHRC, 2020).

Fabian Society, 'The Right to Justice: Final Report of the Bach Commission' (Fabians, 2017).

Faulconbridge, J, 'Alliance "Capitalism" and Legal Education: An English Perspective' (2012) 80 *Fordham Law Review* 2651.

Feenan, D et al, 'Life, Work and Capital in Legal Practice' (2016) 23 *International Journal of the Legal Profession* 1.

Fennell, S, 'Disability Benefits During the Pandemic' (Citizens Advice, 2018).

Fineman, MA, 'Equality, Autonomy, and the Vulnerable Subject in Law and Politics' in Fineman MA and Grear A (eds), *Vulnerability: Reflections on a New Ethical Foundation for Law and Politics* (Routledge, 2013) 12–28.
——'The Vulnerable Subject and the Responsive State' (2010) 60 *Emory Law Review* 251.
——'The Vulnerable Subject: Anchoring Equality in the Human Condition' (2008) 20 *Yale Journal of Law and Feminism* 8.
——'Vulnerability and Social Justice' (2019) 53 *Valparaiso University Law Review* 341.
Fineman, MA and Grear, A, *Vulnerability: Reflections on a New Ethical Foundation for Law and Politics*, 1st edn (Routledge, 2013).
Foster, D and Hirst, N, *Legally Disabled? The Career Experiences of Disabled People Working in the Legal Profession* (Cardiff University, 2020).
Francis, A, 'Legal Education, Social Mobility, and Employability: Possible Selves, Curriculum Intervention, and the Role of Legal Work Experience' (2015) 42 *Journal of Law and Society* 173.
Francis, R and Fleck, J, 'Vicarious Trauma in the Legal Profession: A Practical Guide to Trauma, Burnout and Collective Care' (Legal Action Group, 2021).
Franklyn, R et al, 'Key Findings from the Legal Problem and Resolution Survey 2014–15' (Ministry of Justice Analytical Series, 2017).
Fraser, G, 'Reflections on Changing Family Law Practice During the COVID-19 Lockdown' (2020) 4 *Family Law* 1115.
Forbess, A and James, D, 'Acts of Assistance: Navigating the Interstices of the British State with the Help of Non-Profit Legal Advisers' (2014) 58 *Social Analysis* 73.
Forstenlechner, I and Lettice, F, 'Well Paid but Undervalued and Overworked: The Highs and Lows of Being a Junior Lawyer in a Leading Law Firm' (2008) 30 *Employee Relations* 640.
Gardener, D et al, 'The Effects of Pay Level on Organization-Based Self-Esteem and Performance: A Field Study', (2004) 77 *Journal of Occupational and Organizational Psychology* 307.
Garth, G and Dinovitzer, R, 'After the JD: First Results of a National Study of Legal Careers' (American Bar Foundation, 2004).
Genn, H, *Paths to Justice: What People Do and Think About Going to Law* (Hart, 1999).
Gramatikov, M and Porter, R, 'Yes, I Can: Subjective Legal Empowerment' (2011) 18 *Georgetown Journal on Poverty Law and Policy* 169.
Gray, J and Woodley, M, 'The Relationship between Academic Legal Education and the Legal Profession: The Review of Legal Education in England and Wales and the Teaching Hospital Model' (2005) 2 *European Journal of Legal Education* 1.
Gibbs, P, 'Defendants on Video – Conveyor Belt Justice or a Revolution in Access?' (Transform Justice, 2017).
Greenberg, D, 'Reflections on the New Mexico Conference: What Would You Have Said Before You Came to Law School' (1989) 19 *New Mexico Law Review* 171.
Hanlon, G, *Lawyers, the State and the Market, Professionalism Revisited* (Macmillan, 1999).
Harris, N et al, 'Vulnerability, the Future of the Criminal Defence Profession, and the Implications for Teaching and Learning' (2021) 55 *The Law Teacher* 57.
Harvey, D, *A Brief History of Neoliberalism* (Oxford University Press, 2005).
Her Majesty's Courts and Tribunals Service, 'The HMCTS Reform Programme' (HMCTS, 2021).
Hickie, I, et al, 'Courting the Blues: Attitudes towards Depression in Australian Law Students and Lawyers' (Brain and Mind Research Institute, University of Sydney, 2019).
Hilborne, N, 'Family Lawyers "Disproportionately Female and White"' (Legal Futures, 2020).
Hodgson, C, 'Cruel and Humiliating: Why Fit-for-work Tests are Failing People with Disabilities' (*The Guardian*, 22 May 2017).
Homes, H and Burgess, G, 'Coronavirus has Highlighted the UK's Digital Divide' (Cambridge Centre for Housing and Planning Research: University of Cambridge, 2021).
House of Lords Select Committee, 'Covid-19 and the Courts' (House of Lords, 2021).
Hussain, A, 'Aspiring Lawyers Divided over Career in Legal Aid' (Legal Cheek, 30 June 2021).
Independent Review of Criminal Legal Aid, 'Independent Review of Criminal Legal Aid: Summary Information on Publicly Funded Criminal Legal Services' (Ministry of Justice, 2021).

International Bar Association, 'Mental Wellbeing in the Legal Profession: A Global Study' (International Bar Association, 2021).
Jones, E et al, *Mental Health and Wellbeing in the Legal Profession* (Bristol University Press, 2020).
Justice First Fellowship, 'Supporting the Next Generation of Social Justice Lawyers' (Justice First Fellowship, 2022).
Kadowaki, J, 'Maintaining Professionalism: Emotional Labor Among Lawyers as Client Advisors' (2015) 22 *International Journal of the Legal Profession* 323.
Kalsi, S and Sharpley, D, 'Pathways in Legal Education: Taking the Right Route?' Learning in Law Annual Conference (College of Law, 2010).
Kelk, N et al, 'Courting the Blues: Attitudes Towards Depression in Australian Law Students and Lawyers' (Brain and Mind Research Institute, University of Sydney, 2009).
Kemp, V, 'Transforming Legal Aid: Access to Criminal Defence Services' (Legal Services Research Centre, 2010).
Kennedy, D, 'Legal Education as Training for Hierarchy' in D Kairys (ed), *The Politics of Law: A Progressive Critique* (Pantheon Books, 1990).
Kinghan, J, *Lawyers, Networks and Progressive Social Change: Lawyers Changing Lives* (Hart, 2021).
Krieger, LS and Sheldon, KM, 'What Makes Lawyers Happy? A Data-Driven Prescription to Redefine Professional Success' (2015) 83 *George Washington Law Review* 554.
LawCare, 'LawCare 2020 Figures: Sharp Increase in Legal Professionals Seeking Help for Anxiety' (LawCare, 2020).
—— 'Life in the Law 2020/21' (LawCare, 2021).
—— New Research Into Lawyer Wellbeing Makes the Case For Profession-Wide' Change (LawCare, 2021).
Law Centres Network, 'Law For All: Our New 50th Anniversary Campaign and Report' (Law Centres Network, 2020).
The Law Society of England and Wales, '£500m justice funding boost welcomed, but much more still needs to be done' (The Law Society, 25 November 2020).
—— 'Civil Legal Aid: A Review of its Sustainability and the Challenges to its Viability' (The Law Society, 2021).
—— 'Defending the Future of Criminal Legal Aid: What We are Doing for Members' (The Law Society, 2022).
—— 'Entry Trends: Undergraduates and Graduates in Law' (The Law Society, 2020).
—— 'Law Under Lockdown: The Impact of Covid-19 Measures on Access to Justice and Vulnerable People' (The Law Society, September 2020).
—— 'Legal Aid Deserts' (The Law Society, 22 August 2022).
—— 'Networking Tips For LGBT+ Lawyers' (The Law Society, 18 April 2019).
—— 'Race for Inclusion: The Experiences of Black, Asian and Minority Ethnic Solicitors' (The Law Society, 2020).
—— 'Recommended Minimum Salary for Trainees and SQE Candidates' (The Law Society, 25 July 2022).
—— 'Research to Inform Workforce Planning and Career Development in Legal Services: Skills, Training, Workplace Changes and Job Quality in the Solicitors' Profession' (The Law Society, 2019).
—— 'Written Evidence Submitted by the Law Society of England and Wales to the Justice Select Committee on the Future of Legal Aid' (The Law Society of England and Wales, 2020).
—— 'Women in Law' (The Law Society, 2018).
—— 'Women in Leadership in Law' (The Law Society, 2019).
The Lawyer Portal, 'Course Comparison Table' (The Lawyer Portal, 2022).
Legal Aid Agency, 'Legal Aid Provider Spreadsheet' (Legal Aid Agency, 20 July 2021).
Legal Aid Practitioners Group, 'Joint Open Letter to the Lord Chancellor' (Legal Aid Practitioners Group, 31 March 2022).
The Legal Education Foundation, 'Justice First Fellowship Retention Monitoring Data 2022' (unpublished, on file at the Legal Education Foundation).

Legal Services Board, 'Covid Dashboard Gives Clearest Picture Yet of Pandemic Impact on Legal Services' (Legal Services Board, 2021).

—— 'The State of Legal Services 2020: A Reflection on Ten Years of Regulation' (Legal Services Board, 2020).

—— 'The State of Legal Services 2020 – Evidence Compendium' (Legal Services Board, 2020).

Legal Services Commission, 'Legal Services Commission Annual Report and Accounts 2012–13' (His Majesty's Stationery Office, 2013).

Leighton, P, 'Legal Education in England and Wales: What Next?' (2021) 55 *The Law Teacher* 405.

Llewellyn, KN, *The Bramble Bush: On Our Law and Its Study*, 2nd edn (Oceana, 1960).

Local Government Association, 'Tackling the Digital Divide' (House of Commons, 2021).

Lord Chancellor and Secretary of State for Justice, 'Post-Implementation Review of Part 1 of the Legal Aid, Sentencing and Punishment of Offenders Act 2012 (LASPO)' (His Majesty's Stationery Office, 2019).

Lord Chancellor's Department, 'Striking the Balance: The Future of Legal Aid in England and Wales' (His Majesty's Stationery Office, 1996).

The Low Commission, 'Tackling the Advice Deficit: A Strategy for Access to Advice and Legal Support on Social Welfare Law in England and Wales' (Legal Action Group, 2014).

Mant, J, *Litigants in Person and the Family Justice System* (Hart, 2022).

—— 'Placing Litigants in Person at the Centre of the Post-LASPO Court Process' (2020) 32 *Child and Family Law Quarterly* 421.

Mant, J et al, 'Blended Advice and Access to Justice' (Ministry of Justice and the Access to Justice Foundation 2022).

Marshall, E, 'Almost Four out 10 Legal Aid Firms Do Not Use "Safety Net" Scheme' (The Justice Gap, 2020).

McKee, T et al, 'The Fairness Project: The Role of Legal Educators as Catalysts for Change. Engaging in Difficult Dialogues on the Impact of Diversity Barriers to Entry and Progression in the Legal Profession' (2021) 55 *The Law Teacher* 283.

McManus, S et al, 'Adult Psychiatric Morbidity in England, 2007: Results of a Household Survey' (National Health Service, 2009).

Merton, RK, 'On Sociological Theories of the Middle Range' in RK Merton, *On Theoretical Sociology: Five Essays, Old and New* (Free Press, 1967).

Ministry of Justice, 'Data Compendium: Summary Information on Publicly Funded Criminal Legal Services' (Ministry of Justice, February 2021).

—— 'Diversity of the Judiciary: Legal Professions, New Appointments and Current Post Holders – 2020 Statistics' (Ministry of Justice, 2020).

—— 'Legal Support: The Way Ahead' (Ministry of Justice, 2019).

—— 'Lord Chancellor's Exceptional Funding Guidance (Inquests)' (Ministry of Justice, 2013).

—— 'Proposals for the Reform of Legal Aid in England and Wales' (Ministry of Justice, 2010).

—— 'Response to Independent Review of Criminal Legal Aid' (Ministry of Justice, 2022).

—— 'Transforming Our Justice System' (Ministry of Justice, 2016).

—— 'Transforming Legal Aid: Delivering a More Credible and Efficient System' (CP14/2013, HMSO, 2013).

Montgomery, A and Crittenden, K, 'Improving Coding Reliability for Open-Ended Questions (1977) 41 *The Public Opinion Quarterly* 235.

Moorhead, R, 'Lawyer Specialisation – Managing the Professional Paradox' (2010) 32 *Law and Policy* 226.

—— 'Legal Aid and the Decline of Private Practice: Blue Murder or Toxic Job?' (2004) 11 *International Journal of the Legal Profession* 159.

Moorhead, R and Boyle, F, 'Work in Progress: Quality of Life and Trainee Solicitors: A Survey' (1995) 2 *International Journal of the Legal Profession* 217.

Mulcahy, L, 'The Unbearable Lightness of Being? Shifts Towards the Virtual Trial' (2008) 35 *Journal of Law and Society* 464.

Murphy, E, 'Databases, Doctrine, and Constitutional Criminal Procedure' (2010) 37 *Fordham Urban Law Journal* 803.
Murphy, N, 'Sponsorship, Scholarship or Save: How to Fund the SQE' (Legal Cheek, 10 June 2021).
National Audit Office, 'Reducing the Backlog in Criminal Courts' (National Audit Office, 2021).
Newman, D, 'Are Lawyers Alienated Workers?' (2016) 22 *European Journal of Current Legal Issues* 1.
—— *Legal Aid Lawyers and the Quest for Justice* (Hart, 2013).
Newman, D and Dehaghani, R, *Experiences of Criminal Justice: Perspectives From Wales on a System in Crisis* (Bristol University Press, 2022).
Newman, D and Robins, J, '"The Demise of Legal Aid"? Access to Justice and Social Welfare Law after Austerity' (2022) 3 *Amicus Curiae* 448.
—— *Justice in a Time of Austerity: Stories of a System in Crisis* (Bristol University Press, 2021).
Newman, D and Welsh, L, 'The Practices of Modern Criminal Defence Lawyers: Alienation and Its Implications for Access to Justice' (2019) 48 *Common Law World Review* 64.
Newman, D et al, 'Vulnerability, Legal Need and Technology' (2021) 23 *International Journal of Discrimination and the Law* 230.
Ng, P, 'Delivering a Pro Bono Clinic During the Pandemic: Some Thoughts on Access to Justice, Everyday Problems and the Current Legal Landscape' (2021) 3 *Amicus Curiae* 76.
Nicholson, A, 'The Value of a Law Degree – Part 4: A Perspective from Employers' (2022) 56 *The Law Teacher* 171.
Nicholson, A and Johnson, P, 'The Value of a Law Degree – Part 3: A Student Perspective' (2021) 55 *The Law Teacher* 431.
Nicolson, D, 'Legal Education, Ethics and Access to Justice: Forging Warriors for Justice in a Neo-Liberal World' (2015) 22 *International Journal of the Legal Profession* 51.
Office for National Statistics, 'Exploring the UK's Digital Divide' (Office for National Statistics, 2019).
—— 'Population of England and Wales' (UK Government, 2018).
O'Nions, H, '"Fat Cat" Lawyers and "Illegal" Migrants: The Impact of Intersecting Hostilities and Toxic Narrative on Access to Justice' (2020) 42 *Journal of Social Welfare and Family Law* 319.
Organ, J and Sigafoos, J, 'The Impact of LASPO on Routes to Justice' (Equality and Human Rights Commission, 2018).
Organ, J et al, 'How Legal Advice Can Ameliorate the Unequal Health Impact of Covid-19' (2021) 28 *Journal of Social Security Law* 54.
Otterburn Legal Consulting, 'Transforming Legal Aid: Next Steps – A Report for the Law Society of England and Wales and the Ministry of Justice' (Otterburn Legal Consulting LLP, 2014).
Owens, A, 'Securing Equality Rights and Access to Justice in Wales' (PhD Thesis, forthcoming).
Padel, U, 'The Criminal Justice System Gets Carter' (Centre for Crime and Justice Studies, 2007).
Paterson, A, 'Specialisation and the legal profession' (1986) *New Law Journal* 697.
Patiño, CG et al, 'Global Insights on Access to Justice' (World Justice Project, 2019).
Pereira, I et al, 'The Varying Paths to Justice: Mapping Problem Resolution Routes for Users and Non-users of the Civil, Administrative and Family Justice Systems' (Ministry of Justice Analytical Series, 2015).
Pleasence, P and Balmer, N, 'How People Resolve "Legal" Problems' (Legal Services Board, 2014).
Pleasence, P et al, 'A Time of Change: Solicitors' Firms in England and Wales' (The Law Society, Legal Services Board, Ministry of Justice, 2012).
—— *Causes of Action: Civil Law and Social Justice*, 1st edn (Legal Services Commission, 2006).
—— *Causes of Action: Civil Law and Social Justice*, 2nd edn (Legal Services Commission, 2010).
—— 'How People Understand and Interact with the Law' (Legal Education Foundation, 2015).
—— 'Multiple Justiciable Problems: Common Clusters and Their Social and Demographic Indicators' (2004) 1 *Journal of Empirical Legal Studies* 301.
—— 'Paths to Justice: A Past, Present and Future Roadmap' (UCL Centre for Empirical Legal Studies, 2013).
—— 'Paths to Justice: What People Do and Think About Going to Law' (Legal Services Commission, 2004).
Poulter, K, 'When, If Ever, Is Exploitation Acceptable' (*The Guardian*, 28 May 2010).

Rights of Women, 'Accessible or Beyond Reach? Navigating the Exceptional Case Funding Scheme without a Lawyer' (Rights of Women, 2019).
Rossner, M, 'Remote Rituals in Online Courts' (2021) 48 *Journal of Law and Society* 334.
Rothstein, J and Rouse, C, 'Constrained after College: Student Loans and Early-Career Occupational Choices' (2011) 95 *Journal of Public Economics* 149.
Rowan, E and Vaughan, S, 'Fitting in and "Opting out": Exploring How Law Students Self-Select Law Firm Employers' (2018) 52 *Law Teacher* 216.
The Rushcliffe Committee, 'Rushcliffe Committee Report on Legal Aid and Legal Advice in England and Wales' (CM6641, 1945).
Ryan, CJ, 'Paying for Law School: Law Student Loan Indebtedness and Career Choices' (2021) 1 *University of Illinois Law Review* 97.
Ryan, M, *Remote Hearings in the Family Justice System: A Rapid Consultation* (Nuffield Family Justice Observatory, 2020).
Sadique, H, 'Criminal barristers in England and Wales vote to end strike action' (*The Guardian*, 10 October, 2022), available at www.theguardian.com/law/2022/oct/10/barristers-in-england-and-wales-vote-to-end-strike-action.
Sandefur, RL, 'The Importance of Doing Nothing: Everyday Problems and Responses of Inaction' in P Pleasence (ed) et al, *Transforming Lives* (Legal Services Commission, 2007).
Shapiro, LJ, 'Public Perception of Lawyers: Consumer Research Findings' (American Bar Association, 2002).
Sherr, A, 'Of Superheroes and Slaves: Images and Work of the Legal Professional' (1995) 48 *Current Legal Problems* 327.
—— 'Professional Work, Professional Careers and Legal Education: Educating the Lawyer for 2010' (2000) 7 *International Journal of the Legal Profession* 325.
Sherr, A and Webb, J, 'Law Students, the External Market, and Socialization: Do We Make Them Turn to the City?' (1989) 16 *Journal of Law and Society* 225.
Smith, R, 'Legal Aid on an Ebbing Tide' (1996) 23 *Journal of Law and Society* 570.
Smith, RH, 'Legal Aid and Advice: The Rushcliffe Report as a Landmark' (1947) 33 *American Bar Association Journal* 445.
Solicitors Regulation Authority, 'Cost and Fees' (Solicitors Regulation Authority, 2022).
—— 'How Diverse is the Solicitors' Profession' (Solicitors Regulation Authority, 2022).
—— 'Population of Solicitors in England and Wales' (Solicitors Regulation Authority, 2022).
—— 'Qualifying Work Experience for Candidates' (Solicitors Regulation Authority, 5 April 2022).
Solicitors Regulation Authority and Bar Standards Board, *Academic Stage Handbook* (Solicitors Regulation Authority and Bar Standards Board, 2014).
Sommerlad, H, '"A Pit to Put Women In": Professionalism, Work Intensification, Sexualisation and Work–Life Balance in the Legal Profession in England and Wales' (2016) 23 *International Journal of the Legal Profession* 61.
—— 'Criminal Legal Aid Reforms and the Restructuring of Legal Professionalism' in R Young and D Wall (eds), *Access to Criminal Justice: Legal Aid Lawyers and the Defence of Liberty* (Blackstone, 1996).
—— 'I've Lost the Plot: An Everyday Story of Legal Aid Lawyers' (2001) 28 *Journal of Law and Society* 335.
—— 'Researching and Theorising the Process of Professional Identity Formation' (2007) 34 *Journal of Law and Society* 190.
—— 'Some Reflections on the Relationship between Citizenship, Access to Justice and the Reform of Legal Aid' (2004) 31 *Journal of Law and Society* 345.
—— 'The Implementation of Quality Initiatives and the New Public Management in the Legal Aid Sector in England and Wales: Bureaucratisation, Stratification and Surveillance' (1999) 6 *International Journal of the Legal Profession* 311.
—— 'Women Solicitors in a Fractured Profession: Intersections of Gender and Professionalism in England and Wales' (2002) 9 *International Journal of the Legal Profession* 213.

Sommerlad, H, and Sanderson, PJ, *Gender, Choice and Commitment: Women Solicitors in England and Wales and the Struggle for Equal Status* (Routledge, 1998).

Sommerlad, H et al, 'Diversity in the Legal Profession in England and Wales: A Qualitative Study of Barriers and Individual Choices' (University of Westminster Law Press, 2013).

—— *The Futures of Legal Education and the Legal Profession* (eds) (Bloomsbury Publishing, 2015).

Speak Up for Justice, 'Justice Denied: Impacts of the Government's Reforms to Legal Aid and Court Services on Access to Justice' (Trades Union Congress, 2016).

Spencer, M, 'Public Subsidies without Strings – Labour and the Lawyers at the Birth of Legal Aid' (2002) 9 *International Journal of the Legal Profession* 251.

Susskind, R, *The Future of Law* (Oxford University Press, 1996).

—— *Tomorrow's Lawyers: An Introduction to Your Future* (Oxford University Press, 2013).

The Sutton Trust and the Social Mobility Commission, 'Elitist Britain 2019: The Educational Backgrounds of Britain's Leading People' (The Sutton Trust and the Social Mobility Commission, 2019).

Tague, P, 'Barristers' Selfish Incentives in Counselling Clients' (2008) *Criminal Law Review* 3.

Tata, C, 'In the Interests of Clients or Commerce? Legal Aid, Supply, Demand and "Ethical Indeterminacy" in Criminal Defence Work' (2007) 34 *Journal of Law and Society* 489.

Thomas, PA and Mungham, GM, 'English Legal Education: A Commentary on the Ormrod Report' (1972) 7 *Valparaiso University Law Review* 87.

Thornton, J, 'Is Publicly Funded Criminal Defence Sustainable? Legal Aid Cuts, Morale, Recruitment and Retention in the English Criminal Law Professions' (2020) 40 *Legal Studies* 230.

—— 'The Way in Which Fee Reductions Influence Legal Aid Criminal Defence Lawyer Work: Insights from a Qualitative Study' (2019) 46 *Journal of Law and Society* 559.

Thornton, M, 'Squeezing the Life Out of Lawyers: Legal Practice in the Market Embrace' (2016) 25 *Griffith Law Review* 471.

—— 'The Flexible Cyborg: Work–Life Balance in Legal Practice' (2016) 38 *Sydney Law Review* 1.

—— 'The Law School, the Market and the New Knowledge Economy' (2007) 17 *Legal Education Review* 1.

Tomlinson, J, *Justice in the Digital State* (Policy Press, 2019).

Tomlinson, J and Marshall, E, 'Improving Exceptional Case Funding: Providers' Perspectives' (Public Law Project, 2020).

Twining, W, 'Pericles and the Plumber' in W Twining (ed), *Law in Context: Enlarging a Discipline* (Oxford University Press, 1997).

UK Parliament, 'Legal Aid Scheme: Contracts' (Question for the Ministry of Justice tabled by Afzal Kahn, 21 February 2022).

Vanhala, L, and Kinghan, J, 'The "Madness" of Accessing Justice: Legal Mobilisation, Welfare Benefits and Empowerment' (2022) 44 *Journal of Social Welfare and Family Law* 22.

Wade, M, 'Scottish Defence Lawyers Threaten Strikes Over Legal Aid Fees' (*The Times*, 20 June 2022).

Waters, B, 'The Solicitors Qualification Examination: Something For All? Some Challenges Facing Law Schools in England and Wales' (2018) 52 *The Law Teacher* 519.

Webb, J, 'Regulating Lawyers in a Liberalized Legal Services Market: The Role of Education and Training' (2013) 24 *Stanford Law and Policy Review* 533.

—— 'The LETRs (Still) in the Post: The Legal Education and Training Review and the Reform of Legal Services Education and Training – A Personal (Re)View.' in H Sommerlad et al (eds), *The Futures of Legal Education and the Legal Profession* (Hart, 2018).

Webley, L and Duff, E, 'Women Solicitors as a Barometer For Problems Within the Legal Profession – Time to Put Values Before Profits? (2007) 34 *Journal of Law and Society* 374.

Welsh, L, *Access to Justice in Magistrates' Courts: A Study of Defendant Marginalisation* (Hart, 2022).

Westaby, C, '"Feeling Like a Sponge": The Emotional Labour Produced by Solicitors in Their Interactions with Clients Seeking Asylum' (2010) 17 *International Journal of the Legal Profession* 153.

The Westminster Commission on Legal Aid, 'Inquiry into the Sustainability and Recovery of the Legal Aid Sector' (All-Party Parliamentary Group on Legal Aid, 2021).

Wilding, J, 'Droughts and Deserts: A Report on the Immigration Legal Aid Market' (University of Brighton, 2019).
—— 'Social Welfare and Asylum Legal Aid: A Complex System View of Provider Survival Pre- and Post-Pandemic' (2021) 28 *Journal of Social Security Law* 130.
—— *The Legal Aid Market: Challenges for Publicly Funded Immigration and Asylum Legal Representation* (Policy Press, 2021).
Williams, M et al, 'Research to Inform Workforce Planning and Career Development in Legal Services Employment: Trends, Workforce Projections and Solicitor Firm Perspectives' (Institute of Employment Studies, 2019).
Wizner, S, 'Is Learning to "Think Like a Lawyer" Enough?' (1998) 17 *Yale Law and Policy Review* 589.
Women Barristers' Alliance, 'Written Evidence from Themis: The Intersectional Women Barristers' Alliance' (Women Barristers' Alliance, 2020).
World Health Organization, 'Timeline of WHO's Covid-19 Response' (World Health Organization, 2020).
World Justice Project, 'Global Insights on Access to Justice' (World Justice Project, 2019).
Young Legal Aid Lawyers, 'Covid-19 Report' (Young Legal Aid Lawyers, 2020).
—— 'Second Covid-19 Report' (Young Legal Aid Lawyers, 2020).
—— 'Social Mobility in a Time of Austerity' (Young Legal Aid Lawyers, 2018).
Zaloznaya, M, 'Mechanisms and Consequences of Professional Marginality: The Case of Poverty Lawyers Revisited' (2011) 36 *Law & Social Inquiry* 919.

Legislation/Other

Child and Young Persons (Wales) Measure 2011
Convention for the Protection of Human Rights and Fundamental Freedoms (1950)
Convention on the Elimination of All Forms of Discrimination Against Women
Convention on the Elimination of All Forms of Racial Discrimination
Hansard, HC Vol 459, cc1221–327 (15 December 1948)
International Covenant on Economic, Social and Cultural Rights
Legal Aid and Advice Bill HC Deb 15 December 1948
Legal Aid, Sentencing and Punishment of Offenders Act 2012
Magna Carta (1215)
The United Nations Convention on the Rights of the Child

Case Law

Gudanaviciene and Ors v Director of Legal Aid Casework and the Lord Chancellor [2014] EWCA Civ 1622.
IS v Director of Legal Aid Casework and the Lord Chancellor [2015] EWHC 1965 (Admin) and [2016] EWCA Civ 464.
Public Law Project v Secretary of State for Justice [2014] EWHC 2365.
R (Unison) v Lord Chancellor [2017] UKSC 51

INDEX

Milton Keynes UK
Ingram Content Group UK Ltd.
UKHW020750020823
426189UK00003B/182

9 781509 957804